AF137916

TOWARDS A KNOWLEDGE-AWARE AI

Studies on the Semantic Web

Semantic Web has grown into a mature field of research. Its methods find innovative applications on and off the World Wide Web. Its underlying technologies have significant impact on adjacent fields of research and on industrial applications. This book series reports on the state of the art in foundations, methods, and applications of Semantic Web and its underlying technologies. It is a central forum for the communication of recent developments and comprises research monographs, textbooks and edited volumes on all topics related to the Semantic Web.

Editor-in-Chief:
Prof. Dr. Pascal Hitzler
Department of Computer Science, Kansas State University, Manhattan, KS 66502, USA
Email: hitzler@k-state.edu

Editorial Board:
Eva Blomqvist, Linköping, Sweden; Diego Calvanese, Bolzano, Italy; Oscar Corcho, Madrid, Spain; Michel Dumontier, Maastricht, The Netherlands; Krzysztof Janowicz, Santa Barbara, CA, USA; Carole Goble, Manchester, UK; Frank van Harmelen, Amsterdam, The Netherlands; Markus Krötzsch, Dresden, Germany; Jens Lehmann, Bonn, Germany; Juanzi Li, Beijing, China; Diana Maynard, Sheffield, UK; Mark Musen, Stanford, CA, USA; Axel Ngonga, Leipzig, Germany; Heiko Paulheim, Mannheim, Germany; Valentina Presutti, CNR, Italy; Barry Smith, Buffalo, NY, USA; Steffen Staab, Koblenz, Germany; Rudi Studer, Karlsruhe, Germany; Hideaki Takeda, Tokyo, Japan; Ruben Verborgh, Ghent, Belgium

Volume 55

Previously published in this series:

ISSN 1868-1158 (print)
ISSN 2215-0870 (online)

Towards a Knowledge-Aware AI

SEMANTiCS 2022 — Proceedings of the 18th International Conference on Semantic Systems, 13–15 September 2022, Vienna, Austria

Edited by

Anastasia Dimou

KU Leuven, Belgium

Sebastian Neumaier

University of Applied Sciences St. Poelten, Austria

Tassilo Pellegrini

Institute for Applied Informatics, Dresden, Germany

and

Sahar Vahdati

Institute for Applied Informatics, Dresden, Germany

© 2022 The Authors

This book is published online with Open Access by IOS Press and distributed under the terms of the Creative Commons Attribution License 4.0 (CC BY 4.0).

ISBN 978-3-89838-767-5 (AKA, print)
ISBN 978-1-64368-320-1 (IOS Press, print)
ISBN 978-1-64368-321-8 (IOS Press, online)
doi: 10.3233/SSW55

Bibliographic information available from the Katalog der Deutschen Nationalbibliothek (German National Library Catalogue) at https://www.dnb.de

Publisher
Akademische Verlagsgesellschaft AKA GmbH, Berlin

Represented by Co-Publisher IOS Press
IOS Press BV
Nieuwe Hemweg 6B
1013 BG Amsterdam
The Netherlands
Tel: +31 20 688 3355
Fax: +31 20 687 0019
email: order@iospress.nl

LEGAL NOTICE
The publisher is not responsible for the use which might be made of the following information.

Preface

Anastasia DIMOU[a,0000-0003-2138-7972], Sebastian NEUMAIER[b, 0000-0002-9804-4882], Tassilo PELLEGRINI[b, 0000-0002-0795-0661] and Sahar VAHDATI[c, 0000-0002-7171-169X]

[a] *KU Leuven, nastasia.dimou@ugent.be*
[b] *University of Applied Sciences St. Poelten, Austria, sebastian.neumaier@fhstp.ac.at; tassilo.pellegrini@fhstp.ac.at*
[c] *Institute for Applied Informatics, Dresden, Germany, vahdati@infai.org*

Abstract. This volume contains the proceedings of the 18th International Conference on Semantic Systems, SEMANTiCS 2022 under the title "Towards A Knowledge-Aware AI". SEMANTiCS is the annual meeting place for professionals and researchers who make semantic computing work, who understand its benefits and encounter its limitations. Every year, SEMANTiCS attracts information managers, IT- architects, software engineers, and researchers from organizations ranging from research facilities, NPOs, through public administrations to the largest companies in the world.

Keywords. Semantic Systems, Knowledge Graphs, Artificial Intelligence, Semantic Web, Linked Data, Machine Learning, Knowledge Discovery

SEMANTiCS offers a forum for the exchange of latest scientific results in semantic systems and complements these topics with new research challenges in areas like data science, machine learning, logic programming, content engineering, social computing, and the Semantic Web. The conference is in its 18th year and has developed into an internationally visible and professional event at the intersection of academia and industry.

Contributors to and participants of the conference learn from top researchers and industry experts about emerging trends and topics in the wide area of semantic computing. The SEMANTiCS community is highly diverse; attendees have responsibilities in interlinking areas such as artificial intelligence, data science, knowledge discovery and management, big data analytics, e-commerce, enterprise search, technical documentation, document management, business intelligence, and enterprise vocabulary management.

The conference's subtitle in 2022 was "Towards A Knowledge-Aware AI", and especially welcomed submissions to the following topics:

- Enterprise Linked Data & Data Integration
- Data Fabric: access and sharing of data in a distributed dataenvironment
- Knowledge Graphs
- Business models and Success Factors in applying Semantic Technologies
- Digital Twins and Industry 4.0
- VR augmented by Semantic Technologies
- Semantics on the Web & schema.org
- Terminology, Thesaurus & Ontology Management

- Knowledge Discovery, Semantic Search and Recommender Systems
- Smart Connectivity & Interlinking
- Blockchain and Distributed Ledger Applications
- Machine Learning, NLP & Semantic Computing as a combined approach
- Big Data & Advanced Analytics
- Explainable AI
- Semantically Enriched Digital Experience Platforms
- Data Governance and Data Quality Management
- Data Portals & Knowledge Visualization
- Economics of data, data services, data ecosystems and data strategies
- Community, Social & Societal Aspects
- Apps, services and industry demos that make use of any of the above mentioned topics

In order to properly provide high-quality reviews, a program committee comprising 114 members supported us in selecting the papers with the highest impact and scientific merit. For each submission, at least 3 reviews were written independently from the assigned reviewers in a single-blind review process (author names are visible to reviewers, reviewers stay anonymous). After all reviews were submitted the PC chairs compared the reviews and discussed discrepancies and different opinions with the reviewers to facilitate a meta-review and suggest a recommendation to accept or reject the paper. Overall, we accepted 15 papers which resulted in an acceptance rate of 29%.

In addition to the peer-reviewed work, the conference had four renowned keynote Prof. Olaf Hartig (Associate Professor at Department of Computer and Information Science, Linköping University), Steve Moyle (Founder Amplify Intelligence, Fractional CIO at Freeman Clarke), Adam Keresztes (Business owner IKEA Knowledge Graph), and Jans Aasman (CEO of Franz Inc). Additionally, the program had posters and demos, a comprehensive set of workshops, as well as talks from industry leaders. For the first time in 2022 SEMANTiCS also hosted the co-located conference LT Innovate, an established community event for language and translational technologies.

We thank all authors who submitted papers. We particularly thank the program committee which provided careful reviews in a quick turnaround time. Their service is essential for the quality of the conference.

Sincerely yours,

The Editors

Vienna, September 2022

Program Committee of
SEMANTiCS 2022

Maribel Acosta, Germany, Ruhr University Bochum
Mehwish Alam, Germany, FIZ Karlsruhe - Leibniz Institute for Information
    Infrastructure, AIFB Institute, KIT
Vladimir Alexiev, Bulgaria, Ontotext Corp
Vito Walter Anelli, Italy, Politecnico di Bari
Ghislain A. Atemezing, France, Mondeca
Stefan Bischof, Austria, Siemens AG Österreich
Russa Biswas, Germany, FIZ Karlsruhe, Leibniz Institute for Information
    Infrastructure & KIT Karlsruhe
Carlos Bobed, Spain, everis / NTT Data - University of Zaragoza, Spain
Pieter Bonte, Belgium, Ghent University
Bojan Božić, Ireland, Technological University Dublin
Paul Buitelaar, Ireland, NUI Galway
Pompeu Casanovas, Spain, UAB
Davide Ceolin, Netherlands, CWI
Pierre-Antoine Champin, France, LIRIS, Université Claude Bernard Lyon1
Ioannis Chrysakis, Greece, FORTH-ICS (Greece) and Dept. of Electronics and
    Information Systems, Ghent University - IDLab – imec (Belgium)
Michael Cochez, Netherlands, Vrije Universiteit Amsterdam
Oscar Corcho, Spain, Universidad Politécnica de Madrid
Enrico Daga, United Kingdom, The Open University
Laura Daniele, Netherlands, TNO
Marilena Daquino, Italy, University of Bologna
Victor de Boer, Netherlands, Vrije Universiteit Amsterdam
Ben De Meester, Belgium, Ghent University
Dieter De Witte, Belgium, Ghent University
Christophe Debruyne, Belgium, Université de Liège
Anastasia Dimou, Belgium, Department of Electronics and information systems,
    University of Ghent
Christian Dirschl, Germany, Wolters Kluwer Germany
Milan Dojchinovski, Czechia, Czech Technical University in Prague
Mauro Dragoni, Italy, Fondazione Bruno Kessler - FBK-IRST
Vasilis Efthymiou, Greece, ICS-FORTH
Fajar J. Ekaputra, Austria, Vienna University of Technology
Victoria Eyharabide, France, STIH Laboratory, Sorbonne University
Pavlos Fafalios, Greece, Institute of Computer Science, FORTH-ICS
Catherine Faron Zucker, France, Université Côte d'Azur
Said Fathalla, Germany, Faculty of Science, University of Alexandria and Smart Data
Analytics (SDA), University of Bonn
Agata Filipowska, Poland, Department of Information Systems, Poznan University of
    Economics

Nuno Freire, Portugal, INESC-ID
Michael Färber, Germany, Karlsruhe Institute of Technology
Roberto Garcia, Spain, Universitat de Lleida
Daniel Garijo, Spain, Universidad Politécnica de Madrid
Genet Asefa Gesese, Germany, FIZ Karlsruhe – Leibniz-Institut für
    Informationsinfrastruktur
Paul Groth, Netherlands, University of Amsterdam
Peter Haase, Germany, metaphacts
Nathalie Hernandez, France, IRIT
Fabian Hoppe, Germany, FIZ Karlsruhe, Karlsruhe Institute of Technology
Zhisheng Huang, Netherlands, Vrije Universiteit Amsterdam
Eero Hyvönen, Finland, Aalto University and University of Helsinki (HELDIG)
Shimaa Ibrahim, Germany, Bonn University
Ana Iglesias-Molina, Spain, Universidad Politécnica de Madrid
Antoine Isaac, Netherlands, Europeana & VU University Amsterdam
Marc Jacobs, Germany, Fraunhofer
Naouel Karam, Germany, Fraunhofer
Fahad Khan, Italy, Istituto di Linguistica Computazionale "Antonio Zampolli"
Peter Kieseberg, Austria, St. Pölten University of Applied Sciences
Sabrina Kirrane, Austria, Vienna University of Economics and Business - WU Wien
Dimitris Kontokostas, Greece, Diffbot
Konstantinos Kotis, Greece, University of the Aegean, Dept. of Cultural Technology
    and Comm., Intelligent Systems Lab
Julius Köpke, Austria, Alpen-Adria-Universität Klagenfurt Institute for Informatics
Systems
Jasmin Lampert, Austria, Austrian Institute of Technology
Christoph Lange, Germany, Fraunhofer Institute for Applied Information Technology
FIT and RWTH Aachen University, Germany
Maxime Lefrançois, France, MINES Saint-Etienne
Georgios Lioudakis, Greece, ICT abovo P.C.
Pasquale Lisena, France, EURECOM
Giorgia Lodi, Italy, Istituto di Scienze e Tecnologie della Cognizione (CNR)
Sandra Lovrenčić, Croatia, University of Zagreb, Faculty of organization and
    informatics Varazdin
Andrea Mannocci, Italy, ISTI-CNR
Barbara Mcgillivray, United Kingdom, Alan Turing Institute/University of Cambridge,
    Department of Theoretical and Applied Linguistics
Albert Meroño-Peñuela, United Kingdom, King's College London
Thomas Moser, Austria, St. Pölten University of Applied Sciences
Paul Mulholland, United Kingdom, The Open University
Sebastian Neumaier, Austria, St. Pölten University of Applied Sciences, Austria
Lyndon Nixon, Austria, MODUL Technology GmbH
Andrea Giovanni Nuzzolese, Italy, University of Bologna
D. O'Sullivan, Ireland, Trinity College Dublin
Leo Obrst, United States, MITRE
Francesco Osborne, United Kingdom, The Open University
Monica Palmirani, Italy, CIRSFID
Harshvardhan J. Pandit, Ireland, ADAPT Centre - Trinity College Dublin
Tassilo Pellegrini, Austria, University of Applied Sciences St. Pölten

Catia Pesquita, Portugal, LaSIGE, Faculdade de Ciências, Universidade de Lisboa
Jędrzej Potoniec, Poland, Poznan University of Technology
Torsten Priebe, Austria, St. Pölten University of Applied Sciences
Cédric Pruski, Luxembourg, Luxembourg Institute of Science and Technology
Artem Revenko, Austria, Semantic Web Company GmbH
Giuseppe Rizzo, Italy, LINKS Foundation
Oscar Rodríguez Rocha, France, Teach on Mars
Julian Rojas, Belgium, Ghent University
Anisa Rula, Italy, University of Brescia
Harald Sack, Germany, FIZ Karlsruhe, Leibniz Institute for Information Infrastructure
    & KIT Karlsruhe
Angelo Antonio Salatino, United Kingdom, The Open University
Stefan Schlobach, Netherlands, Vrije Universiteit Amsterdam
Mario Scrocca, Italy, Cefriel
Pavel Shvaiko, Italy, Informatica Trentina
Paulo Silva, Portugal, University of Coimbra
Simon Steyskal, Austria, Siemens AG Austria
Ruben Taelman, Belgium, Ghent University – imec
Ilaria Tiddi, Netherlands, Vrije Universiteit Amsterdam
Tabea Tietz, Germany, FIZ Karlsruhe
Sanju Tiwari, Mexico, Universidad Autonoma de Tamaulipas
Konstantin Todorov, France, LIRMM / University of Montpellier
Francesca Tomasi, Italy, University of Bologna
Riccardo Tommasini, Italy, INSA Lyon - LIRIS
Cassia Trojahn, France, UT2J & IRIT
Jürgen Umbrich, Austria, Vienna University of Economy and Business (WU)
Sahar Vahdati, Germany, InfAI
Dylan Van Assche, Belgium, Universiteit Gent
Herbert Van De Sompel, United States, Data Archiving Networked Services
Frank Van Harmelen, Netherlands, Vrije Universiteit Amsterdam
Miel Vander Sande, Belgium, Meemoo
Maria Esther Vidal, Germany, TIB Hannover
Joerg Waitelonis, Germany, yovisto GmbH
Shenghui Wang, Netherlands, University of Twente
Rigo Wenning, France, W3C
Wolfram Wöß, Austria, Institute for Application Oriented Knowledge Processing,
    Johannes Kepler University Linz, Austria
Umutcan Şimşek, Austria, Semantic Technology Institute Innsbruck

Contents

Learning over Complementary Knowledge

Semantics in Data Quality, Standards, and Protection

Towards a Knowledge-Aware AI
A. Dimou et al. (Eds.)

© 2022 The Authors.
This article is published online with Open Access by IOS Press and distributed under the terms
of the Creative Commons Attribution License 4.0 (CC BY 4.0).

doi:10.3233/SSW220005

Evaluating Web Content Using the W3C Credibility Signals

León Viktor AVILÉS PODGURSKI [a,1], Karolina ZACZYNSKA [b] and Georg REHM [b]

[a] *Technische Universität Berlin, Straße des 17. Juni 135, 10623 Berlin, Germany*
[b] *DFKI GmbH, Alt-Moabit 91c, 10559 Berlin, Germany*

Abstract. The credibility and trustworthiness of online content has become a major societal issue as human communication and information exchange continues to evolve digitally. The prevalence of misinformation, circulated by fraudsters, trolls, political activists and state-sponsored actors, has motivated a heightened interest in automated content evaluation and curation tools. We present an automated credibility evaluation system to aid users in credibility assessments of web pages, focusing on the automated analysis of 23 mostly language- and content-related credibility signals of web content. We find that emotional characteristics, various morphological and syntactical properties of the language, and exclamation mark and all caps usage are particularly indicative of credibility. Less credible web pages have more emotional, shorter and less complex texts, and put a greater emphasis on the headline, which is longer, contains more all caps and is frequently clickbait. Our system achieves a 63% accuracy in fake news classification, and a 28% accuracy in predicting the credibility rating of web pages on a five-point Likert scale.

Keywords. content credibility, credibility assessment, credibility signals, content curation, fake news, NLP

1. Introduction

The digital age continues to transform the ways humankind lives, interacts and communicates. As more and more online information is published and consumed, the trustworthiness of web content has become a major societal issue. Fraudsters, trolls, political activists and state-sponsored actors disseminate misinformation and other unreliable and malicious content commonly described as "fake news" [1]. The proliferation of low-quality information on the web is facilitated by its decentralised and nonrestrictive nature, which enables the publication of content without the limitations or qualitative controls associated with traditional media. In a global study, 62% of respondents felt that fake news was prevalent on online websites and platforms [2].

This work focuses on automatically predicting the credibility of web pages' content. Following the definitions of Navok et al. and Grupta et al. we define credibility as the property of being trusted, i. e., a text is declared credible if a user, e. g., based on common sense, believes that the information it contains is to some extent credible [3,4]. Amidst growing concerns over unreliable online information and fake news, a number

---

[1]E-mail: lv.avilesp@yahoo.de, karolina.zaczynska@dfki.de, georg.rehm@dfki.de

of stakeholders have called for the development of tools, frameworks and technologies to support human credibility judgements on the web [5,6,7,8]. Automated tools can audit information almost instantly and may be deployed for each individual user to flag their consumed content with credibility indicators in real-time. Furthermore, it is vital that users are able to retrace why a given text is classified as (not) credible, and not just given by a black box model trained on a large data set. Previous research has highlighted discriminating structural and linguistic characteristics of web pages with low credibility, such as an increased emotionality [9], shorter average words [10], and less coherent texts [11]. Such properties can be framed as *credibility signals*, measurable units of information that may be used as credibility-indicating heuristics in the credibility assessment process. Each signal represents a certain trait of a web page and may contribute to or detract from its overall credibility. The World Wide Web Consortium (W3C) Credible Web Community Group [12] has published an extensive list with the specifications of more than 200 credibility signals[2]. Studies have shown repeatedly that superficial web page features, like appearance or usability, have a considerable impact on credibility [13,14]. However, we decided to build a credibility assessment system focusing on signals related to the language and actual content of web pages. If our credibility scores are based on properties intrinsic to the evaluated information, the scores will be consistent across platforms for the same content, and should also be much more resistant to adversarial attacks as changes to the content are more costly than modifications of surface characteristics.

The main contributions of this paper are as follows: we present the design and implementation of a software system which calculates the credibility score of a web page through the analysis of (mostly) language- and content-related credibility signals. Although it is a rather popular approach in automated credibility assessment, we decided not to train a machine learning (ML) model for the task. To the best of our knowledge, we are the first to systematically evaluate a subset of the W3C web credibility signals; we develop a web page parsing module and separate evaluation pipelines for a total of 23 credibility signals. Evaluating which credibility signals are particularly relevant to automated credibility assessments, we see that emotional characteristics, various linguistic, especially morphological and syntactical properties, and exclamation mark and all caps usage are particularly indicative. Less credible pages have more emotional, shorter and less complex texts, and put a greater emphasis on the headline, which is longer, contains more all caps and is frequently clickbait. Although there is still ample room for iterative improvements of our credibility evaluation system, we show that a content-focused automated credibility evaluation that is transparent, more robust, domain-independent, modular, and easily expandable is feasible and states a clear added value to existing black-box ML or qualitative approaches. Our system can aid internet users and publishers in their credibility assessments to make more informed credibility decisions about the information at hand; credibility researchers can use the tool to analyse and learn more about web credibility and elements that affect it, as well as study the credibility of specific websites or platforms. The paper is structured as follows: First, we present related work and related sub-fields like fake news (Section 2). Section 3 presents the selected signals and tools used in our system (Section 3.1) and explains how we combine and weight the signals to compute the credibility score (Section 3.2). Section 4 presents the datasets we conducted our test runs on and Section 5 discusses the influence of individual credibility signals for the overall score and the performance of the system.

---

[2]https://credweb.org/signals-20191126. URLs were all last accessed on 2022-01-21.

2. Related Work

Systems that analyse information, helping users regarding different points of view and previously overlooked indicators of credibility, can lead to more holistic and informed credibility judgements. Automated tools can audit information much faster and at larger scale than human reviewers or fact-checkers, while taking features into account that are difficult for humans to evaluate [5,15]. Chen et al. [5] and Lazer et al. [7] suggest a hybrid approach for addressing the problem of fake news: promoting public literacy and critical thinking for the digital space with initiatives and training, such that individuals may consume online content more consciously and validate and cross-check information themselves; and through automated evaluation and verification systems, employed by users or platforms to support credibility assessments and flag suspicious content. To help users recognise filter bubbles, false news or abusive content more easily, Rehm [8] proposes a decentralised infrastructure on top of the World Wide Web, including corresponding metadata standards, smart content and semantic content enrichment following the main principles of the Semantic Web. Our credibility assessment tool can be perceived as one building block of such an infrastructure, aggregating credibility values that can be made available, for example, as Linked Data or as Web Annotations, for example. Horne et al. [16] introduce an open source toolkit intended to facilitate the systematic exploration of the online news ecosystem, where users may consume news articles and simultaneously receive indicators of their reliability. The W3C Credible Web Community Group has published an analysis of the factors, stakeholders and possibilities for improving web credibility assessments, describing promising technical approaches for each of the credibility assessment strategies *inspection, corroboration, reputation* and *transparency* [6]. Furthermore, they published a list of more than 200 credibility signals intended to support the creation of interoperable credibility tools by researchers and software developers [12], which we utilise as the foundation for the design of our system.

Most modern credibility evaluation systems use machine learning and Natural Language Processing (NLP) to analyse the credibility of web pages. Olteanu et al. [17] apply statistical tests to determine 22 particularly important web page features as indicators for credibility (from 37 features identified in the literature), to build an automated credibility evaluation framework. Wawer et al. [18] aim to improve the system by Olteanu et al. [17] through leveraging psychosocial and psycholinguistic cues, and analysing word occurrences using bag-of-words models. Investigating words connected to certain trust levels, they conclude that consumers assign lower credibility to financial services and content generated by users or related to borrowing money, while government- and safety-related content was associated with words implying high trust. Esteves et al. [19] compute credibility ratings after analysing lexical and textual properties, as well as groups of HTML tag occurrences and extracting source reputation cues. Giachanou et al. [9] concentrate on emotional signals, proposing an LSTM model that evaluates textual and emotional indicators for credibility assessment, and determine that the inclusion of emotional signals can improve the performance of credibility assessment systems.

Several publications in automated credibility assessment and fake news detection focus on content-related or linguistic properties of online information. Horne and Adalı [10] evaluate psychological, complexity and stylistic features of legitimate and fake news articles and find significant differences in the language of title and text. They conclude that fake news articles attempt to include all central information in the title, while the text body generally contains only marginally more information. Afroz et al. [20] show that a deceptive writing style can be recognised using stylometry; while authors can intentionally alter their writing style to avoid identification through such an analysis, the actual obfuscation can be detected. Rashkin et al. [21] find that fake news contain more words related to exaggeration, and real news more words related to concrete figures. O'Brien et al. [22] employ a deep neural network for fake news detection based on language features, and discover patterns of language bias, exaggeration and strong rhetoric as corresponding to fake news. Przybyła [23] evaluates a classifier based on stylometric features, and determines sensational and affective vocabulary to be a discriminating factor. Compared to such machine-learning-based credibility evaluation approaches producing one overall score or a binary assessment, our paper follows a different line of argumentation. We calculate the credibility of a web page and evaluate more than 20 credibility signals, defined as small, measurable units of information that may be utilised as credibility-indicating heuristics in the credibility assessment process.

Fake news detection is closely related to, and arguably a sub-domain of automated credibility evaluation, representing a binary classification of the reliability or trustworthiness of web content instead of rating its credibility on a scale. Similarly to automated credibility assessment, fake news detection systems typically utilise machine learning approaches including neural networks to avoid the usage of handcrafted features [1].

3. Methodology

3.1. Signal Selection

In order to build a system which processes web pages and assigns credibility scores, we must identify, extract and analyse relevant information from these web documents. We analysed the list of more than 200 credibility signals by [12] to decide which characteristics of web pages are important for a credibility evaluation and, thus, to be included in our system. Human credibility assessments of web content are often linked to surface signals. Indeed, website appearance, usability and design have frequently been shown to correlate with credibility [24]. We focus on the content and language of web pages rather than surface characteristics for multiple reasons. Several scientific works have focused on language features for credibility classification and fake news detection [10,22,23]. Similarly, we want to investigate the relationship between the credibility of text-based web content and its linguistic features, like a text's vocabulary, tonality, grammar, style and structure. Additionally, we prefer to rely on more robust signals connected to the actual content, rather than superficial indicators. Our credibility ratings are linked strongly to the evaluated data, with ratings being consistent across platforms if the same content is evaluated, i. e., our scores will not change depending on the website that the content was published on. Moreover, precise changes in individual content pieces are more expensive than adapting a website's appearance; as we expect our content-related signals to correlate with credibility and therefore with quality, content providers would have to actually increase the quality of their content to improve its credibility score, and could not just manipulate it by modifying surface properties. Nevertheless, we do include some signals not related to language but pertaining to other characteristics. In the context of the assessment strategies described by the W3C Credible Web Community Group, the credibility evaluation performed by our system is classified as *inspection* [12]. As it is mainly designed to analyse language, it performs best on text-centric content such as news articles and blog posts.

The signals from the W3C Credible Web list were selected according to compliance with the factors *relevance* (expected correlation between signal values and the credibility of the content, based on previous scientific work), *measurement difficulty* (expected difficulty in automatically extracting the needed information from a web page and determining the signal value), *manipulability/feedback risk* (signals should be sufficiently hard to attack, i. e., it should be disproportionately expensive to modify evaluated content to improve the signal evaluation), and *interoperability* (signal evaluation should reach the same result even when performed by several independent systems) [12]. The metrics we opted to use and evaluate are:

Author: This signal represents whether a web page explicitly states the author of its content through a byline or other means. It has been shown that the presentation of author credentials is positively linked to credibility [14,25,26,27]. We implement the signal's automated evaluation by either extracting the author's credentials directly from the web page's HTML code or through the use of a third-party parsing library.

Clickbait headlines are deliberately sensationalist and misleading in an attempt at enticing consumers to click through to the linked article or content. Clickbait has been found to be indicative of web content with poor quality and low credibility, and is frequently linked to fake news [28,29,1]. Karadzhov et al. [30] construct a fake news and clickbait classifier using stylometric, lexical, grammatical and semantic features with a neural model, which we used for our system.

Grammar & Spelling errors are perhaps the most basic language-related form of amateurism, and intuitively indicate lower quality content. Previous studies have found a correlation between such errors and decreased credibility [31]. To determine the amount of spelling and language errors in the headline and text, we utilise the LanguageTool library. A significant problem here was the large amount of false positives, and we perform extensive filtering of the error matches to exclude errors such as using allegedly wrong forms of quotes or dashes, lexical redundancy, and British English orthography. We also conduct entity recognition using spaCy to avoid classifying names as errors, as these were the majority of error matches.

Language structure encompasses several signals related to morphological and syntactical properties of the language which are commonly included in works on credibility and deception detection [32,33,23]. We select the features most frequently deemed effective in predicting credibility: *number of words* in text and title, *average word length* in text and title, and *number of sentences* as well as *type-token-ratio* (TTR[3]) for the text.

External links describes the number of hyperlinks in the text which point to a different website. Linking to additional information, especially from external sources, has been found to increase credibility and be a predictor for legitimate news [19,33].

Readability of a text describes the complexity of its language in syntax and vocabulary, or the linguistic proficiency required to understand it. It is consistently featured in the literature as indicative of credibility or useful feature in fake news classification [19,33,30]. Textual web content with a higher reading level may be considered more professional, and therefore of higher quality, impacting credibility assessments. Using the

---

[3]TTR is the ratio of unique words (types) to total words (tokens) and describes a text's lexical density.

readability[4] library to compare various readability grades, we find that the Coleman-Liau index [34] performs best and use it in our signal evaluation.[5] The same readability index is also utilised by [35] and [33].

Emotional, sensational or affective language: Although previous results are at times inconsistent, researchers are in agreement overall that higher emotionality generally indicates content with lower credibility and an increased likelihood of being fake news [9,36,23]. Highly emotional messages aim at evoking specific feelings, sometimes in an attempt to hide poor argumentation or the absence of supporting evidence, while objective and unbiased information is commonly expected to be presented with little emotion. We decided to use the tool VADER for sentiment analysis and emotional word frequency analysis to target different aspects of language emotionality. For the latter we use the NRC Emotion Intensity Lexicon (NRC-EIL)[6] by [37] to calculate the average intensity per word with regard to eight different emotions.

Subjectivity or bias has been frequently named as a dimension of credibility [38,39,13], and was determined to be an advisable feature in automated credibility evaluation [17]. Like emotional language, this signal is difficult to determine precisely and consistently, nevertheless we opt to evaluate subjectivity due to its widely ascribed relevance to credibility assessments and low manipulability. We use TextBlob (through spaCy)[7] to capture a web page's subjectivity.

Punctuation: Previous research suggests that the analysis of punctuation, in particular question and exclamation mark usage may be beneficial for credibility assessments and fake news detection [32,10]. Increased question or exclamation mark presence – particularly in the headline – might indicate more sensationalist and clickbait'y content.

All caps are employed in informal communication, advertisements and the tabloid press to emphasise parts of text, and typically feel out of place and unprofessional in more formal contexts. Horne and Adalı [10] analysed fake news and determined an increased use of all caps compared to authentic news. Detection of these signals is trivial and they are thus highly interoperable, although it is important to exclude acronyms or initialisms as all-capitalised words.

Top-level domains: We analyse whether URLs include domains like "org", "gov" or "edu" as top- or second-level domain. Studies suggest that websites with these domains are assigned higher credibility ratings by consumers [25,26], which have been found to be a useful evaluation feature for credibility assessment systems [17,19]. While not content-related, this signal is interoperable, very easy to assess, and also difficult to game and therefore we decided to include it as an additional statistic on evaluated data.

Profanity: While insults, slurs or hate speech are discussed rarely in the web credibility literature, there are ample mentions of its negative effect on credibility in other domains [40]. For profanity, we merge a number of suitable word lists available online[8] and manually review the entries, removing those that are not necessarily insults or slurs

---

[4]https://github.com/andreasvc/readability/
[5]This index computes the readability based on on characters per word: $CLI = 0.0588L - 0.296S - 15.8$ where L is the average number of letters per 100 words, S is the average number of sentences per 100 words.
[6]https://saifmohammad.com/WebPages/AffectIntensity.htm
[7]https://spacy.io/universe/project/spacy-textblob
[8]https://github.com/dariusk/wordfilter/blob/master/lib/badwords.json,
https://www.freewebheaders.com/full-list-of-bad-words-banned-by-google/,
https://github.com/RobertJGabriel/Google-profanity-words,
http://www.bannedwordlist.com/lists/swearWords.txt

but perhaps only informal language, e. g., "hell", "crazy", "queer", "insane". Afterwards the text is searched for matching strings, which we find to occur extremely rarely.

A majority of the selected signals are specified precisely in terms of input information and evaluation manner, leading to high interoperability. For example, "misspellings in the text" is clearly defined, and can be consistently evaluated by different systems. On the other hand, a few signals are harder to specify precisely and their evaluation is more implementation-dependent (e. g., "emotionality of the language"). Some signals with lower interoperability, as well as some that are not on the list by [12], were nevertheless included after reviewing relevant publications in the literature, because of their low expected measurement difficulty and proven tie to credibility.

3.2. System Design

We combine pipelines for the measurement of a total of 23 credibility signals, grouped into ten evaluator modules, to assess a web page's credibility (Section 1). Beyond the general functionality of our system ALPACA (Automated Language-focused web page Credibility Assessor), our focus lies on the system's modularity and extensibility (see Figure 1). Subroutines for new signals can be added and modified without much effort, in order to be able to better study the effects of different signals and facilitate iterative improvements of the software.[9] Though a popular approach in automated credibility assessment, we do not train a machine learning model for the overall task. Our system is transparent, domain-independent, as well as modular and easily extensible in contrast to existing ML approaches, which can be considered black boxes.

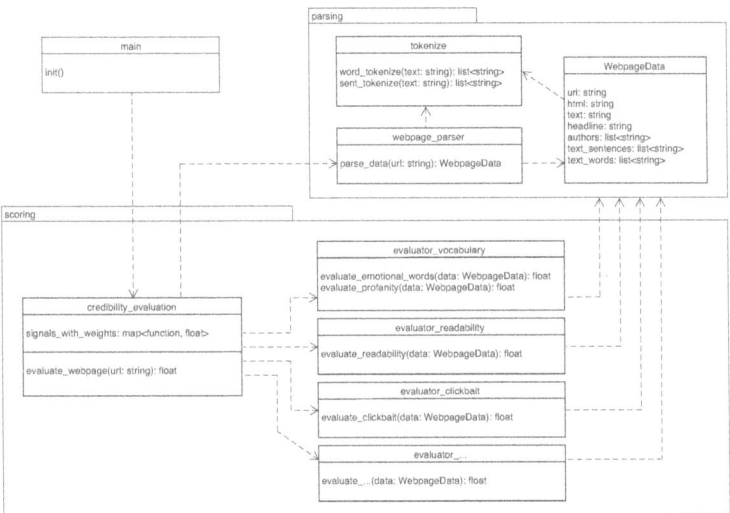

Figure 1. Simplified internal class diagram and architecture of our credibility evaluation system

We implement a web page parsing module and separate evaluation pipelines for the credibility signals, which process the content and return signal sub-scores. These are combined with signal weights through a linear combination function which empha-

---

[9]The data and code is available through our project's GitHub repository: https://github.com/lvap/alpaca.

sises low sub-scores to produce the final score between 0 (low) and 1 (high). We employ our own subroutines and a variety of publicly available tools in the signal evaluation pipelines. For several signals (emotional words, sentiment analysis, readability), we compared different approaches and selected the best-performing method; see Section 4 for the used data sets. Most language metrics are scaled by overall text length, i. e., number of words or sentences.[10]

Table 1. Summary of modules and credibility signals and weights to compute the score. +/− means the signal has a pos./neg. impact on the credibility score for greater values (e. g., more negativity in the headline leads to a lower score). * Domain ending is only weighted as bonus (if sub-score = 1). ** Profanity is only weighted as malus (if sub-score < 1).

Module	Credibility signal	Explanation	Weight
author	author	+ web page states author	0.1
clickbait	clickbait	− headline is clickbait	0.5
errors	errors	− grammar & spelling errors	0.35
language_structure	word_count_text	+ number of words in text	0.3
	word_count_title	− number of words in title	0.35
	sentence_count	+ number of sentences in text	0.4
	ttr	+ type-token-ratio	0
	word_length_text	+ average word length in text	0.3
	word_length_title	+ average word length in title	0.2
links	links_external	+ number of outbound links	0.1
readability	readability	+ Coleman-Liau grade	0.5
sentiment	polarity_text	+ polarity of text (pos. or neg.)	0.35
	polarity_title	− negativity of title	0.35
	subjectivity	− subjectivity	0.25
tonality	questions_text	− question marks in text	0.1
	questions_title	− title contains question mark	0.1
	exclamations_text	− exclamation marks in text	0.4
	exclamations_title	− title contains exclamation mark	0.25
	all_caps_text	− all caps words in text	0.1
	all_caps_title	− all caps words in title	0.4
url	domain_ending*	+ contains .org, .edu or .gov	0.5
vocabulary	profanity**	− no. of profanity words	0.1
	emotional_words	− avg. emotionality per word	0.7

The weights for the signals (Section 1) were determined iteratively, considering prior research results, signal measurement accuracy, and experimental calculations on test data. The type-token-ratio has no definite standing as credibility indicator in the literature and also did not correlate with credibility in our tests, thus it is not weighted in the final evaluation. We decided not to prioritise the domain weighting too much, as our

---

[10]In our repository we have dedicated methods for computing signal subscores, see https://github.com/lvap/alpaca/blob/signal-implementation-analysis/scoring/evaluator_url.py

system should still focus on content evaluation. Profanity only occurs extremely rarely, which is why we only treat it as malus.

We hypothesise that highly credible content scores well on most signals, while less credible web pages will have a mix of low and medium to high signal sub-scores. Therefore, we utilise a linear combination formula for the final score which increases the weight of low signal scores. For scores greater than 0.75, the original weight stays the same, but between 0.75 and 0.25 it linearly increases to twice the weight, and below 0.25 the score is constant again with doubled weight. For any signal α with sub-score $s_\alpha \in [0,1]$ and corresponding preliminary weight w_α from Section 1, the final weight towards the credibility score is:

$$\bar{w}_\alpha := w_\alpha(2 - min(max(2s_\alpha - 0.5, 0), 1)) \tag{1}$$

The system computes the signal sub-scores and final weights depending on the sub-scores and preliminary weights. It then performs a linear combination of the values to determine the overall credibility score between 0 (low credibility) and 1 (high).

4. Data Sets

We conduct test runs on a set of URLs compiled from several data sets with different domains to evaluate the credibility prediction performance of the entire system, of the individual credibility signals, and of the different signal implementations. Some of the data sets showed a variety of issues preventing their use as-is. We discuss the problems pertaining to the individual data sources in more detail in their respective sections. Three data sets contain credibility ratings on a Likert scale from one to five (least to most credible); the fourth contains pages classified as fake or real news; we interpret this as a credibility assertion, equating fake news with low and real news with high credibility.

The **Microsoft data set** [15] contains 1,000 URLs with corresponding Likert credibility ratings, assigned by one author. The authors performed 25 web searches (on 5 overall topics) and selected the top results as data set entries. Several early works in web credibility utilised this data to judge their systems' performance [17,18], but many of the URLs now redirect to unrelated content or point to nonexistent pages. While in theory cached versions of all pages were included, there are numerous practical problems: the cached version does not always match the actual URL, some pages are stored as HTML files and some as PDFs, the folder structure is inconsistent, and not all pages are contained [17,19]. A certain degree of domain and personal bias is expected due to the selection and rating methodology.

The **Reconcile data set** [41], also known as the Content Credibility Corpus (C3), spans 5,691 pages with almost 16,000 crowd-sourced evaluations by more than 2,000 annotators recruited through Amazon Mechanical Turk. The entries were selected manually through RSS feed subscriptions and Google queries by the authors, covering five major domains: politics & economy, medicine, healthy lifestyle, personal finance and entertainment. The annotators evaluated cached pages regarding several dimensions on a five-point Likert scale. Where necessary, we average the credibility ratings to obtain a mean page score. The data set is very diverse, such that we can assume tests on it to generalise well for the English-language web.

The **Credibility Coalition data set** [28] is a corpus of 42 web pages to enable research on credibility indicators. The entries were selected by finding the most shared articles on social media for specific search terms related to public health and climate science. These topics were chosen because the authors believe misinformation to be particularly prevalent in these domains despite an established expert consensus. Five experts for the domains were consulted to produce Likert-scale credibility ratings. On its own, the data set is modest in size, has a limited spectrum of topics, and the credibility ratings originate from just one person each (though they were produced by domain experts).

Lastly, we include the **FakeNewsNet data set** [42]. The fact-checking websites PolitiFact[11] GossipCop[12], automated Google searches and the platform E! Online[13], were utilised to obtain true and false articles in the domains of political news and celebrity gossip. A subset of the data set with roughly 17,400 real and 5,700 fake news pages is published. Although its size is substantial, and the fake news classifications sourced from established fact-checkers are convincing, the data is limited to just two domains.

We decide to use all suitable entries from the Credibility Coalition data set and 100 each (randomly selected) from the Microsoft, Reconcile, FakeNewsNet gossip and politics data sets respectively, for a total of 442 pages, which should yield a fairly robust corpus representative of the English-language web. Every URL was manually checked to confirm that it still links to the presumable original content. Especially older URLs point to unreachable web locations, highlighting the necessity to archive such data sets as HTML files or through online archival services. For broken links, we attempted to find cached versions in the Internet Archive[14]; if available, we chose the version with an archival date close to the release of the respective data set. Infrequently, an archived page instead of the original was selected to avoid cookie banners, pop-ups or redirects. Entries with content that clearly changes often and where the original state at the time of rating could not be determined – such as wiki-style websites, blog homepages, etc. – were discarded. Furthermore, satirical pages and those that are not text-centric, like image collections, link aggregations or video-focused pages, were also skipped.

For the evaluation, we merged the URLs into two data sets: one containing all web pages rated on a Likert scale, and another with the FakeNewsNet fake and real news. We refer to these collections as the "Likert" and "binary" data sets. The binary data contains 100 fake and 100 legitimate news pages. The Likert data set is rather unbalanced, encompassing (when rounding the credibility scores) 16 pages with rating 1, 24 with rating 2, 36 with rating 3, 109 with rating 4, and 57 with rating 5, of a total 242 pages. We process the data sets with our system to collect a variety of statistics pertaining to the different signals, the computed signal sub-scores and the overall web page credibility scores.

5. Results and Discussion

5.1. Individual Credibility Signals

We are particularly interested in the credibility prediction performance of individual signals. Emotional features, several morphological and syntactical text metrics, as well as

---

[11] https://www.politifact.com
[12] https://www.gossipcop.com, redirects to https://www.suggest.com as of 2022-01-21.
[13] https://www.eonline.com
[14] https://web.archive.org

Table 2. Summary data sets

Dataset	Description	#URLS used
Microsoft dataset [15]	1,000 URLs with corresponding Likert credibility ratings assigned by one author; contains websites with different topics and page types	100
Reconcile dataset [41]	5,691 thematically diverse pages with almost 16,000 crowdsourced evaluations by more than 2,000 participants	100
Cred. Coal. dataset [28]	43 web pages with most shared articles on social media related to climate science and public health rated by five domain experts	43
FakeNewsNet dataset [42]	Approx. 17,400 real news and 5,700 fake news in the domains of political news and celebrity gossip	200

the number of exclamation marks in the text and all capitals in the title best predict web content credibility. The domain ending, whether the headline is clickbait, and the sentiment of text and title are also influential. Many signals affirm our assumptions of their relation to credibility on at least one data set, however few produce correlations of statistical relevance for both (Section 3). The two signals that do are also among those with the highest ρ-coefficients: URL domain ending and emotional intensity of the text. The fact that the domain of a web page has such a clear link to credibility points to an influence of properties not related to the communicated information itself. The correlation values for emotional intensity confirm the importance of emotional signals for credibility assessment. We find that pages with more emotionally intense texts are less credible, while neutral or moderate language is linked to more credible content. Although sentiment analysis is rather average among all of our signals in terms of association with credibility, the polarity of the text and headline also show some trends. Specifically, less credible pages have texts and headlines with more negative sentiment on average, and the texts of more credible pages have a more positive sentiment.

Our experiments affirm that more credible web pages have generally longer content with more words and sentences, as well as longer words in the headline and text body. An exception is the length of the title, which is longer for less credible web pages. This coincides with the findings of Horne and Adalı [10], saying that fake news pages put the central claim and as much content as possible in the title, allowing users to skip reading the actual article. Horne and Adalı [10] also determine that fake news articles are repetitive and less complex, leading to a decreased type-token-ratio (TTR) in comparison to legitimate pages. However, we were unable to confirm this assertion, as the calculated TTR values on our data did not correlate positively with credibility. Some of the punctuation and all caps signals affected credibility, although the degree of association and its statistical relevance is small for most tonality signals. Exclamation marks in the text and all capitals in the headline are relatively strong in their correlation to the ratings on one data set respectively, while exclamation marks in the title have a small effect. This is not very surprising, as these features are indicative of more emotional, sensationalist and arguably unprofessional content. Frequency of question marks and all caps did not show a definite trend. Grammar and spelling errors have a negative influence on the credibility ratings of the Likert data set, but the relation on the binary data is not statistically distinctive enough ($p > 0.05$). It might be sensible to construct a more robust error checker if repeating the evaluations, as we suspect that a substantial part of the errors are false matches, contaminating the results. Clickbait is found to correlate with low credibility on the Likert data; the correlation coefficient is similar on the binary data but without

Table 3. Spearman correlation values for the data sets' web page credibility ratings and the underlying data used to compute the signal sub-scores (e. g., for errors the amount of errors per word, for readability the Coleman-Liau index), $*p < 0.05$

Signal	Likert data set		Binary data set	
	ρ	p	ρ	p
domain_ending	0.1746552141*	0.00645	0.2154101092*	0.00219
sentence_count	-0.0395744286	0.54008	0.3288565133*	0.00000
emotional_words	-0.155948275*	0.01517	-0.230712051*	0.00101
exclamations_text	-0.2768877057*	0.00001	-0.0584028802	0.41138
word_count_text	-0.0095320953	0.88272	0.3335141790*	0.00000
all_caps_title	-0.1219136512	0.06094	-0.1997281845*	0.00468
word_count_title	-0.0793427246	0.21972	-0.2014620755*	0.00423
errors	-0.1569651044*	0.01451	-0.1237231099	0.08091
clickbait	0.1362540513*	0.03451	0.1307937102	0.06489
polarity_text	0.035164685	0.58619	0.2280411934*	0.00116
polarity_title	-0.1564103010*	0.01508	-0.0764990174	0.28163
word_length_text	0.2519853282*	0.00007	-0.0055426319	0.93791
subjectivity	-0.1342034708*	0.03695	-0.0883356954	0.21355
readability	0.2375362725*	0.00019	-0.037585972	0.59722
exclamations_title	-0.1236448206	0.05525	-0.0467952685	0.51054
word_length_title	0.0679555930	0.29340	0.0765639770	0.28122
all_caps_text	-0.1059896996	0.09999	-0.0010784989	0.98791
questions_text	-0.0668347009	0.30045	0.0793350012	0.26412
author	0.0938657991	0.14543	-0.1286239389	0.06950
profanity	-0.0049520309	0.93891	0.0593909863	0.40350
questions_title	0.1467793630*	0.02266	-0.0368604890	0.60432
links_external	-0.2065647188*	0.00123	0.0072458950	0.91889
type-token-ratio	0.0229363492	0.72259	-0.3529098958*	0.00000

statistical significance. That clickbait content is less credible becomes apparent when analysing the distribution of clickbait headlines within our data sets: almost two-thirds of both the fake news and 1-rated web pages have titles classified as clickbait, but only 49% of real news and just 30% of 5-rated pages (although 49% still seems like a high number for legitimate content). A weak link is established between increased subjectivity and lower credibility on the Likert data. As the relevance of bias and subjectivity to credibility assessments is emphasised by literary sources [13,17], we believe that the underwhelming overall performance of this signal is due to the simple pre-trained model we employed, and better results might be achievable with a more advanced assessor. Though utilised in many existing credibility classification systems, (Coleman-Liau) readability only predicted credibility on the Likert data. Further analysis reveals that the readability grade distribution is highly similar for both binary data set classes, but follows a trend for the Likert data. It is therefore possible that readability predicts general credibility, but is not able to discriminate between real and fake news content.

Overall, several well-performing credibility signals confirm previous findings regarding their link to credibility, while many further signals show a sound correlation with credibility on one data set but none on the other. This could point to biases in the data selection, but may as well illustrate stylistic differences in the contained web pages.

While we produce a number of results supported by evidence and consistent with the literature, for other signals we did not get statistically significant results such as question mark frequency, author, and outbound links. Although drawn from a plurality of sources, the small size of our data basis (442 pages) is a concern, and we note that our conclusions may not be generally valid. Repeating the evaluation on a sufficiently large and balanced data basis could provide additional insights.

We also analyse co-occurrences of signals, i. e., inter-signal correlations. We calculate the Spearman correlation values for all signal combinations and focus on results with $p < 0.05$. Four signal tuples exhibit particularly strong correlations with each other. Readability and average word length are positively correlated, just like the number of words and sentences. These associations are intuitive: longer words are more complex and lead to a higher readability level, and more demanding texts likely include longer words (the Coleman-Liau index considers letters per words); furthermore, a larger number of sentences obviously correlates with a higher word count, and vice versa. Additionally, TTR is negatively correlated to both the number of sentences and words, which is also easily explainable as longer texts have a much higher potential for lexical repetition.

5.2. System Performance

We analyse the system's credibility assessment performance on the Likert and binary data sets. The calculated scores cluster in the range between 0.45 and 0.7 and fall above a minimum of 0.1986 and below a maximum of 0.9510 (Section 2). The fact that high scores of almost 1 are reached, but barely any under 0.2, might confirm our hypothesis of higher sub-scores being relatively common even among less credible pages, which had motivated our scoring function's design. The distinguishing feature of pages with low credibility is a (small) number of low sub-scores, which should be assigned more weight to be able to affect the overall score. It seems the scoring function is not able to properly leverage the different sub-scores in order to spread the final scores evenly, and therefore a strong bias towards a certain range of values can be observed.

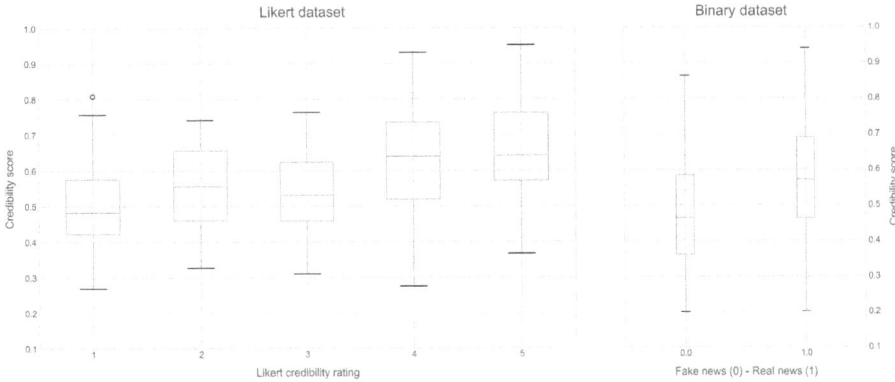

Figure 2. Distribution of computed credibility scores for Likert and binary data sets as box plots (Likert credibility ratings were rounded). The scores cluster in the range between 0.45 and 0.7.

The Spearman correlation coefficients for our credibility scores and the data sets' credibility ratings are $\rho = 0.29123$ (with $p = 0.00041$) for the Likert data and $\rho =$

0.30155 (with $p = 0.00001$) for the binary data. Our scores are undeniably correlated to the ratings, although the degree of correlation is quite weak given that the values should express the same information. The correlation strength is almost the same for the two data sets, suggesting a similar performance on both. To test the system as a credibility classifier, we assign classes to the web pages depending on the computed score. The binary data set's pages are classified as fake news if their credibility score is below 0.5, and as real news otherwise. We predict 94 pages to be fake news and 106 to be legitimate. 60 fake and 66 real news are labelled correctly for a total of 126 correct classifications, resulting in an accuracy of 63% (precision: 62.2%, recall: 66%). The accuracy is therefore above the random baseline but it leaves room for improvement. Web pages in the Likert data set are assigned five classes by multiplying their computed credibility score by five and rounding the resulting values. There are 2 pages with predicted class 1, 59 with class 2, 112 with class 3, 65 with class 4, and 4 with class 5. Comparing these classes to the rounded Likert ratings, we find that 68 out of 242 pages are labelled correctly for an accuracy of 28.1%. The mean offset between a web page's Likert rating and our computed score times five is 1.01828, and the median offset is 0.90077. Thus, our system's credibility scores differ by about 1 on average from the original Likert ratings. The classification performance is clearly better than a random baseline of 20%, but not completely convincing overall. Despite the Likert ratings being very imbalanced, our computed scores roughly follow a normal distribution around the centre class 3, which might be desirable for the general evaluation of web pages. Our system outperforms the random baselines for classifying web page credibility on a Likert scale or as fake/real news. This demonstrates that content-driven credibility evaluation is feasible, and that the corresponding signals are important components of web credibility. The system's performance can still be improved though, such as by adding further signals or improving the credibility score function. Statistics from the evaluation of a large data set could be used to devise an optimal formula for combining sub-scores as well as optimal signal weights.

5.3. Limitations and Future work

Many signals show a correlation with credibility on one dataset but none on the other. This may point to biases in data selection, but may as well illustrate stylistic differences in the contained web pages, e. g., higher readability grades (for all examined readability metrics) were linked to increased credibility on the Likert data, but were not associated with the fake or real news classes. Repeating the evaluation on a sufficiently large and balanced data basis could shed light on the root cause of this behaviour. The overall system outperforms the random baseline for both classifying fake news and web pages into credibility ratings on a Likert scale. This proves that content-focused credibility evaluation is feasible, and that content-related signals are important components of web credibility. However, the overall performance of the system is still in need of improvement.

Besides the addition of further signals, optimisation of the system should focus on the credibility score function and the measurement of individual signals. Theoretically, signal statistics from the evaluation of a large dataset could be used to devise an optimal formula for combining signal sub-scores, including optimal signal weights. We utilised the same datasets to determine the signal weights (through an analysis of the assessment data, together with other factors) and to test the system's performance; ideally, the system should be tested on unrelated data, and our approach could certainly lead to somewhat biased results. Regarding the signal measurements, in general, signal data is often very erratic, with many outliers that introduce unnecessary noise. A common reason for this might be parsing errors or flaws in the signal evaluation, such as in the grammar and spelling error pipeline, which frequently flags passages which are not true errors, or the subjectivity assessment, where we employ a simple pre-trained model, but which could be improved through the use of a better bias and subjectivity detector. Ultimately, while we produce a number of results supported by convincing evidence and consistent with scientific literature, the interpretations should be taken with a grain of salt. While drawn from a plurality of sources, the small size of our data basis (442 pages) is a concern and we must be aware that conclusions drawn from its evaluation may not be generally valid. Therefore, signal-credibility associations (or lack thereof) may not necessarily point to the actual performance of the signals, but could be induced by implementation or dataset specifics for the signals with ambiguous correlation to credibility according to our evaluation. These relationships remain to be further investigated by future research.

6. Summary and Conclusions

The credibility of web content has become an increasingly important public issue as communication and information exchange keeps evolving in the digital age. We believe that computational linguistics and artificial intelligence can play an important role in the development of technologies that help shift the online ecosystem towards more credible content through automated content evaluation and curation tools. When designing such technologies, we must take special care not to devise systems which facilitate censorship and foster social division or echo chambers. We present a system that automatically evaluates the credibility of web pages and produces a web page credibility score, to be utilised by users to inform and support their own assessments. We use the extensive credibility signal list published by the W3C Credible Web Community Group and results from previous research to identify key signals to include in our system. Our focus lies on properties that are linked to the actual content. We evaluate our approach on two data sets, each compiled by selecting a subset of random entries from several publicly available data sets to minimise possible biases. The first contains web pages and their credibility ratings on a five-point Likert scale, while the other consists of real and fake news articles, where the real news are assumed to have high credibility and the fake news low credibility. We can confirm previous findings that link credibility to several signals related to emotion, structural properties of the language, and punctuation and typesetting characteristics. Web pages with lower credibility have a greater emotionality, less complex language, are shorter, and contain more errors and exclamation marks. Headlines of less credible web content are longer, contain more words in all capitals, have more negative sentiment and are frequently clickbait: two-thirds of the web pages with low credibility in our evaluation data sets had clickbait titles. Low quality pages have shorter, less sophisticated content and put more emphasis on the headline, perhaps to allow readers to obtain all necessary information from the title and be able to skip reading the actual text. We use the computed credibility scores to assess the performance of our system, which achieves a classification accuracy of 63% for fake news detection, and a prediction accuracy of 28% for assigning credibility ratings on a five-point scale. Our system outperforms the random baselines of 50% and 20% respectively for both data sets, affirming that content-focused credibility evaluation is feasible. In terms of future work, we intend to incorporate additional signal pipelines (e. g., inter-titles, number and length of paragraphs, photos) and improve the implementation of some existing signals which appear to not yet perform as anticipated. We plan to replicate the evaluation of the signals and the system as a whole on a larger, more robust and balanced data set to obtain more conclusive results. Lastly, some useful signals we analysed – number of sentences, sentiment of text and title, words in all capitals, length of the headline – were not directly covered by the W3C list of credibility signals, but we suggest to include them in any upcoming compilations of credibility signals based on our experimental results.

Acknowledgements

The research presented in this article is partially funded by the German Federal Ministry of Education and Research (BMBF) through the projects QURATOR (Unternehmen Region, Wachstumskern, no. 03WKDA1A) and PANQURA (no. 03COV03E).

References

[1]   Zannettou S, Sirivianos M, Blackburn J, Kourtellis N. The Web of False Information: Rumors, Fake News, Hoaxes, Clickbait, and Various Other Shenanigans. Journal of Data and Information Quality. 2019;11(3):1-37.

[2]   Watson A. Share of adults worldwide who believe fake news is prevalent in selected media sources as of February 2019; 2021. Accessed 2022-01-21. URL https://www.statista.com/statistics/1112026/fake -news-prevalence-attitudes-worldwide/.

[3]   Nakov P, Mihaylova T, Màrquez L, Shiroya Y, Koychev I. Do Not Trust the Trolls: Predicting Credibility in Community Question Answering Forums. In: Proc. of the Int. Conf. Recent Advances in Natural Language Processing, RANLP 2017. Varna, Bulgaria: INCOMA Ltd.; 2017. p. 551-60.

[4]   Gupta A, Kumaraguru P, Castillo C, Meier P. In: Aiello LM, McFarland D, editors. TweetCred: Real-Time Credibility Assessment of Content on Twitter. Cham: Springer; 2014. p. 228-43.

[5]   Chen Y, Conroy NK, Rubin VL. News in an online world: The need for an "automatic crap detector". Proc of the Association for Information Science and Technology. 2015;52(1):1-4.

[6]   W3C Community Group Credible Web. Technological Approaches to Improving Credibility Assessment on the Web; 2018. Accessed 2022-01-21. Sandro Hawke, editor. URL https://www.w3.org/2018/10/cre dibility-tech/.

[7]   Lazer DMJ, Baum MA, Benkler Y, Berinsky AJ, Greenhill KM, Menczer F, et al. The science of fake news. Science. 2018;359(6380):1094-6.

[8]   Rehm G. An Infrastructure for Empowering Internet Users to Handle Fake News and Other Online Media Phenomena. In: Rehm G, Declerck T, editors. Language Technologies for the Challenges of the Digital Age. GSCL 2017. Springer; 2018. p. 216-31.

[9]   Giachanou A, Rosso P, Crestani F. Leveraging Emotional Signals for Credibility Detection. In: Proc. of the 42nd Int. ACM SIGIR Conf. on Research and Development in Information Retrieval. SIGIR'19. Association for Computing Machinery; 2019. p. 877-80.

[10] Horne B, Adalı S. This Just In: Fake News Packs A Lot In Title, Uses Simpler, Repetitive Content in Text Body, More Similar To Satire Than Real News. Proc of the Int AAAI Conf on Web and Social Media. 2017;11(1):759-66.

[11] Karimi H, Tang J. Learning Hierarchical Discourse-level Structure for Fake News Detection. In: Proc. of the 2019 Conf. of the North American Chapter of the Association for Computational Linguistics: Human Language Technologies, Volume 1 (Long and Short Papers). Association for Computational Linguistics; 2019. p. 3432-42.

[12] W3C Community Group Credible Web. Credibility Signals; 2019. Accessed 2022-01-21. Sandro Hawke, editor. URL https://credweb.org/signals-20191126.

[13]   Fogg BJ, Soohoo C, Danielson DR, Marable L, Stanford J, Tauber ER. How Do Users Evaluate the Credibility of Web Sites? A Study with over 2,500 Participants. In: Proc. of the 2003 conference on Designing for user experiences. DUX '03. Association for Computing Machinery; 2003. p. 1-15.

[14]   Rieh SY, Belkin NJ. Understanding Judgment of Information Quality and Cognitive Authority in the WWW. In: Preston CM, editor. Proc. of the 61st Annual Meeting of the American Society for Information Science (ASIS). vol. 35; 1998. p. 279-89.

[15]   Schwarz J, Morris MR. Augmenting Web Pages and Search Results to Support Credibility Assessment. In: Proc. of the SIGCHI Conf. on Human Factors in Computing Systems. CHI '11. Association for Computing Machinery; 2011. p. 1245-54.

[16]   Horne BD, Dron W, Khedr S, Adalı S. Assessing the News Landscape: A Multi-Module Toolkit for Evaluating the Credibility of News. In: Companion Proc. of the The Web Conf. 2018. WWW '18. Int. World Wide Web Conferences Steering Committee; 2018. p. 235-8.

[17]   Olteanu A, Peshterliev S, Liu X, Aberer K. Web Credibility: Features Exploration and Credibility Prediction. In: Serdyukov P, Braslavski P, Kuznetsov SO, Kamps J, Rüger S, Agichtein E, et al., editors. Advances in Information Retrieval. ECIR 2013. Springer Berlin Heidelberg; 2013. p. 557-68.

[18]   Wawer A, Nielek R, Wierzbicki A. Predicting Webpage Credibility Using Linguistic Features. In: Proc. of the 23rd Int. Conf. on World Wide Web. WWW '14 Companion. Association for Computing Machinery; 2014. p. 1135-40.

[19]   Esteves D, Reddy AJ, Chawla P, Lehmann J. Belittling the Source: Trustworthiness Indicators to Obfuscate Fake News on the Web. In: Proc. of the First Workshop on Fact Extraction and VERification (FEVER). Association for Computational Linguistics; 2018. p. 50-9.

[20]   Afroz S, Brennan M, Greenstadt R. Detecting Hoaxes, Frauds, and Deception in Writing Style Online. In: 2012 IEEE Symposium on Security and Privacy. IEEE; 2012. p. 461-75.

[21]   Rashkin H, Choi E, Jang JY, Volkova S, Choi Y. Truth of Varying Shades: Analyzing Language in Fake News and Political Fact-Checking. In: Proc. of the 2017 Conf. on Empirical Methods in Natural Language Processing. Association for Computational Linguistics; 2017. p. 2931-7.

[22]   O'Brien N, Latessa S, Evangelopoulos G, Boix X. The Language of Fake News: Opening the Black-Box of Deep Learning Based Detectors; 2018. Paper presented at the Workshop on "AI for Social Good", NIPS 2018.

[23]   Przybyła P. Capturing the Style of Fake News. Proc of the AAAI Conf on Artificial Intelligence. 2020;34(1):490-7.

[24]   Keshavarz H. Assessing the credibility of Web information by university students: Findings from a case study in Iran. Global Knowledge, Memory and Communication. 2020;69(8/9):681-96.

[25]   Rieh SY, Belkin NJ. Interaction on the Web: Scholars' judgment of information quality and cognitive authority. In: Kraft DH, editor. Proc. of the 63rd Annual Meeting of the American Society for Information Science (ASIS). vol. 37; 2000. p. 25-38.

[26]   Fogg BJ, Marshall J, Laraki O, Osipovich A, Varma C, Fang N, et al. What Makes Web Sites Credible? A Report on a Large Quantitative Study. In: Proc. of the SIGCHI Conf. on Human Factors in Computing Systems. CHI '01. Association for Computing Machinery; 2001. p. 61-8.

[27]   Hong T. The influence of structural and message features on Web site credibility. Journal of the American Society for Information Science and Technology. 2006;57(1):114-27.

[28]   Zhang AX, Ranganathan A, Metz SE, Appling S, Sehat CM, Gilmore N, et al. A Structured Response to Misinformation: Defining and Annotating Credibility Indicators in News Articles. In: Companion Proc. of the The Web Conf. 2018. WWW '18. Int. World Wide Web Conferences Steering Committee; 2018. p. 603-12.

[29]   Bourgonje P, Moreno Schneider J, Rehm G. From Clickbait to Fake News Detection: An Approach based on Detecting the Stance of Headlines to Articles. In: Proc. of the 2017 EMNLP Workshop: Natural Language Processing meets Journalism. Association for Computational Linguistics; 2017. p. 84-9.

[30]   Karadzhov G, Gencheva P, Nakov P, Koychev I. We Built a Fake News / Click Bait Filter: What Happened Next Will Blow Your Mind! In: Proc. of the Int. Conf. Recent Advances in Natural Language Processing. RANLP 2017. INCOMA Ltd.; 2017. p. 334-43.

[31]   Beede P, Mulnix MW. Grammar, spelling error rates persist in digital news. Newspaper Research Journal. 2017;38(3):316-27.

[32]   Pérez-Rosas V, Kleinberg B, Lefevre A, Mihalcea R. Automatic Detection of Fake News. In: Proc. of the 27th Int. Conf. on Computational Linguistics. Association for Computational Linguistics; 2018. p. 3391-401.

[33]   Castelo S, Almeida T, Elghafari A, Santos A, Pham K, Nakamura E, et al. A Topic-Agnostic Approach for Identifying Fake News Pages. In: Companion Proc. of The 2019 World Wide Web Conference. WWW '19. Association for Computing Machinery; 2019. p. 975-80.

[34]   Coleman M, Liau TL. A computer readability formula designed for machine scoring. Journal of Applied Psychology. 1975;60(2):283-4.

[35]   Potthast M, Kiesel J, Reinartz K, Bevendorff J, Stein B. A Stylometric Inquiry into Hyperpartisan and Fake News. In: Proc. of the 56th Annual Meeting of the Association for Computational Linguistics (Volume 1: Long Papers). Association for Computational Linguistics; 2018. p. 231-40.

[36]   Li Q. Clickbait and emotional language in fake news; 2019. Accessed 2022-01-21. Preprint. URL https://www.ischool.utexas.edu/~ml/papers/li2019-thesis.pdf.

[37]   Mohammad SM. Word Affect Intensities. In: Proc. of the Eleventh Int. Conf. on Language Resources and Evaluation. LREC 2018. European Language Resources Association (ELRA); 2018. .

[38]   Metzger MJ, Flanagin AJ, Eyal K, Lemus DR, Mccann RM. Credibility for the 21st Century: Integrating Perspectives on Source, Message, and Media Credibility in the Contemporary Media Environment. Annals of the Int Communication Association. 2003;27(1):293-335.

[39]   Rieh SY, Danielson DR. Credibility: A multidisciplinary framework. Annual Review of Information Science and Technology. 2007;41(1):307-64.

[40]   Jay T. Cursing in America: A psycholinguistic study of dirty language in the courts, in the movies, in the schoolyards and on the streets. John Benjamins; 1992.

[41]   Kakol M, Nielek R, Wierzbicki A. Understanding and predicting Web content credibility using the Content Credibility Corpus. Information Processing & Management. 2017;53(5):1043-61.

[42]   Shu K, Mahudeswaran D, Wang S, Lee D, Liu H. FakeNewsNet: A Data Repository with News Content, Social Context, and Spatiotemporal Information for Studying Fake News on Social Media. Big Data. 2020;8(3):171-88.

Towards a Knowledge-Aware AI
A. Dimou et al. (Eds.)

© 2022 The Authors.
This article is published online with Open Access by IOS Press and distributed under the terms
of the Creative Commons Attribution License 4.0 (CC BY 4.0).

doi:10.3233/SSW220006

Evaluating Quality Improvement Techniques Within the Linked Data Generation Process

Alex Randles[a1] and Declan O'Sullivan[a]

[a] *ADAPT Centre for Digital Content, Trinity College Dublin, Ireland*

Abstract. Linked Data datasets when they are published typically have varying levels of quality. These datasets are created using mapping artefacts, which define the transformation rules from non-graph based data into graph based RDF data. Currently, quality issues are detected after the mapping artefact has been executed and the Linked Data has already been published. It is argued in this paper that addressing quality issues within the mapping artefacts will positively improve the quality of the resulting dataset that is generated. Furthermore, we suggest that an explicit quality process for mappings will improve quality, maintenance, and reuse. This paper describes the evaluation of the Mapping Quality Vocabulary (MQV) Framework, which aims to guide linked data producers in producing high quality datasets, by enabling the quality assessment and subsequent improvement of the mapping artefacts. The evaluation of the MQV framework consisted of 58 participants with varying level of background knowledge.

Keywords. Semantic Web; Mapping Quality; Dataset Quality; Linked data generation.

1. Introduction

Data quality is often referred to as "fitness for use" [1] and is a multidimensional concept which is determined by the stakeholders and factors involved in the creation of the data [2] . The quality of the data will affect how useful data consumers find the data for their application. Currently, quality assessment within the linked data domain is performed on published data and is the responsibility of data consumers rather than the producers [3]. This paper presents the evaluation of the MQV framework [4] that is designed to address the problem of quality earlier in the linked data publication lifecycle. The objective of the framework is to assist data providers in producing high quality linked data by bringing quality improvement procedures earlier into the publication process, thus resolving limitations that exist in the state of the art, where the focus typically is on the quality of the published dataset and not on quality of the mapping artefacts that produce them. The mapping artefacts typically define transformation rules for converting non-RDF data (e.g. excel or relational data) into RDF data. The W3C recommendation for transforming relational databases to RDF data, R2RML [5] is one example of an uplift mapping language. R2RML is used to express customized

---

[1] Alex Randles, ADAPT Centre for Digital Content, Trinity College Dublin, Dublin 2, Ireland; E-mail:alex.randles@adaptcentre.ie.

transformation rules. Creating these mappings is a complex, time-consuming task, which is frequently error prone [2]. Furthermore, creating high quality mappings requires a high level of background knowledge. Oftentimes, quality issues within these mappings are not detected until the dataset has been published. In our research, we argue that introducing quality improvement procedures which focus on these mapping artefacts will allow a significant number of root causes for published dataset quality issues to be identified and resolved. Furthermore, removing quality issues from the rules which generate the dataset will ensure these issues do not appear if the dataset is regenerated. In this paper, we provide a discussion of the structure and results of a usability evaluation of the MQV framework[2] which was conducted with 58 participants. The paper is structured as follows: Section 2 describes the related work within the state of the art; Section 3 presents the MQV framework; Section 4 presents an evaluation of the MQV framework and discusses the results and Section 5 presents final remarks.

2. State of the Art

The state of the art in mapping quality frameworks for linked data has been reviewed. We argue that evaluating the quality of linked data tools with potential end users should be undertaken to demonstrate the usefulness of the design [6]. While several of the approaches in the state of the art have been adopted by users within the community, none of the approaches described have conducted an evaluation which studies user interaction. Most of these approaches have been evaluated using a system evaluation, while the evaluation described within this paper has used a large sample size of users and standardized usability methods.

EvaMap [7] is a mapping quality framework used to assess and improve the quality RDF mappings. The work uses YARRRML mappings, which are a human readable representation of RDF mappings. The framework uses a set of metrics organized into 7 dimensions to assess the quality of the mappings or the resulting datasets when instances are required. Weights can be associated with metrics to provide different importance. Furthermore, a global quality score is generated to represent the overall quality of the mapping. Moreover, feedback is provided to users on how to improve the quality. The reports generated by the framework are human-readable and not machine-readable. An evaluation has not been completed on the framework.

The approach [2] designed by the researchers extends an existing linked data quality assessment framework named Luzzu framework [8]. Noteworthy, the approach focuses only on quality assessment and does not concern quality improvement. R2RML mappings [5] are assessed using metrics which are commonly used to assess dataset quality. Luzzu is extensible which allows the users to add additional metrics to the framework. Four metrics have been implemented by the framework which relate to the representational category [1] of data quality. Luzzu generates two machine-readable reports, however, the problem report is the focus of the work. An evaluation was completed on mappings from a real world uses case. The results show the potential to identify quality issues in certain cases. The approach was found to be reasonably accurate at identify quality issues, however, there was certain cases where ontologies could not be retrieved and queried.

---

[2] MQV framework at https://mqv-framework.adaptcentre.ie/

Resglass [3] provides a rule-driven methodology to detect inconsistencies within the rules used to generate linked data datasets. The approach ranks rules and ontology terms in order that should be inspected by an expert based on a score. Refinements are completed by an expert. Inconsistencies within the dataset are used to refine the rules and ontologies again. The work provides an implementation which targets RML mappings. The inconsistencies are detected using a rule-based reasoning system [9]. The methodology has been applied to two real-life use cases DBpedia and Computer Science bibliograph (DBLP). The researchers discuss manual refinements which could potentially be used to remove these inconsistencies.

The approach [10] provides a test-driven approach for mapping assessment and semi-automatic refinements based on the quality assessment. The implementation targets RML mapping language and extends RDFUnit [11] which is an RDF test-case-based architecture. The RDFUnit test cases are extended to apply to mappings by adjusting the assessment queries. The semi-automatic refinements query the RDFUnit serializations of the quality information which enables triples to be add/delete or suggest actions to the user. The evaluation was applied to diverse use cases which included DBpbedia and iLastic. The mappings collected were assessed which detected a large number of quality issues and a discussion of possible semi-automatic refinements. The results indicated that assessing mappings is more efficient in terms of computational complexity and requires significantly less time compared to assessing the dataset.

3. MQV Framework

The Mapping Quality Vocabulary (MQV) framework[3] [4] is a framework designed for the assessment and refinement of uplift mappings. Uplift mappings specify how to transform non-RDF data into RDF data. The objective of the framework is to improve the quality of these mappings, which will improve quality of the resulting dataset, while promoting mapping maintenance and reuse. The framework represents the quality information generated during the assessment process in RDF format using the Mapping Quality Vocabulary[4] [12,13]. MQV is used to represent and allow interchanging of provenance information relating to the creation, quality assessment and quality refinement of mapping specifications.

3.1. Design

A screenshot of the user interface of the MQV framework displaying the quality information for the mapping used during the evaluation is shown in **Figure 1.**

---

[3] A demonstration of the MQV framework at https://drive.google.com/file/d/1LzO-2CuVv8WLSGE6VaNKqmh3B6Q-osPv/view?usp=sharing

[4] Mapping Quality Vocabulary (MQV) specification at https://alex-randles.github.io/MQV/

Mapping Quality Assessment							Home	Logout

Mapping Quality Information [HIDE]

Violation ID ❶	Metric ID ❶	Result Message ❶	Value ❶	Triple Map Name ❶	Violation Location ❶	Select Refinements ❶	Display violation ❶
0	MP6	Language tag not defined in RFC 5646. ❶	en-GP	TriplesMap1	predicateObjectMap2	Manual ⌄	Display Violation
1	D2	Usage of undefined Property. ❶	prov:values	TriplesMap1	predicateObjectMap2	Manual ⌄	Display Violation
2	D7	Usage of incorrect datatype. ❶	prov:generatedAtTime	TriplesMap1	predicateObjectMap1	Manual ⌄	Display Violation

❶ Create Refinements

Export Quality Report (TTL)   Save result table as PDF

Figure 1: Screenshot of the user interface of the MQV framework

Figure 2 shows the component diagram of the MQV framework, which is designed using a Python web application. The application uses the RDFLib library [14] to query and update the mapping graph using SPARQL queries.

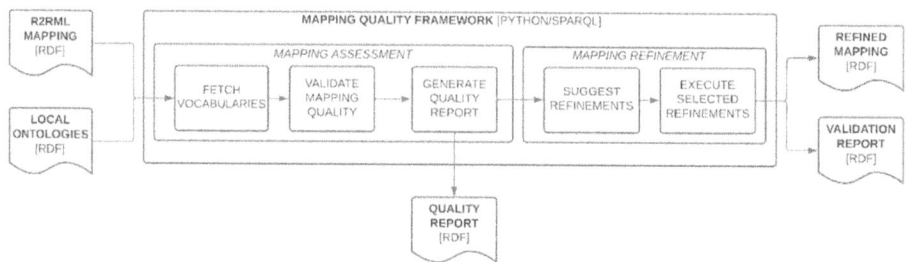

Figure 2: Component diagram of the MQV framework

The process starts with an R2RML [5] mapping and optional local ontology input into the framework. A local ontology refers to an ontology which is not available online, which could be currently being used for testing purposes. The vocabularies used within the mappings are fetched from online and stored in a local cache, which helps improve performance by querying the local copy. These vocabularies are queried using metrics defined as SPARQL queries to validate the quality of the mapping.

For example, the datatype range defined for a predicate within the mapping can be compared against the range within the vocabulary to ensure it is correct. A quality report is generated in MQV format after the mapping quality has been assessed. Refinements are suggested to the user based on quality issues within the mapping. These refinements are semi-automatic refinements which guide the users through the selection and execution. Each refinement has specifically been created for the quality issue. Once the refinements have been executed by the framework, a refined mapping is generated, which is a result of these refinements. Furthermore, a validation report is generated in MQV format which details the quality issues and the refinements which have been executed to resolve these issues. Moreover, the SPARQL query which was executed on the mapping during the refinement process is contained within the report.

3.2. Quality Assessment

The framework assesses the quality of mappings using domain specific metrics. These metrics assess different quality aspects within the mapping, which include Vocabulary, Mapping and Data quality aspects [15]. These metrics and aspects have been inspired from the state of the art in Linked Data quality [1,2,5,15–17].

Mapping Quality Aspect. The aspect ensures the concepts defined within the mapping conform to the specification of mapping language. For example, a join condition must have exactly one parent and child column.

Data Quality Aspect. The aspect focuses on the quality of the output which will be generated when the mapping processor has executed the mapping. For example, a non-dereferenceable class definition within the mapping will result in an exponential number of non-dereferenceable classes within the dataset, thus decreasing the quality of the data.

Vocabulary Quality Aspect. The quality of the vocabularies which are used within the mapping. For example, a class defined within the mapping should contain human-readable labels within the vocabulary.

A **quality violation** is generated when a metric related to one of these quality aspects detects a quality issue within the mapping. Thereafter, the violation can be refined by using the frameworks semi-automatic refinements.

3.3. Quality Refinement

The semi-automatic refinements which involve a human-in-the-loop can be described as three different methods, which have been inspired by previous research [3]. These methods are outlined below.

Insert custom value. Inserting a custom value involves the user entering an IRI or Literal value within a text box. Thereafter, the framework will replace the violation value within the mapping with the value entered. Prefixes are provided on the framework which could help to create the IRI. For example, if an undefined property is used within the mapping, users can select a prefix and enter the remaining IRI within the text box, which will replace the undefined property.

Select from suggested values. Selecting a value from suggested values involves the users browsing a drop-down menu and selecting a value. These values are designed to resolve the quality issues. Thereafter, the framework will replace the quality violation value with the selected value. For example, if an undefined property is used within the mapping, defined properties within the same namespace will be suggested to the user. Thereafter, users will select one of the values and the framework will replace the undefined property.

Insert suggested value. Inserting a suggested value involves the framework suggesting only one value to the user, which could hopefully resolve the quality issue. If the users are satisfied with the suggestion, the value will replace the violation value. For example, if a datatype defined within the mapping does not match the datatype defined within the vocabulary. The datatype from the vocabulary will be suggested to the user.

Once the refinements have been executed, a validation bar chart is displayed which shows the relationship between each quality violation and their corresponding quality dimension. These dimensions have been inspired from previous research [1] in linked data quality. The refined mapping generated by the refinements is available to download on the framework by pressing a button.

4. Evaluation

A usability experiment has been conducted with an implementation of the MQV framework. The usability experiment involved participants interacting with the interface of the framework using a mapping provided. The tasks were designed to test the main functionality of the framework (resolution of issues with a given mapping), followed by the examination of the reports generated.

4.1. Experiment cohorts

The participants were grouped into two cohorts. These cohorts included an expert and student cohort. These cohorts' recruitment process and background knowledge differed. Grouping participants into two cohorts allow them to be characterized based on background knowledge.

Recruitment. The expert participants were recruited based on a discussion with the supervisor of the study who would meet the inclusion/exclusion criteria. These participants were recruited individually through email invitation. These participants completed the experiment to contribute to the research objectives. The participants from the student cohort were recruited from the Knowledge and Data Engineering (CS7IS1) module in Trinity College Dublin. Each member of the class had the option to complete the experiment as a portfolio task for the course.

Background. The participants within the expert cohort are Semantic web researchers who are very knowledgeable with RDF and the R2RML mapping language. These participants have previous experience in creating and executing R2RML mappings. Participants from the student cohort have little knowledge of the theory of the R2RML mapping language. Furthermore, these participants have little experience with creating R2RML mappings, however, they have basic knowledge of semantic web technologies. Each cohort's background knowledge is further described within each of their respective sections.

Number of participants. The expert cohort consisted of 10 participants after the inclusion/exclusion was applied. The student cohort consists of 59 students from the Knowledge and Data Engineering (CS7IS1) module in Trinity College Dublin. The cohort was reduced to 48 participants after the inclusion/exclusion criteria was applied to the cohort.

4.2. Experiment Setup

The experiment setup for each cohort was identical with relation to the information and mapping provided prior to the experiment. However, the setup differed slightly with relation to the completion of the experiment and metrics used to measure the usability. The difference was due to the large sample size of the student cohort. It would not be feasible to arrange a video call with each participant in the cohort and transcribe/analyze their statements.

4.2.1. Experiment Preliminaries

The information sheet/informed consent was provided to all the participants prior to the experiment. Furthermore, the task sheet/mapping used during the experiment interaction were available on the framework. The information sheet and informed consent outlined the procedures and motivation for the experiment. These were provided to participants prior to the completion of the experiment, which would enable them to make an informed decision on whether to participate in the experiment. Furthermore, the participants could withdraw at any time prior to start of the experiment. These documents were reviewed and approved by the School's ethics committee within Trinity College Dublin. Following, the participants signing the informed consent document, a presentation was physically presented to the participants which outlines the motivation of the framework, the objectives of the study, its main contribution to research and an explanation of the mapping which will be used during the participants interaction. Noteworthy, the participants had no prior interaction with the framework before the experiment commenced.

The tasks which the participants completed during the experiment were designed to test the main functionality of the framework, which is the assessment and refinement of mappings. The process involves using a suite of quality metrics and related refinements while capturing information related to these processes in RDF format using MQV. The tasks outlined in the task sheet enable each of these characteristics to be evaluated. Twelve tasks were included within the task sheet. Tasks 1-3 involve the quality assessment of a mapping. Tasks 4-7 involve the selection and execution of refinements to remove quality issues within the mapping. Tasks 8-12 involve the examination of quality assessment information in MQV format and also visually.

The sample R2RML mapping which the participants used to interact with the framework was designed as a realistic use case. The use case of the sample mapping involves provenance information relating to datasets being uplifted to RDF, which can be easily understood by both cohorts as they both have knowledge about datasets. The use case is realistic as the PROV-O [18] documentation includes similar examples. PROV-O was chosen to represent the information as it is the W3C recommendation for capturing provenance information and is widely known. Furthermore, PROV-O includes the necessary data type restrictions to introduce a data type violation into the mapping. Three violations were introduced into the mapping. A quality violation relates to a quality issue within a mapping. The violations introduced into the mapping were chosen from the violations detected in Experiment 1, which indicates these violations occur in real-world mappings. Experiment 1 involved assessing the quality of 30 R2RML mappings, which were collected from semantic web research projects and students. The violations introduced allow the participants to evaluate the various refinement options available on the framework. These refinements involve semi-automatic refinements where the participant can enter a custom value, choose from a drop-down list of restricted values or select a suggested value. The three violations within the mapping are outlined below.

Usage of undefined property. `prov:values` predicate is undefined within PROV-O. The participants can choose a refinement which finds predicates within the same namespace or enter a new predicate within a text box. The predicate must be replaced by the participants with a valid defined predicate to resolve the violation.

Incorrect data type. The `xsd:time` assigned to the predicate object map with predicate `prov:generatedAtTime` is incorrect. The correct data type for the `prov:generatedAtTime` property is `xsd:dateTime`. The participants can choose from a refinement which suggests the correct data type or allows them to enter a data type in a text box. The participants must replace the invalid data type (`xsd:time`) within the mapping with the correct data type (`xsd:dateTime`) to resolve the violation.

Invalid language tag. The language tag "en-GP" is invalid. The participants can choose a refinement which is a drop-down menu with valid language tags. The language tag must be replaced by a valid English language tag to resolve the violation.

4.2.2. Experiment execution

Assistance was available to participants if they were unable to complete an experiment task. The assistance provided and completion of the experiment differed slightly for both cohorts due to the aforementioned reasons.

Completion of experiment. The participants in the expert cohort completed the experiment synchronously using zoom video conferencing platform while their think aloud statements were being recorded. The participants from the student cohort completed the experiment asynchronously by accessing the framework using provided login details. Furthermore, the cohort did not require the use of a video conferencing platform as the think-aloud protocol was not used because it would not be feasible to arrange a zoom meeting for each student and to transcribe/analyze their think-aloud statements.

Experiment Assistance. Each cohort could avail of assistance if they were unable to complete the experiment. The expert cohort was informed at the start of the experiment that assistance could be provided during the call if they are unable to complete a task. The student cohort was informed that assistance could be provided via email if they are unable to complete a task.

4.2.3. Data collected

Data was collected during the experiment from both cohorts in a quantitative and qualitative format.

Quantitative data. The Post-Study System Usability Questionnaire (PSSUQ) [19] was completed by both cohorts. The violation counts, which refers to the number of quality issues present after refined and time taken to complete the experiment was calculated for each cohort.

Qualitative data. The open comment section of the PSSUQ served as a basis of qualitative analysis for both cohorts. The main difference between the qualitative data collected was the use of the Think-aloud protocol [20]. The protocol was used to collect think-aloud statements, where participants verbalize their thoughts while completing the tasks. Only think-aloud statements were collected from the expert cohort as it would not be feasible to collect think-aloud statements from each participant in the student cohort.

4.2.4. Experiment metrics

The experiment metrics used include the usability questionnaire, deriving themes from the qualitative data, time taken to complete each task and count of quality issues remaining in the mapping after the completion of the experiment.

PSSUQ. The Post-Study System Usability Questionnaire (PSSUQ) [19] is widely used to measure users perceived satisfaction of a software system. The questionnaire provides the ability to do standardized comparison with other systems or evolutions of the system. The PSSUQ uses a 7-point Likert Scale where the lower score results in higher satisfaction. The second version of this questionnaire was used for the study, which includes 19 questions.

Thematic analysis. Thematic analysis [21] is designed to analyze qualitative data. The method involves deriving themes from the data. These themes are used to identify patterns within the data. Each theme consists of codes which relate to specific areas within a theme. The frequency of each code is calculated to identify the most commonly occurring themes. Thematic analysis is widely used within the qualitative research field.

Time per task. The time per task can be used as a comparative measure to determine if certain factors such as a worse PSSUQ score have a relationship with their timing.

Violation count. The violation count refers to the number of quality issues which have been resolved by the participant during the experiment. Three violations are present within the mapping provided to participants. The number of violations within the refined mapping generated was used to determine how effective the framework is at improving the quality of mappings.

4.3. Experiment Results

The data collected[5] was analyzed to identify usability issues within the framework. The analysis of data from both cohorts was completed separately and then the results of each cohort were compared. The comparison identifies patterns between both cohorts and determines which cohort found the framework more usable. **Table 1** shows the summary of results for the **expert cohort**.

Table 1: Summary of results for expert cohort

Time taken to complete experiment	*Mean time*	15.4 minutes
	Median time	12.8 minutes
PSSUQ mean metric score (lower number considered better)	*System usefulness (SysUse)*	1.69
	Information quality (InfoQual)	2.43
	Interface quality (IntQual)	2.75
	Overall usability (Overall)	2.11
Number of violations remaining after refinement complete (original mapping had 3 violations)	*0 violations (Best case)*	9 participants (90%)
	1 violation	1 participant (10%)
	2 violations	0 participants
	3 violations (Worst case)	0 participants

The analysis starts by discussing the PSSUQ results, followed by the other quantitative data. The qualitative data is discussed in parallel with the quantitative data. The provenance requirements heading does not directly relate to a metric, however, the heading is included to capture important qualitative data noted during the analysis. The PSSUQ scores have been compared against norms within a previous research study [19] as no previous scores exist for the framework.

Interface & Information quality. The interface quality relates to the quality of the items used to interact with the framework. The interface quality (**IntQual**) metric is the worst scoring metric within the PSSUQ with a mean score of 2.75. Furthermore, previous research [19] states that a score of 2.49 or less for the interface quality metric is sufficient, with the framework scoring lower, which indicates the interface needs to be improved. The qualitative data also indicates that the interface quality as the "Unaesthetic Interface" theme occurs commonly. The information quality relates to the quality of the information which is provided to users by the framework. Previous research indicates a

---

mean score of 3.02 or less for the information quality metric is sufficient, with the framework scoring better than the threshold in the research study. The qualitative data indicates that additional information should be added to describe the refinements.

System usefulness and Overall usability. Only one participant required assistance during the completion of the tasks. The participant skipped a task within the task sheet, which resulted in them being redirected to the incorrect page on the framework. The best scoring metrics related to system usefulness (**SysUse**) and overall usability (**Overall**) with a mean of 1.69 and 2.11 respectively. Furthermore, these metrics both score more than 20% better than the thresholds within the research study. The metric scores and qualitative data indicate the participants found the system useful with an overall positive user experience.

Timing. The mean time for completing the experiment is 15.4 minutes with the fastest time being 11.05 minutes and the slowest time being 24.05 minutes. These results could indicate that not all experts could use the framework equally. Furthermore, noted during the experiment that some experts spent more time exploring the framework while others spent less time. The fastest tasks to complete were related to the assessment process. The participants took longer to choose and execute refinements. Furthermore, the slowest task related to examination of the patterns within the validation report. These results could indicate that the information provided relating to refinements could be improved to enable participants to select a refinement more easily. Furthermore, the layout of the validation report should be improved in future versions to improve the time it takes for participants to interpret the report.

Violation count. 90% of participants have 0 violations in the refined mapping, while 10% have 1 violation in the refined mapping. No participants have 3 violations in the refined mapping. The low violation count within the refined mapping indicates that the framework could be an effective tool for helping an expert user to identify and remove quality violations.

Provenance requirements. The provenance requirements of the framework refer to the quality assessment and refinement information provided by the validation bar chart and validation report. These areas relate to the information quality, however, these areas are more specifically highlighted within the qualitative analysis. The qualitative analysis of the participants' think-aloud statements and questionnaire open comments, indicate that the information provided by these items could be improved. **Table 2** shows a summary of quantitative data results for the **student cohort**. The time for completion, PSSUQ metric mean scores and violation count within refined mapping were calculated.

Table 2: Summary of results for student cohort

Time taken to complete experiment	*Mean time*	10.06 minutes
	Median time	9 minutes
PSSUQ mean metric score (lower number considered better)	*System usefulness (SysUse)*	2.34
	Information quality (InfoQual)	2.42
	Interface quality (IntQual)	2.8
	Overall usability (Overall)	2.42
Number of violations remaining after refinement complete (original mapping had 3 violations)	*0 violations (Best case)*	24 participants (50%)
	1 violation	10 participants (21%)
	2 violations	5 participants (10%)
	3 violations (Worst case)	9 participants (19%)

The analysis starts by discussing the PSSUQ results, followed by the other quantitative data. The qualitative data is discussed in parallel with the quantitative data.

Interface & Information quality. The interface quality relates to the quality of the items used to interact with the framework. The mean score for the interface quality (**IntQual**) metric is 2.8 which is the worst scoring metric. Furthermore, previous research states that a score of 2.49 or less for the interface quality metric is sufficient, however, the framework scores more than 10% worse than the threshold in the research study [19]. Furthermore, questions related to interface quality have the worst scoring third quartile (Q3), with a score of 4 and 3.75 respectively. The poor scoring of the interface quality within the PSSUQ results and the qualitative data indicates that the participants found the interface poor quality. In particular, the aesthetics of the framework needs to be improved in future versions of the framework. The information quality relates to the quality of the information which is provided to users by the framework. Previous research states that a score of 3.02 is sufficient for the information quality metric, with the framework scoring more than 20% better than the threshold. Moreover, the qualitative data was analysed to find data relating to the information displayed on the framework. These results indicate that the information provided by the framework is sufficient for the participants to complete the experiment, however, the qualitative analysis indicates that certain information provided by the framework needs to be improved in future versions. In particular, the information provided for the refinement needs to be improved. The PSSUQ results and qualitative data indicate that the information provided by the framework is sufficient, however, additional information should be added to the refinements to allow users to select and execute the refinements easier.

System usefulness and Overall usability. 48 out of the 59 (81%) students successfully completed the experiment. These results indicate that 81% of the students could successfully interact with the framework. Furthermore, previous research states that a mean score of 2.82 or less is sufficient for the overall usefulness metric and the framework scored 2.42, which is more than 15% better. Moreover, the qualitative data indicates these results also. These results indicate that the framework is fit for purpose and the participants are satisfied by the overall usability. Furthermore, the best scoring metric is the system usefulness with a mean of 2.34. The improvements previously mentioned could further improve the overall usability of the framework.

Timing. The mean time for the student cohort is 10.06 minutes. The maximum time is 23 minutes and the minimum time is 2 minutes. The minimum time of 2 minutes based on the experience of the researcher could indicate certain students were not careful when completing the experiment. The fastest tasks related to the assessment process. The slowest tasks related to the selection/executing of refinements and the examination of the patterns within the validation report. These results indicate that the participants struggled to select refinements and interpret the validation report. The additional information previously mentioned could improve the time taken to select and execute refinements. The patterns within the validation report could be simplified to allow the participants to interpret the report more easily.

Violation count. The original mapping contained 3 violations. 50% of participants have 0 violations. 70% have 1 or 0 violations. 30% have 2 or 3 violations. These results indicate that several students struggled to remove quality issues from the mapping. Several mappings contained violations such as including a data type named `admingeo:a` or `date:xsd`, which are not data types. Other examples of violations include a property named `aair:http://www.w3.org/r2rml#,` which is undefined. These are simple violations and could indicate students who gained more knowledge about semantic technologies during the module were able to remove quality issues easier, as 50% of them had no violations remaining.

Thematic analysis was completed following the six-step process [21] which includes data familiarization, generating initial codes, searching for themes, reviewing the themes, and producing the report. The most common themes and codes within the qualitative data that relate to improvements are shown in **Table 3**.

Table 3: Most common themes and codes discovered through thematic analysis

Themes	Codes
GUI Requirements. The layout and aesthetics of the framework are inadequate.	*Unaesthetic interface.* The look and feel of the interface are inadequate.
	Unclear interface navigation. Guidance provided by the framework interface is hard to understand.
Clarify description and features. Overly complicated and ambiguous text displayed on the framework.	*Clarify text descriptions.* Text descriptions need to be further described.
	Ambiguous refinement options. The refinement options for violations are not described adequately.

The GUI and textual descriptions need to be improved in the next version of the framework. The improvements will focus improving the aesthetics of the framework and adding additional text to describe different components.

4.4. Comparison of each Cohorts Results

The following section compares the main differences between the results of the **student** and **expert** cohorts. The results of the analysis of each cohort's data were compared based on the PSSUQ results, followed by the other quantitative data. The thematic analysis of the qualitative data and a summary of the overall analysis is then discussed.

Interface quality. The mean score for the interface quality (**IntQual**) metric for the expert cohort is 2.75 while the student cohort has a mean score of 2.8 which shows that the expert cohort rated higher satisfaction from the interface. These are the worst scoring metrics for both cohorts, which indicates that the interface needs to be improved for both cohorts. However, the expert cohort could have found the interface easier to use due to their previous experience in using semantic web related interfaces. Furthermore, previous research indicates that a mean score of 2.49 or less is sufficient for the interface quality metric, with both cohorts scoring worse than the threshold. Moreover, the "Unaesthetic Interface" code from the thematic analysis occurs frequently within the qualitative data of both cohorts, which further demonstrates that the aesthetics of the interface need to be improved for both cohorts.

Information quality. The mean score for the information quality (**InfoQual**) metric for the expert cohort is 2.43 while the student cohort has a mean score of 2.42 which shows that the student cohort rated slightly higher satisfaction from the information provided by the framework. Furthermore, 40% of experts rated the information quality a score of 3 or more, while only 20% of students rated the information quality metric with a score of 3 or more. The better scores for the information quality metric could indicate that the background knowledge of the expert cohort allowed them to notice information quality issues more easily. Furthermore, their background knowledge could result in them being more critical of the information displayed on the framework. However, previous research indicates that a mean score of 3.02 is sufficient for the information quality metric, with the information quality metric scoring better than the interface quality metric for each cohort. However, the information quality most frequently noted within the thematic analysis of the cohorts relates to the "Clarify text descriptions" and "Ambiguous refinement options" code. These results could indicate that simplified text and clearer refinement options could benefit both cohorts.

Analysis of each cohort's PSSUQ question scores. The worst scoring metric for both cohorts is the interface quality which indicates the interface should be improved for overall better user experience. The information quality metric scored similarly for both cohorts with a difference of less than 1% which could indicate better quality information is needed for both cohorts. Most median scores of the PSSUQ for the **expert** cohort have a median of 2 (10 out of 19 questions) and a spread below 2 points (5 out of 19 questions). The ease of use and (Q1) and efficiency (Q5) score the best. The questions relate to the error messages (Q9) and the aesthetics of the interface (Q16) score worse. All median scores of the PSSUQ for the **student** cohort have a median of 2. However, questions 16 and 17 have the worst third quartile (Q3), with a score of 4 and 3.75 respectively. These questions relate to the quality of the interface. These results indicate that the aesthetics of the interface should be improved for both cohorts in future versions of the framework.

Violation count. 90% of the expert cohort have 0 violations, while 70% of the student cohort have 0 or 1 violations in the refined mapping, which could indicate that the background knowledge of the expert cohort helped them to identify and remove the quality violations. Furthermore, no expert has 3 violations, while 10% of the student cohort had 3 violations. These results indicate that the effectiveness of the framework is influenced by the background knowledge. However, improvements previously mentioned could help students to identify and remove quality issues more easily.

Timing. The mean time for the expert cohort to complete the experiment is 15.4 minutes while the mean time for the student cohort is 10.06, which is about 5 minutes faster. The student and expert cohort have a median time of 13 and 12 minutes, respectively, which is only a difference of 1 minute. The majority of participants (Q3) completed the experiment in 20 minutes or less. However, the main difference is the maximum value. The student and expert cohort have a maximum time of 23 and 24 minutes, respectively, which could indicate that background knowledge does not influence the time taken to interact with the framework. Most of the task times of the **expert** cohort have a median less than 1 minute (7 out of 12). The other tasks have a median time of more than 1 minute but less than 1 minute and a half (3 out of 12). The longest tasks have a median time of more than 1 minute and a half (2 out of 12) which relate to choosing a refinement value and examining the validation report. Most of the task times of the **student** cohort have a median less than 1 minute (8 out of 12). The longest tasks have a median time of more than 1 minute and but less than a 1 minute and a half (4 out of 12) which related to choosing the refinement and examining the validation report. The task times indicate that both cohorts took the longest time to choose the refinement (Task 4, 5) and examine the patterns within the validation report (Task 12) . These areas could not be influenced by background knowledge and could be simplified in future versions. The reason for the student cohort completing the experiment faster than the expert cohort could be as a result of the expert cohort being more careful while completing each task. Furthermore, the expert cohort was using the think-aloud protocol, which could slow the completion of each task. Moreover, the usability of the framework could require a similar background knowledge, however, the effectiveness could be only influenced by the background knowledge.

Thematic analysis. The thematic analysis is used to discover emerging themes within the data which can be used to guide system improvements. Similar themes occurred within both cohorts, these themes include the "MQV Framework usability", the "GUI Requirements" and the "Clarify descriptions and features". The main areas highlighted within these themes in both cohorts are the poor aesthetics of the framework, unclear interface navigation and the textual descriptions of the refinement options. These are areas that should be improved for overall better usability by each cohort. The main difference between each cohort is the "Provenance usability" theme, which relates to the information provided by the validation report and bar chart. The theme was only noted within the expert cohort, where participants highlighted the patterns used to model the provenance information. The background knowledge of the experts in information modelling could have helped them to discover issues in the information modelling. These patterns should be improved to make them easier to understand by both cohorts.

5. Final Remarks

We would argue that the current approach of improving the quality of Linked Data datasets after the publication stage is more inefficient compared to improving the mapping artefacts that create the dataset in the first place. We introduced the MQV framework, designed to detect and address quality issues of mapping artefacts before they are executed. The framework generates machine-readable quality information represented in a domain specific vocabulary by executing metrics specifically designed for mappings. No previous research could be found within the state of the art where a mapping quality framework has been evaluated with a large sample size of users using standardized methods. The analysis of the results from an evaluation using a real-life use case mapping demonstrates the usability and effectiveness of the implementation. Next steps include the refinement of the framework based on the findings from the evaluation. Furthermore, the framework is currently being applied within a network management use case in Ericsson Software Technology.

Acknowledgements

This research was conducted with the financial support of the SFI AI Centre for Research Training under Grant Agreement No. 18/CRT/6223 at the ADAPT SFI Research Centre (Grant # 13/RC/2106_P2) at Trinity College Dublin.

References

[1]   Debattista J, Lange C, Auer S, Cortis D. Evaluating the quality of the LOD cloud: An empirical investigation. Semant Web. 2018 Mar;9:1–43.
[2]   Junior AC, Debattista J, O'Sullivan D. Assessing the Quality of R2RML Mappings. In: Joint Proceedings of the International Workshop On Semantics For Transport and on Approaches for

Making Data Interoperable co-located with 15th Semantics Conference, Karlsruhe, Germany. CEUR-WS; 2019. (CEUR Workshop Proceedings; vol. 2447).

[3]   Heyvaert P, De Meester B, Dimou A, Verborgh R. Rule-driven inconsistency resolution for knowledge graph generation rules. Semant Web. 2019;10(6).

[4]   Randles A, O'Sullivan D. Assessing quality of R2RML mappings for OSi's Linked Open Data portal. 4th Int Work Geospatial Linked Data ESWC 2021. 2021;

[5]   Das S, Sundara S, Cyganiak R. R2RML: RDB to RDF Mapping Language. W3C Recomm [Internet]. 2012; Available from: http://www.w3.org/TR/r2rml/

[6]   Navarro-Gallinad A, Meehan A, O'Sullivan D. The semantic combining for exploration of environmental and disease data dashboard for clinician researchers. CEUR Workshop Proc. 2020;2778:73–85.

[7]   Moreau B, Serrano-Alvarado P. Assessing the Quality of RDF Mappings with EvaMap. In: 17th Extended Semantic Web Conference (ESWC2020) [Internet]. 2020. p. 164–7. Available from: http://link.springer.com/10.1007/978-3-030-62327-2_28

[8]   Debattista J, Auer S, Lange C. Luzzu-A Framework for Linked Data Quality Assessment. In: 2016 IEEE 10th International Conference on Semantic Computing, (ICSC). Institute of Electrical and Electronics Engineers Inc.; 2016. p. 124–31.

[9]   Arndt D, Meester B De, Dimou A, Verborgh R, Mannens E. Using rule-based reasoning for RDF validation. In: International Joint Conference on Rules and Reasoning. 2017. p. 22–36.

[10]   Dimou A, Kontokostas D, Freudenberg M, Verborgh R, Lehmann J, Mannens E, et al. Assessing and refining mappings to RDF to improve dataset quality. In: Lecture Notes in Computer Science. Springer Verlag; 2015. p. 133–49.

[11]   Kontokostas D, Westphal P, Auer S, Hellmann S, Lehmann J, Cornelissen R, et al. Test-driven evaluation of Linked Data quality. In: WWW 2014 - Proceedings of the 23rd International Conference on World Wide Web. Association for Computing Machinery, Inc; 2014. p. 747–57.

[12]   Randles A, Crotti Junior A, O'Sullivan D. Towards a vocabulary for mapping quality assessment. Proc 15th Int Work Ontol Matching 19th Int Semant Web Conf (ISWC),. 2020;

[13]   Randles A, Junior AC, O'Sullivan D. A Vocabulary for Describing Mapping Quality Assessment, Refinement and Validation. In: 2021 IEEE 15th International Conference on Semantic Computing (ICSC). 2021. p. 425–30.

[14]   Krech D. Rdflib: A python library for working with rdf. Online https://github com/RDFLib/rdflib. 2006;

[15]   Randles A, Crotti Junior A, O'Sullivan D. A Framework for Assessing and Refining the Quality of R2RML mappings. In: Proceedings of the 22nd International Conference on Information Integration and Web-Based Applications & Services. New York, USA: ACM; 2020. (iiWAS2020).

[16]   Poveda-Villalón M, Gómez-Pérez A, Suárez-Figueroa MC. OOPS! (OntOlogy Pitfall Scanner!): An On-line Tool for Ontology Evaluation. Int J Semant Web Inf Syst. 2014;10(2):7–34.

[17]   Zaveri A, Rula A, Maurino A, Pietrobon R, Lehmann J, Auer S, et al. Quality assessment methodologies for linked open data. Submitt to Semant Web J. 2013;1:1–5.

[18]   Lebo T, Sahoo S, McGuinness D, Belhajjame K, Cheney J, Corsar D, et al. PROV-O: the prov ontology. w3c recommendation, 30 April 2013. World Wide Web Consort [Internet]. 2013; Available from: https://www.w3.org/TR/prov-o/

[19]   Lewis JR. Psychometric Evaluation of the PSSUQ Using Data from Five Years of Usability Studies. Int J Hum Comput Interact. 2002 Sep;14(3–4):463–88.

[20]   Fonteyn ME, Kuipers B, Grobe SJ. A description of think aloud method and protocol analysis. Qual Health Res. 1993;3(4):430–41.

[21]   Nowell LS, Norris JM, White DE, Moules NJ. Thematic analysis: Striving to meet the trustworthiness criteria. Int J Qual methods. 2017.

Towards a Knowledge-Aware AI
A. Dimou et al. (Eds.)
© 2022 The Authors.
This article is published online with Open Access by IOS Press and distributed under the terms
of the Creative Commons Attribution License 4.0 (CC BY 4.0).
doi:10.3233/SSW220007

A Semantic Specification for Data Protection Impact Assessments (DPIA)

Harshvardhan J. PANDIT [a,1]

[a] *ADAPT Centre, Trinity College Dublin, Dublin, Ireland*

Abstract. The GDPR requires assessing and conducting a Data Protection Impact Assessment (DPIA) for processing of personal data that may result in high risk and impact to the data subjects. Documenting this process requires information about processing activities, entities and their roles, risks, mitigations and resulting impacts, and consultations. Impact assessments are complex activities where stakeholders face difficulties to identify relevant risks and mitigations, especially for emerging technologies and specific considerations in their use-cases, and to document outcomes in a consistent and reusable manner. We address this challenge by utilising linked-data to represent DPIA related information so that it can be better managed and shared in an interoperable manner. For this, we consulted the guidance documents produced by EU Data Protection Authorities (DPA) regarding DPIA and by ENISA regarding risk management. The outcome of our efforts is an extension to the Data Privacy Vocabulary (DPV) for documenting DPIAs and an ontology for risk management based on ISO 31000 family of standards. Our contributions fill an important gap within the state of the art, and paves the way for shared impact assessments with future regulations such as for AI and Cybersecurity.

Keywords. GDPR, DPIA, Risk Management, ISO, Semantic-Web

1. Introduction

1.1. Motivation

The EU's General Data Protection Regulation (GDPR) [1] requires every Data Controller to assess and document whether their processing is "likely to result in a high risk to the rights and freedoms" of individuals (i.e. *high-risk*[2]), and if so - to carry out a 'Data Protection Impact Assessment (DPIA)'. A DPIA is essentially a three-step iterative risk governance process where the organisation first identifies its activities, then checks whether any DPIA-requiring criteria is met, and if yes - conduct a DPIA (see more in Section 2.1). GDPR does not impose a strict process for how organisations have to conduct their risk and impact assessments, but instead specifies only broad requirements. Data Protection Authorities (DPA), tasked with enforcing GDPR, have published (on respective websites) guidance and tools related to compliance, including DPIA and risk governance.

We identify five important challenges regarding DPIAs present in the current landscape that serve as motivation for this work. (1) DPIAs can involve multiple stakehold-

---

[1] Corresponding Author: Harshvardhan J. Pandit ; E-mail: pandith@tcd.ie
[2] Hereafter, *high-risk* is used as a shortened form of "high risk to the rights and freedoms of natural persons"

ers (e.g. Data Processors) which creates information dependencies (e.g. measures implemented by processors). (2) Since DPIAs must be specific, controllers conducting similar DPIAs will repeat information and tasks. (3) Despite existing standards for risk management, there is variance in methodologies that prevents common universal solutions. (4) Current documentation norms are heavily human-oriented (e.g. spreadsheets, PDF), which severely limit development and application of tools for DPIAs. (5) Solutions do not take into account that high-risk impact assessments are a form of shared activity i.e. they share processing activity information, risks, and impacts with other GDPR requirements (e.g. Register of Processing Activities (ROPA), data transfers), and have overlaps with similar assessments in aligned regulations, e.g. the EU's proposal for AI Act [2].

The state of the art contains multifaceted application-specific solutions for expressing risks, DPIA methodologies, and GDPR compliance. In particular, they demonstrate advantages of semantic web technologies for: (i) specialising for a use-case; (ii) interoperability between stakeholders and tools; (iii) creating shared knowledge-bases; and (iv) developing tooling for machine-based compliance. However, there are two important gaps that have not been addressed: impact assessments and documenting DPIAs.

1.2. Contributions of this Work

We take the first step towards improving the DPIA processes by enabling sharing and reuse of information required for risk/impact assessments through the use of semantic web technologies. Our approach reflects the positioning of DPIAs within a broader framework of information and compliance management associated with GDPR. Thus, rather than creating an ontology solely dedicated to representing DPIA, we extend an existing ontology - the Data Privacy Vocabulary (DPV) produced by the Data Privacy Vocabularies and Controls Community Group[3] (DPVCG) as the state of the art (see Section 2.2). DPV provides a comprehensive taxonomy of data processing related concepts, including rudimentary concepts for risks and DPIA, that are meant to be jurisdiction and domain agnostic, with a separate extension (dpv-gdpr) providing GDPR specific concepts. We identified and proposed concepts currently missing in (core) DPV, and from these developed a DPIA specification as an extension (called DPV-DPIA). For expressing risk/impact assessments - we developed an ontology based on the ISO 31000 family of risk-related standards. For expressing impacts to fundamental rights and freedoms, we created a thesauri from the EU Charter regarding rights and freedoms[4].

To ensure the specification is useful and practical for stakeholders, we based it on DPA guidelines and tools to first ensure important requirements are met (see Section 3.1). We then modelled real-world instances of (publicly available) DPIAs as a form of reflective evaluation, and to demonstrate sharing of knowledge we used the DPV-specified concepts within French DPA's (CNIL) DPIA tool (see Section 4). We conclude with a discussion (see Section 5) on identified and perceived limitations of our work, and the pragmatism of developing shared impact assessments for EU's regulatory landscape.

To summarise, our major contributions are: (i) Machine-readable DPIA specification; and (ii) Enabling reuse and sharing of risks, mitigations, and impacts through linked data. Minor contributions include: (i) Risk ontology based on ISO 31000 family of standards; (ii) Thesauri of EU fundamental rights and freedoms; (iii) Collection of risks, mit-

---

[3]Disclaimer: The lead author currently chairs the DPVCG.
[4]http://data.europa.eu/eli/treaty/char_2012/oj

igations, and impacts from literature; (iv) Extension of DPV and state of the art; and (v) Practical discussions towards developing shared impact assessments.

2. Background and State of the Art

2.1. GDPR and Data Protection Impact Assessments (DPIA)

GDPR's Article 35 prescribes requirements for assessing necessity of DPIAs based on potential for high-risk, and for carrying out a DPIA if a criteria is met. In this, it describes conditions that always need a DPIA and lays down the basis where DPAs can specify further rules on conditions that do/don't require DPIA. It also describes consultation of stakeholders such as Data Protection Officers (DPO) and data subjects where necessary.

In order to determine necessity, controllers require descriptions of processing activities in terms of specific criteria, for example the scale and scope of data (Art.35-3b), or whether automated decision making and profiling operations are involved (Art.35-3a). DPA guidelines provide additional nuanced descriptions of concepts that are relevant for determining risk, impact, and the basis on which DPIAs should be conducted.

While GDPR intends to provide harmonised requirements for DPIAs, individual DPAs have taken different approaches with deviations regarding use of organisational processes related to management practices and risk governance - which are not necessarily directly associated with a DPIA. For example, as part of the DPIA templates, both AEPD (Spanish DPA) and CNIL (French DPA) ask about the organisation's "internal practices and context" which includes " organisation's structure, functions and competencies, adopted policies, norms and standards, organisational maturity objectives and in general the organisation's culture". Owing to this, organisations have difficulties in determining what requirements a DPIA must meet given that the guidance is varied, complex, nuanced, and difficult to judge for sufficiency. Additionally, Georgiadis et al. [3] conducted a systemic literature review on the different privacy and data protection risks specified within the state of the art, with a conclusion on the necessity to further develop better DPIA methodologies due to organisation's limited knowledge on this topic.

2.2. Models for DPIAs and Risk Assessments

There are several domain and application specific approaches for modelling risk in ontological form. Some examples are: Agrawal's [4] ontology based on ISO/IEC 27005:2011 risk management standard, Ameida et al's [5] conceptual enterprise architecture models for organisational risk management based on ISO 31000, Rosa et al's. [6] ontology for IT risk management based on ISO 31000, Vicente et al's. [7] high-level model for organisational risk governance, and Hayes et al's. [8] ontological model of online privacy risks and harms. While these approaches model risk concepts in ontological form, they focus on organisational perspective of risks (e.g. economic), or on generalised concepts (e.g. philosophical) that are not sufficient for expressing impacts as needed for a DPIA.

In approaches that represent DPIA related information, GDPRtEXT [9] provides insufficient concepts related to DPIA. PrOnto [10] specifies DPIA as a workflow with steps and different categorisations of risk. Data Privacy Vocabulary[5] (DPV) [11] provides

---

[5]https://w3id.org/dpv/

comprehensive taxonomies for describing personal data processing activities, which includes DPIA and risk concepts. In approaches related to automating DPIA processes, Dashti et al. [12] explore automation of DPIA based on rule-based mechanisms to identify alternatives for less risky implementations. And Saniei [13] proposes use of semantic web technologies to represent DPIA related knowledge and to use rules and inferences to identify relevant obligations and actions, with ongoing work [14] in collecting competency questions and creating a vocabulary - which was useful for this work.

Of these approaches, none provided all necessary concepts or could be readily used. Of these, DPV was the most suitable choice to extend given that it is: (a) most comprehensive; (b) open access; (c) has a mechanism for updating through DPVCG. This finding is backed by a recent survey by Esteves et al [15] regarding modelling of GDPR related information flows that also included DPIA as a factor in investigation, with favourable reviews for DPV, though it found no suitably complete vocabulary for DPIAs.

3. DPIA Specification

3.1. Requirements and Objectives

For understanding DPIA information requirements, we utilised EU DPA provided guidelines, tools, and templates. For non-English documents, we utilised machine-translation to convert them, and manually inspected them for correctness (relying on the author's familiarity with information). In particular, we focused on identifying requirements regarding: (1) personal data processing activities; (2) DPIA necessity assessment and outcomes; (3) risk/impact assessments and outcome; (4) conditions regarded as high-risk, and requirement for a DPIA; and (5) documentation required for maintaining DPIAs.

As outlined earlier in Section 2.1, these documents provide a wide range of information requirements that do not necessarily relate directly to DPIAs as stated in GDPR Art.35. In particular, the DPAs from Spain, France, and UK have provided comprehensive documentation which does not provide justification for how these are connected to specific legal requirements, and often go well beyond GDPR and into describing internal risk and governance procedures. The scope and breadth of these practices necessitate a much larger study given their complexity, variance, and connection to legal requirements. We focused on representing relevant information at a 'high-level' while also being sufficient in terms of GDPR requirements. This led to identifying the following specific requirements regarding documentation of information: (1) provenance records for DPIA in terms of processes and actors; (2) representing risk/impact assessments; (3) description of processing activities; and (4) risks, mitigations, and impacts.

3.2. Specification Overview

The specification, available online[6], models three categories of information: provenance and status of DPIA, processing activities associated with a DPIA, and the risks/impacts involved in that DPIA. In this, the existing[7] DPV concept dpv:DPIA is reused as a focal point with further specialisation into three aspects: DPIANecessityAssessment repre-

---

[6]https://w3id.org/dpv/dpv-gdpr/dpia
[7]For brevity, concepts presented as contribution are specified without prefix, and existing ones with prefix.

senting determination of whether a DPIA is required; `DPIAProcedure` for risks, impacts, and mitigations being investigated and documented; and `DPIAOutcome` for documenting the outcomes of a DPIA in terms of continuation of processing. Figure 1 represents these along with other core concepts to provide an overview of the specification.

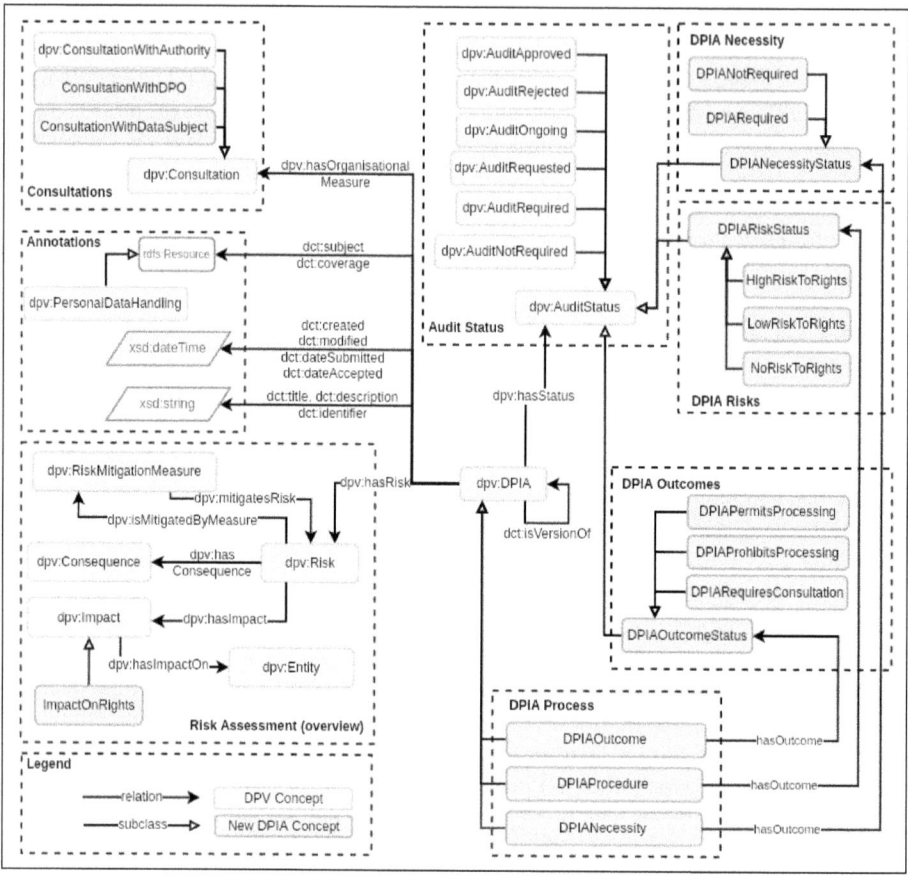

Figure 1. Overview of the DPIA Specification

DPIAs require documentation of provenance information regarding when it took place (temporal information), and who was involved (agents, e.g. approval). For these, we reuse Dublin Core Metadata Innovation[8] (DCMI) terms for temporal information (`dct:created`, `dct:modified`, `dct:dateSubmitted`, `dct:dateAccepted`, `dct:temporal`, `dct:valid`), conformance e.g. codes of conduct (`dct:conformsTo`), descriptions (`dct:title`, `dct:description`), identifier or version (`dct:identifier`, `dct:isVersionOf`), and subject or scope of DPIA (`dct:subject`, `dct:coverage`).

To record outcomes of DPIA processes, we consider a DPIA to be a form of *Audit* and use `dpv:hasStatus` with the appropriate `dpv:AuditStatus`. For example, `DPIANecessityAssessment` with `dpv:AuditRequired` indicates a necessity assessment is required, whereas `DPIAProcedure` with `dpv:AuditApproved` indicates the

---

[8]https://dublincore.org/specifications/dublin-core/dcmi-terms/

DPIA results were approved (e.g. by a DPO). The relation hasOutcome was created to indicate status of each DPIA process as - (i) for dpv:DPIANecessityAssessment: DPIANecessityStatus and specialisations related to whether a DPIA is required or not-required; (ii) for dpv:DPIAProcedure: DPIARiskStatus and specialisations related to level of risk as high, low, or none; and (iii) for dpv:DPIAOutcome: DPIAOutcomeStatus and specialisations for whether processing is permitted or pro-hibited or consultation is required[9]. These represent the broad outcomes to be recorded when carrying out a DPIA in terms of whether risks have been mitigated (or deemed acceptable) and whether processing can (or cannot) be carried out.

For indicating the different stages and processes in conducting and managing DPIA, the concepts Audit, Approval, Investigation, and Review were created with spe-cific relations (e.g. hasAudit) to associate them with the relevant concepts. For indicat-ing specific categories of consultations, the existing concept dpv:Consultation was extended as ConsultationWithDataSubject and ConsultationWithDPO to record their views and inputs within the DPIA process.

For indicating the scope and contents covered within a DPIA, the property dct:coverage is reused with dpv:PersonalDataHandling instances to indicate the specifics of purposes, processing operations, personal data categories, entities (e.g. con-trollers, recipients), technical & organisational measures, legal bases, and other details. Here, dct:subject can be optionally used to indicate a DPIA (and its associated pro-cessing activities) relate to a specific topic, such as a service or a product.

The existing risk concepts in DPV are used as: to indicate risks (dpv:Risk, dpv:hasRisk), mitigations (dpv:RiskMitigationMeasure, dpv:mitigatesRisk), consequences (dpv:Consequence, dpv:hasConsequence), and impacts (dpv:Impact, dpv:hasImpact, dpv:hasImpactOn). For more specific risk assessment information, such as risk levels and severity, the ISO 31000 based risk ontology is used.

3.3. Extending DPV

We found DPV currently has several concepts missing regarding not only DPIAs, but also those related to descriptions of processing activities beyond what is needed from a risk/impact perspective. For example, one of the prominent criteria in determining whether processing is likely to be high-risk is the understanding of scale and scope re-garding personal data, processing activities, and data subjects. Rather than specifying their expression only within what is needed for a DPIA, we consider these concepts to be useful in other tasks and assessments, and thus propose their inclusion in DPV.

An important addition we propose is the indication of certain Scale concepts along with commonly used qualitative terms[10] that relates to a measurement of dimension of some other concept. DataVolume indicates the scale of personal data being pro-cessed with qualifiers (from larger to smaller in context) - {Huge, Large, Medium, Small, Sporadic, Singular}. DataSubjectScale indicates a measurement of the scale of data subjects with the same qualifiers as data volume. GeographicScale indicates the geo-physical scale (e.g. for processing activities or data subjects) as

---

[9]These reflect the possibility where a first iteration of DPIA identifies a high-risk which cannot be mitigated by the second, leading to a consultation with a DPA.

[10]Here concepts are derived from specific obligations, e.g. 'large scale of data', which gives concepts for more/less than 'large'. The specifics of whether something is 'large' is to be interpreted contextually.

{Global, NearlyGlobal, MultiNational, National, Regional, Locality, WithinEnvironment} with the last item referring to instances such as on device. Separate from scale, we also propose the modelling of Scope as a concept referring to the *extent or range* of other concepts such as processing activities. To differentiate between scale and scope, the former refers to a *measurement* such as volume or number whereas the latter relates to *variance* such as categories or dimensions.

Along with scale and scope as new concepts, we also propose remodelling existing concepts that relate to either. These include dpv:Frequency which indicates temporal periodicity, and should be a specialisation of Scale with qualifiers {Continuous, Often, Sporadic, Singular}. Similarly, dpv:Duration should also be a specialisation of Scale with qualifiers {Endless, TemporalDuration, UntilEvent, UntilTime, FixedOccurences} to represent the different categories of durations that are utilised regarding personal data processing activities.

In our analysis of the DPIA documents, a large amount of information was expected to be recorded in the form of *"justification"* for why something was or was not done regarding the requirements set out by GDPR or DPAs. This information would typically be indicated as a textual description (i.e. free-form text) accompanying some question or concept. Given the importance of this concept in legal compliance, and the necessity to record this information in a form more explicit than (mere) descriptions, we propose the property hasJustification for inclusion in DPV. The concept enables associating a textual statement, or document, or specific concept as the justification for its state or existence, and is also useful beyond DPIAs - such as for acknowledging legal compliance obligations or recording a DPO's statements during an investigation.

We also identified concepts missing regarding processing operations: {Access, Assess, Filter, Monitor, Modify, Observe, Screen} - that refer to specific kinds of actions over personal data relevant when conducting a DPIA. Other missing concepts relate to certain categories of purposes, and technical and organisational measures, in particular those that are relevant in determining whether processing activities require a DPIA. Similarly, missing concepts were also identified regarding personal data categories (for the DPV-PD extension[11]) relating to behavioural, financial, professional, and in particular their indication as sensitive and special categories. We have shared these findings with the DPVCG through the public mailing list[12].

3.4. Risk Ontology based on ISO 31000 family of Documents

As stated before, DPV offers a few abstract risk-related concepts that are not sufficient to represent risks, mitigations, consequences, impacts, and their assessments as required within a DPIA. Additionally, the state of the art does not provide a suitable risk ontology that can be used readily or adapted for this work. Due to these reasons, we initiated development of a risk ontology. For this, we looked towards existing standardised forms of risk management, but found no consistent or common modelling of risk or its associated processes. Our experience revealed a fragmented landscape consisting of often conflicting use of terms and a high degree of use-case specific solutions within both academia and industry. The few standardised approaches regarding risk limited themselves to ei-

---

[11]https://w3id.org/dpv/dpv-pd/
[12]https://lists.w3.org/Archives/Public/public-dpvcg/2022May/0003.html

ther providing an organisational perspective of risk or forced the use of domain-specific terms that raised questions regarding its usefulness outside those domains.

Within these, the ISO 31000 family of standards provide a set of harmonised and consensus-building documents that provide guidance, principles, and vocabularies associated with risk management and risk governance. Other approaches also exist that are more systematised - such as the US Government's NIST Risk Management framework[13] [16], or are intuitive for businesses - such as FAIR Risk Management[14].

We decided to utilise the ISO standards due to their global applicability, standardised terminology, involvement and alignment with EU standardisation bodies, and also because one of our future ambitions is to provide a way for expressing utilisation of ISO standards in processing activities, e.g. regarding cloud security. Though it must be noted that the FAIR risk management approach specifies use of an ontology in its modelling of risk concepts, we decided against adopting it in favour of ISO 31000 being standardised.

The two main standards we utilised for our risk ontology were ISO 31000:2018[15] Risk Management Guidelines and 31073:2022[16] Risk Management Vocabulary. From these, we analysed risk-related concepts, definitions, intended uses in these and other documents, and identified relations to create an ontology. Here it is important to state that the resulting ontology is our representation of how the ISO 31000 series can be used for representing risk related information, and that these documents by themselves do not prescribe any specific modelling of relations between the concepts.

We first identified and represented all risk-related concepts from ISO 31073:2022 as a SKOS vocabulary and identified taxonomic (i.e. broader/narrower) relationships between them. This provided us with an overview of what concepts are present in ISO's risk standards and how they relate to each other. We then identified additional relationships between these concepts based on statements from ISO 31073:2022 and ISO 31000:2018 and expressed them as an *OWL* ontology. An overview of the outcome is presented in Figure 2, and the risk ontology is available online[17].

By itself, this risk ontology is sufficient to represent risk-related information required for DPIAs i.e. risk, risk sources, threat actors, consequences and impacts of risks, and their attributes such as likelihoods, severity, and levels. However, in practice, we found variance in how these attributes are used by adopters, for example as differences in risk scale where one set of levels goes from 1 to 5 and another goes from 1 to 10, and yet another that uses only qualitative labels (e.g. high/low). This represented a challenge in modelling use-cases as it prevents a consistent representation of risk-related information.

To address this, we created top-level concepts (e.g. `RiskLevel`) with guidance that any attributes (e.g. risk levels) must follow existing norms where statistical distributions are used to harmonise differences in scales across use-cases. For example, by representing 0 as the lowest possible scale and 1 as the highest, qualitative terms like 'high risk' or 'frequently occurring' are forced to be expressed as values or ranges between 0..1. While the exact values may differ between use-cases (for example, 0.5 may be high-risk in one situation and 0.9 in another), they are useful to compare the actual importance of concepts and harmonise them when information is shared, reused, or imported. To aid

---

[13]https://www.nist.gov/risk-management
[14]https://www.fairinstitute.org/fair-risk-management
[15]https://www.iso.org/standard/65694.html
[16]https://www.iso.org/standard/79637.html
[17]https://w3id.org/riskonto

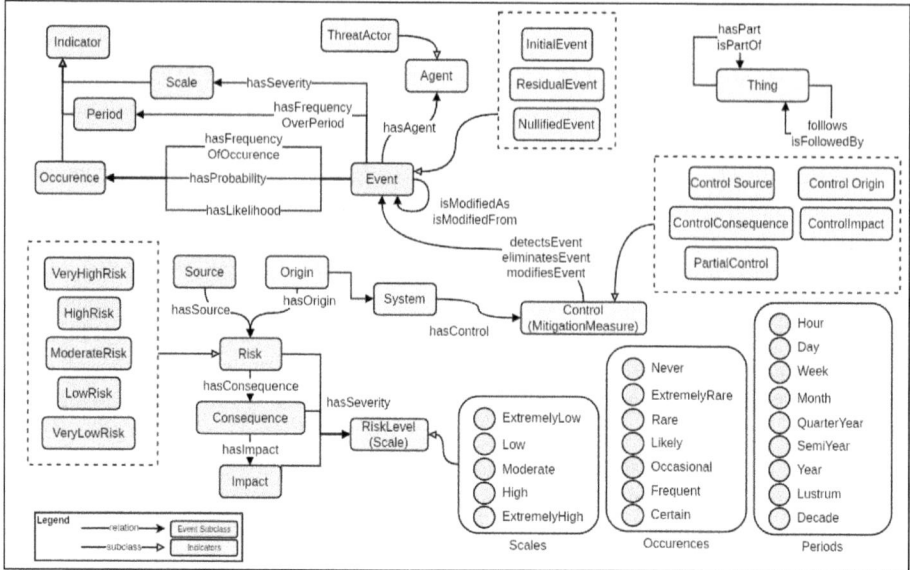

Figure 2. Overview of the Risk Ontology

with the DPIA processes, we provide a list of commonly used scales regarding risk levels and severity based on DPA guidance documents. The risk ontology can thus be used alongside DPV to represent risk-related information with more detail and granularity.

3.5. Thesauri of Fundamental Rights and Freedoms

The consideration of whether processing activities are likely to have an impact on fundamental rights and freedoms of individuals is what determines high-risk within DPIAs. While the actual assessment of whether a use-case has impacts on fundamental rights requires expertise and nuanced interpretations, we focused on the information required for documenting these impacts. This required creating a vocabulary of fundamental rights and freedoms, as defined within the EU Charter of Fundamental Rights, and associating them with impacts of a risk as well as the effect of those impacts.

We started by representing each Article in the document as a skos:Concept (e.g. Article 7 as *RightToPrivacy*), with the Title used to structure them (e.g. Title II as Freedoms). Further distinction between these, in particular regarding what constitutes a *right* and a *freedom* would require philosophical interpretations and their application within the legal domain of EU laws [17]. In future, we aim to expand this vocabulary by modelling the concepts from specific clauses within each article, and investigating whether they can be represented as an ontology. The current iteration is available online[18].

To indicate impacts affecting rights and freedoms, we created the concept ImpactOnRights as a specialisation of dpv:Impact within the DPIA specification, with further specialisations for each identified rights (e.g. ImpactOnRightToPrivacy). The decision on whether concepts related to impact on rights should be part of the main

---

[18]https://w3id.org/rights-vocabulary

DPV vocabulary requires careful deliberation as the notion of *rights* is not uniformly represented or interpreted in laws across the globe.

3.6. Populating Risks and Mitigation Concepts

Along with concepts related to DPIAs, providing commonly used terms related to risks and mitigations would also benefit adopters in representing their use-cases and documentations. As DPA guidance documents provide a small but good number of examples, we looked for additional concepts to better model industry challenges, and to incorporate and represent as much of the commonly utilised terms and 'good practices'.

We first referred to documents published by the European Union Agency for Cybersecurity[19] (ENISA) which provide an expert collection and overview of cybersecurity related incidents, issues, and methods for addressing them. We identified four candidate documents: (i) Risk Management Standards; (ii) Compendium of Risk Management Frameworks with Potential Interoperability; (iii) Interoperable EU Risk Management Framework; and (iv) Guidelines for SMEs on the security of personal data processing.

We also identified three existing privacy risk methodologies and taxonomies that we plan to integrate into our work: Jakobi et al's list of user-perceived privacy risks [18], Solove's Privacy Harms [19], and LINDDUN [20]. Of these, LINDDUN is notable in that it provides a privacy engineering framework that provides knowledge bases and taxonomies for threats and mitigations associated with software systems. It models 7 threat categories and their mitigations, structured according to the LINDDUN acronym as: Linkability, Identifiability, Non-repudiation, Detectability, Disclosure of Information, Unawareness, and Non-compliance. These will be used to categorise and structure risk concepts from other sources for DPIAs, with the 'threats' in LINDDUN modelled as 'risks' in our work, and 'mitigations' modelled as technical and organisational measures in DPV or risk mitigation measures in DPIA (as appropriate).

4. Applying to Real-World Use-Cases and Tools

4.1. Documenting Real-world Use-cases

To better understand how our specification fits its purpose, we looked for publicly available documents and selected three prominent ones based on quality of information, conclusion of investigation, and their topicality. These relate to DPIAs carried out in Netherlands (and involving government bodies and authorities) for use of Zoom [21], Microsoft Office 365 [22], and Google Apps (GSuite) [23]. All three cases represent complex services and infrastructures, and the large length of reports produced reflect the scope and breadth of information that is considered relevant for their DPIAs.

As we stated in the motivation, these DPIAs are also produced as human-readable documents with no ability to extract, query, or reuse their information. First we analysed the kind of information represented in these reports and whether our work (along with DPV) was sufficient in expressing it. We found that we could represent most of the concepts associated with how the processing takes place, e.g. personal data involved or purposes or data transfers. What we could not represent related to complexities of

---

[19]https://www.enisa.europa.eu/publications/

data collections and transfers, such as where Microsoft and Google combine their data across different services and transfer them outside EU/EEA. We also could not represent information about *absence* - such as a specific measure not being present, or *negation* - such as when a company asserted that they do not perform some activity. This resulted in gaps associated with information the DPIA was generated based upon.

The information regarding risks, mitigations, consequences, and impacts in most cases was directly associated with specific implementation details and technologies, and therefore could be represented using DPV and our DPIA and risk ontologies. However some of the consequences and impacts were difficult to quantify since they related to specific behaviours of individuals or groups, and were hypothetical scenarios that could not be specified with likelihood or severity. We observed this pattern in all three documents. We perform a self-reflection on this experience in Section 5.

4.2. Use with CNIL's PIA Tool

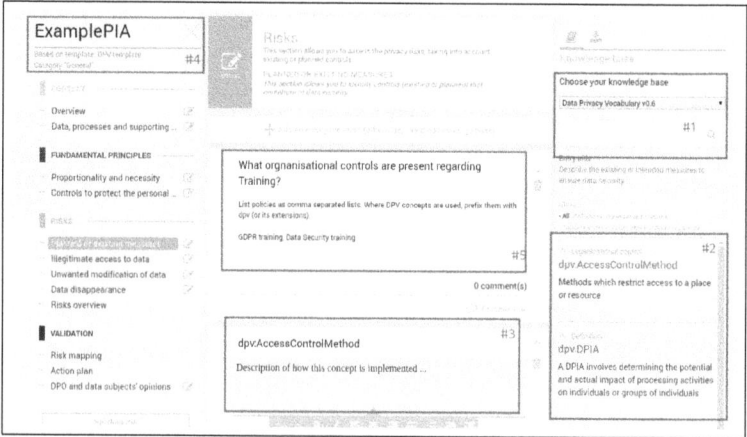

Figure 3. Example of CNIL's PIA tool modified for using DPV as: (1) a knowledge base; (2) providing concepts in relevant sections as controls and definitions; (3) selectively adding concepts to DPIA with description; (4) custom templates explaining how to use DPV concepts; (5) guided data entry for using DPV concepts.

CNIL, the French DPA, has developed the PIA (Privacy Impact Assessment) tool that assists organisations in documenting, reviewing, and sharing information regarding DPIAs. The tool is open source[20], free to use, and can be used as standalone software or on a server (e.g. for sharing). A DPIA is conducted by filling in free-form text or selecting one of specified options within the different form-like sections that relate to description of processing activities, and identifying risks and mitigations. The user can create and select 'templates' that contain pre-populated questions and guidance, and 'knowledge bases' that enable creating concepts for definitions, principles, risks, and mitigations. At the end of input, the tool provides an overview of risk scores based on entered information, and provides the ability for reviewing and approving (e.g. by a DPO).

The PIA tool provides import/export functionality using JSON for DPIA, templates, and knowledge bases. However, it is not documented in terms of structure and content,

---

[20]https://github.com/LINCnil/pia/

as well as how the tool interprets (or *parses*) the content and uses it within the layout. We investigated how our DPV-based DPIA information could be integrated or reused within this tool. This required reverse-engineering the import formats by experimenting with different data exports and analysing them. See Figure 3 for work in progress.

We are investigating the full extent of PIA's undocumented format and attempting to liaise with the developers on how to integrate RDF-based concepts within it. For this work, we used a script to convert and import DPV's concept using JSON. However, this removes the usefulness of DPV's semantics, e.g. identifying relevant risks associated with a parent concept. We hope to utilise (and advance) our DPIA specification so that it can be used within the PIA tool as a knowledge base, to describe various DPIA templates, and to provide consistent and interoperable access to exported information. From this, we also hope to investigate the capability of assisting stakeholders with automated forms of: risk discovery - in particular high-risk, suitable mitigations, and expressing impacts.

5. Discussion

Sufficiency of Concepts in DPV: Sufficiency as a criteria refers to the extent to which our concepts can represent information. The DPIA specification (including DPV) is sufficient to represent the information as specified in GDPR Art.35, but lacks representing concepts associated with other parts of the GDPR - in particular the principles in Art.5. This is because the focus of DPV has been on providing only a *conceptual vocabulary*, whereas tasks such as DPIAs require also *principles* and *controls* - both of which have specific meaning within law and industry practices. In addition, the DPA guidance clearly points to a need to represent organisational processes regarding governance and risk management in the same document as processing activities and GDPR compliance.

We therefore recommend undertaking an evaluation of what aspects of GDPR are currently represented within the DPV, and to prioritise inclusion of concepts such as principles which are important in legal investigations - such as DPIAs. A relevant resource in this is the Standard Data Protection Model (SDM) [24] produced by the German body of DPAs, which provides interpretations of the GDPR in the form of technical and organisational measures. That said, our approach as compared to the SotA definitively is novel, and extends the available methods for conducting and documenting DPIAs as machine-readable information that can be shared and reused. It provides the advantage of machine-readability for using the same information for multiple tasks e.g. to carry out DPIAs (this work) and ROPA - another obligation under GDPR Art.30 [25].

Knowledge Representation vs Practical Considerations: GDPR and DPIAs are a relatively new legal requirement. As a result, both DPAs and organisations are still understanding the intricacies, complexities, and requirements associated with it. We have only laid the groundwork for creating DPIA-related knowledge bases and tools, and there is abundant scope for enriching this work - such as adding more concepts from existing sources. At the same time, the work needs grounding and analysis of specific DPIA approaches to ensure that whatever knowledge is generated is of practical use and beneficial to stakeholders. Our experience with the three DPIAs and the use of the PIA tool shows that automation of processes such as DPIAs have a long road ahead.

We believe impact assessments such as DPIAs are an important aspect of accountability and responsibility, and that completely automating them disregards the intended purpose, and creates false or incorrect notions of safety. Instead, we advocate technology (and technologists) should aim to assist rather than replace a human with related DPIA tasks. Therefore, in addition to adding concepts or using rules or similar mechanisms, DPIA-related approaches should also investigate their role and usefulness in conducting *actual DPIAs* to better understand the disparity between investigation and documentation, and to provide better solutions for capturing the human-generated inputs that can be used for enriching the underlying semantics in future updates. This requires time, financing, and domain expertise - which are difficult to obtain and efficiently utilise in smaller capacities. We therefore recommend undertaking this at larger avenues, such as national and EU frameworks and projects so that a culture of shared knowledge (based on use of semantics) can be established and exploited by public and private bodies alike.

Shared Impact Assessments: The lack of domain-specific knowledge regarding what is being investigated, who it affects, technologies involved, requirements of laws such as GDPR, and governance processes associated with risk management is a challenge in DPIAs. Our motivation was to address this through sharing and interoperability of information by using semantic web technologies. Through this, common shared resources for risks and impact management can be developed and shared for reuse. However, a DPIA is not the only impact assessment that concerns risks, mitigations, and fundamental rights and freedoms. The GDPR itself specifies similar assessments regarding data transfers and legitimate interests. In addition, future regulation proposed by the EU, in particular the AI Act [2] and Health Data Space[21], include impact assessment for high-risk as obligations. Such impact assessments have a large degree of commonality and overlap.

While researchers have investigated the overlap between DPIAs and the proposed AI impact assessment [26], there is no work to date that effectively shows how one can benefit from the other. Instead of developing separate and fragmented approaches for how these risk and impact assessments are carried out, documented, and investigated, a good solution would be to 'share' them as much as possible to reduce the burden on both organisations and auditors. In this, the shared information could relate to risks, mitigations, or categories of impacts, or even the structuring of information for reusing the same tools. This requires undertaking exercises similar to this one for other kinds of impact assessments, which has not been done within the state of the art, and to then identify avenues for shared impact assessments. We plan to undertake such an exercise for combining DPIAs with AI Act's impact assessments in the future.

6. Conclusion

Data Protection Impact Assessments (DPIAs), obligated by the EU General Data Protection Regulation (GDPR), are an important part of ensuring accountability and responsibility of personal data processing, and to identify and minimise harmful impacts to individuals regarding their fundamental rights. We presented the first step towards expressing DPIA and its relevant information as a machine-readable specification that can be used to document risks, mitigations, and their impacts in a formal manner and reused in information systems based on semantic web technologies. To better understand and explore how this work would be of practical use, we utilised three real-world com-

---

[21]https://ec.europa.eu/health/ehealth-digital-health-and-care/

plex DPIAs and identified limitations and important gaps within use of automation and human-involvement in DPIA investigations. Based on this, we have provided discussions on practicality and benefits of our approach in sharing information regarding risks and mitigations, and that this needs to incorporate human-generated information as an important aspect of DPIA documentations. In terms of future work, we have clearly identified concrete steps - such as enrichment of vocabularies based on available sources, and several promising directions - such as the creation of *shared impact assessments* based on commonalities between DPIA and EU's proposed AI Act.

Post-review Changes: We thank the reviewers for comprehensive and useful comments, and have incorporated them in this version. The changes made within DPV during the review period have also been incorporated, and the provided links have been edited to point to the resulting adoption of this work within DPV and DPV-GDPR. The original unedited article is available at `https://doi.org/10.5281/zenodo.6783204`.

Funding Acknowledgements: This work has been funded by Irish Research Council Government of Ireland Postdoctoral Fellowship Grant#GOIPD/2020/790. The ADAPT SFI Centre for Digital Media Technology is funded by Science Foundation Ireland through the SFI Research Centres Programme and is co-funded under the European Regional Development Fund (ERDF) through Grant#13/RC/2106_P2.

Thanks: We thank Rana Saniei for early discussions relevant to DPIAs, Delaram Golpayegani for discussions related to ISO risk management, and Georg P. Krog and other members of DPVCG for discussions on concepts.

References

[1] Regulation (EU) 2016/679 of the European Parliament and of the Council of 27 April 2016 on the Protection of Natural Persons with Regard to the Processing of Personal Data and on the Free Movement of Such Data, and Repealing Directive 95/46/EC (General Data Protection Regulation). Official Journal of the European Union. 2016 May;L119. Available from: `http://eur-lex.europa.eu/legal-content/EN/TXT/?uri=OJ:L:2016:119:TOC`.

[2] Regulation Of The European Parliament And Of The Council Laying Down Harmonised Rules On Artificial Intelligence (Artificial Intelligence Act) And Amending Certain Union Legislative Acts. European Commission; 2021. Available from: `https://eur-lex.europa.eu/legal-content/EN/TXT/HTML/?uri=CELEX:52021PC0206&from=EN`.

[3] Georgiadis G, Poels G. Towards a Privacy Impact Assessment Methodology to Support the Requirements of the General Data Protection Regulation in a Big Data Analytics Context: A Systematic Literature Review. Computer Law & Security Review. 2022 Apr;44:105640.

[4] Agrawal V. Towards the Ontology of ISO/IEC 27005:2011 Risk Management Standard. In: Proceedings of the Tenth International Symposium on Human Aspects of Information Security & Assurance (HAISA 2016); 2016. p. 11.

[5] Almeida R, Teixeira JM, Mira da Silva M, Faroleiro P. A Conceptual Model for Enterprise Risk Management. Journal of Enterprise Information Management. 2019 Sep;32(5):843-68.

[6] Rosa M, Guerreiro S, Pereira R. Designing an IT Risk Management Ontology Grounded on Systematic Literature Review. In: Hawaii International Conference on System Sciences; 2021. .

[7] Vicente P, Mira da Silva M. A Conceptual Model for Integrated Governance, Risk and Compliance. In: King R, editor. Advanced Information Systems Engineering (CAiSE). vol. 141. Cham: Springer International Publishing; 2011. p. 199-213.

[8] Haynes D. Understanding Personal Online Risk to Individuals Via Ontology Development. In: Lykke M, Svarre T, Skov M, Martínez-Ávila D, International Societey for Knowledge Organziation (ISKO), editors. Knowledge Organization at the Interface. Ergon; 2020. p. 171-80.

[9] Pandit HJ, Fatema K, O'Sullivan D, Lewis D. GDPRtEXT - GDPR as a Linked Data Resource. In: European Semantic Web Conference. LNCS. Springer, Cham; 2018. p. 481-95.

[10] Palmirani M, Martoni M, Rossi A, Bartolini C, Robaldo L. PrOnto: Privacy Ontology for Legal Compliance. In: Proceedings of the 18th European Conference on Digital Government (ECDG); 2018. p. 10. Available from: `http://hdl.handle.net/11576/2691050`.

[11]   Pandit HJ, Polleres A, Bos B, Brennan R, Bruegger B, Ekaputra FJ, et al. Creating A Vocabulary for Data Privacy. In: The 18th International Conference on Ontologies, DataBases, and Applications of Semantics (ODBASE2019). Rhodes, Greece; 2019. p. 17.

[12]   Dashti S, Sharif A, Carbone R, Ranise S. Automated Risk Assessment and What-if Analysis of OpenID Connect and OAuth 2.0 Deployments. In: Data and Applications Security and Privacy XXXV. Lecture Notes in Computer Science. Cham: Springer International Publishing; 2021. p. 325-37.

[13]   Saniei R. Challenges in the Implementation of Privacy Enhancing Semantic Technologies (PESTs) Supporting GDPR. In: AI Approaches to the Complexity of Legal Systems XI-XII. vol. 13048. Cham: Springer International Publishing; 2021. p. 283-97.

[14]   Saniei R. Data Protection Impact Assessment (DPIA) Vocabulary v0.1; 2021. Available from: `https://protect.oeg.fi.upm.es/def/gdpia/`.

[15]   Esteves B, Rodriguez-Doncel V. Analysis of Ontologies and Policy Languages to Represent Information Flows in GDPR. Semantic Web J. 2022;Forthcoming.

[16]   National Institute of Standards and Technology. Nist Privacy Framework:: A Tool For Improving Privacy Through Enterprise Risk Management, Version 1.0. Gaithersburg, MD: National Institute of Standards and Technology; 2020. NIST CSWP 01162020.

[17]   van Dijk N, Gellert R, Rommetveit K. A Risk to a Right? Beyond Data Protection Risk Assessments. Computer Law & Security Review. 2016 Apr;32(2):286-306.

[18]   Jakobi T, von Grafenstein M, Smieskol P, Stevens G. A Taxonomy of User-Perceived Privacy Risks to Foster Accountability of Data-Based Services. Journal of Responsible Technology. 2022 Jul;10:100029.

[19]   Citron DK, Solove DJ. Privacy Harms. Rochester, NY: SSRN; 2021. 3782222.

[20]   Wuyts K, Sion L, Joosen W. LINDDUN GO: A Lightweight Approach to Privacy Threat Modeling. In: 2020 IEEE European Symposium on Security and Privacy Workshops (EuroS PW); 2020. p. 302-9.

[21]   DPIA for SURF and Dutch Government on Zoom. Privacy Company; 2022. Available from: `https://www.privacycompany.eu/blogpost-en/new-dpia-for-surf-and-dutch-government-on-zoom-all-high-risks-solved`.

[22]   DPIA Office 365 for the Web and Mobile Office Apps. Privacy Company; 2020. Available from: `https://www.privacycompany.eu/blogpost-en/new-dpia-on-microsoft-office-and-windows-software-still-privacy-risks-remaining-short-blog`

[23]   DPIA Google G Suite Enterprise. Data Protection Authority Netherlands; 2021. Available from: `https://www.privacycompany.eu/blogpost-en/google-mitigates-8-high-privacy-risks-for-workspace-for-education`.

[24]   The Standard Data Protection Model. Conference of the Independent Data Protection Supervisory Authorities of the Federation and the Länder; 2020. Available from: `https://www.datenschutz-mv.de/datenschutz/datenschutzmodell/`.

[25]   Ryan P, Brennan R, Pandit HJ. DPCat: Specification for an Interoperable and Machine-Readable Data Processing Catalogue Based on GDPR. Information. 2022 May;13(5):244.

[26]   Selbst AD. An Institutional View Of Algorithmic Impact Assessments. Harvard Journal of Law & Technology. 2021. Available from: `https://papers.ssrn.com/abstract=3867634`.

Towards a Knowledge-Aware AI
A. Dimou et al. (Eds.)
© 2022 The Authors.
This article is published online with Open Access by IOS Press and distributed under the terms
of the Creative Commons Attribution License 4.0 (CC BY 4.0).
doi:10.3233/SSW220008

AIRO: An Ontology for Representing AI Risks Based on the Proposed EU AI Act and ISO Risk Management Standards

Delaram GOLPAYEGANI [a,1], Harshvardhan J. PANDIT [a] and Dave LEWIS [a]

[a] *ADAPT Centre, Trinity College Dublin, Dublin, Ireland*

Abstract. The growing number of incidents caused by (mis)using Artificial Intelligence (AI) is a matter of concern for governments, organisations, and the public. To control the harmful impacts of AI, multiple efforts are being taken all around the world from guidelines promoting trustworthy development and use, to standards for managing risks and regulatory frameworks. Amongst these efforts, the first-ever AI regulation proposed by the European Commission, known as the AI Act, is prominent as it takes a risk-oriented approach towards regulating development and use of AI within systems. In this paper, we present the AI Risk Ontology (AIRO) for expressing information associated with high-risk AI systems based on the requirements of the proposed AI Act and ISO 31000 series of standards. AIRO assists stakeholders in determining 'high-risk' AI systems, maintaining and documenting risk information, performing impact assessments, and achieving conformity with AI regulations. To show its usefulness, we model existing real-world use-cases from the AIAAIC repository of AI-related risks, determine whether they are high-risk, and produce documentation for the EU's proposed AI Act.

Keywords. AI, Ontology, Semantic Web, Risk, Risk Management, AI Act, ISO

1. Introduction

The adoption of AI has brought many benefits to individuals, communities, industries, businesses, and society. However, use of AI systems can involve critical risks as shown by multiple cases where AI has negatively impacted its stakeholders by producing biased outcomes, violating privacy, causing psychological harm, facilitating mass surveillance, and posing environmental hazards [1,2]. The growing number of incidents caused by (mis)using AI is a matter of concern for governments, organisations, and the public. With the rapid progression of AI technologies and the wide adoption of innovative AI solutions, new forms of risk emerge quickly, which in turn adds to the uncertainties of already complex AI development and deployment processes. According to ISO risk management standards, risk management practices aim to manage uncertainties, in this case regarding AI systems and their risks, by adopting a risk management system for identification, analysis, evaluation, and treatment of risks [3].

---

[1] Corresponding Author: Delaram Golpayegani; E-mail: sgolpays@tcd.ie.

To guide and in some cases mandate organisations in managing risk of harms associated with AI systems, multiple efforts are currently underway across the globe. These activities aim to provide recommendations on development and use of AI systems, and consist of creating ethical and trustworthy AI guidelines [4], developing AI-specific standards such as the AI risk management standard [5], and establishing AI regulatory frameworks - prominently the EU's AI Act proposal (hereafter the AI Act) [6].

The AI Act aims to avoid the harmful impacts of AI on critical areas such as health, safety, and fundamental rights by setting down obligations which are proportionate to the type and severity of risk posed by the system. It distinguishes specific areas and the application of AI within them that constitutes 'high-risk' and has additional obligations (Art. 6) that require providers of high-risk AI systems to identify and document risks associated with AI systems at all stages of development and deployment (Art. 9).

Existing risk management practises consist of maintaining, querying, and sharing information associated with risks for compliance checking, demonstrating accountability, and building trust. Maintaining information about risks for AI systems is a complex task given the rapid pace with which the field progresses, as well as the complexities involved in its lifecycle and data governance processes where several entities are involved and need to share information for risk assessments. In turn, investigations based on this information are difficult to perform which makes their auditing and assessment of compliance a challenge for organisations and authorities. To address some of these issues, the AI Act relies on creation of standards that alleviate some of the compliance related obligations and tasks (Art. 40).

In this paper, we propose an approach regarding the information required to be maintained and used for the AI Act's compliance and conformance by utilising open data specifications for documenting risks and performing AI risk assessment activities. Such data specifications utilise interoperable machine-readable formats to enable automation in information management, querying, and verification for self-assessment and third-party conformity assessments. Additionally, they enable automated tools for supporting AI risk management that can both import and export information meant to be shared with stakeholders - such as AI users, providers, and authorities.

The paper explores the following questions: (*RQ1*) What is the information required to determine whether an AI system is 'high-risk' as per the AI Act? (*RQ2*) What information must be maintained regarding risk and impacts of high-risk AI systems according to the AI Act and ISO risk management standards? (*RQ3*) To what extent can semantic web technologies assist with representing information and generating documentation for high-risk AI systems required by the AI Act?

To address *RQ1* and *RQ2*, in Section 3.2, we analyse the AI Act and ISO 31000 risk management series of standards to identify information requirements associated with AI risks. To address *RQ3*, we create the AI Risk Ontology (AIRO), described in Section 3.3, and demonstrate its application in identification of high-risk AI systems and generating documentation through analysis and representation of real-world use-cases in Section 4.

2. State of the Art

2.1. AI Risk Management Standards

The ISO 31000 family of standards support risk management in organisations by providing principles, guidelines, and activities. ISO 31000:2018 Risk management – Guidelines [3] is the main standard that provides generic principles, framework, and processes for managing risks faced by organisations throughout their lifecycle. Another member of this family is ISO 31073:2022 Risk management — Vocabulary [7] which provides a list of generic concepts in risk management and their definitions to promote a shared understanding among different business units and organisations.

There is ongoing work within ISO to further apply these risk standards within the domains and processes associated with AI. In particular, ISO/IEC 23894 Information technology — Artificial intelligence — Risk management [5] specifically addresses risk management within AI systems. Efforts are also underway to provide agreements on a vocabulary of relevant AI concepts (ISO/IEC 22989 [8]) and addressing ethical and societal concerns (ISO/IEC TR 24368 [9]). These are intended to be utilised alongside recently published standards regarding AI, such as those relating to trustworthiness (ISO/IEC TR 24028:2020 [10]), and bias and decision making (ISO/IEC TR 24027:2021 [11]).

2.2. AI Risk Taxonomies

There is a growing body of literature on discovering types of risk stemming from AI techniques and algorithms. For example, a taxonomy of AI risk sources, proposed in [12], classifies the sources that impact AI trustworthiness into two categories: sources which deal with ethical aspects and the ones that deal with reliability and robustness of the system. The US National Institute of Standards and Technology (NIST) [13] has developed an AI risk management framework which includes a taxonomy of the characteristics that should be taken into account when dealing with risks. The taxonomy identifies three categories of risk sources associated with AI systems, namely sources related technical design attributes such as accuracy, sources related to the way the system is perceived e.g. transparency, and sources associated with principles mentioned in trustworthy AI guidelines e.g. equity. The framework also identifies three types of harmful impacts: harm to people, harm to an organisation/enterprise, and harm to a system.

Andrade and Kontschieder [14] developed a taxonomy of potential harms associated with machine learning applications and automated decision-making systems. The taxonomy identifies the root cause of the harms, their effects, the impacted values, and technical and organisational measures needed for mitigating the harms. Roselli et al. [15] proposed a taxonomy of AI bias sources and mitigation measures, which classifies AI bias into three categories based on the source: bias that arises from translating business goals to system implementation, bias stemmed from training datasets, and bias that is present in individual input samples.

The mentioned studies provide taxonomies without formally modelling the relationships that exist between concepts, e.g. the relation between risk and its controls that indicates which controls are suitable or effective to mitigate the risk. An ontology that expresses the semantic relations between risk concepts enables reasoning over risk information and exploring patterns in the risk management process. This paper goes further than defining a hierarchy of concepts and proposes an ontology for AI risk. The identified concepts and proposed classifications in resources such as the aforementioned studies can be used to populate the AI risk ontology.

2.3. Risk Models and Ontologies

There are attempts to provide a general model of risk such as the common ontology of value and risk [16] which describes risk by associating it to the concept of value and the ontology presented in [17] which models the core concepts and relations in ISO/IEC 27005 standard for infrastructure security risk management.

There are also several studies where ontologies were developed to facilitate risk management in different areas such as construction and health. For instance, Masso et al. [18] developed SRMO (Software Risk Management Ontology) based on widely-used risk management standards and guidelines to address ambiguity and inconsistency of risk terminologies. Hayes [19] created a risk ontology to represent the risk associated with online disclosure of personal information. A key feature of this ontology is separation of consequence of risk from harm. McKenna et al. [20] implemented the Access Knowledge Risk (ARK) platform which employs SKOS data models to enable risk analysis, risk evidence collection, and risk data integration in socio-technical systems.

To the best of our knowledge, there is no ontology available for expressing fundamental risk concepts based on ISO 31000 series of standard, nor one specific to AI risks. Our future ambition is to investigate the state of the art in the areas of (AI) risk modelling as the literature advances and systematically compare our work with the recent advances in an iterative manner.

3. AIRO Development

Given the lack of readily available semantic ontologies regarding risk management and AI systems, answering *RQ3* regarding use of semantic web technologies necessitated creation of an ontology to represent risks associated with AI systems based on ISO risk management standards. The AI Risk Ontology (AIRO) provides a formal representation of AI systems as per the requirements of the AI Act with the risk and impacts being represented based on ISO 31000 family of standards. It is the first step in identifying and demonstrating the extent of semantic web technologies in enabling automation of risk documentation, querying for legal compliance checking, and facilitating risk information sharing for the AI Act and other future regulations.

3.1. Methodology

The development of AIRO followed the "Ontology Development 101" guideline provided by Noy and McGuinness [21] and the Linked Open Terms (LOT) methodology [22]. The steps followed for creating AIRO are as follows:

1. *Ontology requirements specification*: The requirements regarding identification of high-risk AI systems and generating technical documentation are extracted from the AI Act and materialised as competency questions.

2. *Ontology implementation*: To build the ontology we first identify core risk concepts and relations from ISO 31000 series of standards. The top-level AI concepts are derived from the AI Act. Then, the Act and ISO/IEC FDIS 22989 Information technology — Artificial intelligence — Artificial intelligence concepts and terminology [8], which provides a uniform reference vocabulary regarding AI concepts and terminology, are used for further expanding the core concepts.

3. *Ontology evaluation*: To ensure that AIRO fulfils the requirements identified in the first step, the ontology is evaluated against the competency questions and its applicability is evaluated by modelling example use-cases from the AIAAIC repository [2]. The quality of the ontology is ensured by following Semantic Web best practices guidelines, including W3C Best Practice Recipes for Publishing RDF Vocabularies[2] and the OntOlogy Pitfall Scanner (OOPS!) [23].

4. *Ontology publication*: The documentation is created using WIDOCO [24] - a tool for generating HTML documents from ontology metadata. AIRO is available online at `https://w3id.org/AIRO` under the CC BY 4.0 licence.

5. *Ontology maintenance*: Since the proposed AI Act is subject to change, requirements and concepts derived from it will need to be revised as newer versions are published. Additionally, relevant documents including trustworthy AI guidelines and AI incident repositories e.g. AIAAIC, will also influence the design through concepts such as types of AI and known impacts. This leads to an iterative process for updating the ontology, with appropriate documentation of changes.

3.2. AIRO Requirements

The purpose of AIRO is to express AI risks to enable organisations (i) determine whether their AI systems are 'high-risk' as per Annex III of the AI Act and (ii) generate the technical documentation required for conformity to the AI Act.

3.2.1. Describing High-Risk AI Systems

The EU's proposed AI Act aims to regulate the development, deployment, and use of AI systems with the purpose of eliminating harmful impacts of AI on health, safety, and fundamental rights. At the heart of the Act there is a four-level risk pyramid that classifies AI systems into the following categories where the level of risk corresponds to the strictness of rules and obligations imposed: 1) prohibited AI systems, 2) high-risk AI systems, 3) AI systems with limited risk, 4) AI systems with minimal risk.

According to the AI Act, AI systems are software systems that are developed using at least one of the three types of techniques and approaches listed in Annex I namely, machine learning, logic- and knowledge-based, and statistical approaches. High-risk AI systems are either (i) a product or safety component of a product, for example medical devices, as legislated by existing regulations listed in Annex II; or (ii) systems that are intended to be used in specific domains and purposes as mentioned in Annex III.

A major part of the AI Act is dedicated to the requirements of high-risk AI systems and the obligations for providers and users of these systems. To understand their legal obligations regarding the development and use of AI systems, providers need to identify whether the system falls into the category of high-risk. To facilitate this process, we

---

[2]`https://www.w3.org/TR/swbp-vocab-pub/`

analysed the requirements of the AI Act, in particular the list of high-risk systems in Annex III, and identified the specific concepts whose combinations determine whether the AI system is considered high-risk; for example, according to Annex III 6(d), use of AI in the domain of law enforcement (`Domain`) by law enforcement authorities (`AI User`) for evaluation of the reliability of evidence (`Purpose`) in the course of investigation or prosecution of criminal offences (`Environment Of Use`) is high-risk. These are listed in Table 1 in the form of: competency questions, concepts, and relation with AI system.

Table 1. Questions necessary to determine whether an AI system is high-risk according to Annex III

Competency question	Concept	Relation
What techniques are utilised in the system?	AITechnique	usesTechnique
What domain is the system intended to be used in?	Domain	isAppliedWithinDomain
What is the intended purpose of the system?	Purpose	hasPurpose
What is the application of the system?	Application	hasApplication
Who is the intended user of the system?	AIUser	isUsedBy
Who is the subject of the system?	AISubject	affects
In which environment is the system used?	EnvironmentOfUse	isUsedInEnvironment

3.2.2. Technical Documentation

To conform to the AI Act, high-risk AI systems need to fulfil the requirements laid out in Title III, Chapter 2. One of the key obligations is implementing a risk management system to continuously identify, evaluate, and mitigate risks throughout the system's entire lifecycle (Art. 9). To demonstrate conformity to authorities, the providers of high-risk systems need to create a technical documentation (Art. 11) containing information listed in Annex IV. In addition, providers have to identify the information needed to be registered in the EU public database (Art. 60) and provided to the users (Art. 13) [25].

To assist with this process, we identified the information required to be provided as the technical documentation for an AI system as per AI Act Annex IV, with relevant concepts and relations as presented in Table 2. Recording the sources from which the ontology's requirements are identified is helpful in the maintenance process where AIRO should be updated with regard to the amendments that will be applied to the AI Act.

3.3. AIRO Overview

AIRO's core concepts and relations are illustrated in Figure 1. The upper half shows the main concepts required for describing an `AI System` (green boxes), and the lower half represents key concepts for expressing `Risk` (yellow boxes). The relation `hasRisk` links these two halves by connecting risk to either an AI system or a component of the system.

The core concepts related to an `AI System` are: (1) the intended `Purpose` of the system, (2) the `Domain` the AI system is supposed to be used in, (3) the `AI Application` of the system, (4) the `Environment Of Use` which specifies the environment the system is designed to be used in, e.g. publicly accessible spaces, (5) the `AI Technique(s)` utilised by the system such as knowledge-based, machine learning, and statistical approaches, (6) `Output(s)` the system generates and (7) the system's incorporating `AI Component(s)`. Furthermore, the key stakeholders in the AI value chain are modelled

Table 2. Information needed to be featured in the AI Act technical documentation

Annex IV Clause	Required information	Domain	Relation	Range
1(a)	System's intended purpose	AISystem	hasPurpose	Purpose
	System's developers	AISystem	isDevelopedBy	AIDeveloper
	System's date	AISystem	dcterms:date	
	System's version	AISystem	hasVersion	Version
1(c)	Versions of relevant software or firmware	System/ Component	hasVersion	Version
1(d)	Forms in which AI system is placed on the market or put into service	AISystem	isUsedInFormOf	AISystemForm
1(e)	Hardware on which the AI system run	AISystem	hasExecutionEnvironment	AIHardware
1(f)	Internal layout of the product which the system is part of	AISystem	hasDocumentation	Blueprint
1(g)	Instruction of use for the user	AISystem	hasDocumentation	InstructionOfUse
	Installation instructions	AISystem	hasDocumentation	InstallationInstruction
2(a)	third party tools used	AISystem	hasComponent	Tool
	Pre-trained system used	AISystem	hasComponent	Pre-trainedSystem
2(b)	Design specifications of the system	AISystem	hasDocumentation	SystemDesignSpecification
2(c)	The system architecture	AISystem	hasDocumenatation	SystemArchitecture
2(d)	Data requirements	Data	hasDocumentation	Datasheet
2(e)	Human oversight measures	HumanOversightMeasure	modifiesEvent	Event
2(g)	Testing data	AISystem	hasComponent	TestingData
	Validation data	AISystem	hasComponent	ValidationData
	Characteristics of data	Data	hasDocumentation	Datasheet
	Metrics used to measure accuracy/ robustness/ cybersecurity	Accuracy/ Robustness/ CybersecurityMertic	isUsedToMeasure	AISystemAccuracy/ Robustness/ Cybersecurity
	Discriminatory impacts of the system	Consequence	hasImpact	Impact
	Test log	AISystem	hasDocumentation	TestLog
	Test report	AISystem	hasDocumentation	TestReport
3	Expected level of accuracy	AISystem	hasExpectedAccuray	AISystemAccuracy
	Foreseeable unintended outcomes of the risk	Risk	hasConsequence	Consequence
	Sources of the risk	RiskSource	isRiskSourceFor	Risk
	Human oversight measures	HumanOversightMeasure	modifiesEvent	Event
	Technical measures	TechnicalMeasure	modifiesEvent	Event
	Specification of input data	InputData	hasDocumentation	Datasheet
4	Risks associated with the AI system	AISystem	hasRisk	Risk
	Sources of the risk	RiskSource	isRiskSourceFor	Risk
	Consequences of the risk	Risk	hasConsequence	Consequence
	Harmful impacts of the risk	Consequence	hasImpact	Impact
	Probability of risk source/ risk/ consequence /impact	RiskSource/ Risk/ Consequence/ Impact	hasLikelihood	Likelihood
	Severity of consequence/ impact	Consequence/ Impact	hasSeverity	Severity
	Impacted stakeholders	Impact	hasImpactOnAISubject	AISubject
	Impacted area	Impact	hasImpactOnArea	AreaOfImpact
	Risk management measures applied	Control	modifiesEvent	Event
6	Standard applied	AISystem	usesStandard	Standard
	Harmonised standards applied	AISystem	usesStandard	HarmonisedStandard
	Technical specifications applied	AISystem	usesTechnicalSpecification	TechnicalSpecification
7	EU declaration of conformity	AISystem	hasDocumentation	EUDeclarationOfConformity
8	Post-market monitoring system	AISystem	hasPostmarketMonitoringSystem	PostmarketMonitoringSystem
	Description of the post-market system that evaluates the performance	PostmarketMonitoringSystem	dcterms:description	

including (8) AI Users who utilise the system, (9) AI Developers that develop(ed) the AI system, and (10) AI Subjects that are impacted by the system including individuals, groups, and organisations. To specify the area that is impacted by the system the concept of (11) Area Of Impact is defined.

The key risk concepts in AIRO are: (1) Risk Source, indicates an event that has the potential to give rise to risks, (2) Consequence, indicates an outcome of risks, (3)

Impact, represents an effect of consequences on AI Subject(s), and (4) Control, indicates a measure that is applied to detect, mitigate, or eliminate risks. ISO 31000 sees risk as being both an opportunity and a threat. However, in the context of the AI Act the concept of risk, and therefore its consequence and impact, refers to the risk of harm. To reflect this, AIRO only refers to risks in the context of harms. AIRO also distinguishes between Consequence and Impact to indicate consequence as direct outcomes which may or may not involve individuals, which can then lead to an impact (harm) to some AI subjects. Risks, consequences, and impacts can be addressed using Control that can relate to detection, mitigation, and elimination.

To further expand AIRO, the top-level concepts are populated by the classes obtained from the AI Act and ISO/IEC 22989. Then, the classes are categorised using a bottom-up approach. To give an example, the AI Act refers to some of the potential purposes of using AI, such as dispatching emergency services, generating video content (using deepfake), monitoring employees' behaviour, and assessing tests. After identifying sub-classes of Purpose, they are classified into more general categories. In this case, we identified six high-level classes for Purpose namely, Generating Content, Knowledge Reasoning, Making Decision, Making Prediction, Monitoring, and Producing Recommendation. The current version of AIRO incorporates 45 object properties and 276 classes, including 13 AI Techniques, 76 Purposes, 47 Risk Sources, 18 Consequences, 7 Areas of Impact, and 18 Controls.

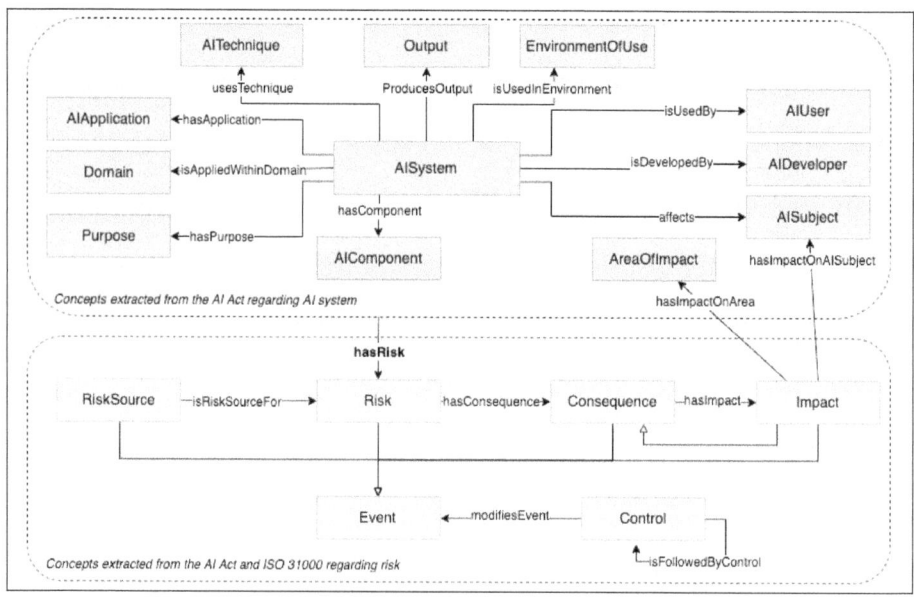

Figure 1. Overview of AIRO's main concepts and relations

4. Applying AIRO by Modelling Real-World Use-Cases

The AI and Algorithmic Incidents and Controversies (AIAAIC) is an ongoing effort to document and analyse AI-related problematic incidents. As of July 2022, it has over

850 incidents collected from news articles, reports, and other sources. Here, we utilise two scenarios from this repository, selected based on availability of detailed information regarding AI system in use and topicality, and manually represent them using AIRO, with potential for automation in future. We then evaluate and demonstrate how AIRO can be used to query relevant information, identify missing concepts, and generate technical documentation - as per the AI Act. RDF representations for both are available online[3].

4.1. Use-case 1: Uber's Real-time ID Check System

This use-case[4] describes an instance where Uber used a facial recognition identification system, known as the Real Time ID (RTID), to ensure that the driver's account is not used by anyone other than the registered Uber driver. If the system failed to recognise a person for two consecutive times, the driver's contract would be terminated and their driver and vehicle licenses would be revoked. Multiple incidents where the system failed to verify drivers of **BAME** (Black, Asian, Minority Ethnic) background proved that the use of the facial recognition system involved risks of inaccuracy which could have lead to unfair dismissal of drivers. Figure 2 illustrates how AIRO is used in modelling the use-case described.

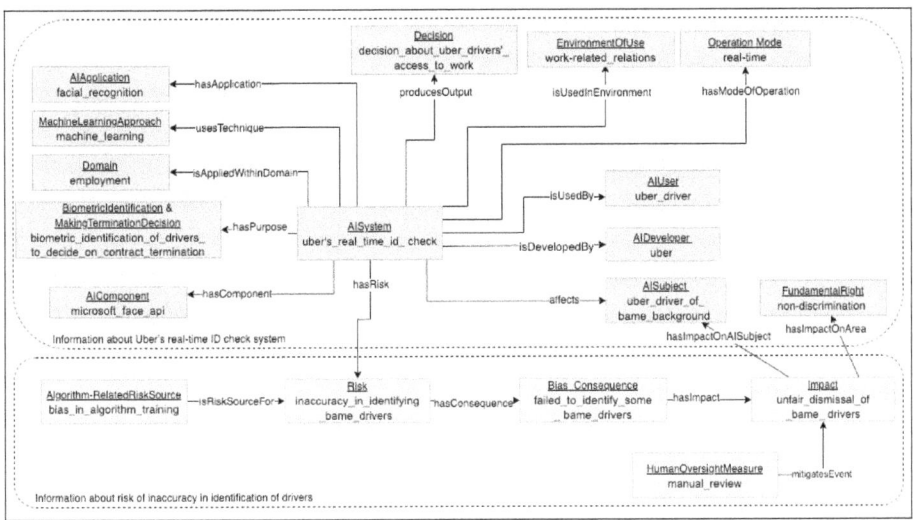

Figure 2. AIRO-based representation of Uber's facial recognition system use-case

4.2. Use-case 2: VioGén Domestic Violence System

This use-case[5] describes the VioGén Domestic Violence System that was used by the Spanish law enforcement agencies to assess the likelihood of a victim of gender violence

---

[3]https://github.com/DelaramGlp/AIRO/
[4]https://www.aiaaic.org/aiaaic-repository/ai-and-algorithmic-incidents-and-controversies/uber-real-time-id-check-racial-bias#h.8t0z8j1p0rj0
[5]https://www.aiaaic.org/aiaaic-repository/ai-and-algorithmic-incidents-and-controversies/viog%C3%A9n-gender-violence-system#h.hh0s4mc5o6ec

to be assaulted by the same perpetrator again, which is used for determining the victim's eligibility for police protection [26].

Its use of statistical models to predict the risk faced by a victim raise questions regarding the accuracy of its predictions since these would be highly dependent on the quality of data fed into the models. The input data was generated based on a questionnaire answered by victims who filed a report. The ambiguity of questions and timing of questionnaire could have lead to inaccurate or biased predictions, and if the score was not modified by police officers - the victim would not required protection. To control this risk, police officers were granted the power to increase the risk score calculated by the system. However, according to [27], in most cases the officers trusted the system's scoring despite warning signs, which led to 'automation bias' i.e. over-reliance on the system's outcomes. Figure 3 shows the representation of this use-case using AIRO.

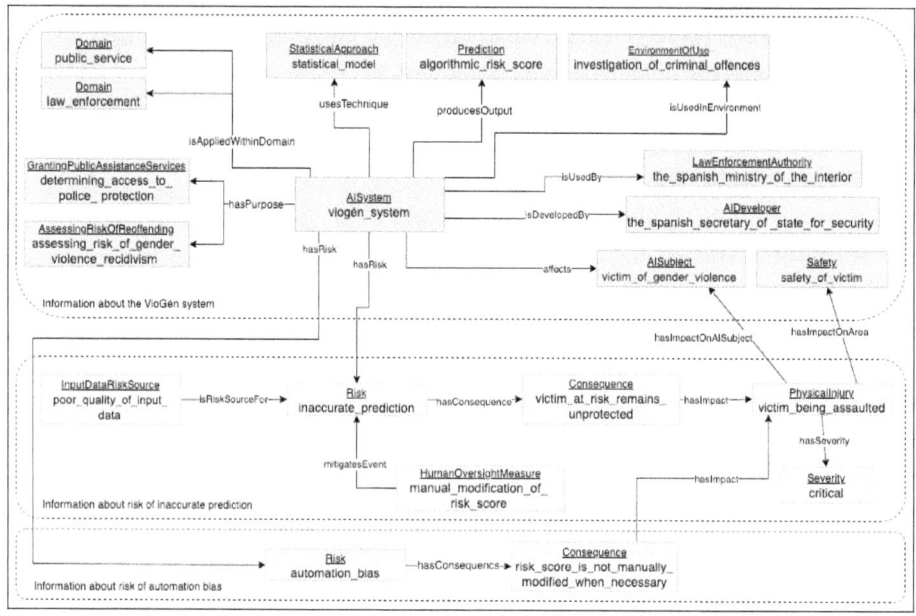

Figure 3. AIRO-based representation of VioGén system use-case

4.3. Identification of High-risk AI Systems

To assist with determination of whether the system would be considered a high-risk AI system under the AI Act, the concepts presented in Table 1 need to be retrieved for the use-case and compared against the specific criteria described in Annex III. This can be achieved through several means: such as using a SPARQL ASK query, SHACL shapes, or any other rule-based mechanism.

For demonstration, we first utilise a SPARQL query, depicted in Listing 1, to list the concepts necessary to determine whether the system is high-risk (see Table 3). It is worth noting that one of the contributions of this paper is translating the high-risk conditions specified in Annex III of the AI Act into 7 concepts which can be retrieved using the SPARQL query depicted in Listing 1. A manual inspection of the use-cases and query results shows that both systems would be considered as high-risk under the AI Act. Uber's system falls within the category of high-risk since it was employed for the purpose of biometric identification of natural persons (Annex III,1-a) and for making decisions on termination of work-related relationships (Annex III, 4-b). VioGén system is considered a high-risk AI system as it is employed by law enforcement authorities as means for predicting the risk of gender violence recidivism (Annex III, 6-a) that in turn is used for determining access to public services, i.e. police protection (Annex III, 5-a).

```
1   PREFIX airo: <https://w3id.org/AIRO#>
2   SELECT  ?system ?technique ?domain ?purpose
3           ?application ?user ?subject ?environment
4   WHERE {
5           ?system a airo:AISystem ;
6                   airo:usesTechnique ?technique ;
7                   airo:isUsedWithinDomain ?domain ;
8                   airo:hasPurpose ?purpose ;
9                   airo:hasApplication ?application ;
10                  airo:isUsedBy ?user ;
11                  airo:affects ?subject ;
12                  airo:isUsedInEnvironment ?environment . }
```

Listing 1: SPARQL query retrieving information for determining high-risk AI systems

Table 3. Information retrieved from the use-cases for identification of high-risk AI systems using the SPARQL query

AIRO concept	Uber's Real-time ID Check	VioGén system
AISystem	uber's_real_time_id_check	viogén_system
AITechnique	machine_learning	statistical_model
Purpose	biometric_identification_of_drivers_to _decide_on_contract_termination	determining_access_to_police_protection & assessing_risk_of_gender_violence _recidivism
Domain	employment	law_enforcement & public_service
AIApplication	facial_recognition	profiling
AIUser	uber_driver	the_spanish_ministry_of_the_interior
AISubject	uber_driver_of_bame_background	victim_of_gender_violence
EnvironmentOfUse	work_relate_relations	investigation_of_criminal_offences
High-Risk?	Yes (Annex III. 1-a & 4-b)	Yes (Annex III. 6-a & 5-a)

To show automation in determination of whether an AI system is high-risk, and to show the usefulness of our analysis and AIRO's concepts, we created SHACL shapes, depicted in Listing 2, representing two of the high-risk conditions defined in Annex III, and then applied them over the use-cases. Annex III defines criteria where systems are high-risk, and SHACL shapes are meant to fail when constraints are not satisfied. Therefore, we modelled these SHACL shapes to check where AI systems are *not high-risk*,

```
1    @prefix dash: <http://datashapes.org/dash#> .
2    @prefix sh: <http://www.w3.org/ns/shacl#> .
3    @prefix airo: <https://w3id.org/AIRO#> .
4    @prefix rdf: <http://www.w3.org/1999/02/22-rdf-syntax-ns#> .
5    :AnnexIII-1
6        a sh:NodeShape ;
7        sh:targetClass airo:AISystem ;
8        sh:message "High-Risk AI System as per AI Act Annex III-1"@en ;
9        sh:description "Biometric Identification of Natural Persons"@en ;
10       sh:not [
11           a sh:PropertyShape ;
12           sh:path airo:hasPurpose ;
13           sh:class airo:BiometricIdentification; ] .
14   :AnnexIII-6a
15       a sh:NodeShape ;
16       sh:targetClass airo:AISystem ;
17       sh:message "High-Risk AI System as per AI Act Annex III-6a"@en ;
18       sh:description "AI systems intended to be used by law enforcement..."
19           "... or the risk for potential victims of criminal offences;"@en ;
20       sh:not [ sh:and (
21           sh:property [
22               a sh:PropertyShape ;
23               sh:path airo:isUsedWithinDomain ;
24               sh:hasValue airo:law_enforcement ;
25           ]
26           sh:property [
27               a sh:PropertyShape ;
28               sh:path airo:hasPurpose ;
29               # omitted (sh:or .. airo:AssessingRiskOfReoffending) here for brevity
30               sh:class airo:AssessingRiskOfReoffending ; ] ) ] .
```

Listing 2: Examples of SHACL shapes identifying high-risk AI Systems from Annex III of the AI Act

that is - they fail when a condition such as purpose being `BiometricIdentification` is met, with the annotation assisting in identifying the source in Annex III-1.

We preferred SHACL since it is a standardised mechanism for expression validations, it always produces a Boolean output, and it can be annotated with documentation and messages. Also, SHACL has been demonstrated to be useful for legal compliance tasks where constraints can first ensure the necessary information is present and in the correct form, and then produce outputs linked to appropriate legal clauses [28].

4.4. Generating Technical Documentation

To demonstrate how AIRO assists with producing technical documentation as required by Art. 11 and described in Annex IV of the AI Act, we utilised SPARQL queries to retrieve the information regarding the two use-cases. The (summarised) results of this

Table 4. Retrieving Information for generating technical documentation using AIRO

Anx.IV. Required Information	Concept	Uber's Real-time ID Check	VioGén system
1(a). System's intended purpose	Purpose	biometric_identification_of_drivers _to_decide_on_contract_termination	assessing_risk_of_gender_violence _recidivism determining_access_to_police _protection
1(a). System's developers	AIDeveloper	uber	the_spanish_secretary_of_state_for _security
1(d). Forms in which AI system is placed on the market or put into service	AISystemForm	service	software
2(e) & 3. Human oversight measures	HumanOversightControl	manual_review	manual_modification_of_risk_score
2(g). Discriminatory impacts of the system	Impact ImpactedArea	unfair_dismissal_of_bame_drivers non-discrimination	lower_risk_scores_assigned _to_women_without_children non-discrimination
3. Expected level of accuracy	AISystemAccuracy	high	high
3. Foreseeable unintended outcomes of the risk 4. Consequences of the risk	Consequence	failed_to_identify_some_bame_ drivers	(1) victim_at_risk_remains _unprotected (2) risk_score_is_not_manually _modified_when_necessary
3 & 4. Sources of the risk	RiskSource	bias_in_algorithm_training	(1) poor_quality_of_input_data (2) N/A
4. Risks associated with the AI system	Risk	inaccuracy_in_identifying_bame _drivers	(1) inaccurate_predictions (2) automation_bias
4. Harmful impacts of the risk	Impact	unfair_dismissal_of_bame_drivers	(1&2) victim_being_assaulted
4. Severity of impact	Severity	N/A	critical
4. Impacted stakeholders	AISubject	uber_driver_of_bame_background	victim_of_gender_violence
4. Impacted area	AreaOfImpact	non-discrimination	safety_of_victim
4. Risk management measures applied	Control	manual_review	(1) manual_modification_of_risk _score (2) N/A

are shown in Table 4. Within the table, the 'N/A' cells represents lack of information in the available sources regarding the related concept. For the sake of brevity, the rows with 'N/A' values for both use-cases are excluded from the table.

In the future, we plan to demonstrate the application of AIRO in modelling multiple, different use-cases where comprehensive information about the AI system and its risks is publicly available.

5. Conclusion & Further Work

In this paper, we presented AIRO - an ontology for expressing risk of harm associated with AI systems based on the proposed EU AI Act and ISO 31000 family of standards. AIRO assists with expressing risk of AI systems as per the requirements of the AI Act, in a machine-readable, formal, and interoperable manner through use of semantic web technologies. We demonstrated the usefulness of AIRO in determination of high-risk AI systems and for generating the technical documentation based on use of SPARQL and SHACL by modelling two real-world use-cases from the AIAAIC repository.

Benefit to Stakeholders

AIRO assists organisations in maintaining risk information in a machine-readable and queryable forms. This enables automating the retrieval of information related to AI systems and their risks, which is necessary to create and maintain technical documentation as required by Art. 11. Furthermore, by assigning timestamp values to the machine-readable risk information expressed by AIRO, organisations can keep track of changes of risks, which is useful for implementation of the post-market monitoring system requirements referred to in Art. 61. Utilising AIRO for modelling AI incidents helps with classification, collation, and comparison of AI risks and impacts over time. This can be helpful in addressing the gaps exist between the ongoing AI regulation and standardisation activities and real-world AI incidents.

Further Work

In the future, the design of AIRO and the SHACL shapes represented for determination of high-risk AI systems will be revisited in the light of the amendments to the proposed AI Act. Our future investigations aim to extend AIRO to (i) represent known categories of AI incidents through their identification within incident reports, such as from the AIAAIC repository, (ii) provide the information required for creating incorporated documents within the technical documentation such as system architecture, datasheet, and the EU declaration of the conformity, (iii) express fundamental risk management concepts from the ISO 31000 family, which are essential for modelling AI risk and impact assessments, and (iv) express provenance of AI risk management activities, which is helpful in the AI Act conformity assessment process and implementation of post-market monitoring systems, by reusing the PROV Ontology [6].

We plan to demonstrate application of AIRO in sharing risk information between entities in the AI governance and value chain. Given the similarity and overlap between the AI Act's risk and impact assessments with the GDPR's Data Protection Impact Assessments (DPIA), we aim to investigate how the use of AIRO can provide a common point for the information management and investigations regarding risks and impacts associated with use of AI.

Acknowledgements

This project has received funding from the European Union's Horizon 2020 research and innovation programme under the Marie Skłodowska-Curie grant agreement No 813497, as part of the ADAPT SFI Centre for Digital Media Technology is funded by Science Foundation Ireland through the SFI Research Centres Programme and is co-funded under the European Regional Development Fund (ERDF) through Grant#13/RC/2106_P2. Harshvardhan J. Pandit has received funding under the Irish Research Council Government of Ireland Postdoctoral Fellowship Grant#GOIPD/2020/790.

References

[1] AI incident database (AIID);. Available from: https://incidentdatabase.ai.
[2] AI, algorithmic and automation incident and controversy (AIAAIC) Repository;. Available from: https://www.aiaaic.org/aiaaic-repository.
[3] ISO 31000 Risk management — Guidelines. International Standardization Organization; 2018.
[4] European Commission and Directorate-General for Communications Networks, Content and Technology. Ethics guidelines for trustworthy AI. Publications Office; 2019. Available from: https://data.europa.eu/doi/10.2759/346720.
[5] ISO/IEC DIS 23894 Information technology — Artificial intelligence — Risk management;. Available from: https://www.iso.org/standard/77304.html.

---

[6]https://www.w3.org/TR/prov-o/

[6] Artificial Intelligence Act: Proposal for a regulation of the European Parliament and the Council laying down harmonised rules on Artificial Intelligence (Artificial Intelligence Act) and amending certain Union legislative acts; 2021. Available from: `https://eur-lex.europa.eu/legal-content/EN/TXT/?uri=CELLAR:e0649735-a372-11eb-9585-01aa75ed71a1`.

[7] ISO 31073:2022 Risk management — Vocabulary. International Standardization Organization; 2022.

[8] ISO/IEC FDIS 22989 Information technology — Artificial intelligence — Artificial intelligence concepts and terminology;. Available from: `https://www.iso.org/standard/74296.html`.

[9] ISO/IEC TR 24368 Information technology — Artificial intelligence — Overview of ethical and societal concerns;. Available from: `https://www.iso.org/standard/78507.html`.

[10] ISO/IEC TR 24028:2020 Information technology — Artificial intelligence — Overview of trustworthiness in artificial intelligence. International Standardization Organization/International Electrotechnical Commission; 2020. Available from: `https://www.iso.org/standard/77608.html`.

[11] ISO/IEC TR 24027:2021 Information technology — Artificial intelligence (AI) — Bias in AI systems and AI aided decision making. International Standardization Organization/International Electrotechnical Commission; 2021. Available from: `https://www.iso.org/standard/77607.html`.

[12] Steimers A, Schneider M. Sources of Risk of AI Systems. International Journal of Environmental Research and Public Health. 2022;19(6):3641.

[13] AI Risk Management Framework: Initial Draft; 2022. Available from: `https://www.nist.gov/system/files/documents/2022/03/17/AI-RMF-1stdraft.pdf`.

[14] Andrade NNGd, Kontschieder V. AI Impact Assessment: A Policy Prototyping Experiment. Available at SSRN 3772500. 2021.

[15] Roselli D, Matthews J, Talagala N. Managing bias in AI. In: Companion Proceedings of The 2019 World Wide Web Conference; 2019. p. 539-44.

[16] Sales TP, Baião F, Guizzardi G, Almeida JPA, Guarino N, Mylopoulos J. The common ontology of value and risk. In: International conference on conceptual modeling. Springer; 2018. p. 121-35.

[17] Agrawal V. Towards the Ontology of ISO/IEC 27005: 2011 Risk Management Standard. In: HAISA; 2016. p. 101-11.

[18] Masso J, García F, Pardo C, Pino FJ, Piattini M. A Common Terminology for Software Risk Management. ACM Transactions on Software Engineering and Methodology. 2022.

[19] Haynes D. Understanding Personal Online Risk to Individuals via Ontology Development. In: Knowledge Organization at the Interface. Ergon-Verlag; 2020. p. 171-80.

[20] McKenna L, Liang J, Duda N, McDonald N, Brennan R. Ark-virus: An ark platform extension for mindful risk governance of personal protective equipment use in healthcare. In: Companion Proceedings of the Web Conference 2021; 2021. p. 698-700.

[21] Noy NF, McGuinness DL, et al.. Ontology development 101: A guide to creating your first ontology; 2001.

[22] Poveda-Villalón M, Fernández-Izquierdo A, Fernández-López M, García-Castro R. LOT: An industrial oriented ontology engineering framework. Engineering Applications of Artificial Intelligence. 2022;111:104755.

[23] Poveda-Villalón M, Gómez-Pérez A, Suárez-Figueroa MC. OOPS! (OntOlogy Pitfall Scanner!): An On-line Tool for Ontology Evaluation. International Journal on Semantic Web and Information Systems (IJSWIS). 2014;10(2):7-34.

[24] Garijo D. WIDOCO: a wizard for documenting ontologies. In: International Semantic Web Conference. Springer; 2017. p. 94-102.

[25] Veale M, Borgesius FZ. Demystifying the Draft EU Artificial Intelligence Act—Analysing the good, the bad, and the unclear elements of the proposed approach. Computer Law Review International. 2021;22(4):97-112.

[26] Álvarez JLG, Ossorio JJL, Urruela C, Díaz MR. Integral Monitoring System in Cases of Gender Violence VioGén System. Behavior & Law Journal. 2018;4(1).

[27] External audit of the VioGén System. Eticas Foundation; 2022. Available from: `https://eticasfoundation.org/wp-content/uploads/2022/03/ETICAS-FND-The-External-Audit-of-the-VioGen-System.pdf`.

[28] Pandit HJ, O'Sullivan D, Lewis D. Test-driven approach towards gdpr compliance. In: International Conference on Semantic Systems. Springer; 2019. p. 19-33.

Representation Learning and Reasoning for Downstream AI Tasks

Towards a Knowledge-Aware AI
A. Dimou et al. (Eds.)
© 2022 The Authors.
This article is published online with Open Access by IOS Press and distributed under the terms
of the Creative Commons Attribution License 4.0 (CC BY 4.0).
doi:10.3233/SSW220010

On a Generalized Framework for Time-Aware Knowledge Graphs

Franz KRAUSE [a,1], Tobias WELLER [a] and Heiko PAULHEIM [a]

[a] *Data and Web Science Group, University of Mannheim, Germany*

Abstract. Knowledge graphs have emerged as an effective tool for managing and standardizing semistructured domain knowledge in a human- and machine-interpretable way. In terms of graph-based domain applications, such as embeddings and graph neural networks, current research is increasingly taking into account the time-related evolution of the information encoded within a graph. Algorithms and models for stationary and static knowledge graphs are extended to make them accessible for time-aware domains, where time-awareness can be interpreted in different ways. In particular, a distinction needs to be made between the validity period and the traceability of facts as objectives of time-related knowledge graph extensions. In this context, terms and definitions such as *dynamic* and *temporal* are often used inconsistently or interchangeably in the literature. Therefore, with this paper we aim to provide a short but well-defined overview of time-aware knowledge graph extensions and thus faciliate future research in this field as well.

Keywords. Knowledge Graph, Dynamic Knowledge Graph, Temporal Knowledge Graph, Time-Aware Knowledge Graph, Semantic Web

1. Introduction

Knowledge graphs (KGs) and their integration into domain-specific use cases represent a topic that has been gaining popularity in recent research. Their inherent information is usually encoded in the form of triples $(h, r, t) \cong (head, relation, tail)$ where a node h has the relation r to another node or attributive literal t. KGs are used to improve the performance in areas like question answering [1] and recommendation [2] regarding various domains, e.g., industrial manufacturing [3] and biomedicine [4]. Furthermore, extension approaches exist which aim at enriching triples with additional metadata [5,6,7], such as annotations or timestamps. However, discrepancies regarding terminology can be found in the literature. For example, the term knowledge graph is often used interchangeably, although enrichment by metadata usually cannot be assumed without loss of generality. Furthermore, especially in the context of time-aware knowledge graph extensions, frequently used terms such as *dynamic*, *temporal*, and *static* are applied inconsistently.

Therefore, in this work, the distinction between standard knowledge graphs by means of stationary sets of triples [8,9] and time-aware KG extensions is elaborated. Reminiscent, mutable and incremental knowledge graphs are introduced as special cases of dynamic and temporal KGs. These definitions should ultimately serve to standardize time-aware KG extensions and thus facilitate future research in this field as well.

---

[1]Corresponding Author. E-mail: franz.krause@uni-mannheim.de

2. Related Work

State of the art knowledge graphs as sets of triples with entries (h, r, t) already provide a limited possibility of expressing time-awareness by assigning additional time-related annotations to nodes [9]. For example, the information that the European Union (EU) was founded in 1951 can be encoded by $(EU, founded, 1951)$ where 1951 is an attributive timestamp literal, in this case the corresponding year. However, time-related node annotations are not sufficient to encode the information that the United Kingdom (UK) joined the EU in 1973 since the year 1973 refers to the edge $(UK, member, EU)$ and not to a single node. To provide the encoded triples with further information, general approaches like RDF* [5] already exist which assign additional metadata to the edges. In the following, we restrict ourselves to time-related metadata in order to standardize time-aware KG extensions. In fact, there are already numerous works dealing with this problem, but most of them consider successive applications such as KG embeddings [6,10] or graph completion [11,12]. However, although knowledge graphs with additional time-related metadata within the edges are always considered, there is no generalized definition for this kind of encoding. As most of these approaches refer to such graphs as temporal KGs, we adopt this notion as well. In particular, temporal extensions represent a local form of time-awareness as timestamps are added to each edge individually.

Additionally, several works exist which consider entire knowledge graphs as being non-stationary, i.e. dynamic, which is to be interpreted as global time-awareness. Similarly to temporal KGs, these apply methods for standard knowledge graphs to dynamic KGs to make them accessible for areas such as KG embeddings [13,14] and KG completion [15]. However, these approaches do not attempt to adapt the original methods to enriched knowledge graphs. Rather, they try to make previous models and results reusable in an efficient way so that, for example, full retraining of an embedding model is not required after the information encoded within the knowledge graph is updated.

To the best of our knowledge, no general definitions of temporal or dynamic KGs exist yet. Usually, respective assumptions are similar but not identical. Furthermore, there are several works where these terms are used interchangeably, inversely, or not at all. Finally, there is no well-defined approach for combining local and global time-awareness.

3. Preliminaries

In this work, the term knowledge graph is used as a generalized notion for approaches that manage semistructured data based on formal conceptualizations, e.g., ontologies, as well as collections of instantiation rules indicating the validity of a graph's topology, i.e., of its inherent edges. However, this generalization is based on the most common implementation form of a knowledge graph as a set of triples, which will be referred to as a standard KG. Furthermore, ontologies which conceptualize a domain by means of triples (h, r, t) are referred to as static ontologies as they allow no further extensions of the triple structure such that facts are to be regarded as final and static. Moreover, a KG may be interpreted in both stationary and dynamic ways, i.e., we allow the consideration of time-related graph evolutions with respect to a set of timestamps $\mathcal{T}$. We assume $\mathcal{T}$ to be of a strict order, so that for $\tau, \tau' \in \mathcal{T}$ with $\tau \neq \tau'$ either $\tau < \tau'$ or $\tau' < \tau$ follows. Therefore, for $\tau < \tau'$ the timestamp τ occurred before τ'. In this context, we also define the closure $\overline{\mathcal{T}} := \mathcal{T} \cup \{-\infty, \infty\}$ such that $-\infty < \tau < \infty$ holds for all $\tau \in \mathcal{T}$.

KNOWLEDGE GRAPH	+	LOCAL EXTENSION	
+		NO	YES
GLOBAL EXTENSION	NO	STANDARD	REMINISCENT	STATIONARY
	YES	MUTABLE	INCREMENTAL	DYNAMIC
		STATIC	TEMPORAL	

Figure 1. Overview of the time-aware knowledge graph extensions regarding possible combinations of local extensions (edge timestamps) and global extensions (consideration of multiple consecutive versions of a graph).

4. Time-Aware Knowledge Graph Extensions

In this section, a generalized framework for extending KGs with time-awareness is introduced, which intends to cover existing and future work in this field. As indicated in Section 2, we are concerned with local extensions, i.e., enriching edges with timestamps, as well as global extensions, i.e., considering the evolution of a graph. The overview in Figure 1 shows the different types of time-aware KGs introduced in this paper. According to the most common terms in the literature, we refer to locally extended KGs as temporal and globally extended KGs as dynamic. If the respective extension is not considered, then the KG is referred to as static and/or stationary. For example, a standard KG is static because all edges in the graph must be interpreted as static triples, and stationary because it models domain knowledge with respect to a fixed point in time.

We investigate different types of KG extensions. A reminiscent KG models the domain knowledge for a fixed point in time, but is provided with memory in the form of additional edge timestamps. Regarding a fixed timestamp, mutable KGs do not contain this memory, but can be observed over the time period $\mathcal{T}$. As a combination, incremental KGs are equipped with additional edge metadata and are observable with respect to $\mathcal{T}$.

4.1. Stationary Knowledge Graphs

Standard KGs represent special cases of static and stationary KGs as they are stationary instantiations of static ontologies $\mathcal{O} = (\mathcal{C}, \mathcal{L}, \mathcal{R}, \rho)$. Such ontologies include concepts $\mathcal{C}$, i.e. entity types, attributive literals $\mathcal{L}$, as well as attributive and contextual relations in $\mathcal{R}$. In addition, ρ denotes the instantiation rules of $\mathcal{O}$ which assess whether triples are valid or not, based on the triples themselves and the topology of the graph. For example, a member of the *EU* must necessarily be a country. Given such an ontology $\mathcal{O}$, a triplestore including a set of entites V and a set of edges E with entries (h, r, t) is called a standard knowledge graph $\mathcal{G} = (V, E)$ if $h \in V$, $r \in \mathcal{R}$, and $t \in V$ or $t \in \mathcal{L}$ holds such that the validity of triples can be assessed using the rules in ρ. In some works, blank nodes are considered as head or tail nodes, but we omit this here without loss of generality, since they can always be added by including the concept of a blank node in $\mathcal{C}$. To extend the facts in $\mathcal{G}$ with additional timestamps, an adaptation of static ontologies is required.

Definition 1 (Temporal Ontology) *Given a time set $\mathcal{T}$ as well as a standard ontology $\mathcal{O} = (\mathcal{C}, \mathcal{L}, \mathcal{R}, \rho)$, a temporal ontology is defined as $\mathcal{O}^+ = (\mathcal{C}, \mathcal{L}, \mathcal{R}, \mathcal{T}, \rho^+)$ such that triples (h, r, t) are replaced by quintuples $(h, r, t, \tau_{start}, \tau_{end})$ with additional timestamps $\tau_{start}, \tau_{end} \in \overline{\mathcal{T}}$, defining the start and end of validity of an edge. Further, the instantiation rules ρ are extended by time-related rules which determine the validity of quintuples.*

Regarding the additional time-related rules in ρ^+, there are some obvious rules, such as the one that $\tau_{start} \leq \tau_{end}$ should always hold. To ensure this rule also for quintuples for which no additional time-related information is available, we assume the previously introduced closure $\overline{\mathcal{T}}$, so that $\tau_{start} = -\infty$ or $\tau_{end} = \infty$ may be used if necessary. By means of $\mathcal{T} = \emptyset$ and $\overline{\mathcal{T}} = \{-\infty, \infty\}$, one also recognizes that static ontologies represent special cases of temporal ontologies. Therefore, with respect to temporal ontologies, we always assume $\mathcal{T} \neq \emptyset$. Accordingly, a real-world instantiation of a temporal ontology for a fixed timestamp is called a reminiscent knowledge graph which is defined as follows.

Definition 2 (Reminiscent Knowledge Graph) *Let $\mathcal{O}^+ = (\mathcal{C}, \mathcal{L}, \mathcal{R}, \mathcal{T}, \rho^+)$ be a temporal ontology. Then a quintuple store including entites V and a set of edges E^+ with entries $(h, r, t, \tau_{start}, \tau_{end})$ is a reminiscent knowledge graph $\mathcal{G}^+ = (V, E^+)$ if $h \in V$, $r \in \mathcal{R}$, $t \in V$ or $h \in \mathcal{L}$, and $\tau_{start}, \tau_{end} \in \overline{\mathcal{T}}$ holds and there are no violations of the rules in ρ^+.*

Similar graph implementations as special cases of the above definition are already used in existing works, for example to optimize KG embeddings with temporal aspects or to integrate past information in a KG and successive applications [10,12]. Since often only single timestamps τ_{start} are considered, we introduce the notion of *semi-temporality* which is present if $\tau_{end} = \infty$ holds for all quintuples. Accordingly, we introduce *semi-reminiscent* KGs as special cases of reminiscent KGs. However, in this case, the deactivation of an edge inevitably leads to its deletion, i.e., only active edges are present.

4.2. Dynamic Knowledge Graphs

Unlike standard and reminiscent knowledge graphs as stationary domain representations, many KG applications are meant to go beyond the original encoding of semistructured data for a fixed point in time. For example, KG embeddings and graph neural networks are supposed to be adaptive such that they can be efficiently reused after the topology of the KG is updated [13,14]. Therefore, it is necessary to consider KG representations that are dynamic with respect to a set of timestamps $\mathcal{T}$, which justifies the following definition of a dynamic KG as a mapping from $\mathcal{T}$ to an appropriate set of KGs.

Definition 3 (Dynamic Knowledge Graph) *We assume a set of timestamps $\mathcal{T}$, a set of either static or temporal ontologies $\{\mathcal{O}_\tau : \tau \in \mathcal{T}\}$ with corresponding sets $\mathbb{G}_\tau$ of all stationary KGs according to $\mathcal{O}_\tau$ and we define $\mathbb{G} := \bigcup_{\tau \in \mathcal{T}} \mathbb{G}_\tau$. Then, a dynamic knowledge graph is defined as a mapping $\Gamma : \mathcal{T} \to \mathbb{G}$ such that $\Gamma(\tau) \in \mathbb{G}_\tau$ holds for all $\tau \in \mathcal{T}$.*

Apparently, Definition 3 does not specify whether static or temporal ontologies are considered. Figure 1 suggests that this may result in different types of time-aware KG extensions, which we discuss in the following. First, we assume static ontologies.

Definition 4 (Mutable Knowledge Graph) *A dynamic knowledge graph Γ is called a mutable knowledge graph if the underlying ontologies $\{\mathcal{O}_\tau : \tau \in \mathcal{T}\}$ are static ontologies and $\Gamma(\tau)$ yields a standard knowledge graph for all $\tau \in \mathcal{T}$.*

A mutable KG thus offers the possibility to infer when triples were added to the graph, i.e., when the inherent information became accessible. However, the stationary images $\Gamma(\tau)$ for $\tau \in \mathcal{T}$ are static and therefore do not contain information about the period of validity of an edge. Thus, regarding time-awareness in general, one has to distinguish between the validity and the accessibility of facts to the knowledge graph.

Definition 5 (Incremental Knowledge Graph) *A dynamic KG* Γ *is called an incremental knowledge graph and is denoted as* Γ^+ *if the underlying ontologies* $\{\mathcal{O}_\tau : \tau \in \mathcal{T}\}$ *are temporal ontologies and* $\Gamma^+(\tau)$ *yields a reminiscent KG for all* $\tau \in \mathcal{T}$.

An incremental KG thus offers the possibility to trace the accessibility of facts as well as their validity. Since deactivated edges are kept in the graph, for timestamps $\tau, \tau' \in \mathcal{T}$ with $\tau < \tau'$, $\Gamma^+(\tau')$ contains at least as many facts as $\Gamma(\tau)$. Therefore, according to the notion of semi-temporality from Section 4.1, we also allow *semi-incremental* KGs as special cases of incremental KGs whose stationary images $\Gamma^+(\tau)$ are semi-reminiscent, i.e., they only contain active facts. However, assuming the prior existence of an edge, the time of its deletion is reconstructable by inspecting the previous versions of the graph.

4.3. Application Example

As indicated in Section 2, standard KGs are not sufficient to encode temporally extended facts like the membership of the UK in the EU from 1973 to 2020. Therefore, reminiscent KGs with additional timestamps $\tau_{start}, \tau_{end} \in \overline{\mathcal{T}}$ are considered so that the fact is encodable as $(UK, member, EU, 1973, 2020)$. In addition, if only active, i.e. currently valid edges are to be contained in the graph, a semi-reminiscent graph can be implemented.

However, stationary KGs do not not trace the time-related evolution of the information encoded within a graph, since they only contain the knowledge available for a fixed timestamp. Therefore, dynamic KGs are introduced in this paper to account for such evolutions. In Table 1, the different dynamic extension types are exemplified. Thus, in 2012, the information that the UK is a member of the EU since 1973 is added to each KG. However, the year 1973 is only explicitly encodable in the (semi-)incremental KGs such that this additional information is still available in 2020. Due to its staticness, this is not the case for the mutable KG. After the Brexit in 2020, the information about the previous membership is removed from the mutable and the semi-incremental KG, since they only contain active edges. In the incremental KG, on the other hand, the fact is updated by means of the new timestamp $\tau_{end} = 2020$, making it available for future timestamps $\tau > 2020$ as well. However, this also leads to a continual expansion of the graph.

4.4. Time-Awareness in Existing Knowledge Graphs and Applications

Many existing and established knowledge graphs such as DBpedia, YAGO, and Wikidata already satisfy certain requirements for time-awareness. Indeed, KGs are mostly based on dynamic domains such that a versioning or the implementation and utilization of a SPARQL update endpoint results in a dynamic KG. However, these dynamics are mostly not explicitly considered, but rather the stationary images of the graphs. In particular, successive applications, such as embeddings and graph neural networks, are developed or trained for stationary images without taking the underlying dynamics into account.

Table 1. Application of dynamic, i.e., **mutable (m)**, semi-incremental (**s-i**) and incremental (**i**) KG extensions.

	2012	...	2020	2021
m	$(UK, member, EU)$		$(UK, member, EU)$	-
s-i	$(UK, member, EU, 1973, \infty)$		$(UK, member, EU, 1973, \infty)$	-
i	$(UK, member, EU, 1973, \infty)$		$(UK, member, EU, 1973, \infty)$	$(UK, member, EU, 1973, 2020)$

5. Summary

This work contributes to the Semantic Web community by providing a generalized framework for time-aware knowledge graph extensions. Current research shows that further progress is needed to establish knowledge graphs in non-stationary and non-static domains. In this context, some promising approaches already exist that extend or adapt methods for standard knowledge graphs to make them usable for dynamic or temporal KGs as well. However, so far, these approaches do not share a common vocabulary to compare their respective results. The definitions introduced in this work provide this kind of vocabulary to facilitate the comparison and integration of existing, but also future works and thus can serve as an accelerator for the desired progress of knowledge graph implementations and applications in time-aware, i.e., dynamic and temporal domains.

Acknowledgements. This work is part of the TEAMING.AI project which receives funding in the European Commission's Horizon 2020 Research Programme under Grant Agreement Number 957402 (www.teamingai-project.eu).

References

[1]   Diefenbach D, Giménez-García J, et al. QAnswer KG: Designing a Portable Question Answering System over RDF Data. In: The Semantic Web: ESWC 2020; 2020. p. 429-45.

[2]   Palumbo E, Rizzo G, et al. Knowledge Graph Embeddings with node2vec for Item Recommendation. In: The Semantic Web: ESWC 2018 Satellite Events; 2018. p. 117-20.

[3]   Bader SR, Grangel-Gonzalez I, et al. A Knowledge Graph for Industry 4.0. In: The Semantic Web: ESWC 2020; 2020. p. 465-80.

[4]   Vidal ME, Endris KM, et al. Semantic Data Integration of Big Biomedical Data for Supporting Personalised Medicine. In: Current Trends in Semantic Web Technologies: Theory and Practice. Springer International Publishing; 2019. p. 25-56.

[5]   Hartig O. Foundations of RDF⋆ and SPARQL⋆ (An Alternative Approach to Statement-Level Metadata in RDF). In: Proceedings of the 11th Alberto Mendelzon International Workshop on Foundations of Data Management and the Web. 2017.

[6]   Liu Y, Hua W, et al. Context-Aware Temporal Knowledge Graph Embedding. In: Web Information Systems Engineering – WISE 2019; 2019. p. 583-98.

[7]   Pelgrin O, Galárraga L, Hose K. TrieDF: Efficient In-memory Indexing for Metadata-augmented RDF. In: Proceedings of the 7th Workshop on Managing the Evolution and Preservation of the Data Web (MEPDaW) co-located with ISWC 2021; 2021. p. 1-10.

[8]   Ehrlinger L, Wöß W. Towards a Definition of Knowledge Graphs. In: Joint Proceedings of the Posters and Demos Track of SEMANTiCS2016 and SuCCESS'16. 2021.

[9]   Hogan A, Blomqvist E, et al. Knowledge Graphs. ACM Comput Surv. 2021;54(4).

[10] Xu C, Nayyeri M, et al. Temporal Knowledge Graph Completion Based on Time Series Gaussian Embedding. In: The Semantic Web – ISWC 2020; 2020. p. 654-71.

[11] García-Durán A, Dumančić S, Niepert M. Learning Sequence Encoders for Temporal Knowledge Graph Completion. In: Proceedings of the EMNLP 2018; 2018. p. 4816-21.

[12] Xu C, Chen YY, et al. Temporal Knowledge Graph Completion using a Linear Temporal Regularizer and Multivector Embeddings. In: Proceedings of the 2021 Conference of the North American Chapter of the Association for Computational Linguistics: Human Language Technologies; 2021. p. 2569-78.

[13] Tay Y, Luu A, et al. Non-Parametric Estimation of Multiple Embeddings for Link Prediction on Dynamic Knowledge Graphs. Proceedings of the AAAI Conference on Artificial Intelligence. 2017;31(1).

[14] Wu T, Khan A, et al. Efficiently Embedding Dynamic Knowledge Graphs. ArXiv. 2019; abs/1910.06708.

[15] Xie W, Wang S, et al. Dynamic Knowledge Graph Completion with Jointly Structural and Textual Dependency. In: Algorithms and Architectures for Parallel Processing; 2020. p. 432–448.

Towards a Knowledge-Aware AI
A. Dimou et al. (Eds.)
© 2022 The Authors.
This article is published online with Open Access by IOS Press and distributed under the terms
of the Creative Commons Attribution License 4.0 (CC BY 4.0).
doi:10.3233/SSW220011

Assigning Systems to Test Environments Through Ontological Reasoning

Petar PARADZIKOVIC [a], Ralph HOCH [b] and Hermann KAINDL [b]

[a] *petar.paradzikovic@gmail.com*
[b] {*ralph.hoch, hermann.kaindl*}*@tuwien.ac.at*
Institute of Computer Technology, TU Wien

Abstract. In the automotive industry, testing for reliability and safety is very important but costly. Due to the deployment of an increasing number of features within
these systems, mapping them to compatible test environments becomes more and
more complex. In this paper, we present a use case for applying ontological reasoning in the automotive industry for supporting testers while making the selection of
test environments. The given task has been to map the software under test together
with test cases to test environments through ontological reasoning. To this end, we
defined an ontology of test environments. It can be used for ontological reasoning,
both by applying instance classification and subsumption reasoning, to assign test
environments. This approach is prototypically implemented in Stardog, in combination with OWL2 and SPARQL. It is deployed alongside existing software at our
industry partner's premises and provides a user interface, which supports testers
while selecting test environments and executing tests.

Keywords. Ontology, subsumption, test environments, automotive software

1. Introduction

In the automotive industry, a variety of test environments for software-based automotive systems are used for testing components and functions of automotive systems. Usually, the choice of the "right" test environment for testing a component and/or its sub-
components is performed manually by an experienced tester. Since a test environment
can be used for different test cases, the goal is to reduce time and costs by reusing test
environments for different functions or components, while at the same time maintaining
the testing quality, such that functional safety is always achieved as required. Specific
test cases sometimes present false positives when executed on a test environment that is
not compatible with these test cases.

For automating the selection of a test environment, we developed an approach based
on ontological reasoning, see [1], which this paper is based upon. It requires a classification of test systems. For this purpose, we created an ontology of test environments within
the scope of automated software testing in the automotive industry.

Figure 1 shows the main entities that had to be specified, which play different roles
within the test environments. One test environment is a combination of one Vehicle-
Model (MDL) and one Hardware-in-the-Loop (HIL) with a connected electronic control

unit (ECU). The HIL with its connected ECU may also be simulated by a Software-in-the-Loop (SIL) system. A software under test is one Program Version (Software) in combination with one Dataset.

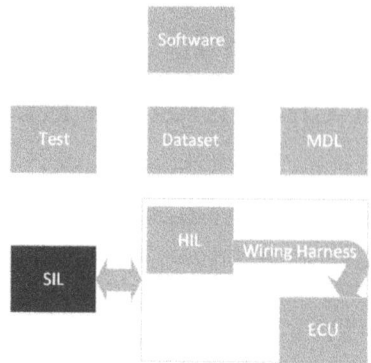

Figure 1. Main entities of test environments.

Since there are a lot of interdependencies between the necessary entities of test environments, we analyzed these dependencies and represented them formally in the ontology. We modeled it using Protégé, whereas for the integration and usage of the ontology the knowledge graph application Stardog was used. Stardog provides an integrated HTTP/REST API and the possibility for storing data from heterogeneous sources in a unified way. Furthermore, it allows querying and manipulation of the knowledge graph using SPARQL and supports built-in reasoning over ontologies.

The overall task has been to map the software under test together with test cases to test environments through automated reasoning. The use case has been defined as follows: given a specific *test case* and attributes of a specific *software under test*, a mapping to a specific *test environment* is to be found that is compatible in the sense that it is configured to be able to correctly perform the test with the software under test.

For supporting the given use case, we provided automated reasoning based on the ontology, both by applying instance classification and subsumption reasoning. For proving this approach to ontological reasoning to the testers, we deployed it at our industry partner's premises and provided a user interface through a REST API. The resulting application features prepared queries, which are called from a separate tool for test automation that outputs their results.

The remainder of this paper is organized in the following manner. First, we sketch some background material on the system test environments in the automotive domain, and on ontological reasoning, in order to keep this paper self-contained. We then describe the developed ontology and, building upon it, we show how ontological reasoning is applied and integrated with tool support. Finally, we discuss our approach and findings as well as related work, before we conclude.

2. Background

We provide here background material on the system test environments in the automotive domain, the ontology language used for their representation, and ontological reasoning as it is used in this work for mapping a specific test case and software under test to a specific test environment. Finally, we present a short introduction of the Stardog tool, which we used for deploying the ontological reasoning approach.

2.1. System Test Environments

Testing hardware and software of Electronic Control Units (ECUs) for automobile engines is essential, and specific test environments are needed for that. In particular, ECUs are running certain software, which is programmed by a development team according to customer requirements. This software is released to storage systems and the information about the attributes of the software is stored in a specific database. The ECU hardware, for testing specific ECU variants of different automobile engine types, has a unique serial number and a company-internal name, which is also stored in specific databases. To be able to test a specific ECU, a suitable software version has to be flashed to the ECU and the test environment components have to be configured for testing that specific ECU. Hence, there are certain dependencies of the hardware and software with the configurations of the test environments.

Test environments are specific workplaces, which usually are preconfigured for testing specific ECU types and functionalities. They are typically shared among testers and maintained by specific persons. Such a test environment consists of a test environment computer, a Real-Time-PC (RTPC), mostly a Hardware-in-the-loop and other hardware. The test environment computer runs a simulation program of the vehicle, where different simulations can be performed using Vehicle-models. This simulation of the vehicle-model is loaded by the RTPC and controls the hardware of the vehicle through the connection of the computer to a Hardware-in-the-loop. The RTPC together with the Hardware-in-the-loop simulate the controlled hardware. Figure 2 roughly depicts an example of a test environment setup.

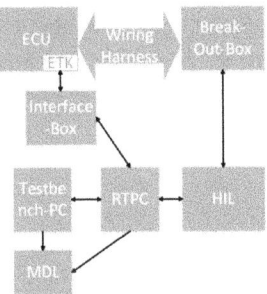

Figure 2. Example of test environment setup.

2.2. Ontology Language

Description Logics (DL) describe a family of logics for knowlegde modeling that are essentially fragments of first order predicate logic [2]. In ontology languages based on DL, semantics are expressed with rules, which relate to a semantically predefined vocabular. For building an ontology based on description logics, concepts, sets of objects, and roles, denoting binary relations between instances of those concepts, are used as semantic entities, which can be atomic or complex. Complex concepts and roles are created using constructors.

OWL (Web Ontology Language), a standard from the World Wide Web Consortium (W3C), is a language for representing an ontology. Currently there are OWL1, where OWL1 DL is the language based on Description Logics, and OWL2, which is an updated version of OWL1 DL.[1] The language builds open XML (Extensible Markup Language) and RDF (Resource Description Framework) and uses a triple structure where a triple consists of subject, predicate and object. Such a triple can be seen as a Node-Edge-Node construct, and a set of triples builds an RDF graph [3].

Using description logics, Gašević et al. [4] describe developing a knowledge base in two parts. The TBox of a knowledge base contains the terminology, which is the vocabulary of the application domain. It defines concepts / classes, semantic relationships and properties. Inside a TBox, concepts are defined in terms of other, previously defined concepts [5]. The ABox contains assertions about concrete instances, using the vocabulary from the TBox.

2.3. Ontological Reasoning

There is a basic distinction in ontological reasoning between subsumption reasoning over concepts and instance checking over instances. Subsumption reasoning is the main reasoning service in the Tbox, and instance checking is the main reasoning service in the ABox.

An ontology represented formally, e.g., in OWL2 enables logical reasoning over concepts using *subsumption* as the basic reasoning technique for the TBox. Subsumption in DL languages is typically written as $C \sqsubseteq D$ [6]. This means, that all objects described by concept C are also objects described by D. The formalism is based on semantics from the mathematical set theory. This encompasses *inheritance* in terms of object orientation.

Reasoning services in the ABox can be defined in terms of instance checking [6], which checks instances for their properties one by one and if the properties are equivalent to the object properties of the defined class they are retrieved as instances of that defined class. For example, "realization" finds the most specific concept of an instance. Querying over ABox data is a core task of DL ontologies [7].

2.4. Stardog

Stardog[2] is an enterprise knowledge application using a graph database with integrated reasoning capabilities and several database connectors for data import. It has built-in features like path querying, where all paths (nodes and edges) between two nodes can be queried. Furthermore, Stardog allows for querying and manipulating the RDF data representing an ontology over the command line interface or an HTTP/REST API. There is also an editor tool called Stardog Studio for creating and manipulating ontologies saved in Stardog.

Stardog uses a *Services Layer* that represents the interfaces to the enterprise applications. In the *Graph Database Layer* are the query engine for processing SPARQL queries and the support for declarative models, which allows the creation of knowledge graphs

---

[1]https://www.w3.org/TR/owl2-new-features/
[2]https://www.stardog.com

without coding. The *Ingest Layer* of Stardog handles different types of data. Structured data is stored in the Stardog storage, semi-structured data is handled with virtual graphs and unstructured data is stored with *BITES*, which is a document storage system for unifying unstructured data like images, voice, etc. Stardog was chosen, because the industry partner is already familiar with it and uses it for other applications.

3. The Ontology

For enabling ontological reasoning, we had to develop an ontology of the domain, i.e., the system test environments and their attributes. It is represented in OWL2, and Figure 3 depicts a top-level view for illustration purposes. The classes shown were specified as main top-level classes. Some of them classify specific segments of expert knowledge like different wiring harnesses, whereas others are more general classes like different databases or repositories containing the actual data, or serving more general purposes. All these classes are subclasses of the owl:Thing class and are further subclassified. Additionally, some classes have object property relationships to other classes on a high level. Since this is very specific domain knowledge, we did not use any upper ontology, but modeled it to our best understanding during knowledge acquisition together with domain experts.

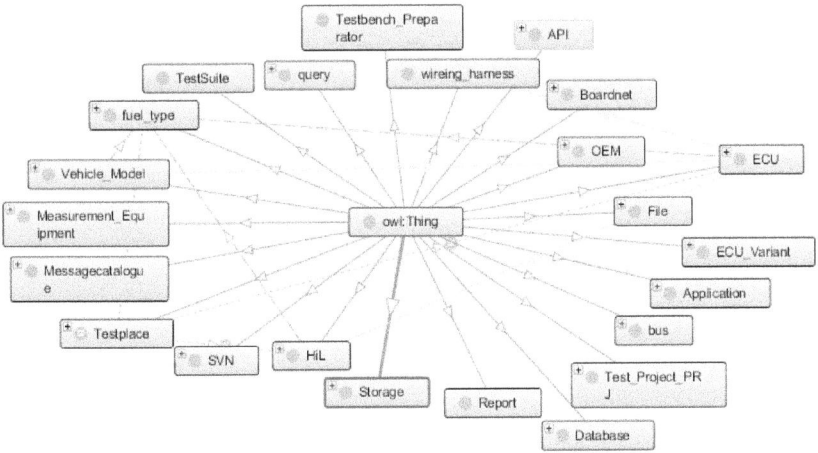

Figure 3. Top-level view of the ontology developed.

Overall, this ontology currently consists of 215 classes, 39 object properties and 3,721 instances. Furthermore, the metrics of Protégé [3] state that there are 14,685 axioms within the ontology.

4. Ontological Reasoning Applied

Based on this ontology, we show how ontological reasoning using instance classification and subsumption can be applied in our use case of assigning a compatible test environ-

---

[3] https://protegewiki.stanford.edu/wiki/Main_Page

ment to the software under test together with test cases. The reasoner performs instance checking over instances, and subsumption reasoning over classes.

4.1. Using Instance Checking

The reasoner infers instances through instance checking with specified rules and retrieves them under a defined class, such that those queried instances can be combined with each other. The information needed for the reasoning consists of the known attributes of an entity, which need to be matched through the same attributes to another entity in the ontology.

Let us illustrate the application of this instance classification approach to our use case. There are two instances given, one instance of a Vehicle-Model and one instance of a Dataset. Their properties are mapped to properties of the test environment, i.e., the properties of its HIL and ECU (or its SIL, respectively).

Furthermore, there is a class "Vehicle_Model_to_Software_Mapping" defined with "equivalent" class axioms, making it a *defined class*. In the following example, the two instances are retrieved as instances of this defined class according to the axioms of the class.

Figure 4 shows an instance of a Vehicle-Model as selected entity in Protégé. The name of the instance is a long identifier and begins with "CDFX_...". The identifier of the selected instance is marked in the top red square, having a purple diamond shape to the left of the instance's name. It has five object property assertions (blue squares), shown in the bottom right red square, and is from class types "Vehicle_Model_Name" and "B47Tue2" (yellow circles), shown in the bottom left red square.

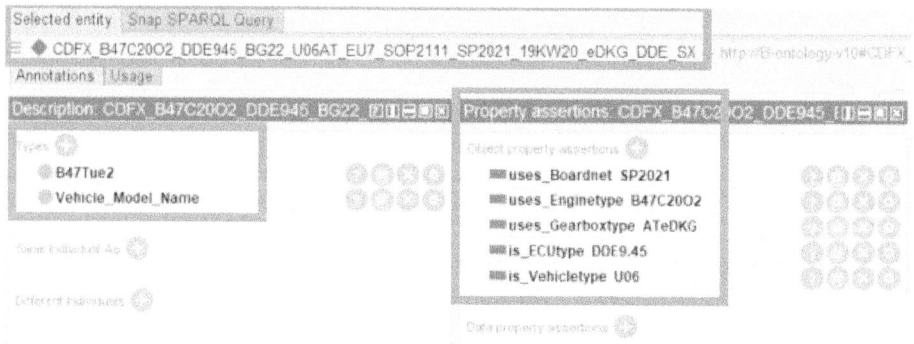

Figure 4. An instance of the class Vehicle-Model with its properties.

Figure 5 shows a selected instance of a Software Dataset with an instance identifier beginning with "J44HFXL...". The identifier of the selected instance is marked in the top red square of the figure. The class type, shown in the bottom left red square, is "Dataset_ID" and there are eight asserted object properties, shown in the bottom right red square.

A defined class "Vehicle_Model_to_Software_Mapping" is shown in Figure 6. The identifier of the selected defined class is marked in the top red square. The selected defined class has an "Equivalent To" field, marked in the middle red square of the figure. This field contains "equivalent" class axioms denoting the classes and properties that are equivalent to the selected class, and thus defining the class. The instances that are retrieved by the semantic reasoner as instances of the selected defined class, are shown in the bottom red square of the figure. In fact, the reasoner retrieves the instances shown in Figures 4 and 5.

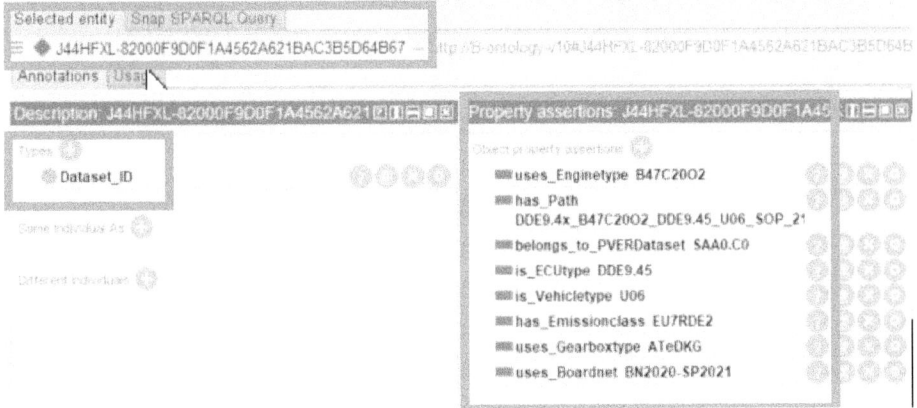

Figure 5. An instance of a Software Dataset with its properties.

Since the properties of the software under test are known for this use case, the defined class should retrieve all instances with these properties to find a match and limit the compatible test environments to use. Therefore, the defined class is set as equivalent to a set of classes, in combination with a set of asserted properties, which define the instances. Thus, under "Equivalent To" this statement is defined:

$$((textscDataset\_ID \text{ or } Vehicle\_Model\_Name \text{ or }$$
$$Vehicle\_Model\_Project) \text{ and }$$
$$(uses\_Boardnet some(\{SP2021\})) \text{ and }$$
$$(uses\_Enginetype some (\{B47C20O2\}))$$
$$\text{and } (uses\_Gearboxtype some (\{ATeDKG\}))) \quad (1)$$

In such a statement, "or" defines the union of concepts, whereas "and" defines an intersection of concepts. The first part of the statement, (Dataset_ID or Vehicle_Model_Name or Vehicle_Model_Project), defines the union of the classes Dataset_ID, Vehicle_Model_Name and Vehicle_Model_Project. Assuming that this part of the statement was given by itself under "Equivalent To", it would denote, that an instance of "Vehicle_Model_to_Software_Mapping" has to be an instance of this union of classes.

The first part of the statement is further intersected with three "equivalent" class axioms, each having an object property, an existential role and a fixed instance. The existential role is defined by the keyword "some" (which can also be read as "at least one of"), i.e., the class expression syntax for an existential restriction. The curly brackets {} describe a class of specific individuals, in this case a single instance. Hence, the first class axiom, "uses_Boardnet some ({SP2021})", defines that every instance of the

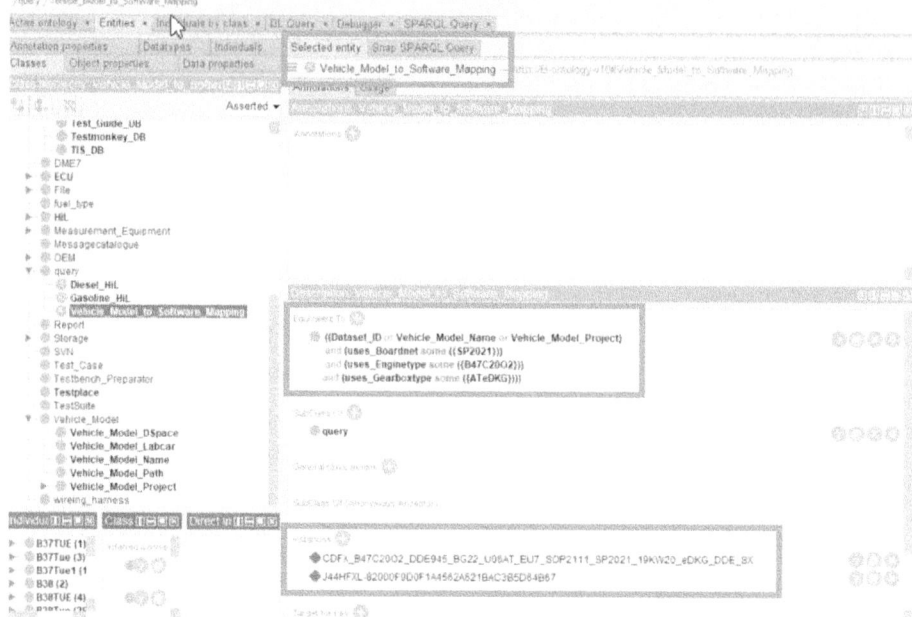

Figure 6. A defined class Vehicle_Model_to_Software_Mapping with queried instances.

class axiom has to have *at least* one object property assignment of uses_Boardnet to an instance {SP2021}. Therefore, the intersection of the first part of the statement with the three "equivalent" class axioms defines the class "Vehicle_Model_to_Software_Mapping" to be the "type of" all instances that are "type of" any of the classes in the union and are connected to fixed instances through the defined object properties.

The semantic reasoner checks and retrieves the instance of a Vehicle Model from Figure 4 and the software under test instance from Figure 5 as instances of this defined class "Vehicle_Model_to_Software_Mapping" from Figure 6, and infers in this way, that this software under test can be tested by the test environment that uses this Vehicle Model.

4.2. Using Subsumption Reasoning

The semantic reasoner also builds a hierarchy and infers information that can be used for subsumption reasoning in the ontology. More specifically, to determine the possible test environments on which an ECU software can be tested, subsumption reasoning can be applied in our use case. We present an example for subsuming a vehicle-model project below an IO Test gasoline project, and other projects under diesel projects, respectively.

The basic idea is to create two classes, each with a special meaning, and define them with the same axioms. These classes will subsume other classes that are subclasses of classes defined by those axioms and, therefore, give them the same special meaning. Since the classes are defined with the same axioms, they are also inferred to be equivalent to each other.

Figure 7 shows a simple presentation of how the vehicle-model class B47Tue is subsumed. On the left hand side of the arrow, the classes are depicted as circles surrounding their class names. Below the circles are the class axioms defining the classes. Only the class B47Tue is not exactly defined by class axiom given below, but it is a subclass of a class defined by that axiom. On the right hand side of the arrow, the inferred result after subsumption reasoning is shown, i.e., that classes IO_Test_for_GasolineProject and Vehicle_Model_GasolineProject subsume the class B47Tue.

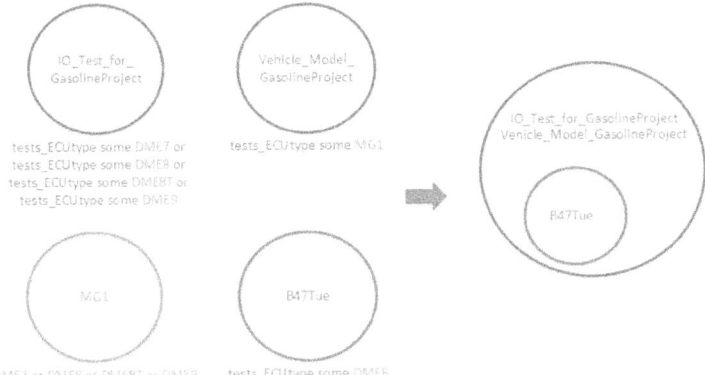

Figure 7. Simplified presentation of how class B47Tue is inferred as a subclass of classes IO_Test_for_GasolineProject and Vehicle_Model_GasolineProject.

From a high-level perspective, the example shows a Vehicle-Model class, which is a subclass of a class axiom (building a superclass for the Vehicle-Model class). This class axiom is specified together with other class axioms as equivalent to other classes in the ontology and *defines* them. The defined classes are an IO Test gasoline project and a vehicle model gasoline project in this example. They represent gasoline projects, whereas other classes are defined for diesel projects, respectively.

Through subsumption reasoning, these classes subsume the vehicle-model class according to their superclass axiom. The IO Tests for gasoline projects are subsumed in the same way. Both, the gasoline IO Tests and the gasoline vehicle-model projects, are subsumed under these defined classes, which declare that they are gasoline projects and are possibly compatible. In other words, the reasoner maps a set of IO Tests – from an IO Test gasoline software project – to a gasoline vehicle-model project running on a test environment that is able to test gasoline ECU types.

Figure 8 shows the class IO_Test_for_GasolineProject, which defines all IO Test projects that test gasoline ECU types.

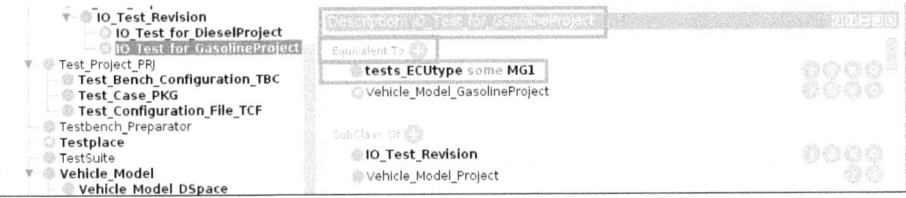

Figure 8. A class IO_Test_for_GasolineProject with its properties in Protégé.

The class is defined through necessary and sufficient conditions in the "Equivalent To" field, marked in the red square. These "equivalent" class axioms specify a class (yellow circles denote classes in Protégé) and define the properties of the class "IO_Test_for_GasolineProject": tests_ECUtype some MG1.

This class specification consists of an asserted axiom, having an object property, an existential role and a class. The class axiom "tests_ECUtype *some* MG1" denotes, that an instance of the class with this "equivalent" class axiom tests *at least* one ECU of type "MG1". Figure 9 shows the class "MG1", which is defined through the "equivalent" class axioms: DME7 or DME8 or DME8T or DME9

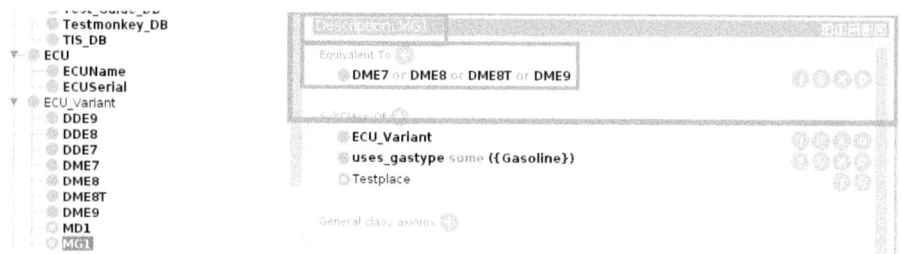

Figure 9. A class MG1 with its properties.

In the class "MG1", these four axioms are linked with the "or"-operator. This operator enables the union (in terms of set theory) of all classes that are defined with one or more of these four axioms.

During the process of hierarchy building through the semantic reasoner, it subsumes the vehicle-model class B47Tue under both the classes IO_Test_for_GasolineProject and Vehicle_Model_GasolineProject, the result can be seen in Figure 10. In Protégé, the inferred reasoning result is shown with yellow background color. This subsumption reasoning, marked in the red square in Figure 10, happens, because class B47Tue was asserted as subclass of "DME7 or DME8 or DME8T or DME9" (equivalent to MG1), and therefore a subclass of IO_Test_for_GasolineProject.

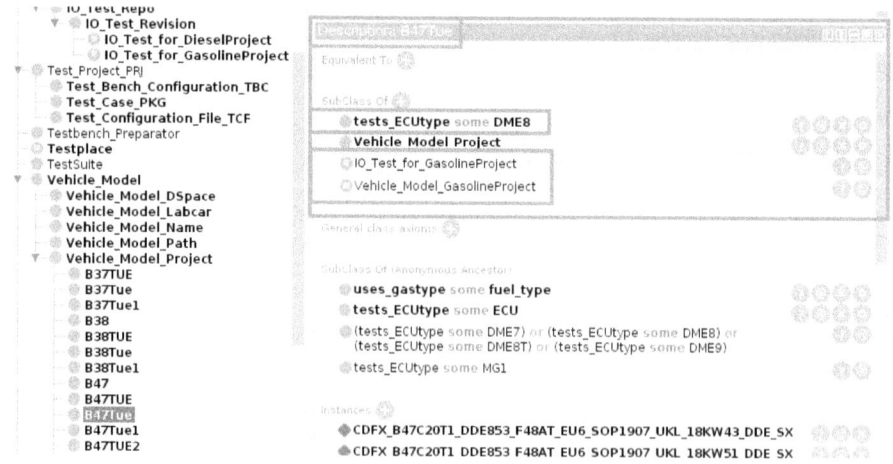

Figure 10. Class B47Tue was inferred as subclass of classes IO_Test_for_GasolineProject and Vehicle_Model_GasolineProject.

Since the vehicle-model project classes use the same ECU type classification (gasoline or diesel) as the IO Test project classes, they are subsumed as well. For instance, the subsumed IO Test projects and vehicle-models in the class "B47Tue" are possibly compatible to each other, but definitely incompatible to diesel software projects and diesel vehicle-models, respectively.

5. Integration and Usage with Tool Support

This section describes the integration of the ontological reasoning approach and its implementation using Stardog and SPARQL. It is deployed at our industry partner alongside existing applications and extends the backend database with an ontology that is queried using Stardog's HTTP API.

Stardog allows configuring the "reasoning type" according to OWL2 *profiles*, which are syntactic subsets of OWL2, offering syntactic restrictions to the language. Any axiom outside the selected type will be ignored by the reasoner. These restrictions result in a trade-off between the language's expressive power and implementational and/or computational benefits. "SL" is a Stardog-specific profile representing a combination of RDFS, QL, RL, and EL axioms (plus SWRL rules) from other OWL2 profiles. The option "SL" was chosen as standard "reasoning type" for the ontology. Another configuration option was "sameAs reasoning", which can be set to ON/OFF. The OWL2 "sameAs" directive denotes that an instance is equivalent to another instance. While other reasoning is performed in a "lazy" (late-binding) way at query-time, "sameAs reasoning" inferences are computed and indexed eagerly, such that these inferences can be used directly at query-time. Since there was a bug with "sameAs reasoning" in Stardog, relatively simple queries timed out with this option turned on. Therefore, "sameAs reasoning" was turned off and for certain cases a work-around had to be implemented using an object property "same_as".

Additionally, an option was configured that enables Stardog to approximate axioms that are outside the supported profile and normally ignored. Some database configurations can be performed with an active database and others require a restart of the database.

For identifying ontologies and their elements, OWL2 uses Internationalized Resource Identifiers (IRI), which can be very long strings. Stardog allows replacing them using a namespace prefix binding configuration. For example, the IRI "http://B-ontology-v10#U06" is the unique identifier for the vehicle-type "U06". The prefix of this IRI ("http://B-ontology-v10#") is used in all other elements and it makes sense to define a prefix binding for it. The prefix "B:" was configured for the IRI "http://B-ontology-v10#" and Stardog replaces this prefix with the IRI in the background. Both can be used in a query, the full IRI and the element with prefix binding.

Interaction with the system is supported through a frontend application, which queries the Stardog API. Predefined SPARQL queries are prepared and stored on Stardog and can be directly invoked. These queries accept input variables (fetched from databases) and allow selecting specific outputs from the ontology, while reasoning is activated. Listing 1 shows an example of a prepared SPARQL query that accepts a Program Version (PVER) and a Dataset as input variables, which define the software under test. This query outputs a Vehicle-Model that has the same dependencies.

```
1  PREFIX B: <http://B-ontology-v10#>
2  SELECT DISTINCT ?proj ?model ?dsvehicletype
3    ?boardnet ?enginetype ?gearbox
4  WHERE {
5    $pver B:belongs_to_project ?proj .
6    ?proj rdf:type ?mproj .
7    ?mproj rdfs:subClassOf B:Vehicle_Model_Project .
8    $dataset B:belongs_to_PVERDataset $pver .
9    $dataset B:is_Vehicletype ?dsvehicletype ;
10         B:uses_Boardnet ?boardnet ;
11         B:uses_Enginetype ?enginetype ;
12         B:uses_Gearboxtype ?gearbox .
13   ?model rdf:type B:Vehicle_Model_Name .
14   ?model B:is_Vehicletype ?dsvehicletype ;
15         B:uses_Enginetype ?enginetype ;
16         B:uses_Gearboxtype ?gearbox .
17 }
```

Listing 1: Sample stored SPARQL query with input variables.

The prepared query is stored with a specific name on Stardog and is called with this name through the API via HTTP GET or POST request. In Listing 1, a PREFIX is set at the beginning (line 1). The sample query accepts two input variables ($pver and $dataset in lines 5 and 8) and selects six output variables (?proj, ?model, ?dsvehicletype, ?board-net, ?enginetype and ?gearbox in lines 2 and 3). Basically, the query retrieves instances of PVER and Dataset and outputs the corresponding software project (?proj), vehicle-model (?model), vehicle-type (?dsvehicletype), boardnet (?boardnet), engine-type (?en-ginetype) and gearbox-type (?gearbox). A triple with the predicate "belongs_to_project" is produced. The Subject is a given PVER in the variable $pver and the object is the corresponding software project in the variable ?proj.

Line 6 shows a triple with the software projects in variable ?proj connected to Vehicle-Model Projects in variable ?mproj through the predicate "rdf:type". The reason is that a Vehicle-Model Project in the ontology is defined as a superclass of RQONE software projects. The next produced triple in line 7 denotes that ?mproj has to be subclass of "Vehicle_Model_Project".

The input variable $dataset is used in the produced triple in line 8 with the predicate "belongs_to_PVERDataset" and the variable $pver. Then, in lines 9-12 a *Predicate List* is produced with $dataset as Subject and some referenced Predicates and Objects.

In line 13, the variable ?model is declared as type of "Vehicle_Model_Name". Finally, a *Predicate List* is produced with Objects ?dsvehicletype, ?enginetype and ?gear-box, which were used above in the Predicate List referencing to $dataset.

The result is serialized in a form defined in the HTTP Header. In this case, JSON was chosen as exchange format. Example results with specific input variables passed to the query in Listing 1 are shown in Listing 2.

```
1  {
2    "head": {
3      "vars": [
4        "proj",
5        "model",
```

```
 6            "dsvehicletype",
 7            "boardnet",
 8            "enginetype",
 9            "gearbox"] },
10    "results": {
11       "bindings": [
12       {
13          "dsvehicletype": {
14             "type": "uri",
15             "value": "http://B-ontology-v10#U06"
16          },
17          "boardnet": {
18             "type": "uri",
19             "value": "http://B-ontology-v10#BN2020-SP2021"
20          },
21          "proj": {
22             "type": "uri",
23             "value": "http://B-ontology-v10#Project_RQONE01071608"
24          },
25          "model": {
26             "type": "uri",
27             "value": "http://B-ontology-v10#CDFX_B47C2002_DDE945_BG22_U06
        AT_EU7_SOP2111_SP2021_19KW20_DDE_SX"
28          },
29          "gearbox": {
30             "type": "uri",
31             "value": "http://B-ontology-v10#ATDKG"
32          },
33          "enginetype": {
34             "type": "uri",
35             "value": "http://B-ontology-v10#B47C2002"
36          }}]}
37    }
```

Listing 2: Example Results in JSON format

The frontend-application, which is completely independent of Stardog, implements the services through passing the prepared query's name and input variables as parameters in the POST request body. Furthermore, it passes the authentication credentials to be able to access the Stardog API. Usually, the frontend-application obtains this from specially created database tables, where the developers try to fill the data accordingly. The Stardog SPARQL queries are used as verification support for different parts of the defined use case. The example above shows how it can be checked which Vehicle-model can test which PVER and Dataset. Another query that works similarly, deals with identifying which IO-Test Project can be tested on which Vehicle-model.

6. Related Work

In technical sciences and industry, ontologies can be used for formal specification of domain knowledge. We provide here an overview of applications of ontologies in the automotive industry.

Alvares-Coello and Gómez [8] discuss how ontologies can benefit vehicle architectures in the automotive industry. They propose an ontology-based approach for integrating vehicle-related data with applications. To this end, application-specific data is annotated with well-defined semantic models and combined with vehicle-related data for facilitating more stable queries over the lifetime of applications.

In [9], an ontology- and rule-based approach using F-Logic [10] is specified and a small prototype is described. The prototype analyses HiL test data with additional formalized rules that are derived from interviews with experts. The test data is recorded during test runs on a HiL system and imported as instances into the ontology. Test instances are checked for rules that are defined in concepts in the ontology and errors are detected and highlighted. In contrast to our work, the authors do not consider using subsumption reasoning nor the use case of mapping test cases to test environments.

An ontological approach for collecting incidents of car breakdowns and connecting them to repair instructions is implemented in [11]. For searching breakdown documents of different vehicle types, a semantic search engine using OWL has been developed.

In [12] and [13], context information is modeled using OWL ontologies and Protégé, for helping drivers handling the car based on contextual information.

7. Discussion

Through specification of knowledge in the ontology, the expert knowledge necessary to assign systems to test environments is gathered at a central place. The landscape of interdependent entities in this domain of interest is both larege and complex.

The granularity of the entity specification can be refined. For instance, test-system components can be further analyzed and fragmented into smaller parts, which can have further dependencies to other parts. This would lead to more detailed dependency management and allow for different use cases within the context of automotive software and hardware testing.

Regularly automated import of relevant data to the ontology is a practical challenge. We have already analyzed import possibilities as well as tooling for gathering and importing of relevant data from heterogeneous sources. Technically, the automated import from such tools can be accomplished by interfacing Stardog.

8. Conclusion

In this paper, we present an approach for improving automated testing in the automotive industry using an ontology and ontological reasoning. We chose to specify the expert knowledge in an ontology and to model dependencies between systems as well. While there are several use cases where an ontology could provide dependency management and decision support, one specific use case was defined for the scope of this paper: for given test cases and software under test, a compatible test environment is found, by taking into account the attributes of the test environment, software and test cases.

For accomplishing this automated mapping, we propose an approach based on ontological reasoning. First, we use instance classification where we infer for specific instances, in our application test environments, to which defined classes they belong, essentially enabling the automatic combination of those queried instances. Secondly, we use subsumption reasoning to determine the test environments compatible with given test cases of a software under test.

We deployed our ontological reasoning approach using Stardog and SPARQL. Stardog provides the means for knowledge graph representation and allows for querying and manipulating the ontology, which is imported and stored as a knowledge graph. Furthermore, reasoning mechanisms that are supported by Stardog were used for the purpose of ontological reasoning.

By doing so, we were able to demonstrate our approach for the defined use case with our prototype deployed at our industry partner. The prototype showed that ontological reasoning can support the process of automated software testing in the automotive industry.

Acknowledgments

Part of this research has been carried out in the VerASoS project (No. 861210), funded by the Austrian Federal Ministry of Transport, Innovation and Technology (BMVIT) under the program "ICT of the Future" of the Austrian FFG.

References

[1] Paradzikovic P. Defining and using an ontology of test environments [Master Thesis]. TU Wien; 2019.

[2] Hitzler P, Krötzsch M, Rudolph S, Sure Y. Semantic Web: Grundlagen. Berlin: Springer; 2008.

[3] Klyne G, Carroll JJ. RDF Resource Description Framework Concepts and Abstract Syntax. W3C; 2004. https://www.w3.org/TR/rdf-concepts/#section-data-model.

[4] Gaševic D, Djuric D, Devedžic V. Model Driven Engineering and Ontology Development. Berlin, Heidelberg: Springer Berlin Heidelberg; 2009. Available from: https://doi.org/10.1007/978-3-642-00282-3_2.

[5] Gruber TR. A Translation Approach to Portable Ontology Specifications. Knowl Acquis. 1993 Jun;5(2):199-220. Available from: http://dx.doi.org/10.1006/knac.1993.1008.

[6] Baader F, Calvanese D, McGuinness DL, Nardi D, Patel-Schneider PF. The Description Logic Handbook: Theory, Implementation and Applications. 2nd ed. New York, NY, USA: Cambridge University Press; 2010.

[7] Pascal H, Markus K, Sebastian R. Foundations of Semantic Web Technologies. 1st ed. Chapman and Hall/CRC; 2009.

[8] Alvarez-Coello D, Gómez JM. Ontology-Based Integration of Vehicle-Related Data. In: 15th IEEE International Conference on Semantic Computing, ICSC 2021, Laguna Hills, CA, USA, January 27-29, 2021. IEEE; 2021. p. 437-42. Available from: https://doi.org/10.1109/ICSC50631.2021.00078.

[9] Syldatke T, Chen W, Angele J, Nierlich A, Ullrich M. How Ontologies and Rules Help to Advance Automobile Development. In: Paschke A, Biletskiy Y, editors. Advances in Rule Interchange and Applications. Berlin, Heidelberg: Springer Berlin Heidelberg; 2007. p. 1-6.

[10] Kifer M, Lausen G, Wu J. Logical Foundations of Object-Oriented and Frame-based Languages. J ACM. 1995 Jul;42(4):741-843. Available from: http://doi.acm.org/10.1145/210332.210335.

[11] Reymonet A, Thomas J, Aussenac-gilles N. Ontology Based Information Retrieval: an application to automotive diagnosis. In: Linköping University, Institute of Technology; 2009. p. 914.

[12] Madkour M, Maach A. Ontology-Based Context Modeling for Vehicle Context-Aware Services. Journal of Theoretical and Applied Information Technology. 2011 12;31.

[13] Lüddecke D, Bergmann N, Schaefer I. Ontology-Based Modeling of Context-Aware Systems. In: Dingel J, Schulte W, Ramos I, Abrahão S, Insfran E, editors. Model-Driven Engineering Languages and Systems. Cham: Springer International Publishing; 2014. p. 484-500.

Towards a Knowledge-Aware AI
A. Dimou et al. (Eds.)
© 2022 The Authors.
This article is published online with Open Access by IOS Press and distributed under the terms
of the Creative Commons Attribution License 4.0 (CC BY 4.0).
doi:10.3233/SSW220012

Adding Domain Knowledge to Improve Entity Resolution in 17th and 18th Century Amsterdam Archival Records

J. Baas [a] , L. van Wissen [b] , J. Reinders [c] , M. M. Dastani [a] and A. J. Feelders [a]

[a] *Utrecht University, Heidelberglaan 8, 3584 CS Utrecht, Netherlands*
[b] *University of Amsterdam, Turfdraagsterpad 9, 1012 XT Amsterdam, Netherlands*
[c] *Huygens Institute for the History of the Netherlands, Oudezijds Achterburgwal 185, 1012 DK, Amsterdam, Netherlands*

Abstract. The problem of entity resolution is central in the field of Digital Humanities. It is also one of the major issues in the Golden Agents project, which aims at creating an infrastructure that enables researchers to search for patterns that span across decentralised knowledge graphs from cultural heritage institutes. To this end, we created a method to perform entity resolution on complex historical knowledge graphs. In previous work, we encoded and embedded the relevant (duplicate) entities in a vector space to derive similarities between them based on sharing a similar context in RDF graphs. In some cases, however, available domain knowledge or rational axioms can be applied to improve entity resolution performance. We show how domain knowledge and rational axioms relevant to the task at hand can be expressed as (probabilistic) rules, and how the information derived from rule application can be combined with quantitative information from the embedding. In this work, we perform our entity resolution method on two data sets. First, we apply it to a data set for which we have a detailed ground truth for validation. This experiment shows that the combination of embedding and the application of domain knowledge and rational axioms leads to improved resolution performance. Second, we perform a case study by applying our method to a larger data set for which there is no ground truth and where the outcome is subsequently validated by a domain expert. Results of this demonstrate that our method achieves a very high precision.

Keywords. Linked Open Data, Digital Humanities, Entity Resolution, Machine Learning, Embeddings

1. Introduction

The project *Golden Agents: Creative Industries and the Making of the Dutch Golden Age*[1] develops a research infrastructure to study relations and interactions between producers and consumers of creative goods during the 17th and 18th century in Amsterdam. It brings together heterogeneous data sets from several content providers as linked open data. However, the independent nature of the institutions that govern these data sets causes them to use different identifiers to refer to the same real-world object, if they pro-

---

[1] https://www.goldenagents.org

vide an identifier for these resources at all. Especially when dealing with archival data the situation is even more complicated, as it is rarely the case that entities are identified as more than a textual reference to e.g. a person or a location. Due to the size and type of this archival data, internal disambiguation or external reconciliation is often not available, which makes every reference an unresolved ambiguous one. In order to use these data sets for prosopographical (common characteristics of a group of people) and biographical research, and ask questions that shed more light on the production and consumption of cultural goods, we need a way to efficiently disambiguate these textual references to entities, thereby making it possible to understand the impact of the Dutch Golden Age on the creative industries and its actors.

The limited availability of ground truth in this type of data is a common problem in the field of the Digital Humanities, which makes it hard to apply supervised machine learning methods to the problem of entity resolution and entity linking. However, unsupervised machine learning methods such as embedding techniques can be applied to this type of data to create sub-symbolic models with which we can attempt to resolve these entity references. Nevertheless, the models may produce errors in the entity resolution outcome, where pairs of entities are identified as identical while in reality they are not. These errors may come about due to inherent weaknesses in the embedding technique, or incomplete and unreliable information in the original data. It is not viable to switch to a supervised method in an attempt to improve performance due to the lack of ground truth. Therefore, it is necessary to use other types of information, such as rational axioms and domain knowledge, to improve the entity resolution method.

We argue that domain-specific knowledge can be used to detect and correct errors and propose an approach to incorporate domain knowledge in an existing entity resolution algorithm. Examples of such domain-specific knowledge are (1) two entities cannot be identical if they occur in the same civil registration record, and (2) two entities, one with birth date x, the other with marriage date y cannot be identical if $x > y$. The purpose of these rules is to cast doubt on the conclusion of a sub-symbolic method that two entities are the same. Furthermore, the use of domain-specific knowledge can involve uncertainty due to the ambiguity in the data. For example, if we want to exploit the fact that a person cannot be born after they have died, one must be able to identify the born and dead persons unambiguously. The difficulty is that in this type of archival sources it is not a given that the person is actively involved in the registration event when they are mentioned. It could even be that the person is already deceased and is solely used as a disambiguating description for someone else (e.g. *Claartje Jans, widow of Cornelis Pieters*). If this happens in a burial registration or the registration of a testament, we need a rule that is aware of this knowledge and we do not treat the fact of a person's death as 100% certain, but see this as relative to the number of persons involved in the event. This uncertainty then propagates to the conclusion of the rule.

The novel contribution of this work is (1) an experiment with the incorporation of these rules with an existing embedding, and (2) a case study where we apply the method to more heterogeneous and voluminous data. In this paper we distinguish the terms 'experiment' and 'case study' to indicate that we have no sufficient ground truth available for the latter and that the main motivation for this case study was to apply the method to our data to make a linkset, which is then incorporated in the Golden Agents infrastructure. The purpose of the experiment is to test whether the inclusion of domain knowledge improves entity resolution performance and to provide estimates for an optimal configuration of the method, which we use for the case study.

We show in our experiment that including the domain knowledge improves overall performance. We show with the case study, applied to a corpus of 84,268 resources, of which 22,073 (not fully disambiguated) persons participating in 7,339 different events, that our method proves to be a useful tool for entity resolution in heterogeneous archival data. We are able to disambiguate 9,151 entities with a precision of around 92%.

2. Related Work

Entity disambiguation on data from archives is a problem that has been around since the first digitisation initiatives of traditional (archival) indices and other entry points. These methods rely on either a strictly defined data model, or on the availability of sufficient data to disambiguate persons easily (e.g. a birth date). While the contribution of this work is on the integration of domain knowledge and rational axioms with embedded data, a selection of other methods for entity resolution on knowledge graphs are, Legato [1], LIMES [2], SILK [3], and Lenticular Lens [4]. These methods assume that there are only two data sets, often called source and target, and that these source and target data sets do not have internal duplicates. An exception is Lenticular Lens, which notes that it can work when the source and target are the same. Another difference is that in the first three methods only literals are used for disambiguation. Our method is more generic in the sense that all nodes related to an entity can act as context and it, in contrast to Lenticular Lens, does not solely rely on pre-defined rules to perform entity resolution. The more heterogeneous a data set is, the less feasible it is to work with a rule-based approach. These are major problems for applying other techniques to our data. Another difference is that our method takes into account the semantics of properties when comparing entities, something that is not done in, for instance, the bag-of-words model of Legato. This is important as we do not want to treat, for instance, death dates and birth dates equally in the context of an entity. That is, the fact that the birth date of an entity is the same as the death date of another entity does not mean they are similar.

In light of the use of integrating domain knowledge with embeddings, Guo et al. [5] have developed KALE, where an embedding is learned by jointly using facts from a knowledge graph and t-norm fuzzy logic. Similarly, Rocktäschel et al. [6] use first-order logic background knowledge to aid the matrix factorisation algorithm in learning dependencies between relations. Domain knowledge can be used with pre-trained embeddings as well, Wang et al. [7] predict new facts (also known as link prediction) by combining the output of an existing embedding with physical and logical rules into an integer linear programming problem. Others have worked on the very similar problem of author name disambiguation, where authors are linked in scholarly data sets such as dblp[2]. For instance, Cen et al.[8] learn stopping criteria to use with hierarchical agglomerative clustering. This method, however, requires a training set, which is often not or very limitedly available when working with cultural heritage data. Furthermore, hierarchical agglomerative clustering has the following drawbacks: its time complexity is high compared with some other clustering methods and it needs to take the number of clusters as input while

---

[2]https://dblp.org/

determining the number of clusters is usually an intractable problem or completely unknown in many digital humanities applications. Work on author name disambiguation seems to have died down, with some efforts ongoing in the medical domain, such as with Sanyal et al. [9].

Others have worked on similar cultural heritage data sets but without the use of embeddings. Raad et al. [10] create a certificate linking method for Dutch civil certificates from the Zeeland region, based on string similarity computations. Furthermore, they propose a contextual identity link [11], as they observe that the `owl:sameAs` link is often misused. Similarly, Idrissou et al. [12,13] have proposed a contextual identity link based on the use of related entities to construct evidence for likely duplicate pairs. An example of evidence is that two entities may co-occur in multiple records under similar names. Koho et al. [14] reconcile military historical persons in three registers. Hendriks et al. [15] use data from the Amsterdam Notarial Archives and Dutch East India Company (VOC) and perform both named entity recognition and record linkage. Finally, Efremova et al. [16,17] perform entity resolution on civil certificates by making use of name similarity (corrected for name popularity), proximity of locations, and limited co-occurrence information as features in regression tree and logistic regression models.

3. Data

The section below describes the data sets used in the experiment and the case study. Each of the data sets either already existed in RDF or was created in the Golden Agents project.

3.1. Amsterdam City Archives

For both the experiment and the case study, the collections of the City Archives of Amsterdam[3] play an important role. Traditionally, the Amsterdam City Archives served the interests of its users by unlocking its sources partially via paper indices that always contain a person's name and the date of the registration in the source. With the scanning of the original sources and the digitisation of the indices starting around 2000, it became easier to find the individuals mentioned in each index. The Golden Agents project has taken these digitised sources and converted and modelled them into RDF so that they are available to be connected to other data sets.

3.1.1. Notice of Marriage registrations

One of the most important indices for early modernists is the index on Notice of Marriage [=Ondertrouw] registrations. Whereas regular Marriage registrations do not contain that much information on the occupations, ages, residency, etc. of the groom and bride-to-be, the Notice of Marriage does contain this. This is crucial information for disambiguating persons. The index counts approximately 1 million person names and distinguishes roles (groom, bride) in the registration event. For 20% of this data, we also have information on among others the witnesses participating in the event. This data is coming from the crowdsourcing project *Ja, ik wil!* [=Yes I do!] [19]. Both the original Notice of Marriage index as well as this enrichment have been reconciled in the Golden Agents project.

---

[3]https://archief.amsterdam/indexen

```
@prefix pnv: <https://w3id.org/pnv#> .
@prefix rdfs: <http://www.w3.org/2000/01/rdf-schema#> .
@prefix roar: <https://data.goldenagents.org/ontology/roar/> .
@prefix sem: <http://semanticweb.cs.vu.nl/2009/11/sem/> .
@prefix thes: <https://data.goldenagents.org/thesaurus/> .
@prefix xsd: <http://www.w3.org/2001/XMLSchema#> .
@prefix deed: <https://archief.amsterdam/indexen/deeds/a74a2bbf-20be-4c27-9d14-d477f5c09ea3?> .
@prefix personName: <https://data.goldenagents.org/datasets/personname/> .

deed:event=Event1 a thes:Begraven ;
    sem:hasTimeStamp "1789-10-24"^^xsd:date .

deed:person=99e87e23-d295-2bb2-e053-b784100a6a2e a roar:Person ;
    rdfs:label "Lucretia Wilhelmina van Merken" ;
    roar:participatesIn deed:event=Event1 ;
    pnv:hasName personName:5289fa40-1a30-5ac9-8583-6a4d01c6443a .

personName:5289fa40-1a30-5ac9-8583-6a4d01c6443a a pnv:PersonName ;
    pnv:baseSurname "Merken" ;
    pnv:givenName "Lucretia Wilhelmina" ;
    pnv:literalName "Lucretia Wilhelmina van Merken" ;
    pnv:surnamePrefix "van" .

deed:person=99e87e23-d294-2bb2-e053-b784100a6a2e a roar:Person ;
    rdfs:label "Nicolaas Simon van Winter" ;
    roar:participatesIn deed:event=Event1 ;
    pnv:hasName personName:b3f66e9f-9f64-5d45-bbe0-24343cd3a90f .

personName:b3f66e9f-9f64-5d45-bbe0-24343cd3a90f a pnv:PersonName ;
    pnv:baseSurname "Winter" ;
    pnv:givenName "Nicolaas Simon" ;
    roar:carriedBy deed:person=99e87e23-d295-2bb2-e053-b784100a6a2e ;
    pnv:literalName "Nicolaas Simon van Winter" ;
    pnv:surnamePrefix "van" .

_:role1 a thes:Geregistreerde ;
    roar:carriedIn deed:event=Event1 .

_:role2 a thes:Geregistreerde ;
    roar:carriedBy deed:person=99e87e23-d294-2bb2-e053-b784100a6a2e ;
    roar:carriedIn deed:event=Event1 .
```

Listing 1: Example RDF Turtle syntax for a single event (Burial registration) in the subset in which two persons participate in the role of 'being registered'. Their name is described as a separate resource using the Person Name Vocabulary (PNV) [18].

3.1.2. Baptism registrations

Containing almost 5 million person names, the index on the Baptism registrations is the largest early modern one the City Archives of Amsterdam has. As does the Notice of Marriage index, the index on the Baptisms includes the roles in which persons are mentioned: child, father, mother, and sometimes witness, if available in the source. Also, the churches where the event took place, are mentioned. This index is highly interesting for those looking for networks of family, friends and of religious congregations.

3.1.3. Burial registrations

One of the oldest indices of the Amsterdam City Archives is the one made on the burial registrations. Although this index is quite a large one, as it contains approximately 1.5 million person names, it cannot be considered trustworthy due to its provenance. For instance, it is unclear which of the mentioned persons is buried, and which person is mentioned as partner, serving as disambiguating description or being the one that declared the burial event. For this reason, the only role persons have in the burial event is the one of 'being registered', which is problematic for the application of rules. Next to this, not all the registration books of burials in churches and on graveyards in Amsterdam survived over time. Although useful as an entrance to the source, one has to be careful in drawing final conclusions in (not) matching records from the burial records with other sources.

3.1.4. Notarial archives

Contrary to the former three mentioned indices, no digitised index was available of the Amsterdam notarial archive up to 2016. Together with the start of the Golden Agents project and for a large part co-financed by it, the City Archives started in 2016 with the indexing of its largest early modern archival collection. From this 3,5 kilometres plank length counting archive almost all early modern deeds have been scanned, delivering nearly 10 million scans. Approximately two million scans of them have been indexed on deed type, person names, date, and locations in the crowdsourcing project 'Alle Amsterdamse Akten' [=All Amsterdam Deeds],[4] resulting in almost 600k unique deeds with over 3 million person names. In this study, three deed types have our special attention: Last Wills [=Testamenten], Prenuptial Agreements [=Huwelijkse Voorwaarden] and Probate Inventories [=Boedelinventarissen]. These deeds are highly interesting because, contrary to the other mentioned indices, each deed gives insight into a complete network of family and friends. Unfortunately, the only role of people in the registration event that is included in the index is the one of 'being registered'. The records in this index resemble the burial registration records in this respect.

3.2. Golden Agents / University of Amsterdam

ECARTICO[5] is a comprehensive collection of biographical data from cultural entrepreneurs, such as painters, writers, book printers, illustrators, goldsmiths and related figures from ca. 1475-1725 in The Netherlands. It aggregates information on persons from this time period and includes references to both primary and secondary sources, among others the sources of the Amsterdam City Archives. The data set thereby provides a basis for the creation of a ground truth for person disambiguation. ECARTICO is hosted by the University of Amsterdam and published as Linked Open Data in the SCHEMA.ORG vocabulary. It is included in the Golden Agents project as one of the main data sets.

3.3. Golden Agents / KB, the National Library of The Netherlands

This data set with Occasional Poetry published in the Dutch Republic between ca. 1600-1800 built by the Royal Library of the Netherlands (KB) contains 6,906 printed poems or collections of poems on a particular type of event, such as marriage (2,433), death (1,049), or various types of anniversaries (474). Work on the data set has been concluded by the KB,[6] and the data set was converted to linked data in the Golden Agents project. It holds bibliographical information on a poem written for an event, together with information on the event's date and participants.

We disambiguated textual references to authors and printers/publishers and connected them to existing resources for metadata: the Dutch Thesaurus of Author names

---

[4]https://alleamsterdamseakten.nl/

[5]https://www.vondel.humanities.uva.nl/ecartico/

[6]https://www.kb.nl/bronnen-zoekwijzers/databanken-mede-gemaakt-door-de-kb/
gelegenheidsgedichten-tot-1800-in-nederland

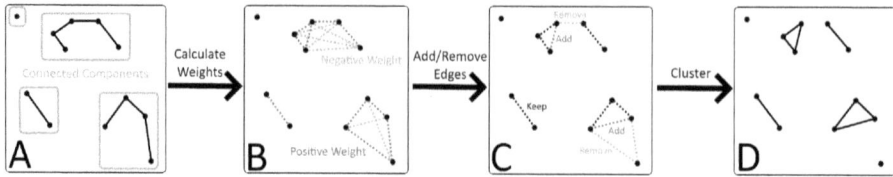

Figure 1. An overview of the entity resolution process.

(NTA)[7] and the STCN printer thesaurus[8] respectively. The same was done, if possible, for persons that are mentioned in relation to the event that the poem is written on, such as the bride and groom in a marriage. In the case that these author and person references could not be found in an existing thesaurus (e.g. the NTA or Wikidata[9]), we tried to find mentions of these actors in archival sources in the above-described data sets of the Amsterdam City Archives and connected them accordingly by making use of a rule-based linking approach using the Lenticular Lens tool [4].

4. Method

We extend the method for identifying duplicate entities previously presented in [20] of which figure 1 gives an overview. This method makes use of an embedding, that is, in our case, an n-dimensional Euclidean space where each (non-unique) person resource is assigned a coordinate based on its neighbouring nodes in the RDF graph. In this research, these neighbouring nodes can be other person entities, events, or names. We call these neighbouring nodes the *context* of a *focus* node. Entities in a context are weighted according to their proximity to the focus node and the number of possible routes from the focus node to a context node in the RDF graph. More detailed information on how this embedding is created can be found in our previous work [21,20].

Following this method, we start with a set of entities that are represented as a (sub-symbolic) embedding $\mathscr{E} = \{v_1, \ldots, v_m\}$ where each vector $v \in \mathscr{E}$ corresponds to a (non-unique) entity (e.g. a person resource in our data set) which may have duplicates (i.e. other resources that refer to the same real-life object). We construct a graph $G = (V, E)$ where each vertex in V corresponds to a vector in $\mathscr{E}$. We then take the k (approximate) nearest neighbours based on euclidean distance between embedding vector of each entity $i \in V$, denoted by the set N_i^k, and create an edge between that entity and its neighbour $j \in N_i^k$ if their cosine similarity $u_{ij} = cosim(v_i, v_j)$ exceeds some threshold θ. Such constructed graphs, which are illustrated in panel A on figure 1, consist of a number of connected components. The number and size of these components depend on the choice of θ: high values of $\theta \approx 1$ result in many small components and lower values result in fewer but larger components. With each possible pair of entities i and j within each component we associate a weight $w_{ij} = u_{ij} - \theta$. Panel B illustrates how these weights can be both positive (blue, similar) and negative (red, dissimilar). Components are subsequently subdivided into cliques using integer linear programming (ILP) and an alternative heuris-

---
[7]http://data.bibliotheken.nl/id/dataset/persons
[8]http://data.bibliotheken.nl/id/dataset/stcn/printers
[9]https://www.wikidata.org/

tic algorithm (panel C). Both algorithms work by associating a cost for omitting a pair with a positive weight and for retaining a pair with a negative weight in a solution. The partitioning with the (approximate) lowest cost is then selected, illustrated in panel D.

In the remainder of this section, we explain our extension to the work described above. That is, how domain knowledge is encoded and integrated into this process at two points. This domain knowledge is encoded as a set of rules provided by domain experts. These rules, which aim at identifying non-duplicate entities, have the general form: *if a certain condition holds for a pair of entities i and j, then it is ruled out that i and j are duplicates*. We assume that we have a data set that contains additional knowledge about the entities on which the condition of these rules can be checked. This data can, for instance, come in the form of an RDF graph, where rules are encoded as filter clauses in SPARQL queries. We have provided an example SPARQL query in our repository[10]. Such rules can be divided into two categories:

1. **Definite Rules:** There are rules for which we know in advance that applying them results in conclusions with high certainty, that is, the two entities on which the definite rule is applied are not duplicates. For example, *if entity i and j both occur in the same marriage event, then it is ruled out that entities i and j are duplicates* as one can not be a bride/groom and witness at the same time.

2. **Probabilistic Rules:** For other rules, we may not be as confident in the evaluation of the premise. This can, for instance, be due to uncertainty or ambiguity in the data. For example, consider the rule *if the burial date of entity i is before the marriage date of entity j, then it is ruled out that entities i and j are duplicates*. The burial record is ambiguous as it contains in addition to entity i also an entity k, without mentioning who was buried. This means that the probability that entity i was the one who died is 50%, and the probability of the conclusion of the rule that entities i and j are ruled out as duplicates also becomes 50%.

We use $\mathscr{S}_{ij}$ to denote the set of all definite rules applied to i and j, and $\mathscr{R}_{ij} = \{r_1, \ldots, r_n\}$ to denote the set of all probabilistic rules that are applied to entities i and j. First, the definite rules are used to further cull the approximate nearest neighbours found in the embedding, next to already removing neighbours that have a similarity which falls below the threshold θ. That is, we only create an edge between entities i and j in the graph G if $u_{ij} \geq \theta$ and no definite rule is satisfied for that pair. Since multiple probabilistic rules could be satisfied on an entity pair, the rules and their probabilities need to be aggregated first. To this end, for $r \in \mathscr{R}_{ij}$, we use $p(r)$ to denote the probability that i and j are ruled out as duplicates, e.g. $p(r) = 0.5$ is read as in 50% of the cases it is ruled out that i and j are duplicates. When evaluating a set of rules on a pair of entities i and j, the outcomes are aggregated as follows:

$$p_{ij} = \prod_{r \in \mathscr{R}_{ij}} 1 - p(r),\qquad(1)$$

where p_{ij} is the total probability that it is *not* ruled out that i and j are duplicates.

---

[10]https://github.com/knaw-huc/golden-agents-occasional-poetry

Here we assume for convenience that rules are independent, as it would be very difficult to quantify the dependencies between all of them. As is, for example, the case with the naive Bayes classifier, we expect that the independence assumption still gives a reasonable approximation.

Using equation (1), we calculate a penalty s_{ij} for considering a given pair of entities i and j as duplicates:

$$
s_{ij} = \begin{cases} 10^6 & \text{if } \mathscr{S}_{ij} \neq \emptyset \\ 0 & \text{else if } \mathscr{R}_{ij} = \emptyset \\ 1 - \sqrt{p_{ij}} & \text{otherwise} \end{cases} \tag{2}
$$

This yields a very large penalty if any definite rule was applied for the pair of entities i and j and no penalty if no rule was applied. This large penalty guarantees that pairs of entities satisfy a definite rule in the final results. In all other cases, it transitions smoothly between $s_{ij} = 1$ for $p_{ij} = 0$, and $s_{ij} = 0$ for $p_{ij} = 1$. The square root is taken to reduce the penalty to prevent the probabilistic rules from acting as definite rules in some edge cases.

Finally, we calculate the updated final weight w_{ij}, used for the partitioning of connected components, with the following equation:

$$
w_{ij} = u_{ij} - s_{ij} - \theta \tag{3}
$$

Note that s_{ij} represents the amount of evidence against the conclusion that i and j are duplicates. Also, note that rule application can never lead to an increase in the weight since a lack of evidence to rule out a pair of entities as duplicates do not constitute evidence that they are the same. At this point, the connected components are then partitioned into cliques as in our previous work. Each clique then corresponds to a unique real-life object (panel D). For example, in our experiment, each vertex (entity) denotes a *reference* to a person, and each clique corresponds to a single real-life person (object).

5. Experimental Setup

For both the experiment and the case study, we use domain knowledge to improve the results. The experiment shows by how much the rules improve performance in both precision and recall, while the case study only gives us precision. The experiment makes it possible to determine reasonable values of θ for the case study when both precision and recall are considered.

5.1. Domain Knowledge Experiment

For our experiment to determine the effectiveness of applying rules we have used four data sets containing real historical data from the cultural heritage domain. We made use of a subset of the above-described registers from the Amsterdam City Archives and a subset of the ECARTICO data set containing information on marriage registrations. Combined, the above-described subsets together form a data set that contains 12,517 entities referring to (non-unique) persons, and a partial ground truth of 1073 clusters, obtained with manual validation by domain experts [22].

We have designed two definite rules based on expert domain knowledge, namely that two entities co-occurring in the same record are not the same, and that two entities originating from ECARTICO (section 3.2) are not the same. The latter rule is based on the knowledge that ECARTICO is an expert-curated biographical data set that contains a single unique entry for a single person. Furthermore, we have constructed 8 probabilistic rules that consider the dates at which the events took place, and how many years occur between them. Below we list three example rules for entities i and j:

1. Entity i is mentioned in the role of groom or bride in a notice of marriage registration at date d_1, and j is mentioned in the role of husband, wife, father, or mother in a marriage or baptism registration respectively at date d_2. If more than 30 years occur between d_1 and d_2, then it is ruled out that i and j are duplicates.
2. i is mentioned in the role of groom or bride at date d_1. If there is less than 17 years between the birth date of j and d_1, then it is ruled out that i and j are duplicates.
3. i is mentioned in the role of groom or bride at date d_1. If there is more than 60 years between the birth date of j and d_1, then it is ruled out that i and j are duplicates.

Note that in many cases, a rule does not apply because one or both attributes are missing for a given pair of persons. All rules are combinations of what the dates represent and how they relate to each other. The rules that contain a burial date in the premise have been given a probability of 0.5 for reasons explained in section 3.1.3. All other rules have been assigned a range of probabilities ranging from 0.25 to 0.95, with the justification that, for cultural reasons, these kinds of rules can be trusted with different levels to be correct in their assessment. We test our method four times, each time with a different set of rules: (a) no rules, (b) only definite rules, (c) only probabilistic rules, and (d) all rules.

We apply a combination of the Correlation Clustering [23] and Vote [24] algorithms, as these algorithms performed best in our previous work [20]. Due to the NP-hardness of the Correlation Clustering (ILP) algorithm, we apply it only to connected components smaller than 100 vertices. Larger components are handled with the Vote algorithm. This is mostly an issue when using low values of θ, where large components can be generated. As θ increases, Correlation Clustering is used more, until it is solely used when $\theta \geq 0.70$. We have shown in previous work [25] that in our setting the Vote algorithm is very competitive with Correlation Clustering. These clusters are then compared to a partial ground truth which has been validated by domain experts.

5.2. Occasional Poetry Case Study

In the case study we focus on combining two data sets that come from two content providers: (1) the indices from the Amsterdam City Archives, and (2) the Occasional Poetry data. The latter is used to make a selection of these data sets by which we create a subset that is both relevant for our case study and is workable in terms of size.

We limit the data to resources related to the actors in the Occasional Poetry data set, in particular only the persons that we reconciled with at least one mention in the Amsterdam City Archives data. We create this subset using a SPARQL query that constructs a copy of the data that only includes events in which at least one disambiguated person was mentioned. For each of these events, it gives the date of the event, the type of event,

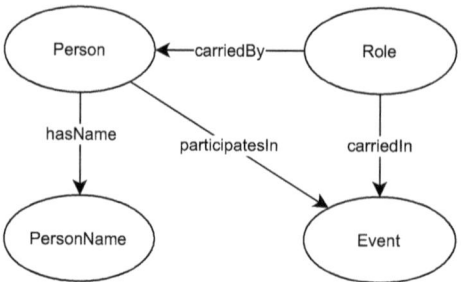

Figure 2. Basic structure of our RDF-model. Persons participate (either actively or passively) in an event. In the event, they carry a specific role: the role in which they are mentioned. Every person has one or more names.

the persons participating in the event, and the role in which they participate (e.g. bride, or witness). In total, this produces a data set that contains 7,339 events and 22,073 persons, of whom 3,839 have been disambiguated (i.e. they participate in at least two events: one from the Occasional Poetry data set, and one from the City Archives' data sets). An example of resources involved in a single event can be seen in Figure 1. The resources are following a basic format that models resources as part of an event in a particular role. The THES: prefixed classes refer to a thesaurus of event and role types. The SPARQL query and the subset itself can be seen in our documentation on GitHub.[11]

In this case study, our goal is to maximise the disambiguation of entities in our subset, so that, ideally, a single (disambiguated) person participates in more than one event. With this, we will be able to gain insight into the lives of persons in this data set, such as their lifespan and their social or professional network, and the motivation behind creative production in the 17th and 18th century in Amsterdam. As mentioned under section 3.3, we already made connections from the Occasional Poetry data set to the data sets of the Amsterdam City Archives using the Lenticular Lens tool [4]. These links were all manually validated and allow us to create the subset described under section 5.2.

Then we extend these links by making use of the graph embeddings method to in particular disambiguate peripheral entities. These are most often entities that do not occur in the role of bride, groom, father, or mother, and that only are mentioned in the Amsterdam City Archives data set. We use three definite rules and no probabilistic rules in the case study. Entities i and j are considered not to be duplicates if any of the following conditions hold:

1. Both i and j participate in the same event.
2. Both i and j are mentioned in the role of child in a baptism record, assuming there are no duplicate baptism records.
3. If i is mentioned in the role of a child in a baptism record and j is mentioned anywhere else in any role at an earlier date.

Finally, a domain expert validates the results of the embedding to assess the quality of the results as well as their usability for future research. This is done by indicating whether or not a person resource (represented by a contextualised URI) refers to the same entity as other URIs in the same cluster. Extra metadata is given to ease the validation process,

---

[11]https://github.com/knaw-huc/golden-agents-occasional-poetry

	Precision						Recall					
θ	0.60	0.65	0.70	0.75	0.80	0.85	0.60	0.65	0.70	0.75	0.80	0.85
previous work	0.65	0.74	0.82	0.86	0.91	0.93	0.69	0.66	0.62	0.58	0.52	0.42
definite	0.87	0.90	0.93	0.93	0.94	0.95	0.68	0.66	0.61	0.57	0.51	0.42
probabilistic	0.69	0.77	0.85	0.89	0.92	0.94	0.68	0.65	0.61	0.57	0.51	0.42
all rules	0.87	0.91	0.93	0.93	0.94	0.95	0.68	0.65	0.61	0.57	0.51	0.42
	F1-Score						$F_{\frac{1}{2}}$-Score					
θ	0.60	0.65	0.70	0.75	0.80	0.85	0.60	0.65	0.70	0.75	0.80	0.85
previous work	0.67	0.70	0.71	0.69	0.66	0.58	0.66	0.72	0.77	0.79	0.79	0.75
definite	0.76	0.76	0.74	0.71	0.66	0.58	0.82	0.84	0.84	0.83	0.81	0.76
probabilistic	0.68	0.70	0.71	0.69	0.65	0.58	0.69	0.74	0.79	0.80	0.79	0.75
all rules	0.76	0.76	0.74	0.71	0.66	0.58	0.83	0.84	0.84	0.83	0.81	0.76

Table 1. Precision, recall, F1 and $F_{\frac{1}{2}}$-Scores for a range of different θ values and rule sets.

such as a person's name, their role, and the type of event they participate in. If necessary, the expert can inspect a scan of the original handwritten document.

Though not needed for the scoring of the method, we do generate an RDF linkset from the result for usage in the Golden Agents project which can be found, together with the data, in the repository.[12]

6. Results

Since we have a ground truth for the experiment on domain knowledge, we report both precision and recall. Then we use the F-Score to determine optimal values for θ. This optimal value is used again in the case study.

6.1. Results of the Domain Knowledge Experiment

Table 1 shows the results of our experiment. High θ values will produce very high precision, as many small (or even singleton) connected components are created. Each component will likely be composed of pairs with similarly high weights, suggesting a high likelihood of them referring to the same real-life object. On the other hand, high θ values will yield a low recall, as we exclude many pairs of entities with lower (but still reasonable) cosine similarities. We discuss each performance metric in more detail below.

6.1.1. Precision

From table 1 we can see that precision increases for all three combinations of rules. For very high values of θ, precision does not increase as the rules are unlikely to exclude pairs with very high cosine similarities, showing that the embedding correctly captured (part of) the likeness between entities. When we lower θ to more reasonable values, the rules start to exclude some of the pairs of entities which the embedding encoded as likely but not certainly referring to the same entity.

---

[12]https://github.com/knaw-huc/golden-agents-occasional-poetry

6.1.2. Recall

Table 1 shows that there is a very slight decrease in recall when rules are applied. We surmise that the decreases in recall are caused by a conflict between the data and the judgement of the domain experts who created the ground truth. For instance, some rules can cause false-negative pairs to be created when a domain expert previously judged a pair to be correct, even though it conflicts with a rule, thereby decreasing recall. This is usually caused by errors or uncertainty in the data, which is not uncommon in these kinds of corpora.

6.1.3. F-Scores

The F-Score can be used to pick an appropriate value for θ based on both precision and recall. It is possible to adjust the F-Score to give greater weight to either precision or recall, depending on the situation. In our case, we report both F1 and $F_{\frac{1}{2}}$-Score, which weights precision twice as high as recall, as in our particular case precision is more important than recall. This is due to the fact that errors in the entity resolution process can complicate the further analysis of the data by historians. A threshold of $\theta = 0.70$ (i.e. the score with the highest $F_{\frac{1}{2}}$-Score) gives the optimum result when precision is valued twice as high as recall, otherwise the threshold $\theta = 0.65$ is best.

6.2. Results of the Occasional Poetry Case Study

We based the choice of $\theta = 0.70$ (as explained in section 5) on the outcome of the experiment, also taking into consideration that this rendered a result size that can be validated in a reasonable time (within a week) by a domain expert. This resulted in 9,151 entities (references to persons) being clustered into 3,400 distinct clusters, where each cluster represents the occurrences of a single real-life person. Of these 9,151 entities, 8,326 were correctly clustered according to the domain expert. Furthermore, 45 entities could not be confidently attributed as either correct or incorrect due to the lack of available information needed for the validation. This means that we achieve a precision between 0.91, if all 45 entities are incorrect, and 0.92 if they are all correct. We are unable to compute the recall, as it is not feasible due to the size, scope, and selection process of the data to determine, for each cluster, which entities are missing. However, we are able to present a list of common errors and points of improvement that were found during the validation process:

- In some cases, the logical ordering of baptism in the role of child, then notice of marriage as husband or wife, then baptism again in the role of father or mother could have been taken into account. Nonetheless, it should be said that people could and did remarry, so strict enforcement of a rule that states that baptism always takes place after a marriage, could introduce additional errors while removing others.
- Some entities were wrongfully clustered. Adding additional relations to other nodes (e.g. religion types, church information) in combination with formulating extra rules could have been used to refine the disambiguation.
- The common occurrence of some patrician family names causes them to be put together into a single cluster, e.g. in the case of the name 'Jan Six' that appears in every generation of this family.

• In some cases, two entities with very different names were put into the same cluster. This type of error can occur when two entities are clustered together with a similarity higher than the threshold θ. It is relatively simple to remove these errors with an additional string similarity check. This is something we plan for future work.

7. Conclusions

We have shown that it is possible to combine symbolic and sub-symbolic knowledge in such a way that it improves the performance of an existing entity resolution method. However, the interaction between the two is not always obvious. Introducing rules which, at first glance, should always improve performance may, in fact, worsen performance if there are errors in the data. In future work we plan on including positive evidence as well, that is, the inclusion of rules which, if applicable, indicate that entities are more likely to be duplicates. This can be done with logical rules, as well as by including information from symbolic methods such as [12].

The case study shows that the method works on a larger data set as well and that it gives good results. In future work, we plan to include more contextual information and distinctive attributes to the resources in the graph, such as religions and locations, which potentially improves the entity resolution outcome. Additionally, having a data set with thousands of disambiguated interconnected entities makes it possible to perform community detection. This could yield previously hidden patterns such as larger networks of people who were somehow connected to each other, either by social or professional relation. In particular, our method of entity resolution shows promise to work well in other deed types of the Amsterdam Notarial Archives, as only contextual information such as co-occurrence of people is available. In fact, this method can be applied to data from other archives in The Netherlands, Flanders, South-Africa, and possibly Suriname and Indonesia as well, as they share a similar structure and carry the same characteristics. Our generic method that can be applied to any (RDF) graph database, combined with tailored domain-rules, makes this tool highly applicable to the domain of cultural heritage.

Finally, We give extra attention to the issue of reproducibility, therefore we have published all the files necessary to run the experiment and case study in a git repository.[13]

References

[1] Achichi M, Bellahsene Z, Ellefi MB, Todorov K. Linking and disambiguating entities across heterogeneous RDF graphs. Journal of Web Semantics. 2019;55:108-21.

[2] Ngomo ACN, Auer S. LIMES—a time-efficient approach for large-scale link discovery on the web of data. In: Twenty-Second International Joint Conference on Artificial Intelligence; 2011. .

[3] Jentzsch A, Isele R, Bizer C. Silk-generating rdf links while publishing or consuming linked data. In: 9Th international semantic web conference (ISWC'10). Citeseer; 2010. .

[4] Idrissou A, Van Wissen L, Zamborlini V. The Lenticular Lens: Addressing Various Aspects of Entity Disambiguation in the Semantic Web; 2022. Graphs and Networks in the Humanities 2022, 3-4 February. Amsterdam, The Netherlands.

---

[13]https://github.com/knaw-huc/golden-agents-occasional-poetry

[5]   Guo S, Wang Q, Wang L, Wang B, Guo L. Jointly embedding knowledge graphs and logical rules. In: Proceedings of the 2016 conference on empirical methods in natural language processing; 2016. p. 192-202.

[6]   Rocktäschel T, Singh S, Riedel S. Injecting logical background knowledge into embeddings for relation extraction. In: Proceedings of the 2015 conference of the north American Chapter of the Association for Computational Linguistics: Human Language Technologies; 2015. p. 1119-29.

[7]   Wang Q, Wang B, Guo L. Knowledge base completion using embeddings and rules. In: Twenty-fourth international joint conference on artificial intelligence; 2015. .

[8]   Cen L, Dragut EC, Si L, Ouzzani M. Author disambiguation by hierarchical agglomerative clustering with adaptive stopping criterion. In: Proceedings of the 36th International ACM SIGIR conference on Research and development in information retrieval; 2013. p. 741-4.

[9]   Sanyal DK, Bhowmick PK, Das PP. A review of author name disambiguation techniques for the PubMed bibliographic database. Journal of Information Science. 2021;47(2):227-54.

[10] Raad J, Mourits R, Rijpma A, Schalk R, Zijdeman R, Mandemakers K, et al. Linking Dutch civil certificates. In: Adamou A, Daga E, Meroño-Peñuela A, editors. WHiSe 2020 Workshop on Humanities in the Semantic Web 2020. CEUR Workshop Proceedings. CEUR-WS; 2020. p. 47-58. 3rd Workshop on Humanities in the Semantic Web, WHiSe 2020 ; Conference date: 02-06-2020.

[11] Raad J, Pernelle N, Saïs F. Detection of contextual identity links in a knowledge base. In: Proceedings of the knowledge capture conference; 2017. p. 1-8.

[12] Idrissou AK, Hoekstra R, Van Harmelen F, Khalili A, Van Den Besselaar P. Is my:sameAs the same as your:sameAs? Lenticular Lenses for context-specific identity. In: Proceedings of the Knowledge Capture Conference; 2017. p. 1-8.

[13] Idrissou A, Zamborlini V, Van Harmelen F, Latronico C. Contextual entity disambiguation in domains with weak identity criteria: Disambiguating golden age amsterdamers. In: Proceedings of the 10th International Conference on Knowledge Capture; 2019. p. 259-62.

[14] Koho M, Leskinen P, Hyvönen E. Integrating historical person registers as linked open data in the warsampo knowledge graph. Semantic Systems In the Era of Knowledge Graphs SEMANTiCS. 2020:118-26.

[15] Hendriks B, Groth P, van Erp M. Recognising and Linking Entities in Old Dutch Text: A Case Study on VOC Notary Records. In: Proceedings of the International Conference Collect and Connect: Archives and Collections in a Digital Age; 2021. p. 25-36.

[16] Efremova I. Mining social structures from genealogical data [PhD thesis]. School of Mathematics and Computer Science Technische Universiteit Eindhoven; 2016.

[17] Efremova J, Ranjbar-Sahraei B, Rahmani H, Oliehoek FA, Calders T, Tuyls K, et al. Multi-source entity resolution for genealogical data. In: Population reconstruction. Springer; 2015. p. 129-54.

[18] Petram L, Dechesne E, Kruithof G. Person Name Vocabulary; 2019. Version 1.1. Available from: https://w3id.org/pnv.

[19] Van Weeren R, De Moor T. Counting Couples: The Marriage Banns Registers of the City of Amsterdam, 1580–1810: Social and Economic History. Research Data Journal for the Humanities and Social Sciences. 2021;6(1):1 45.

[20] Baas J, Dastani MM, Feelders AJ. Entity Matching in Digital Humanities Knowledge Graphs. In: Ehrmann M, Karsdorp F, Wevers M, , Andrews TL, Burghardt M, et al., editors. Proceedings of the Conference on Computational Humanities Research 2021. No. 2989 in CEUR Workshop Proceedings. Amsterdam, the Netherlands; 2021. p. 1-15.

[21] Baas J, Dastani M, Feelders A. Tailored graph embeddings for entity alignment on historical data. In: Proceedings of the 22nd International Conference on Information Integration and Web-based Applications & Services; 2020. p. 125-33.

[22] Idrissou A, Zamborlini V, Latronico C, van Harmelen F, van den Heuvel C. Amsterdamers from the Golden Age to the Information Age via Lenticular Lenses; 2018. Presented at DHBenelux 2018, 6-8 June. Amsterdam.

[23] Bansal N, Blum A, Chawla S. Correlation clustering. Machine learning. 2004;56(1):89-113.

[24] Elsner M, Schudy W. Bounding and comparing methods for correlation clustering beyond ILP. In: Proceedings of the Workshop on Integer Linear Programming for Natural Language Processing; 2009. p. 19-27.

[25] Baas J, Dastani MM, Feelders AJ. Exploiting Transitivity for Entity Matching. In: European Semantic Web Conference. Springer; 2021. p. 109-14.

Ontology Development

© 2022 The Authors.
This article is published online with Open Access by IOS Press and distributed under the terms
of the Creative Commons Attribution License 4.0 (CC BY 4.0).
doi:10.3233/SSW220014

Automatically Drafting Ontologies from Competency Questions with FrODO

Aldo GANGEMI [a,b], Anna Sofia LIPPOLIS [a], Giorgia LODI [a],
Andrea Giovanni NUZZOLESE [a,1,2]

[a] *Institute of Cognitive Sciences and Technologies, Italian National Research Council
(ISTC-CNR), Via San Martino della Battaglia 44, 00184, Rome, Italy*
[b] *Department of Classical and Italian Philology, University of Bologna, Via Zamboni
32, 40126, Bologna, Italy*

Abstract. We present the Frame-based ontology Design Outlet (FrODO), a novel
method and tool for drafting ontologies from competency questions automatically.
Competency questions are expressed as natural language and are a common solution for representing requirements in a number of agile ontology engineering
methodologies, such as the eXtreme Design (XD) or SAMOD. FrODO builds on
top of FRED. In fact, it leverages the frame semantics for drawing domain-relevant
boundaries around the RDF produced by FRED from a competency question, thus
drafting domain ontologies. We carried out a user-based study for assessing FrODO
in supporting engineers for ontology design tasks. The study shows that FrODO is
effective in this and the resulting ontology drafts are qualitative.

Keywords. Ontology Engineering, Ontology, Machine Reading, Knowledge graph,
Knowledge representation

1. Introduction

Competency questions [1] (CQs) expressed as natural language are a common solution
for representing requirements in a number of agile ontology engineering methodologies,
such as the eXtreme Design [2] (XD) or SAMOD [3]. In such methodologies most effort
lies in the design of ontology modules able to address the CQs that have been previously
identified, which is a fully manual activity. Hence, it represents a clear bottleneck for
agile methodologies. This is fairly evident in situations in which ontology drafts need
to be shared among ontology engineers and domain experts or stakeholders for incremental refinements and/or knowledge exchange. Accordingly, it is utmost important that
those ontology drafts, although tentative, must comply with best design practices, e.g.
Ontology Design Patterns, and properties, e.g. cognitive ergonomics, transparency and
flexibility. In this paper we present the Frame-based Ontology Design Outlet (FrODO),
which is a novel method and Web tool for automatically drafting OWL ontologies from
CQs. FrODO builds on and benefits from FRED [4] for *machine reading* [5] aimed at
gathering RDF from natural language. FRED is a formal machine reader that produces

---

[1]Corresponding Author: Andrea Giovanni Nuzzolese; E-mail: andreagiovanni.nuzzolese@cnr.it
[2]The authors are sorted alphabetically as they equally contributed to this paper.

RDF graphs from text, which are (i) domain- and task-independent, and (ii) designed according to the frame semantics [6] and ontology design patterns [7]. Hence, FrODO extends FRED specifically on the case of CQs by tailoring the RDF produced by FRED into domain ontologies by leveraging its formal representation based on the frame semantics. The domain ontologies produced by FrODO are drafts that can be used to feed agile ontology design methodologies. Accordingly, in this work we investigate the following research questions:

- *RQ1*: Is frame semantics fair to be exploited for generating well structured ontology drafts from CQs?
- *RQ2*: Do ontology engineers benefit from ontology drafts that are automatically produced from CQs in their ontology engineering tasks?

In order to address the aforementioned research questions we carried out a user-based study. The participants to the study were asked to use FrODO during the design starting from a set of given CQs. The quality of the resulting ontologies was measured with well known structural metrics. The effectiveness of FrODO was measured in terms of usability within the context of a an ontology engineering workflow. The rest of the paper is organised as it follows: Section 2 surveys some related works; Section 3 describes the methodology implemented by FrODO; Section 4 describes the evaluation, presents and discusses the results; finally, Section 5 presents our conclusions and future works.

2. Related Work

Competency questions (CQs) are questions in natural language that define and constrain the scope of knowledge represented in an ontology. As such, they are used in ontology engineering as requirements useful to evaluate an ontology based on its ability to answer each question, particularly in several agile methodologies, such as, the TOVE enterprise modeling approach [8], eXtreme Design (XD) in [2], SAMOD [3], On-To-Knowledge [9]). All the aforementioned methodologies can be defined as test driven [10,11]. Namely, they assess the commitment of ontologies to the requirements by converting CQs into queries, e.g. SPARQL, DL queries, etc. For example, [12] is a Web application designed for providing the XD methodology with a testing toolbox based on the representation of CQs to SPARQL queries. In this context [13] provides a solution for generating SPARQL queries from CQs. Our solution is meant to be used as a component of the aforementioned agile methodologies. However, it does not automatise the generation of queries for testing purposes, but provides a solution for drafting an ontology from its associated CQs automatically. The latter point can be seen an Ontology Learning and Population (OL&P) task [14,15]. Examples of such methods include [16,17,18]. Most of these solutions are implemented on top of machine learning methods. Hence, they are typically data hungry, i.e. they require large corpora, sometimes manually annotated, in order to learn rules for ontology automatic construction. Such rules are defined through a training phase that can take a long time. On the contrary, our solution does not depend on any training and is unsupervised. Other approaches to OL&P use either lexico-syntactic patterns [19], or hybrid lexical-logical techniques [20]. However, to the best of our knowledge no practical tools have emerged so far for doing it automatically while preserving high quality of results. Finally [4] is a formal machine reader able to transform natural language text into domain-independent formal structured knowledge represented as RDF/OWL. Our solution build on top of FRED for generating domain-dependent ontologies from CQs.

3. The Frame-based ontology Design Outlet

We generate ontologies from CQs by refactoring the RDF graph produced by FRED. This is done by means of graph traversal strategies that exploit the frame semantics [6]. We assume that frames and frame arguments, as represented by FRED, are the key tools to leverage on for drawing domain-relevant boundaries around the classes and properties produced by FRED. This enables the generation of domain ontology drafts. In fact, on one hand frames convey general meaning, i.e. they are bound in FRED to VerbNet frames that are broader and domain-independent concepts. On the other hand, frame arguments enable a solution for specialising such concepts in a specific domain with peculiar knowledge gathered from text directly. Furthermore, frame roles (e.g. agent, patient, theme, etc), that link a frame to its arguments, can be used for introducing peculiar naming conventions, annotations, and axioms in the draft ontologies that are fine-grained to a domain. Frames are represented by FRED in two alternative ways, that is, (i) as *n*-ary relations and (ii) periphrastic relations. Figure 1 depicts the methodology implemented by FrODO through the UML notation for activity diagrams. In such a figure it is fairly evident how FrODO extends FRED (cf. activity 1) by adding frame recognition (cf. activities 2 and 3) and domain ontology generation and enrichment (cf. activities 4 and 5). The activities if Figure 1 are detailed in the subsequent sections.

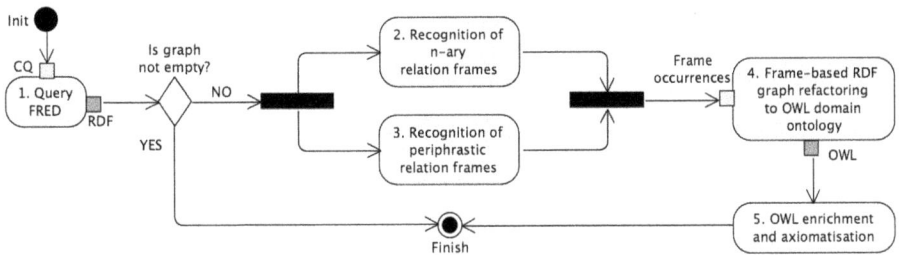

Figure 1. Methodology implemented by FrODO.

3.1. Drafting ontologies from n-ary relations

In the case of *n*-ary relations, a frame occurrence is represented by an individual of a class, which is, in turn, a sub-class of dul:Event. The sub-classing of dul:Event might be not direct. Hence, we need to traverse the rdfs:subClassOf axioms transitively. This can be exemplified with the RDF graph produced by FRED for the CQ *"Who commissioned a component of a system?"*, which is depicted in Figure 2. In such a Figure a frame occurrence based on the *n*-ary pattern is identified by the individual fred:commission_1. This individual is a valid frame occurrence as Equation 1 is matched. In fact, fred:commission_1 is an instance of fred:Commission, which is,

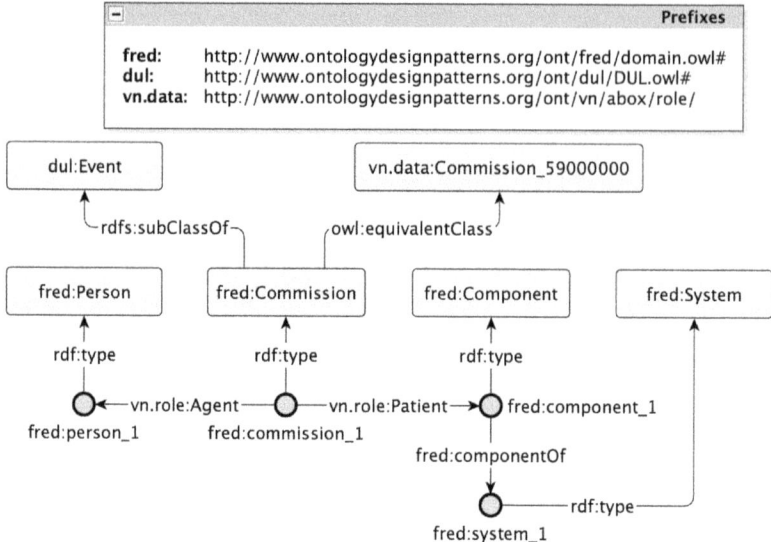

Figure 2. RDF graph produced by FRED for the text *"Who commissioned a component of a system?"*. The graph is drawn with the Graffoo notation [21]

in turn, a sub-class of `dul:Event`. The RDF graph depicted in Figure 2 and the frame identified are possible outputs for the activities 1 and 2 in Figure 1, respectively.

$$F_{n\text{-}ary} \equiv \{f|\ f \in C \wedge C \in \texttt{owl:Class} \wedge C \sqsubseteq^+ \texttt{dul:Event}\} \qquad (1)$$

The arguments of an *n*-ary relation are utmost important for providing the context to an identified frame. In fact, the arguments are the individuals participating in an event, i.e. the frame represented as an *n*-ary relation. These arguments are linked to the event by means of binary predicates, i.e. the frame roles. According to the frame semantics based on VerbNet implemented by FRED possible roles are:

- agentive roles, such as `vn.role:Agent`, `vn.role:Actor`, etc.;
- passive roles, such as `vn.role:Patient`, `vn.role:Patient1`, etc.;
- thematic roles, such as `vn.role:Theme`, `vn.role:Theme1`, `vn.role:Experiencer`;
- oblique roles, such as `vn.role:Asset`, `vn.role:Time`, etc.;
- roles based on periphrastic relations, such as `fred:at`, `fred;composeOf`, `fred:personOf`, etc..

Domain classes in a draft ontology are defined by constructing compound terms from frame occurrences represented with the *n*-ary pattern and their arguments. In this construction the arguments with a passive role are core. In fact, FrODO retrieves the name of the class typing the argument of an *n*-ary that plays a passive role. This class name is then concatenated with the name of the class of the frame occurrence (i.e. the target *n*-ary) itself. The latter name is first declined into gerund form. FrODO does not take into account agentive roles for this construction as they are typically bound to individuals that are typed with classes that are too broader or not constrained to a specific domain, e.g. `fred:Agent`, `fred:Person`, etc. This is due to the fact that the arguments with agentive roles are typically produced from pronouns, e.g. *"Who"*, *"What"*, *"Which"*, etc., by following a shared pattern for defining CQs [22]. On the contrary, arguments with a passive role are typically associated with domain-relevant terms in CQs, e.g. *"component"*. As an example, in Figure 2 the type of the frame occurrence is `fred:Commission`, while the type of its argument playing a passive role is `fred:Component`. Hence, the new class generated by FrODO for representing a domain-relevant *n*-ary in the draft ontology is `:ComponentCommissioning`[3]. The second step of the approach is to define the classes and properties to use as the arguments of the new *n*-ary classes introduced in a draft. This is done by reusing the classes typing the arguments of a frame occurrence in FRED regardless to the specific role played in the *n*-ary relation. Based on our running example, this means that both `:Component` and `:Person` are defined as classes in the ontology drafted by FrODO. Then, those classes are linked to the *n*-ary they belong to by defining new object properties in place of the frame roles provided by FRED. These object properties are constructed by applying a naming convention based on the template `:involves{ClassName}`, where `{ClassName}` is replaced by the actual name of the class being an argument of the target *n*-ary with a camel case notation. For example, the object properties `:involvesComponent` and `:involvesPerson` are generated for the classes `:Component` and `:Person`, respectively. We opt for the term *"involves"* as it evokes the involvement of a participant, i.e. the argument, into a situation, i.e. the frame. The generated object properties are then provided with domain and range axioms. The range axioms are set to the corresponding argument of the *n*-ary, e.g. `:Component` and `:Person` are the range of `:involvesComponent` and `:involvesPerson`, respectively. On the contrary, domain axioms are set to `owl:Thing`, hence they are kept open. The association with the corresponding *n*-ary relation is materialised by means of existential restriction axioms defined locally to the class representing the *n*-ary relation following the pattern defined in Equation 2. This Equation allows FrODO to cope with the activity 2 of Figure 1.

$$C_{n\text{-}ary} \sqsubseteq \exists r_{arg}.C_{arg}, \quad n\text{-}ary \in F_{n\text{-}ary}, \forall \langle p, arg \rangle \text{ s.t. } p(n\text{-}ary, arg) \in G_{FRED} \quad (2)$$

In Equation 2 (i) $C_{n\text{-}ary}$ is the class generated by FrODO from the *n*-ary frame occurrence produced by FRED, which belongs to $F_{n\text{-}ary}$; (ii) C_{arg} is the class generated by FrODO for an argument of the *n*-ary in FRED; (iii) r_{arg} is the object property generated by FrODO for an argument of the *n*-ary in FRED; (iv) p is a frame role, i.e. an RDF predicate, that links the *n*-ary frame occurrence and the corresponding argument in the graph produced FRED, which is G_{FRED}. For each generated object property its corresponding inverse is materialised. The naming convention for inverse object properties is based on the template `:is{ClassName}InvolvedIn`. In this template `{ClassName}` is substituted with the actual name of the class being an argument of the target *n*-ary with a camel case notation. For example, `:isComponentInvolvedIn` and `:isPersonInvolvedIn` are defined as inverse object properties of `:involvesComponent` and `:involvesPerson`, respectively. Addtionally, for each generated class a taxonomy is inferred following the compositional semantics. For example, `:ComponentCommissioning` is declared to be `rdfs:subClassOf` `:Commissioning`. Finally, each class and property defined in the draft ontology is as-

---

[3]In this paper the prefix `:` is reserved for referring to the namespace used by FrODO.

sociated with a human readable label, i.e. `rdfs:label`. The following code is the OWL produced by FrODO for the CQ used so far in our running example. The OWL is serialised with the Manchester syntax. All the solutions explained for generating axioms and labels are part of the activity 5 in Figure 1.

```
ObjectProperty: involvesComponent
    Annotations: rdfs:label "involves component"
    Domain: owl:Thing
    Range: Component
    InverseOf: isComponentInvolvedIn
ObjectProperty: involvesPerson
    Annotations: rdfs:label "involves person"
    Domain: owl:Thing
    Range: Person
    InverseOf: isPersonInvolvedIn
ObjectProperty: isComponentInvolvedIn
    Annotations rdfs:label "is component involved in"
    Domain: Component
    Range: owl:Thing
    InverseOf: involvesComponent
ObjectProperty: isPersonInvolvedIn
    Annotations: rdfs:label "is person involved in"
    Domain: Person
    Range: owl:Thing
    InverseOf: involvesPerson
Class: Commissioning
    Annotations: rdfs:label "Commissioning"@en
Class: Component
    Annotations: rdfs:label "Component"
Class: ComponentCommissioning
    Annotations: rdfs:label "Component commissioning"@en
    SubClassOf: Commissioning,
                involvesComponent some Component,
                involvesPerson some Person
Class: Person
    Annotations: rdfs:label "Person"
```

3.2. Drafting ontologies from periphrastic relations

Periphrastic relations occur in FRED when it generates meaningful object properties by concatenating nouns with their corresponding prepositions, e.g. of, with, for, in, etc. For example, in Figure 2 a periphrastic relation is `fred:componentOf`. In fact, it is the result of the concatenation of the noun *"component"* and the preposition *"of"* as they appear in the input text of the CQ. Periphrastic relations are relevant in our scenario as they express frames as binary relations and not in terms of n-relations. They can be easily identified in the graph as they are OWL object properties defined by FRED using a local namespace. Equation 3 formalises the set of frames evoked by periphrastic relations as $F_{periphrastic}$, thus providing us a method to address the activity 3 in Figure 1. The local namespace[4] is used by FRED for producing URIs from the input textual elements. In Figure 2 the local namespace is associated with the predix `fred:`.

---

[4]The local namespace can be customised by a user in FRED either by means of its API or Web interface. We remark that FRED uses a number of namespaces and prefixes associated with external ontologies and vocabularies used for representing a text as RDF, e.g. DOLCE, VerbNet, DBpedia, etc. We refer the interested readers to [4] for more details about FRED.

$$F_{periphrastic} \equiv \{f \mid f \in \texttt{owl:ObjectProperty} \land namespace(R) = \texttt{fred:}\} \qquad (3)$$

Hence, we explain how FrODO copes with activities 4 and 5 depicted in Figure 1 for periphrastic relation. In the case of a periphrastic relation the frame is the binary relation itself, which produces an object property, while the arguments are the subject and object of the relation that play the agentive and passive roles, respectively. The object property is generated with a naming convention that follows the template `:{relation}{ObjectClassName}` with a camel case notation. In this tamplate (i) `{relation}` is substituted by the name of the periphrastic relation produced by FRED, e.g. `componentOf`, and (ii) `ObjectClassName` is substituted by the name of the class typing the individual that plays the passive role in the relation, e.g. `System`. The object property `:componentOfSystem` is produced for the periphrastic relation in our running example. The naming convention is based on the assumption that arguments that play a passive role convey domain-peculiar knowledge. Then, two classes are generated from the subject and object of the periphrastic relation. The naming convention is based on the template `:{ClassName}`. In such a template `{ClassName}` is a variable to substitute with the actual value being the name of the class typing either the subject or the object of the periphrastic relation. For example, the classes `:Component` and `:System` are produced for the case represented by our example. Accordingly, the object properties resulting from periphrastic relations are enriched with domain and range axioms by following the same rationale adopted for the n-ary relation case. That is, for a given object property the domain and range are set to `owl:Thing` and the class produced from the individual being the object of a periphrastic relation, respectively. In our example, the range of the object property `:componentOfSystem` is `:System`. Furthermore, an inverse relation is materialised for each object property produced. The naming convention used for the inverse object properties is based on the template `:is{ObjectProperty}of` with a camel case notation. In such a template `{ObjectProperty}` is a variable which is substituted with the name of the object property that the current one is an inverse of. For example, is `:isComponentOfSystemOf` is the inverse produced for the object property `:componentOfSystem`. Then, the class generated from subject of the periphrastic relation is axiomatised with an existential restriction by applying the pattern defined in Equation 4.

$$S' \sqsubseteq \exists r_p.O', \qquad p \in F_{periphrastic}, s \in S, o \in O, p(s,o) \in G_{FRED} \qquad (4)$$

In Equation 4 (i) p is a predicate that recognised as a periphrastic relation and holding between a subject s and an object o is a graph G_{FRED}, e.g. the triple $\langle$`fred:component_1,fred:componentOf,fred:system_1`$\rangle$; (ii) S is the class used as the type for the subject s, e.g. `fred:Component`; (iii) O is the class used as the type for the object o, e.g. `fred:System`; S' and O' are the classes generated by FrODO for S and O, e.g. `:Component` and `:System`; (iv) r_p is the binary property produced by FrODO from the input periphrastic relation, e.g. `:isComponentOfSystemOf`.

Finally, FrODO adds `rdfs:label` annotations to generated classes and properties. The following is the OWL produced by FrODO from the periphrastic relation occurring in our running example.

```
ObjectProperty: componentOfSystem
    Annotations: rdfs:label "component of system"
    Domain: owl:Thing
    Range: System
    InverseOf: isComponentOfSystemOf
ObjectProperty: isComponentOfSystemOf
    Annotations: rdfs:label "is component of system of"
    Domain: System
    Range: owl:Thing
    InverseOf: componentOfSystem
Class: Component
    Annotations: rdfs:label "Component"
    SubClassOf: componentOfSystem some System
Class: System
    Annotations:  rdfs:label "System"@en
```

FrODO is implemented as a Python Web application. Its source code is available on a GitHub repository[5] and a running instance is available online[6].

4. Evaluation

4.1. Experimental setup

We designed our experiment as a user-based study in order to address *RQ1* and *RQ2*. Namely, we asked a number of participants to perform an ontology design task starting from a set of identified CQs used as ontological requirements. The ontology design task was composed of two conditions. The first condition, i.e. *C1*, aimed at designing an ontology able to answer the provided CQs without the support of FrODO. On the contrary, the second condition, i.e. *C2*, aimed at designing an ontology able to answer the provided CQs with the support of FrODO. In both conditions the target ontology editor was Protégé. In case of the condition C2 the participants were asked to copy a CQ from the list of CQs they were provided with and paste it into the Web interface of FrODO. Then, they were asked to (i) execute FrODO in order to get the resulting ontology and (ii) import such an ontology into Protégé. This operation had to be executed once per each CQ the participants were provided with. No strategy on the order of CQs to solve for both condition C1 and C2 was imposed to the participants, i.e. they could start from any of the provided CQs by following their preferred order. Additionally, in case of condition C2 (with FrODO), the participants could opt for the implementation strategy the felt more confident with. This means, for instance, a participant might first import all the ontology modules returned by FrODO for each CQs and then refine those modules in the final ontology as a whole. Similarly, a participant might import and refine the ontology modules produced by FrODO for each CQs one-by-one incrementally. For the selection of the CQs we first identified three common CQ patterns out of the set of 12 CQ patterns observed in literature by [22]. The selected CQ patterns capture actors, relations, quantities, and modalities, as well as temporal and spatial elements. Namely the three CQ patterns are:

---

[5]https://github.com/anuzzolese/frodo
[6]https://w3id.org/stlab/frodo that redirects to http://semantics.istc.cnr.it/frodo

Table 1. CQs used as sample in our experiment.

Set	ID	CQ	Pattern
	CQ1	When is the level of a chemical substance recorded in a water body?	P1
S1	CQ2	What is a parameter that represents the quality of water bodies?	P2
	CQ3	Who records the amount of microbiological substances in surface waters in time?	P3
	CQ4	What are the contaminated sites in a geographical area recorded in time?	P1
S2	CQ5	When is the rate of hospitalisation related to a disease registered?	P2
	CQ6	Who monitors the hospitalisations for a disease in geographical area?	P3

- *"When is [object] [relation]?"*, i.e. pattern P1;
- *"What is [object] [relation] [object]?"*, i.e. pattern P2;
- *"Who [relation] [object]?"*, i.e. pattern P3.

For each of the three patterns we randomly picked two CQs from the corpus of CQs we defined in the context of the WHOW project[7]. This allowed us to get two sets of CQs, i.e. *S1* and *S2* having three CQs each. Table 1 reports the CQs selected along with their corresponding set, identifier, and pattern.

We recruited 7 participants for the experiment with all of them being experts in ontology design and patterns. Each participant was asked to perform C1, i.e. ontology design without FrODO, with one of the two CQ sets and C2, i.e. ontology design with FrODO, with the other CQ set. The assignment of the CQ sets to the participants with respect to the two ontology design conditions was performed in order to have the same CQs in S1 and S2 modelled alternatively with FrODO or without FrODO by a a balanced number of participants. Hence, the participants were divided into two groups, i.e. (i) *Group 1* tackling the CQs in the set S1 under the experiment condition C2 and the CQs in the set S2 under the experiment condition C1 and (ii) *Group 2* tackling the CQs in the set S1 under the experiment condition C1 and the CQs in the set S2 under the experiment condition C2. Additionally, we asked 3 participants to carry out the condition C2 as first option and then the condition C1 as second option. The remaining 4 participants were asked to carry out C1 first and then C2. The rationale of this choice was to mitigate possible biases introduced in the experiment by the order that the two conditions were executed by the participants. In fact, a participant, while addressing the experiment condition requested to be the first in the sequence, might acquire, for example, a deeper knowledge of the domain or she might benefit from the re-use of one or more ontology design patterns identified and used in the condition tackled as first option. This might make the condition tackled as second option easier to be solved, thus affecting the veracity of the results. The participants were supervised by an evaluator, who was in charge of (i) introducing FrODO with a brief demonstration, (ii) providing a detailed explanation of the experiment to the participants, (iii) supporting the participants during the experiments, (iv) recording the times taken by the participants for solving conditions C1 and C2. At the end of the experiment each participant was supposed to produce two ontologies as output. That is, one ontology addressing the CQs associated with condition

---

[7]The Water Health Open knoWledge (WHOW) is a project co-financed by the Connecting European Facilities of the European Union under grant agreement 2019-EU-IA-0089. Project website: https://whowproject.eu/

Table 2. Structural metrics used for assessing the ontologies produced by the participants to the experiment for both condition C1 and C2.

Metric	Description
# of annotation assertions	The total number of annotations in the ontology. Values are on ordinal scale.
# of axioms	The total number of axioms defined for classes, properties, datatype definitions, assertions and annotations. Values are on ordinal scale.
# of classes	The total number of classes defined in the ontology network. Values are on ordinal scale.
# of datatype properties	The total number of datatype properties defined in the ontology network. Values are on ordinal scale.
# of inverse object properties	The total number of object properties having a `owl:inverseOf` axiom for representing their inverse properties. Values are on ordinal scale.
# of logical axioms	The axioms which affect the logical meaning of the ontology. Values are on ordinal scale.
# of object properties	The total number of object properties defined in the ontology. Values are on ordinal scale.
# of object property domain axioms	The total number of axioms specifying the domain of an object property. Values are on ordinal scale.
# of object property range axioms	The total number of axioms specifying the range of an object property. Values are on ordinal scale.
# of SubClassOf axioms	The total number of `rdfs:subClassOf` axioms defined in the ontology.
Axiom/class ratio	The ratio between axioms and classes computed as the average amount of axioms per class. Values are computed as $\frac{\text{\# of axioms}}{\text{\# of classes}}$.
Class/property ratio	The ratio between the number of classes and the number of properties. Values are computed as $\frac{\text{\# of classes}}{\text{\# of properties}}$.
Inverse relations ratio	The ratio between the number of inverse relations and all the relations defined in the ontology. Values are on a scale ranging fron 0 to 1 and are computed as $\frac{\text{\# of inv. object properties} + \text{\# of inv. funct. datatype properties}}{\text{\# of object properties} + \text{\# of datatype properties}}$.
Inheritance Richness	The average number of subclasses per class computed as proposed by [23]. Inheritance Richness is expressed on ordinal scale.
Relationship Richness	The ratio between non-inheritance relations and the total number of relations defined in the ontology as proposed by [23]. Inheritance relations are `rdfs:subClassOf` axioms. Values are on a scale ranging from 0 (i.e. the ontology contains inheritance relationships only) to 1 (i.e. the ontology contains non-inheritance relationships only).

C1 and another ontology addressing the CQs associated with condition C2. We remark that the CQs associated with C1 or C2 were either those available for set S1 or set S2.

At the end of the experiment we asked the participants to rate ten statements using a five-point Likert scale (from 1: Strongly Disagree to 5: Strongly Agree). The ten statements are those of the System Usability Scale (SUS) [24]. The SUS is a well-known metric used for evaluating the usability of a system. It has the advantage of being technology-independent, and reliable even with a very small sample size [25] as in our case. It also provides a two-factors orthogonal structure, which can be used to score the scale on independent Usability and Learnability dimensions [25]. The adoption of SUS in our experiment was not meant for assessing neither the usability of FrODO per se nor its integration with Protégé. On the contrary, it was meant for investigating the effectiveness of FrODO and its implemented methodology in supporting ontologists in ontology design tasks.

The ontologies produced by participants were evaluated with respect to the logical and structural dimensions as identified in the ontology evaluation framework formalised by [26]. The logical dimension was assessed by detecting the lack of inconsistencies by means of a DL reasoner. The DL reasoner we opted for is HermiT[8]. The structural dimension was assessed with different metrics that have been defined and used in literature [26,23,27,28]. The structural metrics we used are reported in Table 2. We do not assess the functional dimension, which is the ability of an ontology to address requirements and cover the domain [26]. This is because all the ontologies result from expert ontology engineers that were asked to model ontologies able to address the proposed CQs that identify the target ontological requirements. Hence, we assume that all resulting ontologies are qualitative from the functional perspective.

4.2. Results

All ontologies designed by participants for conditions C1 and C2 are logically consistent. Instead, Figures 3a and 3b show the results computed for the metrics reported in Table 2 for participant groups 1 and 2, respectively. The values reported are averaged among those obtained for each participant to the experiment with regards to the experiment condition. We used OntoMetrics[9] [27] as a tool for computing such metrics automatically. Most metrics we took into account perform better in the experiment condition that includes FrODO (i.e. condition C2) than in the other does not (i.e. condition C2). This observation is valid for both participant groups 1 and 2.

Figure 4a reports the times taken on average by participants to complete the tasks associated with the conditions C1 and C2 regardless to the execution order. Standard deviation values are reported among brackets for each series. On the contrary, Figure 4b reports the same times by taking into account the specific order in which the participants tackled C1 first and then C2. In the first case (cf. Figure 4a) the times recorded are comparable, on average, for the participants of group 1, i.e. 39 minutes for C1 Vs 38.3 for C2. Nevertheless, for the participants of group 2 we recorded longer times when the ontology design process was supported by FrODO, i.e. 32 minutes recorded for condition C2 Vs. 19.7 minutes recorded for condition C1. However, if we limit our analysis to the case having the condition C2 executed after the condition C1 (cf. Figure 4b), then we observe longer times when the ontology design process was not supported by FrODO. That is, for group 1, we recorded on average 37 minutes taken for C2 Vs. 56.5 taken for C1 and, for group 2, we recorded on average 21 minutes taken for C2 Vs. 24 taken for C1.

Figure 5 reports the SUS scores in terms of the overall SUS score and its two orthogonal indicators, i.e. Learnability and Usability. Standard deviation values are reported

---

[8]http://www.hermit-reasoner.com/: last visited on May 2022.
[9]https://ontometrics.informatik.uni-rostock.de/ontologymetrics/ last visited on May 2022.

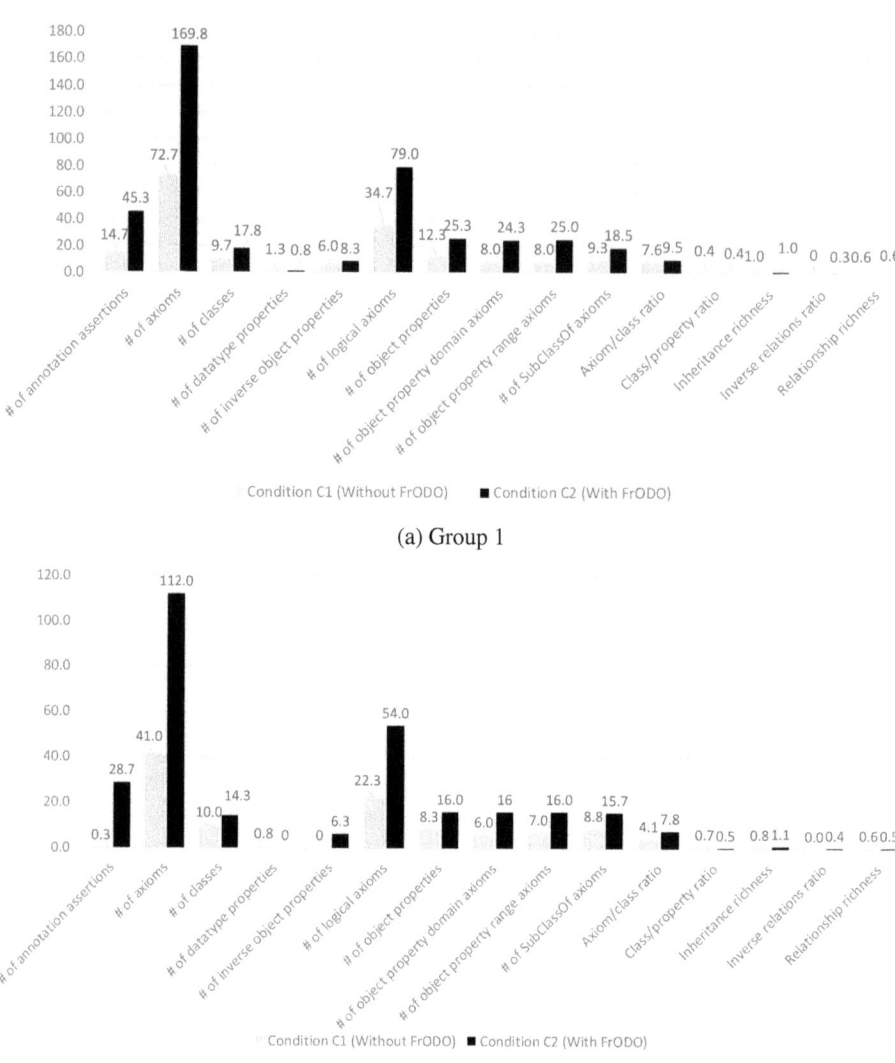

(a) Group 1

(b) Group 2

Figure 3. Results computed for all structural metrics reported in Table 2

among brackets. We report separates perspectives over the results obtained with the SUS along with the global scores by distinguishing between two cases: (a) the condition C2 (with FrODO) was executed before C1 (without FrODO) and (b) vice versa, the condition C1 (without FrODO) was executed before C2 (with FrODO). For the global perspectives the sores are 73.9, 85.87, and 69.9 for SUS, Learnability, and Usability, respectively. For perspective (a) the sores are 68, 82, and 63.3 for SUS, Learnability, and Usability, respectively. Finally, for perspective (b) the sores are 88.8, 95, and 86.6 for SUS, Learnability, and Usability, respectively. All the ontologies generated by the participants for both conditions C1 and C2 are available on GitHub[10]. Simirlarly, the CSV data con-

---

[10]https://github.com/anuzzolese/frodo/tree/main/evaluation/ontologies

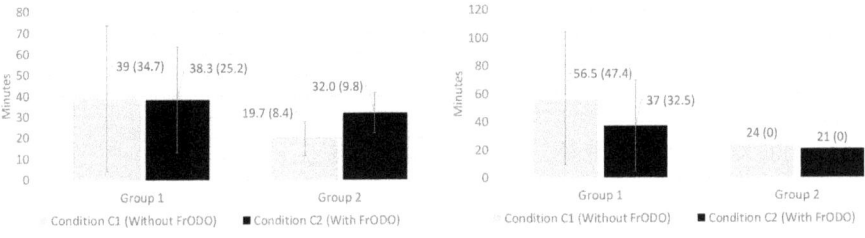

(a) All participants.   (b) Participants that tackled Condition 2 after Condition 1.

Figure 4. Times required on average for completing the tasks associated with condition 1 and 2, respectively. The times are expressed in minutes.

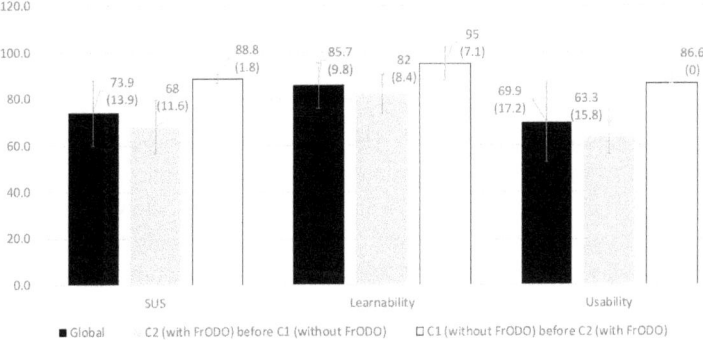

Figure 5. SUS, learnability and usability scores.

taining the metrics computed with OntoMetrics, times, and SUS results are published on Zenodo [11].

4.3. Discussion

The analysis based on the structural metrics computed over the ontologies generated for cases C1 and C2 suggests that the ontologies produced with the support of FrODO (i.e. case C2) are richer in terms of (i) axioms, (ii) annotations, (iii) classes, (iv) taxonomic relations (i.e. rdfs:subClassOf relations), (v) object properties, and (vi) inverse object properties. This richness is confirmed by analysing the results for the class/property ratio, inheritance richness, inverse relation ratio, and relationship richness. In fact, for all these metrics we recorded higher values from the experiment condition involving FrODO (i.e. condition C2) into the development process for both participant groups 1 and 2. This addresses *RQ1*. The SUS-based analysis shows that an ontology design methodology based on FrODO can be considered usable regardless to the specific order in which conditions C1 and C2 were set in the experiment. In fact, based on empirical studies [46], a SUS score of 68 represents the average usability value even in case of a small number of participants [25]. Additionally, we observed, on average, that the adoption of FrODO in

---

[11]https://doi.org/10.5281/zenodo.6574273

an ontology design workflow is not time-consuming. This is satisfactory and addresses *RQ2*.

5. Conclusions and future work

In this work we present the Frame-based Ontology Design Outlet (FrODO), which is a method and tool able to draft ontologies from competency questions (CQs) automatically. First, we provide a background about ontology design methodologies and automatic solutions for generating ontologies from text. Then, we describe the method implemented by FrODO that builds on top of FRED for leveraging frame semantics to gather domain knowledge and formalise it into OWL ontology drafts. Those drafts can be used by ontology engineers to make agile ontology design methodologies (e.g. XD, SAMOD, etc.) smoother. The effectiveness of FrODO was assessed by means of a user-based study that involved 7 participants all of them being expert ontology engineers. The aim of the a study was twofold, that is, evaluating: (i) the quality of the ontology drafts produced by FrODO from the logical and structural perspectives; and (ii) the usability of FrODO when used for an ontology design task. The experiment shows that FrODO produces richer ontologies if compared to the ontologies designed without the support of FrODO from the same set of CQs. The System Usability Scale (SUS) shows excellent usability scores for all the perspective we analysed. Future works include the evaluation of the ontologies produced with the support of FrODO from the functional perspective. Then, we aim at designing and developing a plug-in for Protégé able to embed FrODO inside the popular ontology design framework, thus strengthening the cohesion between the two systems. Additionally, we plan to extend FrODO in order to provide better support to the generation of datatype properties, inverse functional datatype properties, and disjoint axioms, which are overlooked in the current version of the tool. Among the others the implementation of disjoint axioms will benefit from the alignment with foundational ontologies, such as DOLCE+DnS Ultralite, which is already provided by FRED.

Acknowledgements

This work has been supported by the Water Health Open knoWledge (WHOW) project co-financed by the Connecting European Facility programme of the European Union under grant agreement INEA/CEF/ICT/A2019/206322.

References

[1] Grüninger M, Fox MS. The role of competency questions in enterprise engineering. In: Benchmarking—Theory and practice. Springer; 1995. p. 22-31.
[2] Presutti V, Daga E, Gangemi A, Blomqvist E. eXtreme Design with Content Ontology Design Patterns. In: Blomqvist E, Sandkuhl K, Scharffe F, Svátek V, editors. Proc. of WOP 2009. vol. 516 of CEUR Workshop Proceedings. CEUR-WS.org; 2009. .
[3] Peroni S. A Simplified Agile Methodology for Ontology Development. In: Dragoni M, Poveda-Villalón M, Jiménez-Ruiz E, editors. Proc of OWLED 2016. vol. 10161 of Lecture Notes in Computer Science. Springer; 2016. p. 55-69. DOI: 10.6084/M9.FIGSHARE.3189769.V2.

[4] Gangemi A, Presutti V, Recupero DR, Nuzzolese AG, Draicchio F, Mongiovì M. Semantic Web Machine Reading with FRED. Semantic Web. 2017;8(6):873-93. DOI: 10.3233/SW-160240.

[5] Etzioni O, Banko M, Cafarella MJ. Machine Reading. In: AAAI Spring Symposium: Machine Reading. AAAI; 2007. p. 1-55. DOI: 10.5555/1597348.1597430.

[6] Fillmore CJ, et al. Frame semantics. Cognitive linguistics: Basic readings. 2006;34:373-400.

[7] Gangemi A, Presutti V. Ontology design patterns. In: Handbook on ontologies. Springer; 2009. p. 221-43.

[8] Grüninger M, Fox M. Methodology for the Design and Evaluation of Ontologies. In: IJCAI'95, Workshop on Basic Ontological Issues in Knowledge Sharing; 1995. .

[9] Sure Y, Staab S, Studer R. In: Staab S, Studer R, editors. On-To-Knowledge Methodology (OTKM). Berlin, Heidelberg: Springer Berlin Heidelberg; 2004. p. 117-32. DOI: 10.1007/978-3-540-24750-0_6.

[10] Keet CM, Lawrynowicz A. Test-Driven Development of Ontologies. In: Sack H, Blomqvist E, d'Aquin M, Ghidini C, Ponzetto SP, Lange C, editors. ESWC. vol. 9678 of Lecture Notes in Computer Science. Springer; 2016. p. 642-57. DOI: 10.1007/978-3-319-34129-3_39.

[11] Wiśniewski D, Potoniec J, Ławrynowicz A, Keet C. Analysis of Ontology Competency Questions and their formalisations in SPARQL-OWL. Journal of Web Semantics. 2019 11;59. DOI: 10.1016/j.websem.2019.100534.

[12] Carriero VA, Mariani F, Nuzzolese AG, Pasqual V, Presutti V. Agile Knowledge Graph Testing with TESTaLOD. In: ISWC Satellites; 2019. p. 221-4.

[13] Wisniewski D. Automatic translation of competency questions into sparql-owl queries. In: Companion Proceedings of the The Web Conference 2018; 2018. p. 855-9. DOI: 10.1145/3184558.3186575.

[14] Cimiano P. Ontology learning and population from text: algorithms, evaluation and applications. vol. 27. Springer Science & Business Media; 2006.

[15] Al-Aswadi FN, Chan HY, Gan KH. Automatic ontology construction from text: a review from shallow to deep learning trend. Artificial Intelligence Review. 2020;53(6):3901-28. DOI: 10.1007/s10462-019-09782-9.

[16] Cimiano P, Völker J. A framework for ontology learning and data-driven change discovery. In: Proceedings of the 10th International Conference on Applications of Natural Language to Information Systems (NLDB). Springer; 2005. p. 227-38. DOI: 10.1007/11428817_21.

[17] Witte R, Khamis N, Rilling J. Flexible ontology population from text: The owlexporter. In: Proceedings of LREC 2010; 2010. .

[18] Tanev H, Magnini B. Weakly supervised approaches for ontology population. In: Proceedings of 11th Conference of the European Chapter of the Association for Computational Linguistics; 2006. p. 17-24.

[19] Hearst M. Automatic acquisition of hyponyms from large text corpora in proc. In: 14th International Conference Computational Linguistics, Nantes France; 1992. .

[20] Völker J, Rudolph S. Lexico-Logical Acquisition of OWL DL Axioms - An Integrated Approach to Ontology Refinement. In: Proceedings of ICFCA 2008. vol. 4933 of Lecture Notes in Artificial Intelligence; 2008. .

[21] Falco R, Gangemi A, Peroni S, Shotton DM, Vitali F. Modelling OWL Ontologies with Graffoo. In: Presutti V, Blomqvist E, Troncy R, Sack H, Papadakis I, Tordai A, editors. ESWC (Satellite Events). vol. 8798 of Lecture Notes in Computer Science. Springer; 2014. p. 320-5. 10.1007/978-3-319-11955-7_42.

[22] Ren Y, Parvizi A, Mellish C, Pan JZ, Deemter Kv, Stevens R. Towards competency question-driven ontology authoring. In: European Semantic Web Conference. Springer; 2014. p. 752-67.

[23] Tartir S, Arpinar IB, Sheth AP. Ontological evaluation and validation. In: Theory and applications of ontology: Computer applications. Springer; 2010. p. 115-30. DOI: 10.1007/978-90-481-8847-5_5.

[24] Brooke J. SUS - A quick and dirty usability scale. Usability evaluation in industry. 1996;189(194):4-7. DOI: 10.1201/9781498710411-35.

[25] Sauro J. A practical guide to the system usability scale: Background, benchmarks & best practices. Measuring Usability LCC; 2011.

[26] Gangemi A, Catenacci C, Ciaramita M, Lehmann J. Modelling ontology evaluation and validation. In: European Semantic Web Conference. Springer; 2006. p. 140-54. DOI: 10.1007/11762256_13.

[27] Lantow B. OntoMetrics: Putting Metrics into Use for Ontology Evaluation. In: KEOD; 2016. p. 186-91. DOI: 10.5220/0006084601860191.

[28] Carriero VA, Gangemi A, Mancinelli ML, Nuzzolese AG, Presutti V, Veninata C. Pattern-based design applied to cultural heritage knowledge graphs. Semantic Web. 2021;12(2):313-57. DOI: 10.3233/SW-200422.

Towards a Knowledge-Aware AI
A. Dimou et al. (Eds.)
© *2022 The Authors.*
This article is published online with Open Access by IOS Press and distributed under the terms
of the Creative Commons Attribution License 4.0 (CC BY 4.0).
doi:10.3233/SSW220015

Plow: A Novel Approach to Interlinking Modular Ontologies Based on Software Package Management

Maximilian GOISSER, Daniel FIEBIG, Sebastian WOHLRAPP and Georg REHM

Field 33 GmbH, Berlin, Germany – firstname@field33.com

Abstract. Ontology development offers many challenges, with some of the most prominent being modularization and evolution of ontologies over time. Based on lessons learned from popular programming language package managers, we present a novel approach to package management of OWL ontologies. Most prominently we integrate a dependency resolution algorithm based on the popular SemVer versioning scheme with tooling support for dependency locking, which allows for decoupling publication and consumption of ontologies, reducing the need for coordination in ontology evolution. To complete our unified approach, we additionally provide an integrated registry, which serves as a domain-agnostic repository for ontologies (https://registry.field33.com).

Keywords. Semantics, Ontology Management, Ontology Modularization, Ontology Repositories, Knowledge Representation, OWL2, Package Management

1. Introduction and Motivation

More than a decade ago, the essay "Why Software is eating the world" [1] succinctly outlined how software is increasingly making its way into our everyday lives and how it is even being picked up in the value chains of primarily 'analogue' companies with business models rooted in the production of physical goods. Since 2011, this trend has continued with software growing in amount and complexity, which is why the field of software engineering has seen an increase in professionalization. With software being deeply entangled with business processes and, consequently, with business success, the requirements to reduce the risk of software projects have also grown. At the same time, threats to software production supply chains have increased, with malicious actors targeting them due to their high-value nature, using, for example, ransomware, as well as an increased reliance on third parties. To fulfill some of those requirements, new structured processes and tooling to support these processes have been established, primarily addressing the reuse of software by independent parties using programming language package management.

In the same time frame, industry adoption of ontologies and other semantic technologies has *not* seen the same level of growth, nor has it seen the same advances as other fields in software engineering in terms of robust tooling. Actual production use of ontologies is still largely relegated to a few domains in which they have demonstrated a track record to justify developing bespoke tooling, with little success in other areas. With recent large-scale initiatives like Industrie 4.0 [2] or Gaia-X [3], interest in providing ontologies across and also as a basis for a wide variety of domains has been reignited.

When it comes to ontology engineering, the current model for package management is based on dependencies between ontology packages that are modelled solely using URIs, and package updates are handled via manual processes. This current state-of-the-art in ontology management is no longer adequate to fulfil the needs of modern software engineering workflows because the inclusion of ontologies in larger software projects can pose a significant risk to the project's success.

In this article, we present our approach, *Plow*, as a solution to bring well-established practices and tooling from programming language package management to ontology management while adapting it to the unique characteristics of knowledge representation through ontologies. By closing the gap between ontology engineering on the one hand and software engineering on the other, we are able to provide a robust foundation that projects relying on ontologies can build on and benefit from cross-fertilisation between the two fields moving forward.

The remainder of this article is structured as follows. First, Section 2 describes related work, especially with regard to modular ontologies, OWL, ontology repositories and programming language package management. Section 3 presents our overall approach, including the broad requirements we have. Section 4 describes, in detail, the implementation of Plow. Afterwards we explain the use of the tool (Section 5) and its limitations (Section 6). The article finishes with several conclusions and future work.

2. Related Work

2.1. Web Ontology Language (OWL)

The Web Ontology Language (OWL) [4] is one of the most commonly used languages for knowledge representation. Many ontology engineering tools support OWL and use the concept of an IRI-identified ontology as the fundamental unit of modularization. OWL2 [5] introduces a "version IRI" to identify a single version of an ontology.

To specify dependency relations between ontologies, the OWL specification establishes the concept of "imports" together with a number of annotation properties (e. g., `owl:imports`). Additional annotation properties allow for specifying the version of an ontology as well as specifying version order, compatibility and the incompatibility between different versions of an ontology. While these features provide a framework for expressing basic dependency relations, the specification intentionally leaves the semantics for the annotations under-specified, making them unfit as a source of truth for a fully-featured ontology management system on their own.

One area where the provided primitives are lacking is the ability to specify abstract dependency relationships. One can either express the relationship on any version of an ontology via an Ontology IRI or express the relationship on a single version of an ontology via an Ontology Version IRI. This results in a situation where one has to choose between under-specifying the compatibility to specific versions of the dependency and risk accidental upgrades or over-specifying the dependency by providing an exact version and making upgrading between versions a manual process.

OWL2 also leaves open how an ontology file should be retrieved, even though it does outline a loading mechanism. This can lead to a multitude of problems when trying to retrieve the ontology document backing an IRI. There is no guarantee that any two requests to retrieve the ontology file by URL result in the same document due to a lack of mechanisms for testing its integrity, like, e. g., Subresource Integrity [6]. Since there is no guarantee that the machine serving the URL will be continuously online, a server going offline can result in an unretrievable ontology and an incomplete set of dependencies. A growing amount of dependencies from different sources means that the reliability of the retrieval process is subject to an increasing number of points of failure.

As a prominent standard, OWL forms the basis for ontology formalization in Plow, while supplementing its dependency management primitives with ones suitable to resolve the outlined shortcomings.

2.2. Ontology Repositories

Ontology repositories help improve the discoverability of ontologies. They vary in sophistication, with some consisting of a simple static HTML page linking to a list of Ontology IRIs and more sophisticated ones including fully interactive web applications through which users can publish ontologies in a self-service manner. A recent overview of related work in this area is provided by [7].

As Plow contains a registry component that most closely resembles existing self-publishing repositories like BioPortal, we survey the existing solutions in that space. While ontology repositories like DBpedia Archivo do not fit our model as closely, they are also of interest as inspiration on how to keep compatibility with the existing ecosystem and how the registry could be provided with an initial set of ontologies.

2.2.1. Self-Publishing Repositories

BioPortal [8] is a repository of approx. 1000 ontologies from the biomedical domain. It features a web UI for searching and discovering ontologies, through which it exposes many of the core metadata and statistics that can be of interest when evaluating an ontology for its quality and an entity explorer that can be used to explore the contents of an ontology. BioPortal incorporates access control, which can be used to restrict the visibility of an uploaded ontology to a certain set of users, and it exposes a REST API, which can be used with an API key for programmatic ontology submission and retrieval.

Ontohub [9] is a self-service ontology repository providing distributed version-control based on Git, following the standards of the Open Ontology Repository Initiative (OOR). It uses the Distributed Ontology, Modeling and Specification Language (DOL) to enable uniform support for all kinds of formal knowledge representation languages.

2.2.2. Harvesting Ontology Repositories: DBpedia Archivo

One notable recently added ontology repository is DBpedia Archivo [7]. Archivo is a repository of ontologies based upon discovery via existing ontology repositories, as well as inspecting all previously discovered ontologies for imports. It continuously crawls all known ontologies and creates new archival snapshots when a change is detected. As an additional source of ontologies, new URLs can be submitted for harvesting, which will be added to the repository for continuous checking upon a successful initial crawl. One unique feature is Archivo's support for Semantic Versioning (SemVer) [10]. As the original ontologies do not provide SemVer versions, Archivo compares the changes between the new snapshot and a previous one. Based on the observed changes, it tries to derive an appropriate version through a set of rules that mimic the SemVer rules and provides that version as a semantic versioning "overlay".

2.3. Programming Language Package Management

Plow's dependency management is based on recent advances in tools for dependency management in programming languages. These vary greatly in sophistication and size of ecosystem. We take a look at the most recent and prominent ones, to identify the core mechanics that Plow can utilize to support a rapidly evolving ecosystem of ontologies.

2.3.1. NPM and other Package Managers

In the JavaScript/Node.js ecosystem, the Node Package Manager (npm) project provides CLI package management tooling, as well as a public repository of npm packages [11]. With almost 2 million published packages [12], it has also been the subject of research for open source software development methodologies. In terms of functionality, it reads a set of abstract dependency requirements in the form of SemVer version ranges from a manifest file (`package.json`), runs its dependency resolution algorithm and writes the resulting set of package versions into a Lockfile (`package-lock.json`).

Many recent programming language communities have recognized the importance of establishing package management tooling (as well as an integrated registry) early in the lifetime of the language ecosystem. By providing integrated tooling usually consisting of a CLI interface for package consumption and publication, a centrally hosted self-service package registry with a REST API and web UI to allow for package discovery, all core needs for package management are met. Since some features can involve components of the package management solution, having a common party maintain those components together can greatly simplify the evolution of the package management.

2.3.2. OntoMaven

OntoMaven [13] is a tool for managing transitive dependencies of modular ontologies based on the build automation tool Apache Maven [14] and its accompanying repository system. In addition to resolving transitive ontology dependencies and downloading a copy for local use, OntoMaven also includes functionality to create an OASIS XML-Catalog file, in which the local copies of external URIs are referenced. This file can be read by Protégé and other tools to allow them to load an ontology by reading it from disk instead of trying to retrieve the ontology file via HTTP. As Maven is traditionally used in software development utilizing Java (and other JVM-based languages), OntoMaven is well suited for software engineers with prior experience in that area. OntoMaven (like Maven) is only available via a command-line interface, which can make it inaccessible to ontology engineers who are used to GUI-based workflows and have little to no experience with command-line interfaces.

OntoMaven builds on top of Maven repositories, for which multiple commercial hosting offerings exist, which should provide low operating complexity when running an OntoMaven repository. In practice, the lack of an official repository to be used when starting a new ontology development project can negatively impact the solution's adoption due to the necessary effort of having to set up a repository before publishing an ontology.

3. General Approach

3.1. Simplifying Ontology Reuse

While ontology reuse is a well-established concept in general, the concrete reuse of ontologies can be challenging [15, 16]. Current primitives are not sufficient to support and automate the maintenance of ontologies that depend on a large number of other ontologies. By providing a framework that simplifies the inclusion and maintenance of external dependencies, the effort required to maintain an individual ontology can be reduced. This approach would finally make it possible to maintain a set of smaller, modular ontologies where previously, one single bigger ontology would have been used – out of sheer necessity – to reduce the overhead of manual maintenance processes. The implementation of tooling that additionally can assist in avoiding common pitfalls of ontology reuse and that streamlines the publication process can lower the barrier for enabling domain experts to provide their formalized knowledge to third-parties.

In Plow, we reduce the effort required for maintenance and consumption of ontology packages by specifying dependencies in abstract terms via SemVer ranges, which can automatically be resolved and updated through an automated version resolution mechanism. By providing this mechanism to end-users through a CLI and a GUI, we can cover a wide spectrum of use cases from deep integration into automatic software delivery pipelines facilitated by developers to the development of ontologies by ontology engineers with little or no software engineering experience.

3.2. Industry-Readiness in Consumption and Publication of Ontologies

Current solutions for building and consuming ontologies do not offer the same level of sophistication as their programming language counterparts, hindering the adoption of ontology-based systems in industry. Given that in many scenarios, ontology contents are being interpreted to guide the dynamic execution of software systems or display data to end-users, they can act as a potential delivery method for malware.

The careless inclusion of dependencies maintained by third-parties can allow for the delivery of malicious payloads without the application's maintainer being aware of this. Thus, package managers which serve as the central component for managing external dependencies, have become crucial for ensuring safety with regard to attacks against software supply chains. Furthermore, to ensure compliance with intellectual property rights, package managers have adopted functionalities to allow for the automated analysis of the licenses of all transitive dependencies of a project.

In Plow, we aim to meet these requirements by providing a dependency resolution mechanism that, at its core, is designed to be reproducible via the production of Lockfiles. Furthermore, in many aspects, Plow's design is hardened against cyber-security threats. This includes cryptographically secure integrity hashes that prevent undetectable tampering with package versions during their retrieval, which allows for delivery via third-party content delivery networks as well as using them for offline caching solutions. In addition, we integrate security features like multi-factor authentication into the service registry to prevent account takeover attacks. The availability of a Lockfile that contains the fully resolved dependency tree also allows for deeper transparency into the ontology supply chain, enabling automatic license conformance checks via SPDX 2.1 license expressions [17], which are enforced as required metadata on submission to the registry service. As ontologies created in a business context may be considered valuable intellectual property, the registry provides the option to publish private packages with access control, which by default are only available to the package maintainer.

3.3. Domain and Programming Language Agnosticism

For some of our requirements (see above), partial solutions exist in some domain-specific ontology building ecosystems, which have invested in tooling to support these requirements. As these tools are often tailored to the needs of the specific domains, they do not generalize well to other domains. Similarly, in the past, implementation efforts were mostly focused on the JVM [18] and Python [19] programming language ecosystems.

Using our approach for building a package management solution, that at its core is agnostic to domains and programming languages, the upfront cost to establish ontology building and publication in new domains and programming languages can be significantly reduced. Plow supports making ontologies of different domains available on a common platform, building ontologies that span multiple domains and simplifying the reuse of established ontologies of each of the respective domains, increasing the utility of domain-specific ontologies through reuse.

3.4. Compatibility with Existing Ecosystem

As a lot of valuable work has gone into the development of ontologies in the past, a new system should try to be compatible with existing ecosystems. In Plow, we build upon OWL and provide a solution existing ontology maintainers can migrate towards. Plow is also designed in a way that makes it easy to integrate into existing workflows.

One aspect where Plow can break compatibility with an existing ecosystem is regarding its stance to the HTTP retrieval aspect of the Linked Data principles. In Plow, ontologies are not retrieved via HTTP from their URIs (from potentially different parties) – a property that in practice many ontology maintainers struggle to uphold. Instead it relies on a single known source of truth with built-in measures for reliability.

4. Implementation

The implementation of Plow has been inspired by Cargo [20], the official package manager for the Rust programming language, and its corresponding official registry crates.io [21]. To the best of our knowledge, technical descriptions of these tools are not available, so we attempt to outline the major architectural decisions that we adopted from their system alongside our novel additions. We deviate from Cargo's architecture with regard to our implementation's support for private ontology packages, which enables a mixed public-private registry service. Our implementation of dependency resolution is also different due to the nature of the preexisting ontology ecosystem.

4.1. Ontology Package

In its current implementation, an *ontology package* is equivalent to a Turtle-serialized [22] file containing a single OWL ontology. To match the agricultural-inspired naming of Plow, an ontology package is nicknamed a *field*. All metadata utilized for package management is added as annotations to the `owl:Ontology` entity in the ontology, with the annotation properties (Table 1) defined in our ontology[1] with the prefix `registry`.

Annotation Property	Purpose	Repeatable
`:ontologyFormatVersion`	Version identifier for the ontology format itself	No
`:packageName`	Identifier for the ontology package	No
`:packageVersion`	SemVer version for the ontology package version	No
`:dependency`	Name and SemVer version range of a package this package depends on	Yes
`:canonicalPrefix`	Canonical prefix to be used in place of the ontology IRI when importing this ontology in another ontology	No
`:licenseSPDX`	SPDX 2.1 license expression	No
`:license`	Free-form field for non-standard license information	Yes
`:author`	Name and contact information for a author of the package	Yes
`:homepage`	URL for a homepage of the ontology	Yes
`:documentation`	URL for a page with documentation for the ontology	Yes
`:repository`	URL for a VCS repository where the ontology is maintained	Yes
`:category`	Category according to the categorization system defined by the Registry	Yes
`:keyword`	Self-defined keyword to be used in discovery mechanisms of the Registry	Yes

Table 1. Overview of annotation properties defined in the `registry` ontology

Packages are identified through a combination of a *namespace* (prefixed by @) and a *package name*, e. g., the package `infrastructure` in the namespace `software` can be referred to by the identifier `@software/infrastructure`. Namespaces allow the grouping of packages that have a common set of authors allowed to publish packages belonging to that namespace. This property should be ensured by the registry service. Organizing packages in namespaces reduces the attack surface for "typosquatting" [23], where a malicious party publishes malicious code under a package name that is a common misspelling of a popular package, one of the most common supply chain attacks on package managers.

Ontology Package Version and Dependencies

To identify a specific version of a package, we use the *SemVer* [10] versioning scheme. Each version is assigned a *version number* that is unique across all versions of the same ontology package inside a registry (a combination of package name and version number). In SemVer, a version number follows the MAJOR.MINOR.PATCH format, where the version number sections are incremented for a newly published version based on the level of compatibility of the changes made to the package since the previously published version. This level of compatibility is derived from categorizing changes to the public API of the package to be one of "backwards compatible bugfixes" (increase in PATCH

---
[1]http://field33.com/ontologies/REGISTRY/

version), "backwards compatible addition of new features" (increase in MINOR version), and "breaking changes" (increase in MAJOR version).

By encoding information about the "compatibility" in the version number, this enables a package consumer to answer the question of whether it is possible to upgrade between package versions by looking only at the package version, without a need to inspect the whole set of changes that have been applied between the package versions. This simplification allows for a more streamlined approach to upgrading the versions of the packages one depends on, which was previously a labour-intensive manual process.

Programming language package managers have also been exploiting this property by using *SemVer version ranges* for specifying the acceptable set of versions for a dependency. As an example, by specifying a *dependency requirement* for the package `@foo/bar` with the version range `>=1.2.3, <2.0.0`, we can tell that the package with the version `1.7.1` falls within the specified range and satisfies the dependency requirement. Conversely, we can also tell that the version `1.1.0` does not satisfy the requirement, as according to the semantics of the MINOR position in the SemVer version number, it lacks new functionality introduced in version `1.2.0`.

4.2. Registry Service

A *Registry* is an abstract entity consisting of an *Index* and an *Artifact Store*. This interface can be implemented with different characteristics, fitting different use cases, e. g., for non-collaborative development purposes, a registry can be constructed where Index and Artifact Store exist in their entirety on disk on a single machine, while for collaborative development on the same Registry, the bulk of the Index and Artifact Store contents are stored on a remote server, and only the required resources are copied to the local machine. In particular, in our implementation, we developed a *Registry Service*, which runs as a remote HTTP server, to serve the requests from a GUI or CLI client. In addition to supporting the core registry functionality required for package dependency resolution, it also provides a Web UI for searching and discovering published ontology packages.

4.2.1. Index

The *Index* contains the metadata for all published packages and their versions that were published to the Registry (Listing 1 shows an example). By restricting itself to contain only the metadata required for dependency resolution, the total size of the Index stays small enough to fit on a local development machine easily. By storing the Index in a Git repository, we can leverage the existing synchronization mechanism of Git to efficiently synchronize the Index between machines. To support private packages, a separate Index served via authenticated REST endpoints of the Registry Service is employed. The Index records a cryptographic checksum for a package version under the `cksum` key.

Listing 1: Example of an Index metadata file for a package with a single published version and a single dependency

```
{
  "versions": [
    {
      "name": "@test/package1",
      "version": "0.1.0",
```

```
      "cksum": "ef7118...5704f04",
      "ontology_iri": "http://example.com/@test/package1/",
      "deps": [
        {
          "name": "@test/package2",
          "req": ">=0.1.0"
        }
      ]
    }
  ]
}
```

4.2.2. Artifact Store

The *Artifact Store*, which complements the Index, does not have any knowledge of ontology package metadata. It contains all the original copies of the published packages and makes them available for download.

4.2.3. Additional Metadata Storage

To support functionality related to package ownership, user authentication, access control for private packages and mapping package versions to artifacts, the Registry Service also maintains an additional metadata storage in the form of a relational database management system (RDBMS).

4.3. Ontology Management Lifecycle Actions

Based on the components outlined in Section 4.2, we can now define the major process steps [24] for package management. At the core is the pipeline of *extract, resolve* and *retrieve* (Figure 1), which is completely automated. As each of the steps is independently reproducible, the whole pipeline is reproducible given the same state of the ontology document, Lockfile and Registry. In the common case of no changes to the ontology document, an existing Lockfile, and previously retrieved ontology packages, the need for communication with the Registry is completely eliminated, enabling the same pipeline to be reused in an offline environment.

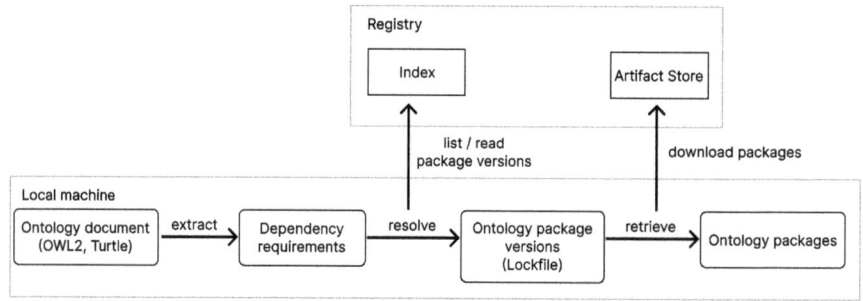

Figure 1. Outline of the package management process steps and their interaction with the registry

4.3.1. extract

The *extract* step extracts all *dependency requirements* from the ontology source file by parsing the file according to its serialization format (in our case Turtle), and reading triples with the `registry:dependency` predicate.

4.3.2. resolve

The *resolve* step takes the *dependency requirements* from the *extract* step, and computes a set of *concrete dependency versions*, which is serialized and persisted as a *Lockfile*. To do this, a dependency resolution algorithm, which has read access to the Index, is run to determine a set of dependency versions in a way that the dependency requirements for all transitive dependencies are satisfied. If the resolve step has been run previously, the existing Lockfile will be used as an additional input to the resolve step, which allows previously selected package versions to take precedence in the dependency resolution. In the case of an existing Lockfile and no changes to the dependency requirements, this results in the step being reduced to a No-Op, as all dependency requirements are already fulfilled, eliminating the need to read from the Index and making this common case fully reproducible. In the case of an existing Lockfile and a change to the dependency requirements, this results in only the required amount of (transitive) dependencies being updated to satisfy the changed dependency requirements. This increases the stability of addition, removal, and update operations to the dependency requirements, as it prevents unintended updates of dependencies unrelated to the change in requirements.

Our implementation is built on an implementation of the PubGrub version solving algorithm [25, 26]. One aspect that many dependency resolution algorithms differ in is the decision what to do about conflicting package versions in the dependency trees, with the two main options being a) allowing multiple different versions of a package to be present in the dependency tree, which allows some sets of dependency requirements to be successfully solved, or b) ensuring that only a single version of the package is present in the dependency tree.

Allowing for multiple versions of a package to be present as dependencies, is an option that is often chosen in package management for compiled languages, where at compile time the identity of an imported entity can be traced back to one specific package version and usage of that entity is restricted to only occur with other entities from the same package (e. g., type `Foo` of package version `1.2.0` can be used as an argument for function `bar` of package version `1.2.0`, but it cannot be used with function `bar` of incompatible package version `2.0.0`). As many ontology tools today rely on using the IRI (which is the same across different versions of an ontology package) for identifying an ontology, importing multiple versions of an ontology dependency is generally not supported. As we want to keep compatibility with those tools, we chose the option of only permitting a single version of an ontology package in the dependency tree for Plow.

4.3.3. retrieve

The *retrieve* step takes the *concrete dependency versions* resulting from the *resolve* step, and downloads the package versions from the Artifact Store for local usage. This step may have slight variations (or steps that run directly after it), depending on the use case. For the local editing of ontologies, we provide a variation of the step with similar functionality to the *OntoMvnImport* plugin of OntoMaven [13], where an XMLCatalog file is created with locations of the local copies of ontology packages.

4.3.4. update

With the *update* action we can update the dependencies as specified in the ontology. As this operation may result in an unresolvable set of dependency requirements, this should be modeled as a fallible operation, where a backup of a previous state with good dependency requirements is kept, which can be restored in case of failure.

4.3.5. publish

In the *publish* action, an ontology maintainer submits an ontology package version to the Registry for inclusion in the Index and Artifact Store, making it available to other users and consumers of the Registry. During submission, the Registry Service validates the presence of all metadata required for dependency management.

4.4. CLI and GUI

To make these actions available to end users, we provide the CLI command `plow`, which targets developers and continuous integration and continuous delivery (CI/CD) use cases. For less tech-savvy users we also provide a GUI application. Both support all lifecycle actions (Section 4.3).

4.5. Availability of the Tool

The code for the CLI, GUI, the library with their common logic, as well as a reference implementation of the registry service that outlines the REST API are open sourced under a permissive license and made available on GitHub.[2] We also provide a fully-featured hosted version of the registry service,[3] for which we decided not to open-source the underlying code, as it is tightly integrated with our infrastructure and relies on paid third-party services.

5. Plow in Use

Through the interaction with business clients, we are able to highlight the advantages of Plow for maintaining a set of ontology packages. By sharing our experience in building a Software as a Service (SaaS) product which integrates Plow we can also highlight how Plow enables a highly dynamic usage of ontologies in a user-facing product.

5.1. Dependency Tree Maintenance

For multiple of our clients we maintain a set of roughly 30 ontology packages related to the domain of software development, agile software development practices and related metrics. This set of packages is strongly interlinked, with the two most pathological cases being the ontologies that define the core concepts of software development and metrics, which are used by most of the other packages either directly or indirectly.

---

[2]https://github.com/field33/plow
[3]https://registry.field33.com

As each of the clients has separate release cycles during which the package contents are fixed, and even during a new release only a subset of the ontologies is supposed to be updated, the naive approach of just maintaining a single "current" version for each ontology was not an option, as updating that ontology could accidentally deliver changes to customers that should not receive them. To satisfy these requirements, the predecessor system to Plow was introduced, which could handle package management of ontologies with transitive dependencies, but with the limitation that only exact version requirements between ontologies could be specified.

While this system worked well, with an increasing number of ontologies, it put more strain on the ontology maintainers. Due to the fixed version requirements, even a minor change (e. g., fixing a typo) to one of the core packages that many other packages depended on became cumbersome to fix. When a new version of the core package was released, the fixed version requirement in all dependant packages had to be adjusted and a new version of them released, and then the same had to be done for the packages dependant on them, and so on. This meant that a change in one of the core ontologies triggered a cascade of manual changes and releases in the dependency tree, increasing the work the ontology maintainers had to do, and increasing the delay of new ontology-based features to the clients, as changes started to be batched into bigger releases.

Through the introduction of Plow, with its SemVer-based dependency requirements, this problem was completely resolved, allowing ontology maintainers to focus their time on expanding the scope of ontologies and focusing on breaking changes between ontology versions. Smaller bug fixes and backwards-compatible feature additions are now published under the appropriate increases of MINOR and PATCH version, and can be updated by re-running the dependency resolution.

5.2. Field 33: An Integrated Use Case

Plow is one of the central components of the Field 33 platform, a SaaS knowledge graph product. Each customer or user (in the form of an organization) maintains their own knowledge graph, with a different set of ontologies loaded for each of them. As users are not expected to have prior knowledge of semantic data technologies or ontology management, they are presented with a set of options in the form of domain packages like "Software Development", which they can load into their knowledge graph, together with a desired level of version stability towards automated updates.

With the help of Plow, this is translated into a set of SemVer-based dependency requirements, which are resolved to a set of ontology package versions that are loaded into the customer's graph (see Figure 2). To make new versions of ontologies available to customers, a curation layer is employed that builds on top of the stable identifiers for Plow package versions. By providing the Plow Registry as the interface for publication and consumption of the ontologies and reducing the involvement of our company to the role of a platform provider, the task of ontology maintenance can also be done by public contributors, contracted third-parties or customers if they have specialized staff.

6. Evaluation and Limitations

To evaluate Plow, we compare it with four similar solutions that provide state-of-the-art capabilities in their respective areas. The comparison focused upon selected features in

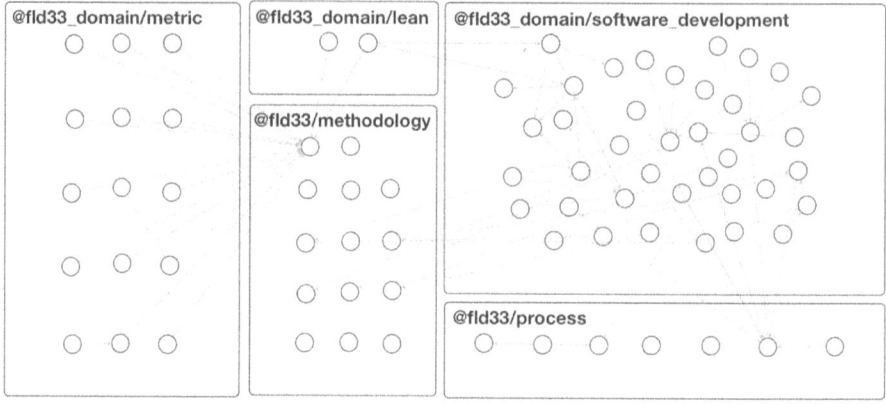

Figure 2. Plow package network visualization, showing package boundaries and contained ontology concepts, for a subset of the Software Development domain in the Field 33 product

the categories of access to ontologies and usability in industry-ready ontology engineering (see Section 3) in a comparison matrix (Table 2, adapted from [7]).

Plow is the only solution providing an integrated approach to ontology management by providing a state-of-the-art registry service and bundling it with tooling for ontology engineers to enable first-party publishing and consumption of ontology packages. While both Archivo and Plow provide unified SemVer version numbers, there is a difference in approach, where Plow relies on version numbers provided by maintainers, where Archive has to try and derive a fitting version number from the ontologies it scrapes. OntoMaven has the biggest workflow similarities when it comes to the publication and consumption of ontology packages, though OntoMaven is lacking reproducibility, as well as a hosted public instance of its repository.

Table 2. Solution comparison based on features in the areas of access and usability

Dimensions			Access				Usability			
Solution	TY	DO	SM	OV	OF	MA	MT	DR	SC	HS
Plow	R,D	I	–/●[1]	●/●	●	●/–	●/●	●/●	●	●
Archivo	R	I	●/○	●/●	●	○/●	–/–	–/–	–	●
BioPortal	R,D	S	–/●[1]	○/–	○	●[1]/●	–/–	–/–	–	●
Ontohub	R,D	I	–/●[1]	○/–	○	●[1]/–	–/–	–/–	–	●
OntoMaven	D	I	–/●[1]	○/–	●	○[2]/–	●/–	●/○[3]	–	–

● = provides property; ○ = provides property partially; – = does not provide property; **TY**: Solution type: (R)egistry/Repository/Archive, (D)evelopment platform; **DO**: ont. domain focus: (S)pecialized vs. (I)ndependent; **SM**; mode of (automated) ont. submission: *inclusion request/direct upload*; **OV**: ont. version numbers: *unified/SemVer*; **OF**: access to ont. in one unified format; **MA**: ont. metadata access via *REST API/SPARQL*; **MT**: maintainer tools: *CLI/GUI*; **DR**: *dependency resolution/including Lockfile*; **SC**: supply-chain security measures; **HS**: hosted public instance

[1] account/login required;   [2] depending on used Maven repository service;
[3] can be achieved via a Maven plugin;

As we have focused on establishing the functionalities required for full end-to-end package management workflows, Plow is currently limited in the variety of supported ontology languages and serialization formats, by only supporting OWL ontologies serialized as Turtle. We also recognize that parts of the assumptions regarding programming language managers and their inherent connection to their respective ecosystems are based on subjective experience by interacting with them, which is why we would welcome additional research in these areas.

7. Conclusions and Future Work

This article first outlines the broad requirements for a state-of-the-art package management solution for ontologies and our specific approach. We then highlight details of the implementation of the individual components that make up our unified approach, Plow. By taking a look at how our tool has been used in a production setting, we illustrate its ease of use with regard to maintenance of a set of interlinked ontologies and integration into a user-facing application.

With the core functionality of our package management solution established, our next steps include the implementation for support of a wider range of established ontology formats, to allow for consuming most existing popular ontologies as Plow packages. We will also add support for consuming packages from multiple registries at the same time, as well as adding automated mirroring of indices and artifacts between registries, to be able to support a wider range of industrial use cases.

References

1. Andreessen M. Why Software Is Eating the World. 2011 Aug. Available from: https://a16z.com/2011/08/20/why-software-is-eating-the-world/
2. Grangel-Gonzalez I, Baptista P, Halilaj L, Lohmann S, Vidal ME, Mader C, and Auer S. The Industry 4.0 Standards Landscape from a Semantic Integration Perspective. *22nd IEEE International Conference on Emerging Technologies and Factory Automation (ETFA)*. Limassol, Cyprus: IEEE, 2017 :1–8
3. GAIA-X Open Work Package Self-Description. GAIA-X Core Ontology. Rev.: 21/12. 2022. Available from: https://gaia-x.gitlab.io/gaia-x-community/gaia-x-self-descriptions/core/core.html
4. Smith MK, Welty C, and McGuinness DL. OWL Web Ontology Language Guide. Available from: https://www.w3.org/TR/owl-guide/
5. W3C OWL Working Group. OWL2 Web Ontology Language Document Overview (Second Edition). Available from: https://www.w3.org/TR/owl-overview/
6. W3C Recommendation: Subresource Integrity. Available from: https://www.w3.org/TR/SRI/
7. Frey J, Streitmatter D, Götz F, Hellmann S, and Arndt N. DBpedia Archivo: A Web-Scale Interface for Ontology Archiving Under Consumer-Oriented Aspects. *Semantic Systems. In the Era of Knowledge Graphs*. Ed. by Blomqvist E, Groth P, de Boer V, Pellegrini T, Alam M, Käfer T, Kieseberg P, Kirrane S, Meroño-Peñuela A, and Pandit HJ. Vol. 12378. Cham: Springer, 2020 :19–35

8. Noy NF, Shah NH, Whetzel PL, Dai B, Dorf M, Griffith N, Jonquet C, Rubin DL, Storey MA, Chute CG, and Musen MA. BioPortal: Ontologies and Integrated Data Resources at the Click of a Mouse. Nucleic Acids Research 2009; 37:W170–W173

9. Codescu M, Kuksa E, Kutz O, Mossakowski T, and Neuhaus F. Ontohub: A Semantic Repository Engine for Heterogeneous Ontologies. Applied Ontology 2017 Nov; 12. Ed. by Baclawski K and Bennett M:275–98

10. Preston-Werner T. Semantic Versioning 2.0.0. Available from: https://semver.org

11. Npm – Package Manager and Registry for the JavaScript Community. Available from: https://www.npmjs.com

12. Module Counts. Available from: http://www.modulecounts.com

13. Paschke A and Schäfermeier R. OntoMaven – Maven-Based Ontology Development and Management of Distributed Ontology Repositories. *Synergies Between Knowledge Engineering and Software Engineering.* Ed. by Nalepa GJ and Baumeister J. Vol. 626. Cham: Springer, 2018 :251–73

14. Apache Maven. Available from: https://maven.apache.org

15. Shimizu C, Hammar K, and Hitzler P. Modular Ontology Modeling. Semantic Web Journal 2022. Available from: http://www.semantic-web-journal.net/content/modular-ontology-modeling-1

16. Verborgh R, ed. The Semantic Web: 18th International Conference, ESWC 2021. Lecture Notes in Computer Science 12731. Cham: Springer, 2021

17. Software Package Data Exchange (SPDX) Specification Version: 2.1. 2016. Available from: https://spdx.dev/wp-content/uploads/sites/41/2017/12/spdxversion2.1.pdf

18. Horridge M and Bechhofer S. The OWL API: A Java API for OWL Ontologies. Semantic Web Journal 2011; 2:11–21

19. Jean-Baptiste L. Ontologies with Python: Programming OWL 2.0 Ontologies with Python and Owlready2. Berkeley, CA: Apress, 2021

20. Cargo – The Rust Package Manager. Available from: https://github.com/rust-lang/cargo

21. Crates.io – Rust Package Registry. Available from: https://crates.io

22. Beckett D, Berners-Lee T, Prud'hommeaux E, and Carothers G. RDF 1.1 Turtle. W3C Recommendation. https://www.w3.org/TR/turtle/

23. Duan R, Alrawi O, Kasturi RP, Elder R, Saltaformaggio B, and Lee W. Towards Measuring Supply Chain Attacks on Package Managers for Interpreted Languages. *28th Annual Network and Distributed System Security Symposium, NDSS.* 2021

24. Boyer S. So You Want to Write a Package Manager. 2017. Available from: https://medium.com/@sdboyer/so-you-want-to-write-a-package-manager-4ae9c17d9527

25. Weizenbaum N. PubGrub: Next-Generation Version Solving. 2018. Available from: https://nex3.medium.com/pubgrub-2fb6470504f

26. PubGrub Version Solving Algorithm Implemented in Rust. 2022 May. Available from: https://github.com/pubgrub-rs/pubgrub

Towards a Knowledge-Aware AI
A. Dimou et al. (Eds.)
© 2022 The Authors.
This article is published online with Open Access by IOS Press and distributed under the terms
of the Creative Commons Attribution License 4.0 (CC BY 4.0).
doi:10.3233/SSW220016

Modelling Business Agreements in the Multimodal Transportation Domain Through Ontological Smart Contracts

Mario Scrocca [1], Marco Comerio, Alessio Carenini, and Irene Celino

Cefriel – Politecnico di Milano
Viale Sarca 226, 20126 Milano, Italy
e-mail: name.surname@cefriel.com

Abstract. The blockchain technology provides integrity and reliability of the information, thus offering a suitable solution to guarantee trustability in a multi-stakeholder scenario that involves actors defining business agreements. The Ride2Rail project investigated the use of the blockchain to record as smart contracts the agreements between different stakeholders defined in a multimodal transportation domain. Modelling an ontology to represent the smart contracts enables the possibility of having a machine-readable and interoperable representation of the agreements. On one hand, the underlying blockchain ensures trust in the execution of the contracts, on the other hand, their ontological representation facilitates the retrieval of information within the ecosystem. The paper describes the development of the Ride2Rail Ontology for Agreements to showcase how the concept of an ontological smart contract, defined in the OASIS ontology, can be applied to a specific domain. The usage of the designed ontology is discussed by describing the modelling as ontological smart contracts of business agreements defined in a ride-sharing scenario.

Keywords. business agreement, ontological smart contracts, multimodal transportation

1. Introduction

In the context of multimodal transportation, a wide set of stakeholders should cooperate to provide passengers with a seamless travel experience. The Shift2Rail Innovation Programme 4[2] (IP4) investigated the design and implementation of an ecosystem of transportation stakeholders relying on an *Interoperability Framework* to support the communication among them and the definition of new services for the users. In this context, the Ride2Rail project[3], focused its attention on the integration of ride-sharing alternatives.

The introduction of new transportation modes, such as ride-sharing, poses additional challenges related to a business environment blending companies and private actors. For this reason, Ride2Rail investigated the usage of blockchain technology to offer suitable

---

[1]Corresponding Author. E-mail: mario.scrocca@cefriel.com
[2]Shift2Rail IP4, https://rail-research.europa.eu/research-development/ip4/
[3]Ride2Rail, https://ride2rail.eu/

guarantees for trust in a multi-stakeholder scenario involving the definition of business agreements. Ride2Rail developed a specific software module for the definition of business agreements as smart contracts, i.e, executable software applications that implement self-executing logic in a blockchain. A smart contract could be implemented as a tool to automate the execution of an agreement that will run when certain conditions are met.

To foster the semantic interoperability of the developed module within the IP4 ecosystem, we designed and adopted an ontology to model the defined agreements through a shared semantic and decoupling the specification of the agreements from its technological implementation. This paper describes the development of such ontology and its application within the Ride2Rail project to describe business agreements in the considered ride-sharing scenario. The main contributions of the paper are: (i) analysis of the literature surveying approaches for an ontological representation of smart contracts, (ii) design and development of an ontology for the definition of business agreements in a multimodal transportation scenario, and (iii) validation of the ontology and exemplification of its usage.

The developed *Ride2Rail Ontology for Agreements* leverages the concept of *Ontological Smart Contract* defined in the OASIS ontology [1] and investigates how it can be extended to model the semantic of business agreements. Although we focused our work on the transportation domain, the proposed approach can be generalised to model ontological smart contracts in different domains.

The remainder of the paper is structured as follows: Section 2 discusses preliminaries regarding the context, terminology and methodology followed; Section 3 frames the work considering the state-of-the-art; Section 4 describes the ontology engineering process and the implemented ontology; Section 5 exemplifies the usage of the ontology reporting how it is used to describe the agreements defined within the Ride2Rail project; Section 6 draws the conclusions, discusses how the proposed approach can be generalised and future work.

2. Preliminaries

This section presents a preliminary introduction to the context and terminology analysed in the paper and the methodology adopted.

2.1. Context

The Ride2Rail project investigated the specific requirements of ride-sharing for its integration in the multimodal transport ecosystem defined in IP4. The idea behind Ride2Rail is to consider each driver (i.e., a user offering a shared ride with her/his car) as a private transport service provider (TSP) offering transportation services on a specific route. The challenges of such an integration are multiple, for example, the need for a user application that could allow passengers to become a driver offering a ride with their own vehicle, or the need for a dynamic update of shared rides published by drivers for the multimodal journey planning. Moreover, a major challenge is related to how to guarantee trust in an environment where private actors can offer, along with companies, a paid transportation service to passengers. For this reason, the *Agreement Ledger Module* was designed and developed in Ride2Rail exploiting the blockchain technology to guarantee trust in the definition of agreements between parties (TSPs, drivers and passengers). The *Agreement Ledger Module* is a software module exposing through an API a set of functionalities relying on smart contracts deployed on a distributed ledger for the digital representation and execution of business agreements. The overall design and implementation of the *Agreement Ledger Module* is documented in the project deliverable [2].

The objective of the ontology engineering activity described in this paper is not to transpose ontologically the content of the ledger, but to identify and provide a *semantic description* of the contracts implemented so that they can facilitate interoperability within IP4 and their comprehension from IP4 stakeholders.

For this purpose, the *Ride2Rail Ontology for Agreements* aims at identifying a set of classes and properties to represent the agreements between parties that could be implemented through the *Agreement Ledger Module*. In this paper, we demonstrate how the following agreements could be described using the ontology:

- The *Ridesharing Booking*, as an agreement between a driver and a passenger.
- The *Incentive*, as an agreement between different parties to grant, according to a set of conditions, a reward that could promote more sustainable transportation alternatives.

2.2. Terminology

In the IP4 scenario, a user with a mobility need can interrogate an application for passengers that is able to process a mobility request and return a set of multimodal offers to cover the itinerary between the required origin and destination. Each *offer* is associated with a *trip* and a set of *offer items* that the passenger can book to be entitled to travel according to the proposed trip. In the general case, a trip is composed of multiple *travel episodes*, i.e., multimodal trip legs, offered by different *travel expert* systems, provided by different operators and combined to generate a trip.

In this context, the following terminology is introduced for the considered scenario:

- a *lyft* is defined as a ride-sharing leg in the (multi-modal) trip of a passenger, therefore, it is a travel episode for ridesharing;
- a *ride* is the transportation service offered by a *driver* that enables a travel episode for one or more passengers;
- a *ridesharing booking* represents the booking made by a passenger of an offer item associated with a ride offered by a driver;
- a *Crowd-based Travel Service Provider* is a travel expert system handling offer items for the rides offered by a set of drivers;
- an *incentive* is an agreement between parties that is offered by an *incentive provider* defining the *incentive mechanism* and *incentive conditions* for granting it.

A more detailed discussion of the presented terminology can be found in the Ride2Rail deliverables [3,4,5].

2.3. Methodology

The methodology adopted for the definition of the ontology is based on *Linked Open Terms* (LOT) [6], a consolidated industrial method to develop ontologies and glossaries.

The LOT methodology is divided into four steps: ontology requirements specification, ontology implementation, ontology publication and ontology maintenance. In the following paragraphs, we briefly discuss the first three steps of the methodology performed to design and implement the *Ride2Rail Ontology for Agreements*.

The ontology requirements specification consists of the definition of the ontology requirements considering the purpose and scope of the ontology, domain analysis and an investigation of the existing data flows. The activity starts with the identification of a set of *use cases* and *user stories* for the ontology. A *use case* should answer the following questions: *Who will be the actors interested in querying the ontological data? What are the expected usages of data modelled through the ontology?*

Considering the *use cases* and *user stories* defined and the domain analysis performed, then the ontological requirements are specified in the form of *competency questions* and *facts*. The set of *competency questions* defines, in the form of hypothetical questions associated with a *user story*, the information that should be possible to retrieve from data modelled using the ontology. The set of *facts* describes the semantics and the requirements associated with the domain-specific terminology (e.g., attributes describing a specific term, etc.). In this phase, domain experts and stakeholders, are involved to ensure a comprehensive set of ontological requirements is specified.

The second step is the implementation of the ontology. Considering the requirements, a first conceptual model is produced with the required set of classes and properties. Then, in line with the best practices of ontology engineering, the relevant and already existing vocabularies are analysed to assess the possibility of reusing them.

Finally, the actual ontology is coded in the OWL language and it is validated with the support of automatic diagnosis tools and by manually assessing it with respect to the ontological requirements specified.

The third step is the documentation and publication of the ontological model.

3. Related work

Blockchain-based solutions and Semantic Web technologies are complementary and may benefit each other. Many researchers are investigating how to combine these technologies and also the European Commission is supporting this research area. As an example, we cite the H2020 ONTOCHAIN[4] project financed under the Next Generation Internet initiative.

Different approaches combining these two areas are reported in the literature. J. Cano-Benito et al. discuss in [7] six different scenarios: (a) blockchain with semantic meta-data, (b) blockchain with RDF content, (c) blockchain and virtual RDF service to publish its content, (d) blockchain with external pointers to RDF data, (e) blockchain referencing another blockchain through RDF, (f) semantic blockchain implemented relying on Semantic Web.

The implementation of the mentioned scenarios relies on the definition of ontologies to model the content of the blockchain. In Ride2Rail, we were interested in investigating how smart contracts implemented on the blockchain could be described using an ontology. This approach addresses two interoperability needs: (i) the description in

---

[4]https://ontochain.ngi.eu/

an implementation-independent way of the smart contracts defined according to a specific blockchain-based solution, and (ii) the adoption of proper and shared terminology to describe domain entities and their relationships. Moreover, even if out of scope for the Ride2Rail project, it can foster the implementation of virtual RDF services to query the content of the blockchain using the ontology (scenario *c.*).

In the following paragraphs, we analyse existing vocabularies that were considered to evaluate their re-use in the implementation of the ontology.

3.1. Smart Contracts and Ontologies

In the analysis of the literature, we found relevant related work regarding the definition of ontologies for smart contracts.

The paper *Ontologies for Commitment-Based Smart Contracts* [8] defines a platform-independent conceptualization of smart contracts, however, as mentioned also by the authors in their conclusions, it represents an initial model that should be refined and evaluated before being finally implemented and published as an ontology.

Kruijff and Weigand in *Understanding the Blockchain Using Enterprise Ontology* [9] adopt an ontology-based approach to formalise the terminology related to the blockchain, including smart contracts, but the proposed modelling considers a higher level of abstraction and doesn't allow for the detailed description of a specific smart contract. Moreover, the authors mention that the presented ontology is still an initial model to be validated and finalised.

Similarly, the *Ontology for Smart Contracts* proposed by McAdams [10] identifies the basic terminology for a conceptualisation of smart contracts that could aid in implementing formal reasoning over their behaviour. The proposed contribution is, however, not implemented as an ontology yet.

Finally, the paper *Ontological Smart Contracts in OASIS* [1] defines the concept of Ontological Smart Contract extending the OASIS ontology for agents, systems, and integration of services [11]. The proposed ontology defines the concept of a smart contract as an entity to define agreements between agents and specify their terms, independently from the specific blockchain implementation. Differently from the other work in the literature, the OASIS ontology is fully implemented in OWL, published online and its usage is documented and exemplified by the authors. Moreover, we contacted the authors that provided us with additional documentation to re-use the vocabulary and confirmed that a plan for the maintenance of the ontology is in place. For these reasons, we decided to adopt this vocabulary as a basis for our work.

In this paper, we discuss how the OASIS ontology can support the modelling of ontological smart contracts considering different blockchain technologies, and how it can be extended and leveraged to model business agreements in different domains. Indeed, the usage of the OASIS ontology is exemplified in [1] considering a trading agent selling stocks and the Ethereum platform, while, in Section 5, we consider agreements in the transportation domain implemented through the Hyperledger Fabric API[5].

---

[5]https://github.com/hyperledger/fabric-contract-api-go

3.2. IP4 Ontologies

To support the definition of domain-specific classes and properties, and to support interoperability within IP4, we analysed the current status of the ontologies for the multimodal transportation domain defined in the context of IP4.

The IP4 ontology is currently undergoing an in-depth process of modularization and extension [12] considering already standardized formats (e.g., Transmodel[6], OSDM[7], TRIAS[8], GTFS-RT[9] etc.). A preliminary release of the new modules of the IP4 ontology, currently under finalisation is available on Github[10]. The two already available modules of the IP4 ontologies address the *Transmodel* concepts (Core, Commons, Fares, Facilities and Journeys submodules) [13] and the *Open Sales and Distribution Model* (OSDM) specification to model the booking process.

4. Ontology for Agreements

The objective of the *Ride2Rail Ontology for Agreements* is to provide a conceptualization of the basic terms for the description of the business agreements defined in the multimodal transportation context discussed in Section 2.1. The ontology takes into account the terminology (Section 2.2) and the ontologies already defined within IP4 (Section 3.2) to support interoperability through shared semantics.

The following sections describe the application of the presented methodology (Section 2.3) for the design, implementation and publication of the *Ride2Rail Ontology for Agreements*.

4.1. Ontological Requirements Specification

This section describes the ontological requirements identified for the *Ride2Rail Ontology for Agreements*. The collection of requirements leveraged the analysis of the overall requirements defined for the Ride2Rail project and the specific ones identified for the implementation of the Agreement Ledger Module. Furthermore, additional stakeholders from the transportation domain were involved to take into account additional considerations from the project consortium and other IP4 actors.

Two use cases were identified to support the definition of the ontology.

UC1 – Dispute Resolution about Ridesharing
Description: in case of a dispute between a driver and a passenger regarding a booked ride, the responsible authority wants to access trusted data to resolve it.
Stakeholders: Driver, Passenger, Authority
Workflow: The responsible authority analyses the details of the booking agreement between the driver and the passenger obtaining trusted information that can help in solving the dispute.

---

[6]https://www.transmodel-cen.eu/
[7]https://unioninternationalcheminsdefer.github.io/OSDM/
[8]https://github.com/VDVde/TRIAS
[9]https://developers.google.com/transit/gtfs-realtime
[10]Working repository https://github.com/oeg-upm/mobility

UC2 – Incentives to promote Ridesharing
Description: travellers (both drivers and passengers) are given incentives to involve ride-sharing in their multimodal rides.
Stakeholders: Passenger, Driver, Travel Service Provider
Workflow: Incentives are represented as ontological smart contracts and can be queried to get information about the conditions and mechanisms of available incentives within IP4.

For each use case, different user stories considering the stakeholders involved were identified. Finally, a set of facts and competency questions was defined considering: (i) the use cases and user stories defined, (ii) the analysis of the business agreements modelled on the blockchain, and (iii) the relevant terminology in the considered domain.

Table 1 contains the competency questions identified for the two use cases, terms starting with a capital letter are concepts described in facts. The complete list of user stories, facts and competency questions is reported in the ontology repository[11].

Competency Question	Expected Result	Use case
What is the origin/destination of the Ridesharing Leg offered by the Driver and booked by the Passenger?	Origin/Destination of the Ridesharing Leg involved in the Ridesharing Booking	UC1
What is the price agreed upon between the Driver and the Passenger?	Price agreed for the Ridesharing Leg involved in the Ridesharing Booking	UC1
What is the number of seats declared by a Driver offering a Ride?	Number of seats associated with a Ride	UC1
What are the incentive agreements involving a TSP as an incentive provider?	Incentives involving a TSP in the agreement	UC2
What are the conditions defined for a given Incentive?	Conditions defined for the applicability of the Incentive	UC2
Is there a tangible good or benefit associated with a given Incentive?	Benefit associated with the Incentive	UC2

Table 1.: Competency Questions identified for the Ontological Requirements Specification

4.2. Ontology Implementation

To support the ontology implementation phase, we adopted the *Chowlk*[12] notation and converter [14] that allows building the conceptual model graphically and then to directly obtain a first serialization of the ontology in OWL.

The design of the conceptual model, starting from a glossary of terms extracted from the ontological requirements, went through several iterations considering also the outcomes of the review of already available ontological and non-ontological data formats.

To facilitate the description of the final conceptual model, we first discuss the reused vocabularies to model the ontological smart contracts and the domain terminology. Then,

---

[11]https://github.com/Ride2Rail/agreement-ledger-ontology/tree/main/requirements
[12]https://chowlk.linkeddata.es/

we present the final version of the ontology through the *Chowlk* notation. Using the diagram, we motivate our design decisions by describing the introduced classes and properties and the alignment with the re-used vocabularies.

4.2.1. Ontological Smart Contracts

The Ontology for Agents, Systems, and Integration of Services (OASIS) is published online[13] with the namespace http://www.dmi.unict.it/oasis.owl# (oasis: prefix).

An ontological smart contract in OASIS (*oasis:SmartContract*) is modelled defining the set of entries involved in the agreement (*oasis:SmartContractEntry*) and the set of conditionals (*oasis:ConditionalSet*) specifying the terms of the agreement. Agreement instances are modelled through the class *oasis:SmartContractInstance* and they are associated with a specific *oasis:SmartContract*.

A *oasis:SmartContractEntry* can be of class *oasis:SmartContractEntryParticipant*, describing a participant involved in the agreement, or class *oasis:SmartContractEntry Value*, describing values involved. Each *oasis:SmartContractEntry* can be described using the property *oasis:refersExactlyTo*, if it refers to a specific individual for each instance of the described agreement, or using the property *oasis:refersAsNewTo*, if it describes an individual through an *oasis:EntryTemplate*. An *oasis:EntryTemplate* allows to specify the features that an *oasis:SmartContractEntry* should have in an *oasis:SmartContractInstance* of the modelled *oasis:SmartContract*.

The terms of the agreements are modelled using *oasis:Conditional*, which represent an implication between an antecedent (*oasis:ConditionalBody*) and consequent (*oasis:ConditionalHead*). Whenever the conditions specified in the antecedent hold, then the conditions specified in the consequent must also hold. Both an *oasis:ConditionalBody* and an *oasis:ConditionalHead* can specify multiple conditions modelling different *oasis:ConditionalAtom*. All the *oasis:ConditionalAtom* should be satisfied to satisfy the antecedent/consequent. A *oasis:ConditionalAtom* can be described through:

- *oasis:ConditionalSubject*: representing the subject;
- *oasis:ConditionalObject*: representing the object;
- *oasis:ConditionalOperator:* representing actions (*oasis:Action*) from subject(s) to object(s);
- *oasis:ConditionalParameter*: representing a parameter of the action described by the operator (the two subclasses *oasis:ConditionalInputParameter* and *oasis:ConditionalOutputParameter* representing an input and an output parameter, respectively);
- *oasis:ConditionalOperatorArgument*: representing operator arguments for a subordinate characteristic of the operator

Also in the modelling of conditionals, an *oasis:EntryTemplate* can be leveraged to specify the features that the entities involved in the conditional.

4.2.2. Domain Terminology

For the definition ontology, considering the elicited requirements, we focused mainly on the *OSDM* module of the IP4 ontologies. The namespace for the considered ontology is https://w3id.org/mobility/

---

[13]OASIS ontology https://www.dmi.unict.it/santamaria/projects/oasis/oasis.php

`osdm/core#` (`osdm:` module), but the publication process is not finalised yet. In particular, we reused classes and properties related to the concepts of:

- *osdm:Offer*: defined as "a response to a customer mobility request as a result of the travel shopping process, it is composed of offer item(s) for service(s) designed to cover each proposed journey, and, optionally, ancillary services".
- *osdm:Booking:* defined as "an operational process as part of the sales process to commit to a sales transaction binding the customer and supplier to the offer".

To complement the set of classes and properties already available in the IP4 ontologies, the MaaSive Glossary and the conceptualisation effort made in Ride2Rail WP2.1 (Deliverable D2.1 [3] and D2.4 [4]) and WP3.1 (Deliverable 3.1 [5]) were taken into account as non-ontological resources to improve the semantic interoperability of entities modelled in our ontology.

4.2.3. Ride2Rail Ontology for Agreements

The implementation of the *Ride2Rail Ontology for Agreements* is based on the decision to reuse the *oasis:SmartContract* as the class to model a business agreement. Our claim is that concept of *oasis:SmarContract* is modelled in the OASIS ontology using a generic approach that can be extended and applied to different domains once identified a suitable vocabulary for the representation of the domain terminology. An *oasis:SmarContract* not only enables the representation of the agreement and the entities involved a *oasis:SmartContractEntry*, but also a detailed model of the terms of the agreements as *oasis:Conditionals*. The main objective of the ontology is to complement the current IP4 ontologies and extend the OASIS ontology providing the needed terminology to model ontological smart contracts in the multimodal transportation domain.

Figure 1 adopts the Chowlk notation to describe the classes and properties modelled and their relations with reused vocabularies. The namespace selected for publication is `https://w3id.org/ride2rail/terms#` (`r2r:` prefix).

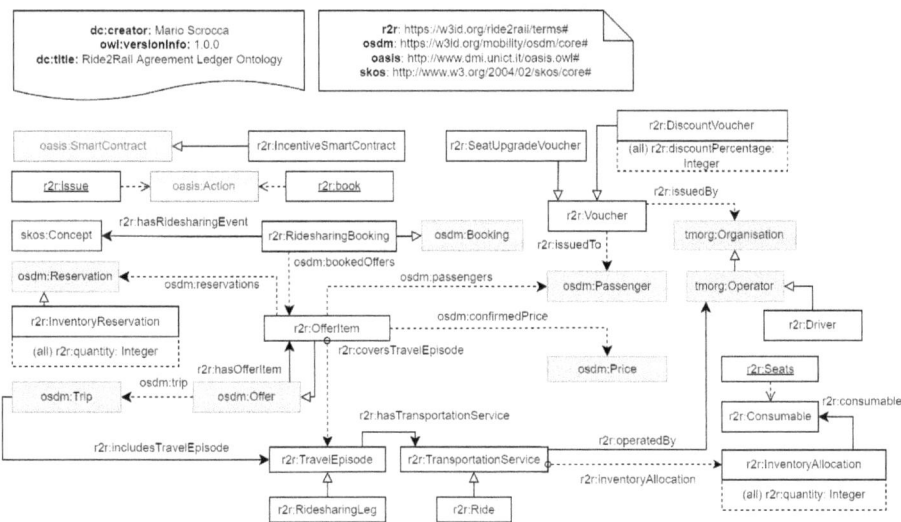

Figure 1. Chowlk diagram for the Ride2Rail Ontology for Agreements

To support the modelling of the *oasis:SmartContract* for a ridesharing booking, the class *r2r:RidesharingBooking* is defined as a subclass of *osdm:Booking*. An *osdm:Booking* is associated with the booked *osdm:Offer* and the *osdm:Price* paid for the offer. *An osdm:Offer* represents the pair between a computed *osdm:Trip* and the set of products (*osdm:OfferPart*) offered to an *osdm:Passenger* and required to perform the trip.

The ontology extends the concept of *osdm:Offer* defining an *r2r:OfferItem* to model the corresponding term in the IP4 glossary (an offer item is part of an offer, which is provided by a single TSP). As a result, *r2r:RidesharingBooking* is associated with an *r2r:OfferItem* provided by a ridesharing TSP, i.e. the Crowd-based TSP in the ridesharing scenario.

The ontology also defines two classes, *r2r:TravelEpisode* and *r2r:TransportationService* to model, respectively, the IP4 concepts of *travel episode* ("part of a trip operated with the same vehicle") and *transportation service* ("service that provides transportation on a travel episode"). An *osdm:Trip* may include multiple *r2r:TravelEpisode* (possibly aligned with the concept of *osdm:Segment*), an *r2r:TravelEpisode* may be operated by an *r2r:TransportationService*.

An *r2r:OfferItem* for an *r2r:RidesharingBooking*, is associated with an *r2r:RidesharingLeg* (subclass of *r2r:TravelEpisode*) that is made possible through an *r2r:Ride* (subclass of *r2r:TransportationService*) operated by an *r2r:Driver*. In this sense, *r2r:Driver* extends the concept of *tmorg:Operator*.

As specified in the requirements, an *r2r:Ride* may specify an *r2r:InventoryAllocation* that indicates a given quantity of available consumables (*r2r:Consumable*). The ontology defines *r2r:Seat* as an individual of the class *r2r:Consumable*. An *r2r:InventoryReservation* (subclass of *osdm:Reservation*) can be associated with an *r2r:OfferItem* defining the number of consumables reserved by the corresponding booking.

To support the modelling of incentives, the class *r2r:IncentiveSmartContract* is defined as subclass of *oasis:SmarContract*. The ontology also models the concept of *r2r:Voucher* to define a redeemable good issued by a *tmorg:Organisation*. Two subclasses are defined for *r2r:Voucher* to model the mechanisms of the incentives implemented in Ride2Rail: a *r2r:DiscountVoucher* allowing to model a certain percentage of discount granted to the beneficiary of the voucher, and a *r2r:SeatUpgradeVoucher* granting an upgrade of seat class for the beneficiary.

To express the incentive conditions defined in the requirements, the ontology also defines two *oasis:Action* individuals, *r2r:issue* and *r2r:book*, that can be used as *oasis:ConditionalOperator* in the modelling of conditionals for an *oasis:SmartContract*.

Finally, to model the events that can be associated with a ridesharing booking we decided to implement a SKOS[14] Concept Scheme.

As defined in the requirements, five events are identified in the first level of the taxonomy: *RidesharingStarted* for the start of the ride associated with the ridesharing booking, *RidesharingCompleted* for the completion of the ride associated with the ridesharing booking, *RidesharingCancelled* for the cancellation of the ridesharing booking by the passenger or by the driver, *RidesharingDelayed* for a delay in the ride due to the passenger or to the driver, *RidesharingNoShow* for a passenger or a driver not showing as expected for the booked ridesharing.

---

[14]https://www.w3.org/2004/02/skos/

The modelled ontology was validated against the ontological requirements and using OOPS! [15] as the state-of-the-art tool for automatic diagnosis of anomalies in the ontology[15].

4.3. Ontology Publication

The *Ride2Rail Ontology for Agreements* is published online following the best practices for ontology publication at `https://w3id.org/ride2rail/terms#` (r2r: prefix). We adopted the *w3id* service for permanent identifiers[16], and we implemented content negotiation to serve the ontology in different human-readable and machine-readable formats[17]. The Widoco [16] tool was used to generate the ontology documentation, then complemented through diagrams and the description of the main design decisions. The SKOS taxonomy for ridesharing booking events is published at `https://w3id.org/ride2rail/rb-events#` (rbe: prefix) using a similar approach.

The license adopted is the Creative Commons with Attribution right (CC-BY), which allows licensees to copy and distribute the work and make derivative works, giving the authors proper credits.

All the material related to the ontology and the artifacts produced during the ontology engineering process are hosted on Github under the Ride2Rail organisation in the repository `https://github.com/Ride2Rail/agreement-ledger-ontology`.

5. Modelling Business Agreements

In this section, we exemplify the usage of the defined *Ride2Rail Ontology for Agreements* discussing the RDF representation of the business agreements implemented through the Agreement Ledger Module in the Ride2Rail project, i.e., the ridesharing booking and the incentives. We decided to distinguish between the ontology and the agreements since the definition of different business agreements (e.g. different conditionals and incentives) is made possible by relying on the implemented ontology.

The RDF dataset is published at `https://w3id.org/ride2rail/agreements#` (ag: prefix) and hosted on Github[18]. A Chowlk diagram is provided in the ontology documentation for each *oasis:SmartContract*[19]. In the following, we discuss the defined agreements and the expected usage of the terms in the considered scenario.

The first agreement is the *ag:RidesharingBookingSmartContract* that defines the entities associated with a ridesharing booking and their relations. Figure 2 represents the Chowlk diagram describing the modelled *oasis:SmartContract*. An *ag:RidesharingBookingSmartContract* involves an *r2r:Driver* and an *osdm:Passenger* as participants in an *r2r:RidesharingBooking*. The agreement specifies that the *r2r:RidesharingBooking* is associated with an *r2r:OfferItem* for the passenger, that has a specific *osdm:Price*, is associated with an *r2r:RidesharingLeg*, and includes an *r2r:InventoryReservation*. The

---

[15]A report of the validation is available in the ontology repository `https://github.com/Ride2Rail/agreement-ledger-ontology`

[16]`https://w3id.org/`

[17]Recipe 3 from `https://www.w3.org/TR/swbp-vocab-pub`

[18]`https://github.com/Ride2Rail/agreement-ledger-ontology/tree/main/agreements`

[19]The Chowlk diagrams for the defined *r2r:IncentiveSmartContract*s are available also in the repository `https://github.com/Ride2Rail/agreement-ledger-ontology/tree/main/docs/diagrams`

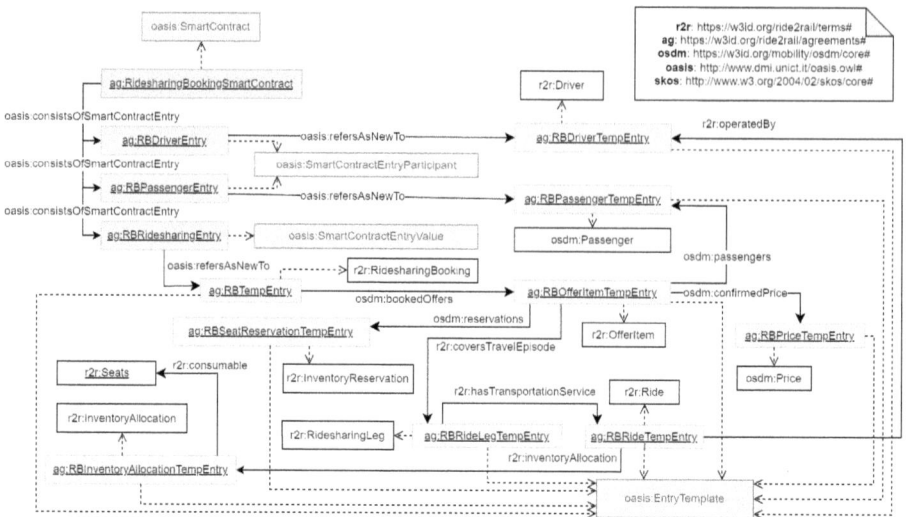

Figure 2. Diagram describing the *RidesharingBookingSmartContract* agreement.

r2r:RidesharingLeg has as transportation service an *r2r:Ride* offered by the driver with a specific *r2r:InventoryAllocation*.

The *ag:RidesharingBookingSmartContract* does not define any *oasis:Conditional* since the terms of the agreement are not directly modelled through the Agreement Ledger Module. Table 2 defines examples of *oasis:Conditional* that can be defined exploiting the ontology, in particular, leveraging the ride-sharing booking events taxonomy. Example 1 describes the fact that the money from the passenger should be transferred to the driver if the ride is correctly started and ended, examples 2 and 3 describe potential refund policies if the driver doesn't show up or cancels the ride.

Conditional		*example-1*	*example-2*	*example-3*
Entities	Participant	Passenger Driver	Passenger Driver	Passenger Driver
	Value	Ridesharing Booking	Ridesharing Booking	Ridesharing Booking
Body	Subject	Ridesharing Booking	Ridesharing Booking	Ridesharing Booking
	Operator	is associated with	is associated with	is associated with
	Object	Start Event, End Event	Cancelled Driver	No Show Driver
Head	Subject	Passenger	-	-
	Input Parameter	Price	-	-
	Operator	pay	refund	refund
	Output Parameter	-	Price	Price
	Object	Driver	Passenger	Passenger

Table 2.: Example of *oasis:Conditional* for a ride-sharing booking smart contract.

The Agreement Ledger Module implemented in Ride2Rail defines three agreements related to incentives, i.e., three *r2r:IncentiveSmartContract*: Ride with other passengers (*ag:RideWithOtherPassengersIncentive*), Multimodal discount (*ag: MultimodalDiscountIncentive*), Multimodal repetition discount (ag:*MultimodalDiscountIncentive3*). Table 3 summarises the defined agreements reporting the *oasis:SmartContractEntry* involved and the modelled *oasis:Conditional*. All the agreements are between an *osdm:Passenger* and a *tmorg:Operator,* then:

- *ag:RideWithOtherPassengersIncentive* defines a conditional specifying that if the passenger books a ride also booked by another passenger, then the TSP issues an *r2r:SeatUpgradeVoucher* to the passenger;
- *ag:MultimodalDiscountIncentive* defines a conditional specifying that if the passenger books a multimodal ride involving an *r2r:RidesharingLeg* and at least another leg, then the TSP issues an *r2r:DiscountVoucher* of 10% to the passenger;
- *ag:MultimodalDiscountIncentive3* defines a conditional specifying that if the passenger books a multimodal ride involving an r2r:RidesharingLeg and at least another leg for three times, then the TSP issues an r2r:DiscountVoucher of 20% to the passenger.

Incentive Smart Contract		*Ride With Other Passengers Incentive*	*Multimodal Discount Incentive*	*Multimodal Repetition Discount Incentive*
Entities	Participant	Passenger P1 Travel Service Provider TSP	Passenger P1 Travel Service Provider TSP	Passenger P1 Travel Service Provider TSP
Body	Subject	Passenger P1, Passenger P2	Passenger	Passenger
	Operator	makes a booking	makes a booking	makes a booking
	Operator Argument	-	-	3 times
	Object	Ride R1	Offer for a Trip involving a Ridesharing Leg and another Leg	Offer for a Trip involving a Ridesharing Leg and another Leg
Head	Subject	TSP	TSP	TSP
	Operator	issue	issue	issue
	Object	Seat Upgrade Voucher for Passenger P1	10% Discount Voucher for Passenger	20% Discount Voucher for Passenger

Table 3.: *IncentiveSmartContract*s implemented in Ride2Rail

The described *oasis:SmartContract*s not only enable the sharing of the modelled business agreements between the IP4 stakeholders, but also the representation of smart contract instances stored on the blockchain to support the use cases defined.

6. Conclusions

In an ecosystem comprehending various stakeholders, the implementation of business agreements through a distributed ledger provides several benefits regarding information trust and the automatic execution of the agreed terms modelled as smart contracts. This approach, however, doesn't provide any guarantee about the interoperability of the defined agreements from a technological and semantic perspective. On one hand, the domain terminology shared among the involved stakeholders should be referenced by the modelled entities, on the other hand, other software systems can benefit from a machine-readable representation of the agreements.

The concept of ontological smart contract, defined in the OASIS ontology, supports the representation of business agreements independently from their implementation and relying on standardised vocabularies. The defined *Ride2Rail Ontology for Agreements* enables the application of this concept to support the interoperability of business agreements in the multimodal transportation scenario considered by the Ride2Rail project. Two use cases were considered: the representation of the ride-sharing booking as an agreement between the driver and the passengers for dispute resolution, and the definition of incentives as agreements between different stakeholders to promote the usage of multimodal transportation. In the paper, we validated and exemplified the usage of the ontology by modelling the specific business agreements implemented in the project on the ledger.

The discussed approach can be generalised to support an ontological representation of smart contracts in different domains. The following steps summarise the discussed activities: (i) investigation of the business agreements to be modelled in the considered scenario (use cases and user stories), (ii) analysis of the domain terminology covered by the business agreements (facts and competency questions), (iii) identification of existing vocabularies covering the relevant domain entities and relationships, and/or implementation of an ontology supporting their representation, (iv) modelling of each business agreement as an ontological smart contract identifying the involved entities and the terms of the agreement, and, optionally, (v) representation of specific entities of the business agreement stored on the ledger using the ontology. In this way, different stakeholders are able to access through uniform terminology a description of the smart contracts and, possibly, their instances.

In future work, we will investigate the materialisation/virtualisation of smart contracts and/or related instances from the blockchain to enable querying according to the defined ontology. In particular, we will explore the configuration of semantic conversion pipelines [17] and the exploitation of the obtained knowledge graph. Moreover, we would like to extend the scope of the defined ontology to enable the representation of heterogeneous agreements in the multimodal transportation domain, for example, considering requirements for the sharing and electric mobility [18]. Finally, the evolution of the suite of IP4 ontologies will be taken into account to extend and update the defined ontology.

Acknowledgements

The presented research was supported by the RIDE2RAIL project (Grant Agreement 881825), co-funded by the European Commission under the Horizon 2020 Framework

Programme. We would like to thank Daniele Santamaria for his support regarding the OASIS ontology.

References

[1] Cantone D, Longo CF, Nicolosi Asmundo M, Santamaria DF, Santoro C. Ontological Smart Contracts in OASIS: Ontology for Agents, Systems, and Integration of Services. In: Intelligent Distributed Computing XIV. Studies in Computational Intelligence. Cham: Springer International Publishing; 2022. p. 237-47.

[2] Ride2Rail Project. D3.5 - Ride-sharing Agreements Ledger Module; 2022. Project Deliverable (pending approval by EC). Available from: https://ride2rail.eu/resources-library/.

[3] Ride2Rail Project. D2.1 - First conceptualization of choice criteria and incentives; 2020. Project Deliverable. Available from: https://doi.org/10.5281/zenodo.4537031.

[4] Ride2Rail Project. D2.4 - Final conceptualization of choice criteria and incentives; 2021. Project Deliverable. Available from: https://doi.org/10.5281/zenodo.4607203.

[5] Ride2Rail Project. D3.1 - Quantitative Estimate of Service Quality Factors; 2021. Project Deliverable. Available from: https://doi.org/10.5281/zenodo.6803935.

[6] Poveda-Villalón M, Fernández-Izquierdo A, García-Castro R. Linked Open Terms (LOT) Methodology; 2019. Publisher: Zenodo. Available from: https://zenodo.org/record/2539305.

[7] Cano-Benito J, Cimmino A, García-Castro R. Towards Blockchain and Semantic Web. In: Business Information Systems Workshops. Lecture Notes in Business Information Processing. Cham: Springer International Publishing; 2019. p. 220-31.

[8] De Kruijff J, Weigand H. Ontologies for Commitment-Based Smart Contracts. In: On the Move to Meaningful Internet Systems. OTM 2017 Conferences. Lecture Notes in Computer Science. Cham: Springer International Publishing; 2017. p. 383-98.

[9] De Kruijff J, Weigand H. Understanding the Blockchain Using Enterprise Ontology. In: Advanced Information Systems Engineering. Lecture Notes in Computer Science. Cham: Springer International Publishing; 2017. p. 29-43.

[10] McAdams D. An Ontology for Smart Contracts. IOHK paper; 2017. p. 3. Accessed online at https://cryptopapers.info/assets/pdf/ontology_for_smart_contracts.pdf.

[11] Cantone D, Longo CF, Nicolosi-Asmundo M, Santamaria DF, Santoro C. Towards an Ontology-Based Framework for a Behavior-Oriented Integration of the IoT. In: Proceedings of the 20th Workshop "From Objects to Agents". vol. 2404 of CEUR Workshop Proceedings. Parma, Italy: CEUR; 2019. p. 119-26. ISSN: 1613-0073. Available from: http://ceur-ws.org/Vol-2404/#paper18.

[12] CONNECTIVE Project. D1.2 – Architectural Principles and Design A-REL; 2020. Project Deliverable. Available from: https://projects.shift2rail.org/s2r_ip4_n.aspx?p=MaaSive.

[13] Ruckhaus E, Anton-Bravo A, Scrocca M, Corcho O. Applying the LOT Methodology to a Public Bus Transport Ontology aligned with Transmodel: Challenges and Results. Semantic Web. 2021 Jan;Prepress:1-19. Publisher: IOS Press. Available from: https://doi.org/10.3233/SW-210451.

[14] Feria SC, García-Castro R, Poveda-Villalón M. Converting UML-based ontology conceptualizations to OWL with Chowlk; 2021. Available from: https://openreview.net/forum?id=u1Vp2y_QE1.

[15] Poveda-Villalón M, Suárez-Figueroa MC, Gómez-Pérez A. Validating Ontologies with OOPS! In: Knowledge Engineering and Knowledge Management. Lecture Notes in Computer Science. Berlin, Heidelberg: Springer; 2012. p. 267-81.

[16] Garijo D. WIDOCO: A Wizard for Documenting Ontologies. In: The Semantic Web – ISWC 2017. vol. 10588. Springer International Publishing; 2017. p. 94-102. Series Title: Lecture Notes in Computer Science. Available from: http://link.springer.com/10.1007/978-3-319-68204-4_9.

[17] Scrocca M, Comerio M, Carenini A, Celino I. Turning Transport Data to Comply with EU Standards While Enabling a Multimodal Transport Knowledge Graph. In: Proceedings of the 19th International Semantic Web Conference. vol. 12507. Springer; 2020. p. 411-29. Available from: https://doi.org/10.1007/978-3-030-62466-8_26.

[18] Scrocca M, Baroni I, Celino I. Urban IoT ontologies for sharing and electric mobility. Semantic Web. 2021 Jan;Pre-press:1-22. Publisher: IOS Press. Available from: https://doi.org/10.3233/SW-210445.

Learning over Complementary Knowledge

Towards a Knowledge-Aware AI
A. Dimou et al. (Eds.)

155

© 2022 The Authors.
This article is published online with Open Access by IOS Press and distributed under the terms of the Creative Commons Attribution License 4.0 (CC BY 4.0).

doi:10.3233/SSW220018

Learning Ontology Classes from Text by Clustering Lexical Substitutes Derived from Language Models [1]

Artem REVENKO [a] Victor MIRELES [a] Anna BREIT [a] Peter BOURGONJE [b]
Julian MORENO-SCHNEIDER [c] Maria KHVALCHIK [a] Georg REHM [c]

[a] *Semantic Web Company GmbH, Austria.*
{firstname}.{second.name}@semantic-web.com
[b] *Morningsun Technology GmbH, Germany.*
peter.bourgonje@morningsun-technology.com
[c] *DFKI GmbH, Germany. {firstname}.{second.name}@dfki.de*

Abstract.

Many tools for knowledge management and the Semantic Web presuppose the existence of an arrangement of instances into classes, i.e. an ontology. Creating such an ontology, however, is a labor-intensive task. We present an unsupervised method to learn an ontology from text. We rely on pre-trained language models to generate lexical substitutes of given entities and then use matrix factorization to induce new classes and their entities. Our method differs from previous approaches in that (1) it captures the polysemy of entities; (2) it produces interpretable labels of the induced classes; (3) it does not require any particular structure of the text; (4) no re-training is required. We evaluate our method on German and English WikiNER corpora and demonstrate the improvements over state of the art approaches.

Keywords. Ontology Learning, Knowledge Discovery, Language Models

1. Introduction

The assignment of entities into a hierarchy of semantically coherent classes is the basis of knowledge organization systems, and is useful for many information and text processing tasks. Such classifications are usually created manually (a labour intensive task), but can also be identified in semi-automatic ways from a corpus. Specifically, the ontology learning task dealt with in this paper, seeks to create the class hierarchy *de novo* from a corpus, along with an assignment of entities into the induced classes. This approach constitutes a translation of the distributional semantics captured in corpus-wide statistics, into the explicit semantics described in the class hierarchy of an ontology.

Making corpus-based ontology learning effective on small domain-specific corpora, enables small organizations to tackle specific problems in reduced times. The resulting

---

[1]The work presented in this article has received funding from the German Federal Ministry for Economic Affairs and Climate Action (BMWK) through the project SPEAKER (no. 01MK19011), and the Austrian Research Promotion Agency (FFG) through the Project OBARIS (Grant Agreement No 877389)

ontologies can be useful for creating data models or powering search applications, among myriad other applications. In particular, the use of domain-specific ontologies in enabling knowledge-based transfer learning in information extraction systems (e.g., [14,27]) is a promising method for industrial applications. For these and other applications, ontology learning has been approached from different angles, as reviewed in Section 2.

The assignment of entities into semantically coherent classes relies on some method for recognizing these in text, such as Named Entity Recognition (NER) or Entity Linking (EL) tools, which have a variety of associated costs. Therefore, an effective corpus-based class induction method should be *able to work with the output of any annotation tool*. In turn, since many of these methods are not able to *handle polysemous words*[2], ontology learning also must include some means of disambiguation. Another important consideration is that any subdivision of a corpus into documents or similar structures might not necessarily follow the semantic categorization of entities. That is, the assumption –which e.g., topic modelling approaches build on– that semantically similar concepts are often co-occurring across documents, induces already a notion of semantic similarity which might not correspond to the task at hand or the different uses of entities by the authors of the corpus. For this reason, ontology learning methods that *don't make use of any notion of document* have a larger range of applications. Finally, since ontologies are meant to be consumed not only by machines, but rather help inform human-centered knowledge managing, it is desirable that any automatically identified classes be *interpretable by humans*, for example, by being accompanied by a natural language description.

In this work, we present a method for learning ontology classes that leverages large pre-trained language models, in order to reduce the amount of training data required and make it applicable to corpora of different sizes. We use lexical substitutes derived from the language models to capture representations of annotated entities in context. By analyzing the substitutes of different entities in different contexts we identify and cluster the different contextualized usages of entities, and propose a class hierarchy for them. By clustering contextualized usages, as opposed to entities themselves, the system also disambiguates between different senses of an entity, in particular between general and domain-specific ones. The details of the method are presented in Section 3. Finally, the learned classes are assigned descriptors, which can aid a human in distinguishing them and, eventually, assigning a label to each. Our proposal is compared to state of the art approaches to the same task in Section 4.3, according to evaluation criteria presented in Section 4.

2. Related Work

Ontology Learning   Ontology learning is the process of deriving an ontology from natural language or structured data [16,4,8]. In general ontology learning includes many tasks such as identifying terms, grouping them into classes, extracting hierarchical (taxonomical) and non-hierarchical relations between classes, and discovering more complex axioms. In this work we aim at grouping the entities (terms) into a hierarchy of classes, and moreover we assume that entities are already identified and annotated in the corpus. Our tasks correspond to the third and fourth layer of the Ontology Learning Layer Cake

---

[2]For example, "Apple" as fruit or as a brand name.

[8]. These tasks are especially important as the class hierarchy defines the backbone of an ontology [1]. Common approaches combine linguistic features with statistics and machine learning [11,13,29,23]. These methods often have low recall and are affected by noise [7]. Also such methods often assume significant human intervention and are language-specific.

Modern end-to-end deep learning models have a chance to overcome these limitations. First, it is not necessary to provide explicit features to such systems. Second, intrinsic language understanding might overcome noise in the data. In [9,2] authors exploit static (not contextualized) word embeddings to extract ontologies. However, to the best of our knowledge (and see also [1,16]) none of the existing ontology learning approaches exploits lexical substitutes produced by pre-trained, deep learning-based, Language Models (LM) to identify classes of entities.

Induction of Topic Taxonomies   A closely related field is induction of topic taxonomies [35]. Topic taxonomies can be defined as lightweight ontologies that only include class hierarchies and assertions of instances to classes. Hence, this task exactly matches the task we solve in this work. The creation of topic taxonomies has often been approached by means of clustering methods, interpreting the resulting clusters as topics. In order to use common clustering methods, a mapping from terms to vectors is required, for example by the use of word embeddings pre-trained on large corpora such as word2vec [22,33]. These approaches, however, fail to capture the idiosyncratic use of terms in a given domain[3], and so context-specific embeddings have been proposed. In this respect, contextualised embeddings, such as those underlying recent LMs, have been exploited to produce vectors that are to be fed into statistical classifiers to detect is-a relations [10,18], as well as more general relation extraction [31]. Unfortunately, the use of the LMs in existing work does not properly capture the polysemy of terms and studies have shown that the only is-a relations found are those which the model acquired during training [20]. A more careful use of contextualised embeddings can be found in TaxoGen [35] and its derivatives [30], however, its usability is limited by the need of retraining embeddings on specific sub-corpora, and sense disambiguation is not explicitly handled.

To the best of our knowledge, none of the existing methods tackles the polysemy of entities. The polysemy of terms is especially important in domain-specific corpora, as it is common for words to be adopted and given new senses in each domain. However, retention of the original sense is not uncommon, and constitutes a challenge which might degrade the quality of the resulting ontology. Often these models rely on the notion of document as a single coherent piece of text, which itself induces a notion of semantic similarity which might be more related to the process of producing and editing the corpus, than to the meanings of entities themselves. The method we introduce in this paper does not require partitioning of the corpus into documents.

Topic Modeling   Topic modeling is a frequently used text-mining tool for discovery of hidden semantic structures in a text body. The goal of topic modeling is to cluster a corpus of documents into thematically coherent groups of documents and keywords [32]. These clusters of keywords could be used to produce new classes of an ontology. Therefore, this method is compatible with our task and we will use the results for comparison.

---

[3]For example, the action of the verb "to host" is applied on software or services in the field of Computer Science, but in the field of product reviews, it is usually applied on people.

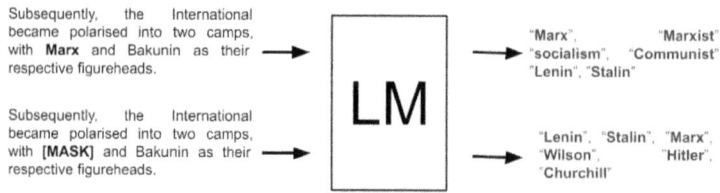

Figure 1. Top $m = 6$ substitutes predicted by a language model for an unmodified (top) and masked (bottom) context of "**Marx**".

However, the initial goal is to discover latent topics in the corpus, therefore the grouping of the terms relies more on the distribution of words across documents rather than specific patterns of the usage of words.

Language Modeling   In our experiments, we exploit modern language modeling techniques. Recently, neural network architectures, in particular the Transformer architecture, have progressed the state-of-the-art in many benchmark Natural Language Processing (NLP) tasks [25,26,12]. The pre-training usually happens on Wikipedia or on news articles (due to their wide availability), though domain-specific incarnations also exist, e. g., BioBERT [17], SciBERT [6] and ClinicalBERT [15]. One essential feature of language models used in this work, is their ability to predict a word or sequence which has been masked in a text. For this particular task, the contextualized representation inherent in modern language models yields better results[25,26] than earlier vector representation-based language models [21], and bidirectionality can further improve these results [12]. These predictions, can be interpreted as lexical substitutes of the masked section.

3. Method

We start from a corpus which has been annotated with entities, for example using an NER tool, an entity linking tool or a gazetteer. Based on these entity annotations, we set out to induce a classification of the entities and produce a set of interpretable descriptors for each class. This is done in a three-step process: first we generate lexical substitutes for the entity in context, second, we induce sense representations of entities, and finally, we group these senses into classes. See Figure 2 for a graphical summary of the procedure.

Create Substitutes   We consider a set of entity annotations, each with a context c consisting of a window of w words before and after the entity mention. For each of these annotations, we generate two inputs that are fed into a language model: the original unmodified context c, and the context c_{masked} in which the entity mention has been masked (see Figure 1 for an example). For each of these inputs, we obtain the top m substitutes, where m allows us to balance between a low number of high quality substitutes and high number of potentially lower quality substitutes.

Extract Senses   Next, we generate a set of binary matrices $\{M^e\}$, one for every entity. Each of the matrices M^e has one row per context in which the entity e is mentioned, and one column per substitute suggested by the language model. Thus, the entry $M_{i,j}$ is 1 if and only if the language model predicts substitute j as one of the m best ranked substitutes for any of the contexts c_i, c_{i_masked}. In total, we obtain as many binary matrices as unique entities can be found in the corpus.

It is possible that a given entity is used in more than one sense throughout the corpus. In order to identify those senses, we factorize each of the binary matrices M^e using Algorithm 2 from [5], in a fashion that has also been used for word sense induction (e.g., [3]). This algorithm outputs a set $S^e = \{s_1, s_2, \ldots\}$ of factors, which we call *senses*. Each sense s consists of a set of contexts and a set of substitutes D_s, such that for each context, the annotated entity can be substituted by any of the substitutes from D_s. We call D_s the *sense descriptors* of s. We consider only at most k descriptors for each sense. Similar to m, higher values of k produce larger sense descriptions. Finally, heuristically we identified that if an entity appears less than five times it is unlikely that more than a single sense would be induced. Therefore, for such infrequent entities, a single representative cluster is produced by taking the most common substitutes for the entity.

Induce Classes   Once we have produced a set of senses, we proceed to cluster these in order to induce classes. For this, we generate a second binary matrix $\mathcal{M}$ whose rows correspond to all senses of all entities, and whose columns correspond to all descriptors of all senses, and factorize it using the same method from [5]. The result of this factorization is a set of tuples of the form $C = (E, D)$ where E is a set of entity senses and D a set of entity descriptors. Each of these tuples represents a class, where E is a set of entity senses belonging to it, and the descriptors in D provide and interpretable representation of the class. To enforce longer class descriptions, we introduce a new parameter th and filter out clusters with less than th descriptors. Examples of the resulting classes can be seen in Examples 2 (English) and 3, 4 (German).

Note that the maximum possible size of the matrix $\mathcal{M}$ is $N_s \times (k \times N_s)$, with N_s being the total number of senses for all entities. In practice we observe smaller values for the second dimension, as descriptors for different senses overlap; which also indicates that we can expect better results for the entire procedure as many different senses share substitutes and could be efficiently grouped.

We perform the matrix factorisation twice: First for each entity separately and then for the obtained senses and their descriptors. One could skip the first factorisation and just collect all *occurrences* of entities and their respective substitutes into a single binary matrix. However, the distribution of entities is far from normal, so the over-represented ones would dominate such a matrix. In preliminary experiments we have observed that this leads to the discovery of various sub-senses of the popular entities rather than a meaningful grouping of different entities. To favor the semantic grouping of various senses we deem double factorisation necessary.

3.1. Hierarchies of Classes

It is possible to generalize the introduced method to induce hierarchies of classes. Namely, we see two possibilities to reveal hierarchies, whose evaluation is left outside the scope of this paper:

Iterative application of the method. Given a class of interest we apply the method to entities of this class. The induced classes are sub-classes of the initially given class.

Control the granularity of the class with th. Larger numbers of th produce more specific classes, smaller values of th produce more general classes with more entities. Comparing the classification with different th allows to extract hierarchies between those classes. For an example see EN-11-th3 and EN-9-th6 in Example 1 and 2.

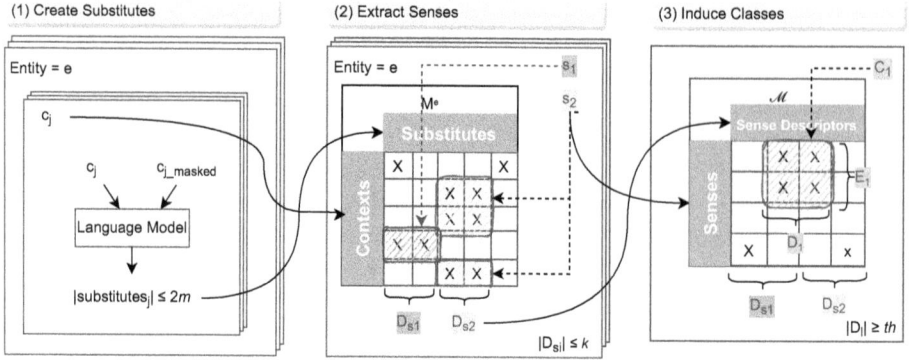

Figure 2. Class induction diagram. c_j represents the jth context. s_i is the ith induced sense; D_{s_i} are the descriptors of s_i. C_l is one of the induced classes; D_l are the descriptors of C_l, and E_l are the entity senses belonging to C_l. k, m and th are hyperparameters.

4. Experiments

4.1. Experimental Setup

We showcase the method presented here by applying it to two corpora in which named entities have been annotated. We use the first 120k tokens (including approx. 10k entities) from both the English and the German sections of the WikiNER data set [24]. While both of these corpora have been annotated for entities and their type, we ignore the specific type of each annotation/entity (except for the evaluation). In total, the German corpus contains 15,207 occurrences of 10,478 unique entities, and the English section contains 10,273 occurrences of 4,485 unique entities.

We choose the WikiNER dataset because class induction on it can be evaluated using the first method described above, using the original NER types as categories. To make evaluation by the second method possible, we link the annotated entities to Wikidata. Entity Linking (EL) was performed before executing class induction, in order to normalise the different surface forms that a putative entity can have. The linking was done using Entity Fishing[4], and resulted in a modest amount of normalisation, as shown in Table 1. One side effect of Entity Linking with modern tools is that senses are potentially disambiguated, but we observed this happening in only a small number of instances (see Table 1).

In the reported experiments, we use DistilBERT [28] as Language Model, using the HuggingFace implementation [34]. Our implementation is available online[5].

4.2. Evaluation Setup

Given a set of entities, finding the best assignment of them into classes is not a well-defined problem. In general, several of the criteria to consider when the assignment is made are independent of any corpus and are more related to the final task the categorization is

---

[4]https://github.com/kermitt2/entity-fishing/ visited on April 18, 2021.
[5]https://github.com/semantic-web-company/ptlm_wsid

to help solve. Since the candidate classes produced by the method presented here are not specific to any downstream task, we consider three different methods to evaluate their quality, all of which are also task-agnostic.

The first evaluation method is based on the manual NE annotations originating from the used corpora. The associated entity types are relatively coarse-grained, covering *Persons, Locations, Organizations*, and *Other*.

The second evaluation method compares the candidate classes derived from the corpus by out class induction approach with other large, task-agnostic and crowd-sourced ontologies, which are manually curated but not derived from any particular corpus. This comparison is made on two assumptions: (i) said pre-existing ontology represents the collective understanding of the entities' *meaning* which is consistent with that contained in almost any corpus, and (ii) the corpus which the method was executed on is a representative sample of a putative universal corpus that informs the creation and maintenance of the preexisting ontology. Such an ontology is the Wikidata class structure, as represented by predicates P:31 and P:279 (*instance of*, and *subclass of*, respectively).

The third evaluation method is purely a qualitative one, in which the candidate classes resulting from the method presented here are inspected and commented upon. This method, while not capable of giving any numerical measure, does take into account several sources of knowledge (as summarized in the background knowledge of the human commentator) and gives a more complete interpretation of the results.

The first and second methods both allow for a numerical value to be assigned to any set of candidate classes produced by the method presented here, or by any other producing groupings of entities. In order to aid the explanation of the computation of this value in these cases, in the following we refer to both Wikidata classes, and to NER types, as categories, and we assume that the entities present in the corpus can be linked to members of said categories (in the experiments performed, this assumption holds most of the time, as detailed in Table 1). The quality of the match is quantified using a well-known enrichment analysis method [19]. For every candidate class C and every possibly matching category K, *enrichment* is the probability of a randomly chosen candidate class of the same size as C to contain as many entities of K as C does. If we define $N(K,C)$ as the number of entities in candidate class C that also belong to category K, enrichment is computed using a binomial test according to:

$$P(K,C) = \sum_{k=N(K,C)}^{|C|} \binom{|C|}{k} P(K)^k (1 - P(K))^{|C|-k} \qquad (1)$$

where $P(K) = \frac{|K|}{|E|}$, and E is the set of all entities in the corpus. Since we compute such probability for several categories K, we account for multiple testing by using Bonferroni correction (i.e. dividing by the number of different categories K that contain at least one entity in common with C).

Using the resulting p-value, we can compute the percentage of candidate classes which are significantly enriched for a category of each of the knowledge sources. In brief, this number tells us how many of the classes suggested by our method are linked to entities contained in one of the categories of the knowledge source, compensating for the overall distribution of the entities in the corpus across the categories. We now present a parameter exploration evaluated using the first and second methods, as well as a quantitative analysis of the results with several combinations of parameters.

4.3. Quantitative Analysis

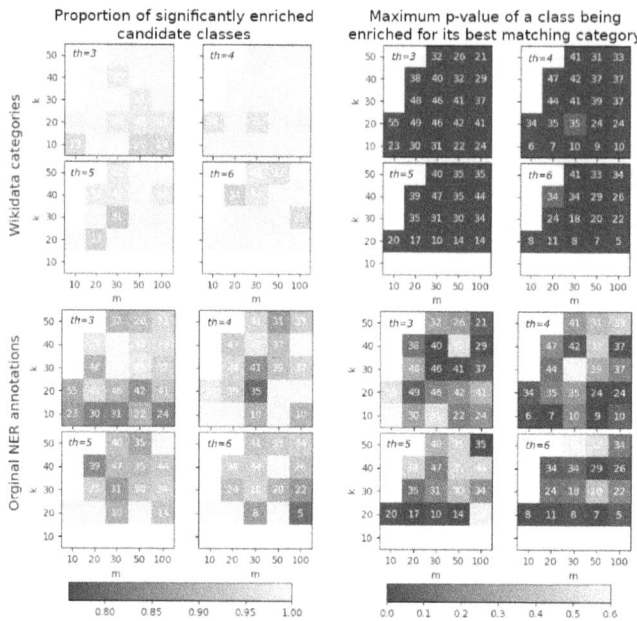

Figure 3. Quantitative evaluation of English candidate classes. Left shows the proportion of candidate classes which are significantly enriched (p-value < 0.05 according to Eq. 1 after Bonferroni correction) for at least one Wikidata category (top) or of the original NER types the dataset was annotated with (bottom); higher is better. Right shows the maximum p-value of this enrichment, lower is better. Shown in white is the number of candidate classes produced with each combination of parameters.

Using the first two evaluation methods presented earlier, we evaluate the behaviour of our method using different combinations of hyperparameters m, k and th. The number of senses produced in the second step of our method (factorisation of the first binary matrices) is dependent on m, but does not show much variance: for English we produce at most 45 polysemous entities with $m = 20$ and at least 33 with $m = 10$; for German – at most 30 polysemous entities with $m = 30$ and at least 23 with $m = 20$. Many polysemous entities only appear a few times and it is expected that our method will not induce different senses for such infrequent entities.

The results of the parameter exploration are shown in Figure 3 and Figure 4. For both the German and English corpus, most combinations of parameters lead to a good amount of candidate classes which are significantly enriched in Wikidata categories. For the English corpus, the candidate classes are not always fully contained within the original NER types, although at least 80% are, for all but two parameter combinations, see

Normalisation. Number of URIs with N entities					Disambiguation. Number of entities with N URIs				
N	**1**	**2**	**3**	**4**	**≥5**	**1**	**2**	**3**	**4**	**≥5**
English	3,972	320	40	10	13	4,099	306	37	6	1
German	9,566	397	55	23	12	10,111	286	7	0	1

Table 1. Normalisation and Disambiguation by linking to Wikidata.

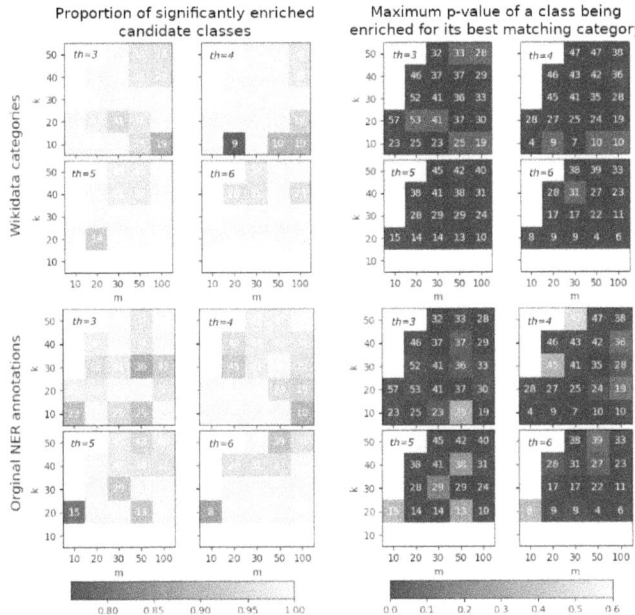

Figure 4. Quantitative evaluation of German candidate classes. Left shows the proportion of candidate classes which are significantly enriched for at least one Wikidata category (top) or of the original NER types the dataset was annotated with (bottom); higher is better. Right shows the maximum p-value of this enrichment, lower is better. Shown in white is the number of candidate classes produced with each combination of parameters.

Figure 3 lower left. It is worth noting that for most parameter combinations, even those candidate classes which are not significantly enriched for Wikidata categories are still close to statistically significant (p-value less than 0.1), see Figure 3 upper right. For the German corpus, both the Wikidata categories and the original NER types are significantly enriched in the candidate classes, see Figure 4 left.

The parameters m and k regulate the number of substitutes and sense descriptors, respectively. Therefore, by increasing these parameter values, we might expect better quality of sense and class descriptors. We do observe these effects in the quantitative analysis. However, with too high parameter values this effect gets smaller as the language model produces less relevant substitutes. Moreover, the computational time increases as the binary tables get larger. The other parameter th introduces a threshold on the minimum number of class descriptors. Thus, a larger th yields finer-grained classes.

The granularity of the classes can be assessed by inspecting the Wikidata categories for which they are enriched. When the threshold th is small, the most enriched-for categories are very wide. A close analysis of this can be seen in Figure 5. As the value of th increases, more of the candidate classes found are enriched on Wikidata categories which are smaller than the mean category size (for those categories whose entities are present in the corpus). These smaller categories are more specific, so that instead of a candidate class being enriched with, for example, $Human_{Q5}$, a class could be enriched with $Heads\ of\ state_{Q48352}$. Obtaining candidate classes of different levels of specificity is one of the strong points of the method presented here.

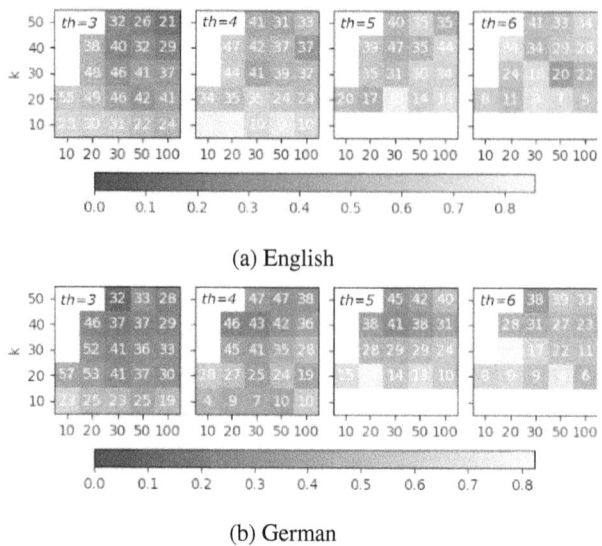

(a) English

(b) German

Figure 5. Proportion of candidate classes which are enriched with small Wikidata categories. We consider a Wikidata category to be small if the size of its intersection with the terms in the corpus is below the mean. For every combination of parameters k and m, the ratio of candidate classes which are enriched for such small categories is shown. The number of candidate classes is given in white.

4.4. Qualitative Analysis of Induced Classes

In order to gain a better understanding of the quality of the proposed approach, we manually checked the classes that resulted from the presented experiments when $m = 30$ and $k = 40$, as the quantitative results for these values showed stable high-quality outcomes over different settings. We investigated the results for $th = 3$ (see Examples 1 and 3) and $th = 6$ (see Examples 2 and 4) both in the English and German dataset.

EXAMPLE 1 (some English Candidate Classes *for m=30 k=40 th=3*)

<u>EN-6-th3</u> *Descriptors:* **Greek, Greece, Athens**
  Entities: sparta, bozcaada, cyprus, spitamenes, olympias, Aegean Sea, thessaloniki, athenian empire, . . .
<u>EN-8-th3</u> Descriptors: **Hercules, Jupiter, Prometheus, Zeus, Apollo**
  Entities: zeus, saturn, Athena, heracles, ajax, mt. olympus, 28 bellon . . .
<u>EN-11-th3</u> Descriptors: **film, Oscar, Film**
  Entities: william c. demille, 80th Academy Awards, the lady vanishes, sight & sound, douglas fairbanks, golden lion, Best Original Song, . . .
<u>EN-18-th3</u> Descriptors: **Macintosh, Home, iPhone, Apple**
  Entities: Macworld, apple lisa, apple usb modem, wireless keyboard, game boy color, apple, iphone 3g, magic mouse, . . .
<u>EN-22-th3</u> Descriptors: **Nadal, Masters, Davis, Wimbledon, Serena, Murray, set, Federer**
  Entities: michael stich, david wheaton, robby ginepri, patrick rafter, Federer, john mcenroe, arnaud clément, . . .
<u>EN-37-th3</u> Descriptors: **Mercury, Gemini, space, NASA**
  Entities: saturn v, vostok 6, apollo 13, Mercury, command/service module, sts-95, ufo, . . .

EXAMPLE 2 (some English Candidate Classes for *m=30 k=40 th=6*)

EN-9-th6 Descriptors: director, Newman, Oscar, film, Hollywood, Film

william c. demille, alfred hitchcock presents, jean vigo, robert bresson, laurence olivier, henry fonda, grace kelly, john ford, hitchcock, …

EN-11-th6 Descriptors: Switzerland, Germany, Europe, Poland, Austria, England

Entities: iceland, Germany, great britain, Holland, norway, estonia, sweden, Israel, …

EN-27-th6 Descriptors: Pluto, Mars, Orion, Galileo, Uranus, Titan, Jupiter, Apollo, Mercury

Entities: Mars, 2 Pallas, janus, 944 Hidalgo, 28 bellona, saturn, 37 fides, 52 europa, Phobos, near shoemaker…

EXAMPLE 3 (some German Candidate Classes for *m=30 k=40 th=3*)

DE-10-th3 Descriptors: Verein, Club, Fußball

Entities: fc bayern münchen, vfr aalen, tsv crailsheim, fc valencia, fußball-bundesliga der frauen, sc heerenveen, first vienna fc, asiens fußballer des jahres, saison 1977/78…

DE-30-th3 Descriptors: Militär, Reich, Volk

Entities: französische heer, kaiserlich russischen marine, nationalen widerstandsrates im iran, bayerische justizministerium, waffen-ss, nationalen volksarmee, heer, …

DE-31-th3 Descriptors: Eisenbahn, Strecke, Insel

Entities: turmbergbahn, u-bahn-linie u6, bahnstrecke braunschweig-magdeburg, brücke, pariser métro, b 173, mariazeller straße b20, themse, …

EXAMPLE 4 (some German Candidate Classes for *m=30 k=40 th=6*)

DE-8-th6 Descriptors: Bach, Donau, Rhein, Fluss, Saale, Elbe

Entities: mittellandkanal, seille, oder, omerbach, tauber, europäische hauptwasserscheide, …

DE-14-th6 Descriptors: Schule, Halle, Universitat, Akademie, Fakultät, Universität, Hochschule

Entities: technische universität chemnitz, universitätssternwarte wien, cambridge university, eth zürich, hochschule für musik detmold, …

DE-26-th6 Descriptors: Karlsruhe, Stuttgart, Baden, Tübingen, Heilbronn, Württemberg

Entities: stuttgart, baden-württemberg, cannstatt, heilbronn, ulm, alpirsbach, rottweil, konstanz, …

DE-28-th6 Descriptors: Anna, Katharina, Maria, Mathilde, Agnes, Helene

Entities: maria von beuthen, dorothea becker, zabel, beatrix von luxemburg, irina walentinowna moissejewa, anna friessnegg, …

DE-30-th6 Descriptors: Louis, Marie, François, Jean, Paul, Joseph

Entities: françois rude, charles-françois von velbrück, aurel emile joliat, auguste de montferrand, jean baptiste janssens, …

Overall, produced classes are of high quality, with only a very small number of classes where the assigned entities could not be semantically grouped in an obvious way. Furthermore, their semantic characteristics are quite diverse: One the one hand, classes covering sub-categories of locations were produced, such as countries (e.g, EN-11-th6[6]) and municipalities (e.g., DE-26-th6), as well as geographical entities such as rivers (DE-8-th6), and infrastructural elements such as railway tracks and streets (DE-31-th3). On the other hand, persons were subdivided due to their gender (e.g., DE-28-th6), profession (e.g., EN-9-th6), the origin of their name(DE-30-th6), or their membership to a specific group, such as Greek deities (EN-8-th3). Furthermore, classes of organisations (e.g., sports clubs DE-10-th3, armed forces DE-30-th3, or universities DE-14-th6) were produced. However, some classes also provided a wider view, e.g., EN-6-th3 combines Greece-related entities, both persons and locations. Also, very focused classes such as class EN-18-th3 (technology) and class EN-37-th3 (space) were identified.

The examples show that the specificity of different classes varies a lot (different entities that relate to Greece in EN-6-th3 compared to cities in a single German State in DE-26-th6). As seen in the quantitative analysis, the granularity of the classes is dependent

---

[6]We use the convention {LANGUAGE}-{CLASS NUMBER}-th{THRESHOLD}

on *th*, where higher values lead to more specific classes. While classes that already had a high degree of specificity with a lower threshold would remain quite stable with higher thresholds e.g., class EN-22-th3 about tennis stars is identical –both in terms of descriptors and entities– to EN-15-th6, increasing *th* in more coarse-grained classes can lead to the creation of sub-classes: $th = 3$ resulted in a class (EN-11-th3) about film awards, which includes different awards themselves (Golden Lion, Academy Award) as well as winning (or nominated) actors, directors, and movies. By increasing *th* to 6, EN-9-th6 is created, which only includes award-winning directors and actors. Another example in this regard is EN-8-th3, which includes Greek gods, but also celestial bodies named after them (Saturn::LOC, 28 Bellona). When increasing the threshold to 6, these two kinds of entities can be successfully separated (see EN-27-th6).

Taking a look at the produced descriptors, we see that for some classes, these descriptors come close to class names, scope of the class can be understood by reading the descriptors only, e.g., DE-14-th6 has the descriptors *School, Hall, University, Academy, Faculty* and summarises higher education facilities. However, for others, additional background knowledge is needed, in order to get an understanding of their content, e.g., to recognise the tennis stars theme in class EN-22-th3 with descriptors *Nadal, Masters, Davis, Wimbledon, Serena, Murray, set, Federer*. Even though the concrete granularity of a class can be only determined by taking a look at the entities, in almost all of the cases, the descriptors provided helpful insights into the class content.

For retrieving the additional background knowledge to understand the class content, it can be helpful to consider the best matching Wikidata category as it provides some useful insights for possible semantic connections between the entities. For example, while at first glance the descriptors *(Austria, Uzbekistan, Uganda, San Marino)* might only share the shallow relation of being countries, the common Wikidata link *Landlocked country*$_{Q123480}$ reveals a non-obvious, more specific connection. The same holds for DE-26-th6, where –for a non-expert– it might be difficult to see that all entities are towns located in the German state of Baden-Württemberg when not provided with the Wikidata link to *city district of Baden-Württemberg*$_{Q2327515}$. Still, in most cases, the best matching Wikidata category seems too broad to provide helpful insight (e.g., for almost all person-related classes, the category *Human*$_{Q5}$ or *Common Names*$_{Q502895}$ is provided), and sometimes it is even confusing (EN-11-th6 has the common broader *Legal science*$_{Q382995}$).

4.5. Benchmark and comparison to other methods

The work presented here produces sets of semantically coherent entities from an annotated corpus. This task is, in a wide sense, equivalent to the tasks solved by two different approaches: topic modeling (TM), and topic taxonomy induction (TTI). The former is well-known and has many different solutions, and the latter deals specifically with the construction of hierarchies and state of the art solutions make also use of embeddings. Both approaches make the additional assumption that the corpus is partitioned into documents, and derive from this partition information about the semantic relatedness of entities. In order to gauge the performance of our method, we compare to both approaches.

For TTI, the state of the art TaxoGen[35] method was used, as per the original author's implementation. For TM, a standard approach using count-based vectorisation followed by LDA, both using the Scikit-learn library, was performed, and an entity was deemed part of a topic by thresholding the resulting row-normalised term-topic matrix

Table 2. Comparison to other methods. We compare the best sets of topics produced by different methods according to three criteria. The best values are marked in **bold**. TTI stands for the TaxoGen implementation of Topic Taxonomy Induction, and TM for topic modelling.

Optimized for:	Enrichment with small Wikidata categories			Many classes enriched with Wikidata categories			Max. p-value of enrichments to Wikidata categories		
Method	our	TTI	TM	our	TTI	TM	our	TTI	TM
Number of candidate classes	7	5	36	14	17	12	26	19	10
Average candidate class size	15.7	10.0	88.0	16.4	10.0	390.5	80.8	10.0	461.2
Prop. enriched with small Wikidata categories (HIB)	0.86	**1.0**	0.75	0.71	**0.76**	0.0	0.27	**0.74**	0.0
Prop. significantly enriched (HIB)	**1.0**	**1.0**	0.83	**1.0**	**1.0**	**1.0**	**1.0**	**1.0**	**1.0**
Max. p-value of enrichment (LIB)	**4.5e-4**	5.5e-4	1.9e-3	3.7e-4	8.7e-5	**2.9e-16**	9.9e-9	2.9e-5	**5.4e-18**

with thresholds 0.01, 0.1, 0.2, and 0.5. In both cases, each document in the corpus was represented as a list of entities (as per the annotations), and the number of topics (clusters, in TTI) was varied from 5 to 50 in increments of two. For each criteria, the best decomposition by each method was selected, and basic statistics on topic size were computed (see Table 2). Comparison was done only for the English language corpus.

The results of the comparison (Table 2) show that TM tends to generate very large topics, which makes it an unfavorable choice when trying to find collections of entities with very specific similarities. Therefore, our method outperforms TM in finding groups of entities matching small Wikidata categories, while TM yields very good p-values for enrichment. In contrast, both our method and TaxoGen lead to smaller classes (clusters), which are also very good matches to Wikidata categories. Our method achieves results comparable to the state-of-the-art, while neither requiring specific re-training of embeddings, nor assuming the corpus to be partitioned into documents.

Our method more often produces more classes that are better populated with entities than the results of TaxoGen. In the second column of Table 2, though our method outputs only 14 candidate classes as opposed to 17 by TaxoGen, the coverage of original entities is 35% higher than by TaxoGen because our candidate classes on average have 64% more entities. In other columns the difference is even larger. Therefore, the method presented here covers the given entities better and produces a more complete classification. This feature is specifically important when working with small corpora or with corpora with little annotations.

5. Conclusions

We present a method to automatically induce classes from an entity-annotated corpus. Our method exploits the ability of modern language models to predict lexical substitutes for a target in a given context, to tackle potential polysemy of the annotated entities to induce senses of the annotations on the fly. The generated entity senses are grouped into coherent classes with human-interpretable class descriptors. Importantly, our method requires no additional supervision, can work with annotations coming from different kinds of tools, and does not require the partitioning of input corpus into documents.

With different parameter combinations, this method allows for classes to represent differently grained classifications of entities. This allows, for example, recognizing particular entities as belonging to the coarse topic of *persons* and, with a different combination of parameters, as belonging to more fine-grained subclasses of people, such as *Presidents of the United States*, or *19th century painters*. Generalizations of our method are capable of extracting hierarchies of classes.

We evaluate our method on large general-purpose corpora in two languages. Quantitative and qualitative evaluations show our method's ability to induce a set of classes that is in agreement with external classification schemes in Wikidata. The quality of the results from our method is comparable to one of the state of the art methods (TaxoGen), however our method covers the original annotations better and yields more a complete classification of the original entities.

Our method is also applicable to small domain-specific corpora, since the usage of pre-trained language models on short contexts (as opposed to documents for other methods) allows for capturing the contextual semantics of previously unseen domain-specific words. Additionally a good coverage of the original entities in the output classification makes efficient use of smaller quantities of input data.

References

[1] Al-Aswadi, F.N., Yong, C.H., Gan, K.H.: Automatic ontology construction from text: a review from shallow to deep learning trend. Artif. Intell. Rev. **53**(6), 3901–3928 (2020)

[2] Albukhitan, S., Helmy, T., Alnazer, A.: Arabic ontology learning using deep learning. In: Proceedings of the International Conference on Web Intelligence. p. 1138–1142. WI '17, Association for Computing Machinery, New York, NY, USA (2017)

[3] Amrami, A., Goldberg, Y.: Word Sense Induction with Neural biLM and Symmetric Patterns. In: Proceedings of EMNLP 2018. pp. 4860–4867. Brussels (2018)

[4] Asim, M.N., Wasim, M., Khan, M.U.G., Mahmood, W., Abbasi, H.M.: A survey of ontology learning techniques and applications. Database **2018** (2018)

[5] Belohlavek, R., Vychodil, V.: Discovery of optimal factors in binary data via a novel method of matrix decomposition. Journal of Computer and System Sciences **76**(1), 3 – 20 (2010)

[6] Beltagy, I., Lo, K., Cohan, A.: Scibert: A pretrained language model for scientific text. In: Proceedings of the 2019 Conference on Empirical Methods in Natural Language Processing and the 9th International Joint Conference on Natural Language Processing (EMNLP-IJCNLP). pp. 3606–3611 (2019)

[7] Browarnik, A., Maimon, O.: Ontology learning from text: Why the ontology learning layer cake is not viable. Int. J. Signs Semiot. Syst. **4**(2), 1–14 (2015)

[8] Buitelaar, P., Cimiano, P., Magnini, B.: Ontology learning from text: An overview (2005)

[9] Casteleiro, M.A., Prieto, M.J.F., Demetriou, G., Maroto, N., Read, W.J., Maseda-Fernandez, D., Des Diz, J.J., Nenadic, G., Keane, J.A., Stevens, R.: Ontology learning with deep learning: a case study on patient safety using pubmed. In: SWAT4LS (2016)

[10] Chen, C., Lin, K., Klein, D.: Inducing Taxonomic Knowledge from Pretrained Transformers. arXiv preprint arXiv:2010.12813 (2020)

[11] Cimiano, P., Hotho, A., Staab, S.: Learning concept hierarchies from text corpora using formal concept analysis. J. Artif. Intell. Res. **24**, 305–339 (2005)

[12] Devlin, J., Chang, M.W., Lee, K., Toutanova, K.: Bert: Pre-training of deep bidirectional transformers for language understanding (2018)

[13] Drymonas, E., Zervanou, K., Petrakis, E.G.M.: Unsupervised ontology acquisition from plain texts: The ontogain system. In: NLDB (2010)

[14] Geng, Y., Chen, J., Zhuang, X., Chen, Z., Pan, J.Z., Li, J., Yuan, Z., Chen, H.: Benchmarking Knowledge-driven Zero-shot Learning. arXiv e-prints arXiv:2106.15047 (Jun 2021)

[15] Huang, K., Altosaar, J., Ranganath, R.: Clinicalbert: Modeling clinical notes and predicting hospital readmission. arXiv preprint arXiv:1904.05342 (2019)

[16] Khadir, A.C., Aliane, H., Guessoum, A.: Ontology learning: Grand tour and challenges. Comput. Sci. Rev. **39**, 100339 (2021)

[17] Lee, J., Yoon, W., Kim, S., Kim, D., Kim, S., So, C.H., Kang, J.: Biobert: a pre-trained biomedical language representation model for biomedical text mining. Bioinformatics **36**(4), 1234–1240 (2020)
[18] Liu, H., Perl, Y., Geller, J.: Concept placement using BERT trained by transforming and summarizing biomedical ontology structure. Journal of Biomedical Informatics **112** (Dec 2020)
[19] Mi, H., Muruganujan, A., Casagrande, J.T., Thomas, P.D.: Large-scale gene function analysis with the PANTHER classification system. Nature protocols **8**(8), 1551–1566 (2013)
[20] Michael, J., Botha, J.A., Tenney, I.: Asking without Telling: Exploring Latent Ontologies in Contextual Representations. In: Proceedings of the 2020 Conference on Empirical Methods in Natural Language Processing (EMNLP). pp. 6792–6812. Association for Computational Linguistics, Online (Nov 2020)
[21] Mikolov, T., Sutskever, I., Chen, K., Corrado, G.S., Dean, J.: Distributed representations of words and phrases and their compositionality. In: Burges, C.J.C., Bottou, L., Welling, M., Ghahramani, Z., Weinberger, K.Q. (eds.) Advances in Neural Information Processing Systems 26, pp. 3111–3119. Curran Associates, Inc. (2013)
[22] Nikishina, I., Logacheva, V., Panchenko, A., Loukachevitch, N.V.: RUSSE'2020: Findings of the First Taxonomy Enrichment Task for the Russian language. CoRR **abs/2005.11176** (2020)
[23] Nivre, J.: Incrementality in deterministic dependency parsing. In: Proceedings of the Workshop on Incremental Parsing: Bringing Engineering and Cognition Together. pp. 50–57. Association for Computational Linguistics, Barcelona, Spain (Jul 2004)
[24] Nothman, J., Ringland, N., Radford, W., Murphy, T., Curran, J.R.: Learning Multilingual Named Entity Recognition from Wikipedia. Artif. Intell. **194**, 151–175 (Jan 2013)
[25] Peters, M.E., Neumann, M., Iyyer, M., Gardner, M., Clark, C., Lee, K., Zettlemoyer, L.: Deep contextualized word representations. arXiv preprint arXiv:1802.05365 (2018)
[26] Radford, A., Narasimhan, K., Salimans, T., Sutskever, I.: Improving language understanding by generative pre-training. URL https://s3-us-west-2. amazonaws. com/openai-assets/researchcovers/languageunsupervised/language understanding paper. pdf (2018)
[27] Revenko, A., Breit, A., Mireles, V., Moreno-Schneider, J., Sageder, C., Karampatakis, S.: Annotating entities with fine-grained types in austrian court decisions. In: Further with Knowledge Graphs, pp. 139–153. IOS Press (2021)
[28] Sanh, V., Debut, L., Chaumond, J., Wolf, T.: DistilBERT, a distilled version of BERT: smaller, faster, cheaper and lighter (2019)
[29] Shamsfard, M., Barforoush, A.A.: Learning ontologies from natural language texts. Int. J. Hum. Comput. Stud. **60**, 17–63 (2004)
[30] Shang, J., Zhang, X., Liu, L., Li, S., Han, J.: Nettaxo: Automated topic taxonomy construction from text-rich network. In: Proceedings of The Web Conference 2020. pp. 1908–1919 (2020)
[31] Sousa, D., Couto, F.M.: BiOnt: Deep Learning Using Multiple Biomedical Ontologies for Relation Extraction. In: Jose, J.M., Yilmaz, E., Magalhães, J., Castells, P., Ferro, N., Silva, M.J., Martins, F. (eds.) Advances in Information Retrieval. pp. 367–374. Springer International Publishing, Cham (2020)
[32] Vayansky, I., Kumar, S.A.: A review of topic modeling methods. Information Systems **94**, 101582 (2020)
[33] Vedula, N., Nicholson, P.K., Ajwani, D., Dutta, S., Sala, A., Parthasarathy, S.: Enriching taxonomies with functional domain knowledge. In: The 41st International ACM SIGIR Conference on Research & Development in Information Retrieval. p. 745–754. SIGIR '18, Association for Computing Machinery, New York, NY, USA (2018)
[34] Wolf, T., Debut, L., Sanh, V., Chaumond, J., Delangue, C., Moi, A., Cistac, P., Rault, T., Louf, R., Funtowicz, M., Brew, J.: HuggingFace's Transformers: State-of-the-art Natural Language Processing. CoRR **abs/1910.03771** (2019)
[35] Zhang, C., Tao, F., Chen, X., Shen, J., Jiang, M., Sadler, B., Vanni, M., Han, J.: TaxoGen: Unsupervised Topic Taxonomy Construction by Adaptive Term Embedding and Clustering. In: Proceedings of the 24th ACM SIGKDD. p. 2701–2709. KDD '18, Association for Computing Machinery, New York, NY, USA (2018)

Towards a Knowledge-Aware AI
A. Dimou et al. (Eds.)
© *2022 The Authors.*
This article is published online with Open Access by IOS Press and distributed under the terms
of the Creative Commons Attribution License 4.0 (CC BY 4.0).
doi:10.3233/SSW220019

Metadata Based Contextual Summarizer for Technical Conversations in Public Forums

Gyan Ranjan [a], Abinaya Govindan [b] and Amit Verma [c]

[a] *Neuron7.ai, Bangalore, India*
[b] *Neuron7.ai, Bangalore, India*
[c] *Neuron7.ai, California*

Abstract. In recent years, the task of sequence to sequence based neural abstractive summarization has gained a lot of attention. Many novel strategies have been used to improve the saliency, human readability, and consistency of these models, resulting in high-quality summaries. However, because the majority of these pretrained models were trained on news datasets, they contain an inherent bias. One such bias is that most of these generated summaries originate from the start or end of the text, much like a news story might be summarised. Another issue we encountered while using these summarizers in our Technical discussion forums usecase was token recurrence, which resulted in lower ROUGE-precision scores. To overcome these issues, we present a unique approach that includes: a) An additional parameter to the loss function based on ROUGE-precision score that is optimised alongside categorical cross entropy loss. b) An adaptive loss function based on token repetition rate which is optimized along with the final loss so that the model may provide contextual summaries with less token repetition and successfully learn with the least training samples. c) To effectively contextualize this summarizer for technical forum discussion platforms, we added extra metadata indicator tokens to aid the model in learning latent features and dependencies in text segments with relevant metadata information. To avoid overfitting due to data scarcity, we test and verify all models on a hold-out dataset that was not part of the training or validation dataset. This paper discusses the various strategies we used and compares the performance of fine tuned models against baseline summarizers n the test dataset. By end-to-end training our models with these losses, we acquire substantially better ROUGE scores while being the most legible and relevant summary on the Technical forum dataset.

Keywords.
natural language processing, abstractive summarization, sequence-to-sequence models, multiple loss optimization, rouge-based learning, information systems

1. Introduction

With the massive increase in available information due to the growth of the Internet, meaningful data consumption has always been a difficult endeavour. The tremendous growth in the quantity of blogs, articles, research papers, and reports is particularly combustible. Due to the abundance of data, extensive study into various summarising techniques - both abstractive and extractive - has been conducted. According to Radef et al. [3], a summary is "a text that is constructed from one or more texts, contains crucial information in the original text(s), and is no longer than half of the original text(s) and frequently, substantially less than that." Having such contextual brief summaries can help people grasp material better, which can lead to more efficient text processing and comprehension. A summary might be extractive or abstractive in nature. The summary is simply a reduced version of the text by picking important sentences, segments, and paragraphs from the original text block. Abstractive summarising techniques rely on the semantic knowledge of the text to provide semantically coherent, factually and logically valid summaries.

At Neuron7.ai we're building a Service Intelligence platform that, when presented with information about defective hardware, suggests actions and offers actionable insights to the end user. It is critical for us to be able to deliver as many relevant insights as possible during this process of enabling clients to draw meaningful insights from device malfunction logs and repair notes. To accomplish so, we employ technical data sources found in every organization's ecosystem, such as product manuals, knowledge articles, and internal technical forums. Our application allows users to interact with the system and ask questions about any technical problem they are having, and it then recommends appropriate course correction procedures based on the knowledge gained from the technical documents. The user query often has multiple dimensions, including information on device types, recurrence history, efforts done to resolve the issue to date, and any additional parameters that they believe might help us deliver a better solution. When these parameters are treated as a whole, they can cause highly particular issues, which can add to the model's confusion rather than help it better its outcomes. As a result, we require a sophisticated and domain-specific summariser capable of making sense of such technical data and condensing it into a format that can be consumed by downstream natural language processes.

We begin by establishing a baseline performance using current state-of-the-art summarizers. From the experiments using these out-of-the-box models, we faced the following issues -

- The input query's technical terminology and words frequently lacked grammatical structure and were frequently found in the generated summaries in inappropriate circumstances.
- We noticed a lot of token duplication and repetition in the generated summary, which is a frequent problem with many natural language generation tasks.
- Because of the structure of the dataset on which these models were trained, the majority of the produced summaries came from the beginning or conclusion of the text. This presumption is false in our technical discussion forums, as participants frequently express their problems in no particular sequence.

To solve the above issues, we designed and developed a system which

- **Pre-processing stage** - Because the summarizer's main purpose is to feed our Technical forum Search with summarised user queries (Heterogeneous QA framework in Govindan et al. [2]), the first stage of the pre-processor included custom modules to clean technical phrases that don't add value to the context of the question.

- **Hierarchical metadata extractor** - The metadata extractor, which is used to extract hierarchical metadata using an unsupervised named entity recognizer as proposed by Govindan et al, [20], is the second portion of the pre-processor.
- **Modeling stage** - To help the framework perform well in the Technical forum domain, we included two new loss parameters: the ROUGE precision-based loss function and the token repetition rate-based loss function, which are learnt in addition to the category cross entropy loss to provide short and targeted summaries.
- **Post-processing stage** - Because we utilise the produced summaries in the Technical Search forum ([2]), we execute a few post-processing processes to assist us give the best search results and suggestions to users.

This paper investigates and compares the proposed approach with various summarising approaches and evaluates performance criteria such as ROUGE-precision, recall, and F1 to assess the quality of the generated summaries. We also use other metrics to assess the length and quality of summaries, such as token average lengths and lengths at different percentiles, to choose the optimum model.

2. Related work

Many methods for extracting summaries from text have been proposed, according to Moratanch et al. [4], using a range of weighting mechanisms such as content, word, and sentence level features in various graph based, fuzzy logic, and Latent semantic analysis based techniques. Recent transformer-based advancements, like as BERT, have led to strategies like leveraging BERT embeddings in combination with clustering algorithms to create extractive summaries, as proposed by Biswas et al. [14].

Sequence to sequence based models have been successfully deployed in applications including neural machine translation, headline generation, and text summarization in recent years. The majority of these models may provide abstractive summaries using just appropriate neural network models like recurrent neural networks RNNS, long short term memory LSTMs (Sepp et al. [6]), or gated recurrent units GRUs. These models are based on the encoder-decoder architecture (Sutskever et al. [10]), in which the encoder accepts an input sequence of words and the decoder emits an output sequence of tokens that make up the resulting summary. These networks are often trained on a large corpus of training text-summary pairs, learning to generate summaries of incoming text as a result.

Another state-of-the-art model is a hybrid pointer-generator network that combines pointing and coverage metrics to replicate words from the source text. These enhancements result in accurate information replication while the generator continues to generate fresh words. Due to the coverage metric [9], these summaries had a lower word repetition rate. Other techniques, such as [7], employ attentional transformers to construct summaries that capture sentence-to-word hierarchy to achieve best-in-class performance in abstractive text summarization.

Basic seq2seq models may be enhanced further by incorporating an attention mechanism (Bahdanau et al. [1]), resulting in attention-based encoder decoder models being a standard architecture for all sequence to sequence tasks, particularly text summarization (Lin et al. [11]). The attention mechanism seeks to "attend" to the most significant words in the sequence, resulting in the most meaningful summaries based on the order of most

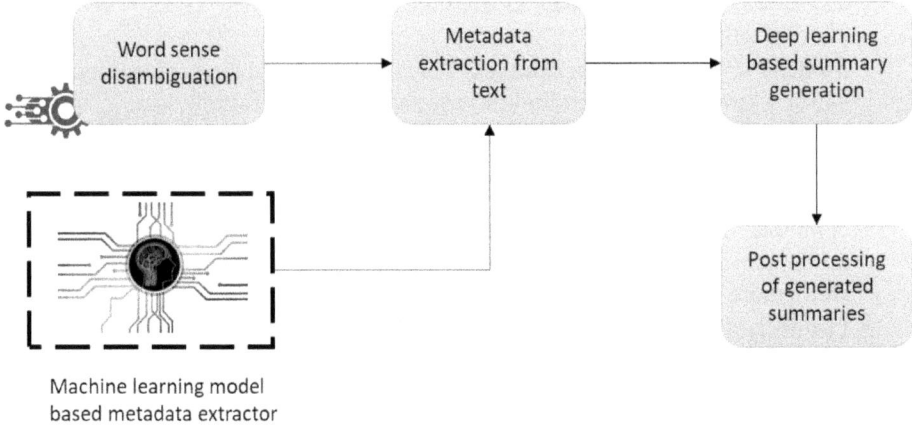

Machine learning model
based metadata extractor

Figure 1. Detailed overview of proposed workflow

important words in the text. This is accomplished by learning and feeding a context vector that quantifies the value of each token in the sequence to the decoder when constructing the summaries. You et al. [13] presented a transformer-based encoder-decoder architecture with an encoder-integrated focus-attention mechanism and a separate saliency-
selection network that regulates the information flow from encoder to decoder. To predict
generalised and resilient summaries, Kouris et al. [8] uses a coping and coverage strategy
in encoder-decoder based models, as well as reinforcement learning.

As previously said, the bulk of these models are trained using publicly available
datasets such as news datasets, which have a clear grammatical framework and a consistent structure across several news sources. These models, on the other hand, ignore the
technical character of inquiries for technical forums, as well as the repetitive structure
of the resulting summary. As a result, this research focuses on using current methodologies for the technical forum domain by integrating technical metadata during the data
preparation stage and loss functions that can tackle token repetition difficulties during the
modelling stage. The suggested framework's core component is a sequence-to-sequence
deep learning neural network, which is helped by a metadata-based technique, as detailed
below.

3. Our Work

The overall framework is illustrated in 1. The input to the framework consists of single
document text, along with a few metadata information, while the output is a human-
readable summary. The various sections that comprised the framework are :

- **Pre-processor** - The pre-processor module performs a few custom steps to handle the technical nature of the dataset - in terms of cleaning unwanted tokens to
  improve quality of input text
- **Hierarchical metadata extractor** - The hierarchical metadata extractor has been
  trained to extract metadata information at two levels and add it to metadata input

text in order enable the model to learn metadata-based latent features in the data more effectively.

- **Modeler** - We included an extra loss function based on the token repetition rate, which was optimized in addition to the category cross entropy loss, to increase the quality of the output summaries. The model was able to create summaries with a lower token repetition rate attributed to this function. We also introduced an extra loss function derived from the Rouge-precision score was introduced and optimised. Since this loss is predicated on precision, extraneous tokens that appear in summaries along with the correct tokens, are penalised, allowing the model to create more focused summaries.

- **Postprocesser** - Since we use the generated summary as a user query in downstream Technical Forum Search [2], we execute a few post-processing processes such as reinforcing segment which has metadata, adding PII information to guarantee that the created summaries have all the required data to deliver the best query results and suggestions to the end user.

3.1. Data Pre-processor

We created a comprehensive pre-processor with numerous modules, as below:

3.1.1. Technical data cleaner

The data source for our usecase came from Slack-like technical forums, necessitating the deployment of the following bespoke data cleansing modules:

- To extract and eliminate URLs that led to resolutions attempted by the user or other associated information, we employed regular expression-based processors.
- Image processors that detect and remove screenshots of user errors from the query text
- Using the Python library spacy [12], we used out-of-the-box named entity recognizers to extract named entity types like PERSON. Because they don't provide any useful information to the user inquiry, these named entities were eliminated from the input text.
- Motivated by the work of Kouris et al. [8], we use a word sense disambiguator to provide additional meaning to ambiguous statements. For words that are too specialised to the issue, the disambiguator provides further information to the user question. *SLA*, *VDI* and *VNC* are examples of acronyms used in the technical sector that have no relevance to the model until more information is provided. We extract acronyms using word parsers and thoroughly evaluate the most essential ones with business stakeholders. We established a word taxonomy and dictionaries, which are then fed into the preprocessor to provide extra context for the words.

3.2. Hierarchical metadata extractor

The technical nature of the data is the key reason why typical summarizers fail to perform adequately in our scenario. We intended to create a system that could recognise metadata related information in the data to assist the model in making sense of such noisy data. One common observation in this data is The intent is that when a section of text, such as a phrase, has information related to metadata associated with it, that sentence frequently includes useful information that should be kept in the summary. For example, if a user has a problem with their *VDI*, the query might include information such as the time when it stopped operating, the methods taken to resolve the problem, and so on.However, if one were to find the most important pieces of this query, the sentence that includes *VDI* relevant information should be the first place to search. We picked a few entity types that would make the most sense for the domain we want to target. However, technical forum data frequently contained two levels of metadata - for example, a a *mobile* can be the first level, and additional particular information such as *android* or *ios*, if available in the text, can assist provide more depth to the suggested resolution. As a result, the named entity recognizer needed to save hierarchical information and be able to deliver metadata at both levels.

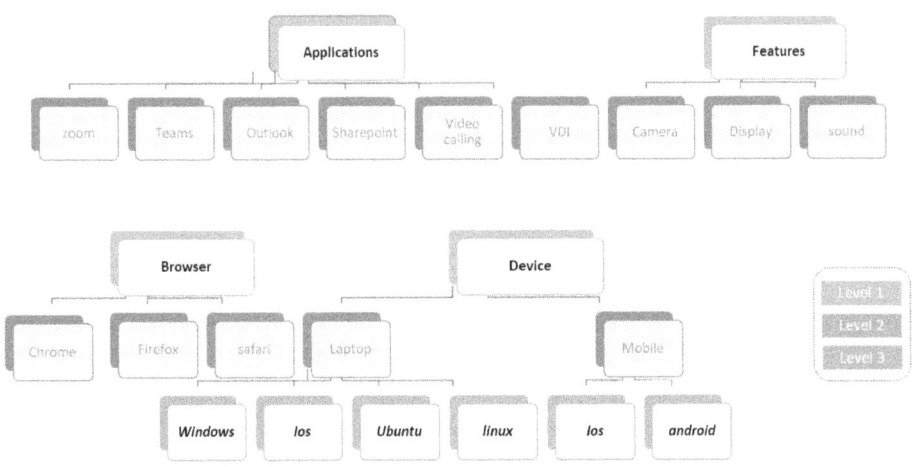

Figure 2. Sample hierarchical structure of metadata extracted

3.2.1. Heuristic metadata extractor

As seen in 3, the final metadata extractor is a combination of heuristic models and semi-supervised named entity extractors. Heuristic engines can handle metadata kinds that are rather straightforward. These metadata categories included things like *browser* and others that had extremely restricted values and all of these exhaustive values were already pre-defined and made accessible, either as a result of domain intelligence obtained before or as a result of business definition.

3.2.2. Semi-supervised named entity extractor

Semi-supervised named entity extractors were used to extract metadata types with more complex values and various variants and values. We intended to use a semi-supervised data formulation method to annotate and train the entity recognizers, as proposed in Govindan et al, [20]. We employed a two-level classification to manage the data hierarchy: one model predicted the Level-1 of metadata type, and this entity label, along with the text, was used to train the second level of entity recognizer. In 4, the whole NER training mechanism is described. There are two main modules in the system.

- The Level 1 entity recognizer is the initial component of the trainer, and it uses transformer-based named entity recognizers to identify the first level kind of information. We won't go into depth about this model because it's already been covered in Govindan et al, [20]
- The second component of the trainer consists of a Level 2 named entity recognizer that was trained using the Level 1 labels, as well as text that is used to predict the Level 2 entity kinds. For each of the level 1 types, additional tokens that are not part of the current vocabulary are defined, and these tokens are appended before the relevant entity token in the text and supplied as input to the model.
- Negative examples containing only Level 1 types, such as *My mobile does not work*, are also used to train the model so that it can recognise when the second level of metadata is missing in the text.

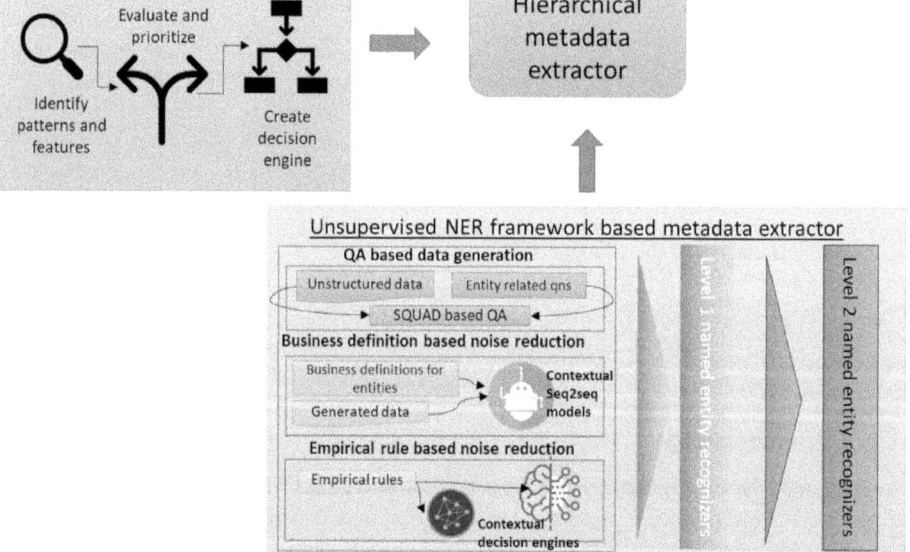

Figure 3. Hierarchical metadata extractor

We identify the highest level of entity type contained in each phrase once our models have been fine-tuned to recognise Level 1 and 2 entity types. We return Level 1 type if a phrase contains Level 1 entity type. Level 2 entity type is returned if the text has granular Level 2 type. This entity type indicator token was previously defined and added to the transformer's tokenizer's vocabulary before being inserted before each phrase in the text. As mentioned below, this content is used as input text, and the summary is used as a target for the decoder to learn.

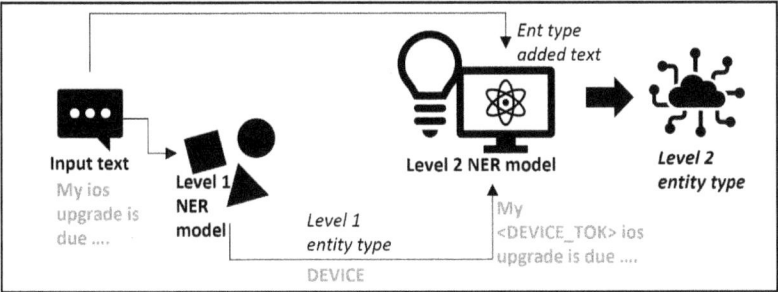

Figure 4. Hierarchical metadata extractor

3.3. Modeler

A deep sequence to sequence model based on Transformer encoders and decoders is used to generate the summary. This model, in more formal terms, predicts the output sequence of summary tokens as defined as :

$$Y' = (y_1', y_2', y_3', .., y_m')$$

given an input sequence of tokens

$$X = (x_1, x_2, ..x_n)$$

We have built our proposed approach on Transformer based architecture such as DistilBert and T5 since transformer-based models (proposed by Vaswani et al. [17] , Zhang et al. [18] and Song et al. [19]) have been highly popular for numerous natural language processing problems. Refer to 5 to see the suggested model architecture. The modeller goes through several stages:

3.3.1. Input layer

We fragment the input into phrases or logical blocks to feed it to the transformer encoder-decoder (specific to use cases). We next determine if each of the segments has metadata-related information, and if so, we keep the metadata name as well as the granularity level (Level 1 or Level 2). We extract the matching token identification from the metadata classes and append the token to the beginning of each segment. Label encoded values make up the metadata classes. The following structure is now supplied as input to the model:

$$\text{Input} : X = (x_1, x_2, x_3 .... x_n)$$

$$\text{Metadata extracted} : M = (m_1, m_{11}, .., m_n)$$

where m_1 signifies the first Level 1 metadata and

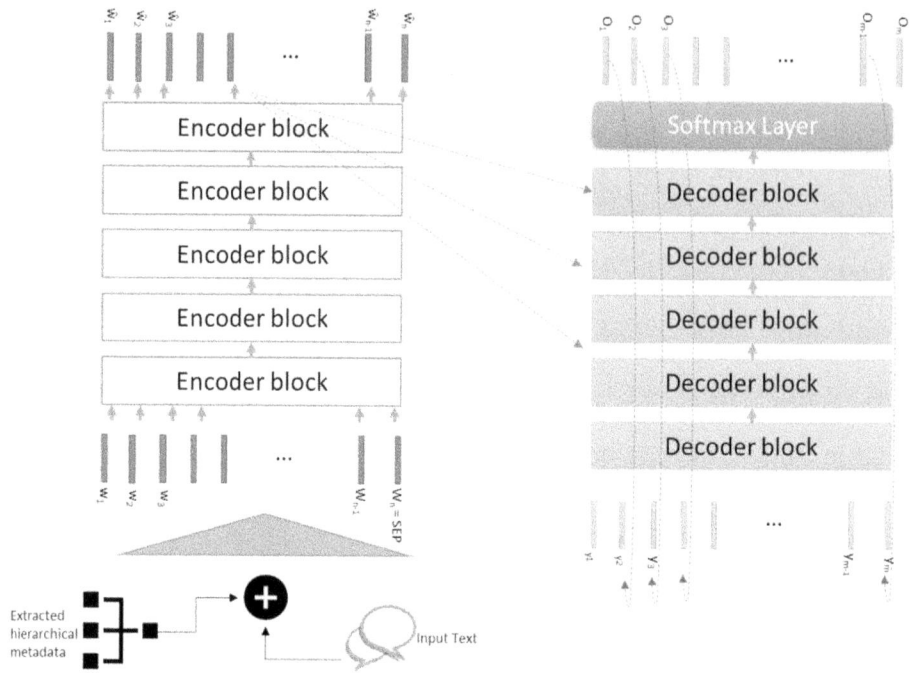

Figure 5. Proposed model architecture

m_{11} corresponds to 1st sub entity in 1st entity class.

Final metadata infused input : $X(M) = (m_1 x_1, m_n x_n)$

3.3.2. Pretrained transformer model

The various variants of the model that we tried are :

DistilBert based trainer.   We fine-tuned our summarizer based on DistilBert since we wanted the model to be computationally cheap.

Distilled T5 based trainer.   The difficulty of deploying very deep neural network models is especially pertinent for edge devices with limited memory and processing power. To address this issue, Hinton et al. [21] created a model compression strategy to transfer information from a large model into training a smaller model with no substantial performance loss. We used teacher-student training, in which the learner strives to imitate the instructor model and leverage the information to reach similar, if not superior, accuracy. On a t5-base (Raffel et al. ([22])) pretrained model, we attempted knowledge distillation, and the distiled t5-base model was then utilised to fine tune our summarizer.

T5-based trainer.   The third variant was based on t5-small proposed by Raffel et al. [22]. We fine-tuned the model's weights using the pre-trained weights from t5-small.

The weights of these models were fine-tuned for our dataset for all of the aforementioned model variants.

3.3.3. Loss functions

In the proposed system, we defined the following losses :

Cross entropy loss.   One of the loss functions we use is the classic cross entropy loss which is defined as

$$Loss_{CE}(y,\hat{y}) = -\sum_{i=1}^{N_c} y_i \log(\hat{y}_i) \tag{1}$$

where $y \in \mathbb{R}^{|V|}$ is a one-hot label vector and N_c is the number of classes.

ROUGE based loss.   This innovative loss function was developed to decrease the amount of wrong tokens and token repetition in the generated summary, which is a prevalent problem in natural language production. The loss function is created as follows:

$$Precision = TP/(TP+FP)$$
$$\hat{Precision} = min(Precision, 100) \tag{2}$$
$$Loss_{PRE} = 1/\hat{Precision}$$

Repetition rate based loss.   The repetition rate based loss has been designed to identify and promote the number of unique tokens in the resulting summary. This is calculated using the total number of tokens in the summary and the number of unique tokens in the summary.

$$Loss_{Rep} = n(\hat{A})/n(A)$$
$$\text{where } \hat{A} = set(A) \text{ and} \tag{3}$$

A is number of tokens in generated summary

During the training phase, all of these losses are trained and optimised as individual functions. We didn't aggregate these individual losses to produce an ensembled or single loss since we didn't want any of the loss values to dominate the final loss. Individual training guarantees that each function contributes evenly to the overall loss function.

3.4. Postprocesor of generated summaries

3.4.1. PII extractor

We have observed that Technical forum user queries often include information personal to the user such as device type, username, location, and team names. We extract all of these personal identification identifiers using PII parsers and add these parameters as a JSON which is then passed to the downstream Technical Forum Search platform for better user recommendations.

4. Performance evaluation and Inference

4.1. Parameter settings

We employed 256 and 512 word embeddings and hidden states (of encoder and decoder) in all of our tests since we fine-tuned utilising BERT/t5 based models. The weights of the transformer encoder and decoder were also learnt throughout the training. For stochastic optimization, Adam (Kingma et al. [15]) was employed with the hyperparameters $beta1=$ 0.9 and $beta2$=0.999. We utilised a 5e-5 learning rate and a mini batch of 4. Due to the fact that ROUGE-precision loss employs the inverse of ROUGE precision score, very low precision scores result in an extremely high value, hence leading to poor learning by the model. To circumvent this, we set a threshold defined by heuristics for the ROUGE loss. All of the models were trained for a total of 20 epochs. We executed a train-test split of the training dataset, and at the end of each epoch, we evaluated the ROUGE score on the validation set. The input text had a maximum sequence length of 512 characters, and the target summary length was 32, with any longer summaries being truncated. This length was chosen after considering a number of parameters, including the length that allows for the optimal performance in indexed searches and downstream question answering tasks. By comparing the final training and validation losses of multiple fine-tuned models, the influence of ROUGE and token repetition rate based losses is first investigated. In 6, the training and validation loss for models fine-tuned based on distilbert, distiled t5-base, and recommended framework based on t5-small are presented.

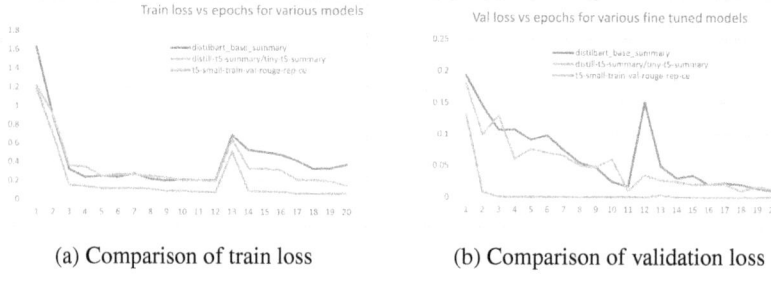

(a) Comparison of train loss   (b) Comparison of validation loss

Figure 6. Comparison of train and validation loss during fine tuning of various models

4.2. Evaluation metrics

In our test experiments, we validated the baseline models (Wolf et al. [5] huggingface's distilbert-based summarizer) performance on our dataset. To compare the models' performance, the following variables were used:

(A) **Evaluation at runtime** In 7, we use the average run time of summary generation as a first assessment criterion. This is an important statistic for our use case since real-world practical systems must answer in near-real-time, because the user expects a definitive response from the system as soon as he enters his query.

(B) **Succinctness of summary assessment** We evaluate token lengths at various percentiles to determine the model that can provide summaries that are the most comparable to the predicted summaries to assess the quality of summaries in terms of redundant information and additional tokens mentioned.

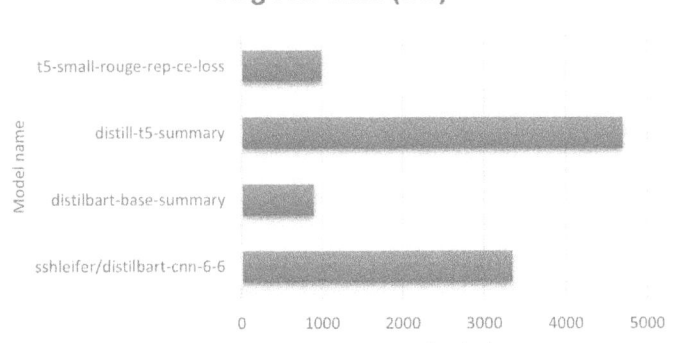

Figure 7. Comparison of runtime for different models

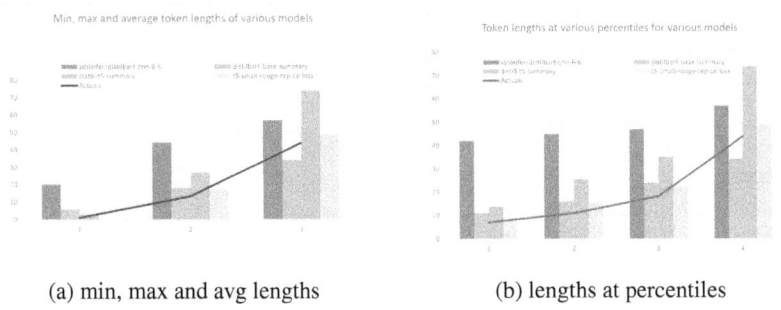

(a) min, max and avg lengths   (b) lengths at percentiles

Figure 8. Comparison of generated summary lengths at various percentiles for different models

(C) **Lexical similarity evaluation** ROUGE scores, or Recall-Oriented Understudy for Gisting Evaluation, were first introduced by Chin et al. [16] and have since become standard metrics for evaluating various text summarization algorithms. To test the quality of summarization, they quantify the number of overlapping units (i.e., n-grams, word sequences, and word pairs) between machine-generated and golden-standard (human-written) summaries. ROUGE-1 (unigram), ROUGE-2 (bigram), and ROUGE-L are the most commonly utilised ROUGE measures for single-document abstractive summarization (longest common subsequence). The pyrouge package, which gives accuracy, recall, and F-score for these metrics, is used to evaluate several models in this article. On our hold-out dataset, we use ROUGE-L scores to evaluate the models' overall lexical performance. As seen in 1, the system proposed surpasses baseline and other finetuned models by a significant margin. We compare our findings to those of other fine-tuned models to demonstrate that fine-tuning any out-of-the-box model may not always produce the best results, especially if training data is scarce.

Model name	Rouge1			Rouge2			RougeL		
	Precision	recall	fmeasure	Precision	recall	fmeasure	Precision	recall	fmeasure
sshleifer/distilbart-cnn-6-6	0.2573	0.9125	0.3714	0.1966	0.7116	0.2832	0.2265	0.8175	0.3277
distilbert	0.1844	0.2488	0.1975	0.0867	0.1203	0.0953	0.1625	0.2263	0.1766
distil-t5	0.4369	0.7891	0.5211	0.3454	0.6171	0.4086	0.4057	0.7250	0.4808
t5-small-rouge-rep-ce-loss	0.6313	0.7801	0.6742	0.5388	0.6233	0.5576	0.6009	0.7262	0.6359

5. Future Work

Our current work focuses on designing a system that provides the most appropriate input format and exploiting token-related scorings to improve the transformer-based model's performance. While our method beats baseline models on test data, we want the summarised query to be constructed as a hybrid of extractive and abstract methods, with the model being able to paraphrase and infer information over a large number of words. This needs the training data to be curated in such a mixed-format. So we would want to apply an active-learning framework, as provided by Govindan et al. [23] in which the proposed model may generate abstractive summaries after sufficient training and the user can edit the summary to create a semi-extractive summary, which can then be used to train hybrid summarizers. We also want to apply loss functions based on decoder-encoder attentions to improve learning of important features while summarizing.

References

[1] Bahdanau, D., Cho, K. and Bengio, Y., 2022. Neural Machine Translation by Jointly Learning to Align and Translate. [online] arXiv.org. Available at: ¡https://arxiv.org/abs/1409.0473¿ [Accessed 9 May 2022].

[2] Govindan, A., Ranjan, G. and Verma, A., 2021. Question Answering Module Leveraging Heterogeneous Datasets. [online] http://dx.doi.org/10.5121/ijnlc.2021.10601.

[3] Dragomir R Radev, Eduard Hovy, and Kathleen McKeown, "Introduction to the special issue on summarization," Computational linguistics 2002. 28, 4 (2002), 399–408.

[4] Moratanch, N. and Gopalan, Chitrakala, "A survey on extractive text summarization",2018 1-6.10.1109/ICCCSP.2017.7944061.

[5] Wolf, T., Debut, L., Sanh, V., Chaumond, J., Delangue, C., Moi, A., Cistac, P., Rault, T., Louf, R., Funtowicz, M., Davison, J., Shleifer, S., von Platen, P., Ma, C., Jernite, Y., Plu, J., Xu, C., Scao, T., Gugger, S., Drame, M., Lhoest, Q. and Rush, A., 2022. HuggingFace's Transformers: State-of-the-art Natural Language Processing. [online] arXiv.org. Available at: ¡https://arxiv.org/abs/1910.03771

[6] Sepp Hochreiter and J¨urgen Schmidhuber. 1997. Long short-term memory. Neural computation 9, 8 (1997), 1735–1780

[7] Ramesh Nallapati, Bowen Zhou, Cicero dos Santos, C¸ a glar Gulc¸ehre, and Bing Xiang. 2016. Abstractive Text Summarization using Sequence-to-sequence RNNs and Beyond. CoNLL 2016 (2016), 280.

[8] Kouris, Panagiotis and Alexandridis, Georgios and Stafylopatis, Andreas, "Abstractive Text Summarization: Enhancing Sequence-to-Sequence Models Using Word Sense Disambiguation and Semantic Content Generalization", Computational Linguistics, 2021.

[9] See, Abigail, Peter J. Liu, and Christopher D. Manning. 2017. Get to the point: Summarization with pointer-generator networks. arXiv preprint arXiv:1704.04368. https://doi.org/10.18653/v1/P17-1099

[10] Sutskever, I., O. Vinyals, and Q. V. Le. 2014. Sequence to sequence learning with neural networks. Advances in NIPS.

[11] Lin, Hui and Vincent Ng. 2019. Abstractive summarization: A survey of the state of the art. In Proceedings of the AAAI Conference on Artificial Intelligence, volume 33, pages 9815–9822. https://doi.org/10.1609/aaai.v33i01.33019815

[12] Honnibal M, Montani I. spaCy Natural language understanding with Bloom embeddings, convolutional neural networks and incremental parsing. 2017.

[13] You, Yongjian, Weijia Jia, Tianyi Liu, and Wenmian Yang. 2019. Improving abstractive document summarization with salient information modeling. In Proceedings of the 57th Annual Meeting of the Association for Computational Linguistics, pages 2132–2141. https://doi.org/10.18653/v1/P19-1205

[14] Biswas, P. and Iakubovich, A., 2022. Extractive Summarization of Call Transcripts. [online] arXiv.org. Available at: https://arxiv.org/abs/2103.10599¿

[15] Kingma, D. and Ba, J., 2022. Adam: A Method for Stochastic Optimization. [online] arXiv.org. Available at: ¡https://arxiv.org/abs/1412.6980¿ [Accessed 12 May 2022].

[16] Chin-Yew Lin. 2004. ROUGE: A package for automatic evaluation of summaries. Text Summarization Branches Out (2004).

[17] Vaswani, Ashish, Noam Shazeer, Niki Parmar, Jakob Uszkoreit, Llion Jones, Aidan N. Gomez, Łukasz Kaiser, and Illia Polosukhin. 2017. Attention is all you need. In Advances in Neural Information Processing Systems, pages 5998–6008.

[18] Zhang, Haoyu, Jianjun Xu, and Ji Wang. 2019. Pretraining-based natural language generation for text summarization. arXiv preprint arXiv:1902.09243. https://doi.org/10.18653/v1/K19-1074

[19] Xu, Song, Haoran Li, Peng Yuan, Youzheng Wu, Xiaodong He, and Bowen Zhou. 2020. Self-attention guided copy mechanism for abstractive summarization. In Proceedings of the 58th Annual Meeting of the Association for Computational Linguistics, pages 1355–1362. https://doi.org/10.18653/v1/2020.acl-main.125

[20] Govindan, A., Ranjan, G. and Verma, A., 2021. Unsupervised Named Entity Recognition for Hi-Tech Domain [online] http://dx.doi.org/10.5121/csit.2021.111917.

[21] Hinton, G., Vinyals, O. and Dean, J., 2022. Distilling the Knowledge in a Neural Network. [online] arXiv.org. Available at: ¡https://arxiv.org/abs/1503.02531¿ [Accessed 15 May 2022].

[22] Raffel, C., Shazeer, N., Roberts, A., Lee, K., Narang, S., Matena, M., Zhou, Y., Li, W. and Liu, P., 2022. Exploring the Limits of Transfer Learning with a Unified Text-to-Text Transformer. [online] arXiv.org. Available at: ¡https://arxiv.org/abs/1910.10683¿ [Accessed 15 May 2022].

[23] Govindan, A., Ranjan, G. and Karthik, A., 2019. Continuous learning mechanism of NLU-ML models boosted by human feedback [online] http://dx.doi.org/10.1109/ICCIDS.2019.8862102.

Towards a Knowledge-Aware AI
A. Dimou et al. (Eds.)
© *2022 The Authors.*
This article is published online with Open Access by IOS Press and distributed under the terms
of the Creative Commons Attribution License 4.0 (CC BY 4.0).
doi:10.3233/SSW220020

esT5s: A Spanish Model for Text Summarization

Adrian VOGEL-FERNANDEZ, Pablo CALLEJA and Mariano RICO [1]

Ontology Engineering Group, Universidad Politécnica de Madrid (UPM), Spain

Abstract. Deep Learning models based on the Transformer architecture have revolutionized the state of the art of NLP tasks. As English is the language in which most significant advances are made, languages like Spanish require specific training, but this training has a computational cost so high that only big corporations with servers and GPUs are capable of generating them. This work has explored how to create a model for the Spanish language from a big multilingual model. Specifically, a model aimed at creating text summarization, a very common task in NLP. The results, concerning the quality of the summarization (ROUGE score), point out that these small models, for a specific language, achieve similar results than much bigger models, with a reasonable training in terms of time required and computational power, and are significantly faster at inference.

Keywords. Deep learning, T5, Spanish, Text summarization

1. Introduction

Summarization is a Natural Language Processing task that consists of condensing the most relevant information from a document. This task can be divided into two categories: extractive summarization and abstractive summarization. Extractive summarization consists of identifying and copying the most relevant and useful information pieces (typically sentences) from the original content. In contrast, abstractive summarization requires a deeper understanding of the language to summarize the most relevant content, paraphrasing the original sentences, combining and using synonyms or new words, without losing information and preserving cohesion and coherence [1]. Thus, abstractive summarization is a difficult task in natural language processing.

Currently, the state-of-the-art of language models based on transformers [2] have reached a high level of language comprehension. However, all research is mainly focused on the English language and then applied to other languages. Even important languages such as Spanish, which is the second language spoken in the world, has an enormous

---

[1]Corresponding Author: Mariano Rico; E-mail:mariano.rico@upm.es.
The authors gratefully acknowledge the computer resources at Artemisa, funded by the European Union ERDF and Comunitat Valenciana as well as the technical support provided by the Instituto de Física Corpuscular, IFIC (CSIC-UV). Also we acknowledge the Universidad Politécnica de Madrid for providing computing resources on Magerit Supercomputer. This work was funded partially by the project Knowledge Spaces (PID2020-118274RB-I00), funded by MCIN/AEI/ 10.13039/501100011033; and project HCommonK (RTC2019-007134-7, funded by MCIN/AEI/ 10.13039/501100011033).

gap in their language models compared to English [3]. For example, the T5 model [4] is one of the best language models, which exploits the features of text-to-text transfer learning and it is usually used for the text summarization task, it is only trained for English language, and there is no Spanish version yet.

Despite this lack of models for non-English languages, there are multilingual models (also including English). This is the case of the multilingual T5 (mT5) [5] which is trained in 101 languages, including English and Spanish among them. These multilingual approaches outperform monolingual models because similar languages have positive transfer between them [6]. However, the effort required to create (and also execute) these multilingual models is very high. Our approach takes advantage of these multilingual models to create a single-language model, much more efficient in training and execution.

Despite there are several summarization models for Spanish publicly available (specifically in HuggingFace), after testing them and, to the best of our knowledge, there is only one model supported by a peer reviewed publication, the so named NASES model. However, this model is intended for small texts (up to 512 tokens), achieving low quality values in the tests carried out.

This work presents the creation of a Spanish model for text summarization based on the T5 model, specifically designed for Spanish for text summarization affordable in terms of computational requirements. We want to emphasize that this method is generic and can be applied to **any other** language, not only Spanish.

Our method is capable of creating a summarization model for the Spanish language in less than 1 hour of computing time, using a single GPU and a the T5 multilingual language model. In our case, a NVIDIA V100 16 GB, that many organizations or individuals can afford. As an alternative, Google Colaboratory [2] allows you to train for free neural models using a similar GPU for a maximum of 1 hour for small model versions. The Pro version of Colaboratory allows you to train bigger models (longer execution time) for a small fee (10 USD/month) with even better GPUs.

The simplest version of the resulting models of this work was trained in 49 minutes, and it is capable of summarizing a Spanish text with a reasonable quality: the summary does not have typos and always produces sentences lexically and grammatically correct. The quality of this model is close to the performance of the state-of-the-art model in terms of the ROUGE score [7], the standard quality metric in this field.

Also, we have developed other models with different configurations that obtain a better performance, but with training time above 1 hour. The training of these slightly bigger models is affordable by institutions or individuals since the computation time is below 24 hours (specifically 17 hours) with a single GPU.

Concerning the time required to summarize a Spanish text, in general terms, the bigger the model is, the longer execution time it requires. All resulting models presented in this work are faster than the models in the state of the art. The experiments show summarization time faster (between x6.56 and x1.43).

For the sake of reproducibility, the source code is available [3]. The models will be publicly available at our page in HuggingFace https://huggingface.co/oeg.

---

[2] https://colab.research.google.com/
[3] https://github.com/oeg-upm/t5-spanish-news-summarization

2. State of the Art

The state of the art in abstractive summarization is the PEGASUS model [8]. It introduces Gap Sentence Prediction (GSP) as a pre-training mechanism. This model achieves the highest ROUGE scores, but it is only for the English language, and it is not feasible to reproduce it for other languages given its computational cost.

The state of the art for Spanish text abstractive summarization is the model published by Hasan et al. [9] based on the mT5 model (this model will be referred as mT5Hasan) and NASES [10], both reporting the highest ROUGE scores. It is important to mention that mT5Hasan ROUGE scores are calculated with the XL-Sum dataset, while NASES scores are calculated with a dataset that is not public and authors do not point out any indication on the dataset used. In order to test the model and compare it to the proposed models, it is needed to calculate the ROUGE scores in the test partition of the XL-Sum dataset. Moreover, it is important to notice that the training of the NASES model has a maximum input size of 512 tokens, but mT5Hasan and the proposed models can handle up to 768 tokens. This makes the proposed models much better to deploy in real life applications since they can handle longer input texts.

The NASES model creates a generic Spanish language model (from a Spanish corpus) trained using the GSG (Gap Sentences Generation) [8] technique (used by the Google PEGASUS model). This technique is specifically designed to improve the performance of the summarization task. However, the proposed model does not train any generic model but specializes a reduced version of the multilingual generic model T5. The NASES model, to our best knowledge, is the only Spanish summarization model trained from scratch, without a pretrained language model.

mT5Hasan [9] is a multilingual T5 summarization model based on mT5 and trained on all 44 languages of the XL-Sum dataset, which makes the model performance better for each of the individual languages since different languages can have a positive transfer between them [11]. This model is currently the best performing Spanish summarization model, but it is important to notice that this model was trained using 1 million examples of text and summary pairs of 44 languages during 4 days using an 8 GPU cluster. Both state of the art models have been used to compare results with the resulting models of this work.

The evaluation in this work has been performed with the three ROUGE score metrics: ROUGE-1 measures the number of 1-grams that are equal in the reference and the model summary, ROUGE-2 with 2-grams, and ROUGE-L with the longest common subsequence between the model summary and the reference. Although ROUGE has its limitations [12,13].

For the Spanish language, there are not so many publicly available datasets for text summarization. The best datasets available for Spanish, with an evaluated quality, are multilingual. The main multilingual datasets are XL-Sum [9] and MLSUM [14]. XL-Sum contains summaries obtained from BBC news, but its Spanish portion only has 44,413 examples and MLSUM has 290,645 examples obtained from *El País*, a Spanish newspaper. However, only XL-Sum dataset has been evaluated by humans following an answering template [9]. Thus, we consider XL-Sum a higher quality dataset and it will be used for the fine-tuning process.

3. Methodology

This section presents the process of converting the multilingual T5 model into a single language model (pruning) and then, specialize (fine-tune) the model to perform abstractive summarization. Figure 1 shows an overview of the whole process.

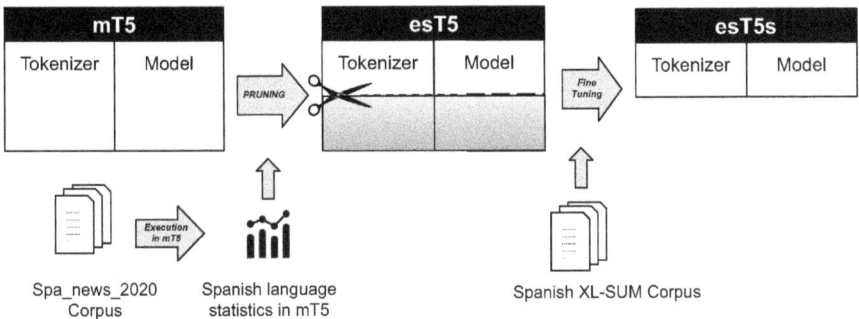

Figure 1. Overview of the method: pruning of mT5 + fine tunning process from the mT5 model.

3.1. Model pruning

The process starts taking the original mT5, a big trained multilingual model for 101 languages (Spanish among them). From this model, we have applied the pruning method [15] but specialized for mT5. This method removes the embeddings of other languages to perform a lossless compression over the multilingual model into a single language.

As mT5 is distributed in different sizes, which refers to the maximum length of the input tokens, we have used the mT5-small and the mT5-base models (512 and 768).

The idea of the pruning method is to reduce the number of parameters of embeddings that are not used and reduce the size of the vocabulary. In the mT5-small model, the 85.2% of the model parameters are used for embeddings and in the mT5-base model, the 65.96% of the model parameters are used for embeddings.

The method needs a reference corpus of the target language to analyze the vocabulary used and how is represented in the multilingual model. For the Spanish language, the corpus used has been spa_news_2020_1M-sentences which is a sentence corpus from Leipzig corpora collection[4]. The corpus contains more than 19,000 sentences about Spanish news. Then, the tokenizer of the mT5 is used to tokenize the sentences of the corpus. This process finds out that only 25.9% of the vocabulary of the multilingual tokenizer is used and that the 25,000 most frequent Spanish tokens comprise 99% of the Spanish vocabulary of the corpus.

To prune the original tokenizer of the mT5, the following tokens have been selected: the first tokens from the original tokenizer which include some special tokens and subwords or characters and the 25,000 most frequent Spanish tokens detected in the analysis of the corpus. The resulting tokenizer vocabulary has only 10% of the original tokens.

---

[4]Available at https://corpora.uni-leipzig.de/es?corpusId=spa_news_2020

To reduce the number of model's parameters, the unused embeddings from non-Spanish languages of the encoder, decoder and the language model head are removed. This process is made by adjusting the length of the embeddings to keep only the Spanish language representation. This reduces the mT5-small model size from 1.2GB to 274MB and the mT5-base model size from 2.3GB to 928MB, which represents the 22% and the 40.34% of the original size respectively. The resulting models are named esT5-small and esT5-base.

3.2. Fine-tuning process

The last process is fine-tuning the language models to perform abstractive summarization. The resulting models will be referenced with the name esT5s. This process is performed using the dataset partitions provided by XL-Sum dataset of training and validation corpora.

First, a model has been trained using the small version (esT5-small) for 3 epochs with a batch size of 8, an AdamW optimizer [16] with a learning rate of 0.0001 into a single GPU. This is the simplest model presented in this work which contains the main targets: it is trained in less than one hour and has achieved enough evaluation results. Also, the small model has been trained for different epochs to study future improvements or limitations of the size of the model. The selection strategy was to keep the model with lowest validation loss for each epoch during the experiments.

Moreover, the esT5-base model has been used to train different models with different epochs in order to explore the possible performance obtained in a single GPU. However, the batch size has been reduced to 4 to fit in the GPU memory. The GPU used for these experiments was a NVIDIA V100 with 16GB of memory.

4. Evaluation

Table 1 presents the ROUGE scores obtained for the resulting models and for the referenced models of mT5Hasan and NASES evaluated with XL-Sum dataset. The XL-Sum test set contains 4,763 examples. The simplest version of esT5s model using the small model language esT5 and 49 minutes of training (3 epochs) achieves considerable good results in comparison with the results provided with mT5Hasan, which needed 96 hours of training. Moreover, different experiments have been performed with the small model language to see the improvements over time with 9 and 15 epochs. The results show a continuous improving trend, meaning that better results can be achieved with more training time but, in this case, this work studies methods to produce results with limited resources.

Also, similar experiments have been performed with the base model esT5 in order to see its performance with similar epochs. The results show an improvement of ROUGE values of these models. The last experiment performed with the esT5-base model has been to do a fine-tuning without time restrictions in order to create the best possible model. In this case, the best ROUGE results have been achieved at epoch 17, closer to the results of the mT5 model. Beyond this number of epochs there is no significant improvement in the model.

The evaluation shows also that the size of the model limits the quality of summarization, as shown in the differences between models trained with the small model or

Model	Dataset	Epochs	Time	ROUGE-1	ROUGE-2	ROUGE-l	max length	exec. time
esT5s-small	XL-Sum	3	49'	22.21	5.28	17.44	512	80 min.
esT5s-small	XL-Sum	9	210'	22.54	5.86	17.74	512	80 min.
esT5s-small	XL-Sum	15	267'	23.30	6.48	18.47	512	80 min.
esT5s-base	XL-Sum	3	180'	23.91	7.16	19.09	768	310 min.
esT5s-base	XL-Sum	9	9h	24.26	7.86	19.68	768	310 min.
esT5s-base	XL-Sum	17	17h	**25.30**	**8.21**	**20.29**	768	310 min.
mT5Hasan	XL-Sum	-	96h*	26.21	8.74	21.06	768	460 min.
NASES	DACSA	-	NA	16.63	2.64	13.32	512	-

Table 1. ROUGE metric for different models. Note: *The mT5Hasan model reports a training time of 4 days (96h) in a cluster of 8 GPUs. Our models use a much modest hardware (1 GPU).

with the base one. The ROUGE scores for NASES model are lower that expected. This is because NASES model was trained using the DACSA dataset. This dataset is not public but, looking at some examples in their work, seems that the dataset is comprised of news and summaries shorter than the ones contained in XL-Sum. As a result, the knowledge obtained during their training process is not transferred as much as expected in the summarization process of the XL-Sum texts. This explains the low ROUGE score achieved in the experiments when compared with the results published by their authors.

Also, an evaluation of the execution time that models need to generate summaries have been performed. This evaluation has focused on the generation of the summaries of test set of XL-Sum (4,763 examples) to calculate the different ROUGE values. The models used in the evaluation has been the esT5s-small (15 epochs), the esT5s-base (17 epochs) and the mT5Hasan. The results are shown in column *Execution time* in table 1.

The mean processing time for the esT5s-small model is 1 hour 20 minutes and 5 hours and 10 minutes for the esT5s-base model. As mT5Hasan model time is 7 hours 40 minutes, we conclude that both models are faster not only for training times but also for summary generation, with a significant difference for the esT5s-small model.

5. Conclusions

The computational effort required to create summarization models is beyond the scope of any ordinary company or research laboratory. The proposed methodology creates models archiving a performance similar to big models with less computation cost.

Specifically, the proposed method outperforms the training time and computation power required to generate an abstractive summarization model. For small companies or research labs it is important to reuse and adapt big models that cannot be generated from scratch. Our models outperforms in execution time: they can summarize the test portion of the XL-Sum dataset in 1 hour 20 minutes (for the small model) and 5 hours 10 minutes (for the base model) while the state of the art model takes 7 hours 40 minutes.

Also it is important to take into consideration model sizes: mT5Hasan is 2.3GB in size, while the resulting models esT5s is 274MB in size for the small and 928MB in size for the base. Taking into account the faster computation times and the smaller sizes, these models are much easier to deploy in a web or portable applications.

References

[1]	Gupta S, Gupta S. Abstractive summarization: An overview of the state of the art. Expert Systems with Applications. 2019;121:49-65.

[2]	Vaswani A, Shazeer N, Parmar N, Uszkoreit J, Jones L, Gomez AN, et al. Attention is all you need. Advances in neural information processing systems. 2017;30.

[3]	Gutiérrez-Fandiño A, Armengol-Estapé J, Pàmies M, Llop-Palao J, Silveira-Ocampo J, Carrino CP, et al. Spanish language models. arXiv preprint arXiv:210707253. 2021.

[4]	Raffel C, Shazeer N, Roberts A, Lee K, Narang S, Matena M, et al. Exploring the limits of transfer learning with a unified text-to-text transformer. arXiv preprint arXiv:191010683. 2019.

[5]	Xue L, Constant N, Roberts A, Kale M, Al-Rfou R, Siddhant A, et al. mT5: A massively multilingual pre-trained text-to-text transformer. arXiv preprint arXiv:201011934. 2020.

[6]	Lample G, Conneau A. Cross-lingual language model pretraining. arXiv preprint arXiv:190107291. 2019.

[7]	Lin CY. Rouge: A package for automatic evaluation of summaries. In: Text summarization branches out; 2004. p. 74-81.

[8]	Zhang J, Zhao Y, Saleh M, Liu P. Pegasus: Pre-training with extracted gap-sentences for abstractive summarization. In: International Conference on Machine Learning. PMLR; 2020. p. 11328-39.

[9]	Hasan T, Bhattacharjee A, Islam MS, Samin K, Li YF, Kang YB, et al. XL-sum: Large-scale multilingual abstractive summarization for 44 languages. arXiv preprint arXiv:210613822. 2021.

[10]	Ahuir, Vicent and Hurtado, Lluís-F and González, José Ángel and Segarra, Encarna. NASca and NASes: Two Monolingual Pre-Trained Models for Abstractive Summarization in Catalan and Spanish. Applied Sciences. 2021;11(21). Available from: https://www.mdpi.com/2076-3417/11/21/9872.

[11]	Conneau A, Khandelwal K, Goyal N, Chaudhary V, Wenzek G, Guzmán F, et al. Unsupervised Cross-lingual Representation Learning at Scale. In: Proceedings of the 58th Annual Meeting of the Association for Computational Linguistics. Online: Association for Computational Linguistics; 2020. p. 8440-51. Available from: https://aclanthology.org/2020.acl-main.747.

[12]	Dorr B, Monz C, Schwartz R, Zajic D. A methodology for extrinsic evaluation of text summarization: does ROUGE correlate? In: Proceedings of the ACL Workshop on Intrinsic and Extrinsic Evaluation Measures for Machine Translation and/or Summarization; 2005. p. 1-8.

[13]	Schluter N. The limits of automatic summarisation according to ROUGE. In: Proceedings of the 15th Conference of the European Chapter of the Association for Computational Linguistics: Volume 2, Short Papers. Valencia, Spain: Association for Computational Linguistics; 2017. p. 41-5.

[14]	Scialom T, Dray PA, Lamprier S, Piwowarski B, Staiano J. MLSUM: The multilingual summarization corpus. arXiv preprint arXiv:200414900. 2020.

[15]	Abdaoui A, Pradel C, Sigel G. Load What You Need: Smaller Versions of Multilingual BERT. CoRR. 2020;abs/2010.05609. Available from: https://arxiv.org/abs/2010.05609.

[16]	Kingma DP, Ba J. Adam: A method for stochastic optimization. arXiv preprint arXiv:14126980. 2014.

Towards a Knowledge-Aware AI
A. Dimou et al. (Eds.)

© 2022 The Authors.
This article is published online with Open Access by IOS Press and distributed under the terms
of the Creative Commons Attribution License 4.0 (CC BY 4.0).

doi:10.3233/SSW220021

A Joint Model for Detecting Causal Sentences and Cause-Effect Relations from Text

Tirthankar DASGUPTA [a,1], Abir NASKAR [a] and Lipika DEY [a] Mohammad SHAKIR [a]

[a] *TCS Research, India*

Abstract. Text documents are rich repositories of causal knowledge. While journal publications typically contain analytical explanations of observations on the basis of scientific experiments conducted by researchers, analyst reports, News articles or even consumer generated text contain not only viewpoints of authors, but often contain causal explanations for those viewpoints. As interest in data science shifts towards understanding causality rather than mere correlations, there is also a surging interest in extracting causal constructs from text to provide augmented information for better decision making. Causality extraction from text is viewed as a relation extraction problem which requires identification of causal sentences as well as detection of cause and effect clauses separately. In this paper, we present a joint model for causal sentence classification and extraction of cause and effect clauses, using a sequence-labeling architecture cascaded with fine-tuned Bidirectional Encoder Representations from Transformers (BERT) language model. The cause and effect clauses are further processed to identify named entities and build a causal graph using domain constraints. We have done multiple experiments to assess the generalizability of the model. It is observed that when fine-tuned with sentences from a mixed corpus, and further trained to solve both the tasks correctly, the model learns the nuances of expressing causality independent of the domain. The proposed model has been evaluated against multiple state-of-the-art models proposed in literature and found to outperform them all.

Keywords. Causal sentence detection, Causal information extraction, Joint modeling, Evaluation

1. Introduction

Detecting causal information from text documents is an important language processing task that has a wide range of applications. Causal information abounds in scientific articles that report reasons behind various observed phenomena, along with details of the study based on which the conclusions are obtained. Similarly, analyst notes contain explanations about various economic or political phenomenon. Mining these rich repositories of documented knowledge provides valuable authoritative information that can be used for downstream decision making applications. Causality extraction from text is

---

[1] Corresponding Author.

rapidly gaining speed as the extracted cause-effect pairs are found to play a significant role in several downstream analytical and predictive tasks like identification of actionable items, question-answering, isolation of confounding variables and predictive variables for predictive systems [1,2]. Curating causal relations from text documents can also help in building repositories of causal insights which are useful for reasoning tasks [3].

The concept of causality can be informally introduced as a relationship between an antecedent e_1 and a consequence e_2, expressed as e_1 *causes* e_2 [4,5]. However, natural language texts contain an abundance of such relations appearing in different forms [6,7]. Even a single sentence expressing causal relations can be arbitrarily complex in structure, which makes the extraction task challenging. Below is a high-level categorization of causal sentences, depicted with examples which highlight the variability in the use of linguistic constructs.

- Single cause-single effect - Let us consider the sentence - *Leukocytosis is caused by bacterial infection.* In this sentence, Leukocytosis is cited as the effect while bacterial infection is cited as a cause. The positions of the cause and effect can be inter-changed as shown in the following example - "Intravenous azithromycin causes ototoxicity", where the causal phrase *Intravenous azithromycin* appears before the effect, *ototoxicity.*
- Multiple cause-multiple effect - The following sentence from a business news article - *The recent market falls have been the result of big budget deficits, as well as the US's yawning current account gap,* depicts the presence of multiple causes for one effect.
- Causal chains - Sometimes a causal chain which expresses causal effects as a series of events can be observed, as illustrated by the following sentence: - *Unavailability of IT infrastructure support team has hugely impacted development and support activities thereby affecting customer relations.*

Causality is expressed within text documents in arbitrarily complex ways. The expression of causality may be implicit or explicit. Sometimes causal expressions are easy to detect as sentences that contain clauses related by "caused" or "because of". However, there are many other ways in which causalities may be expressed, as illustrated in examples like "climate change induced by rise in greenhouse gases", or "ribavirin was associated with lower incidence of acute respiratory distress syndrome". Causality detection from text requires identification of causal sentences as well as isolation of the cause and effect phrases from it. It is often viewed as a relation classification and argument extraction problem. Causality detection from text is challenging since the number of sentences containing causal relations are few and far-between [8]. The number of non-causal sentences far outnumbers the causal sentences.

In this paper, we have proposed a joint model for causal sentence classification and cause-effect relation extraction using a multi-tasking architecture, which learns to do the tasks simultaneously. Most of the earlier works have focused on extracting the cause-effect components from a given causal sentence only. Our observation is that a joint modeling for classifying causal sentences and detection of the components can yield a more effective model, that also has more practical use. Another significant aspect of the proposed model is that, unlike many of its predecessors, the model doesn't require the entities to be provided as input. Rather, the model learns to effectively isolate cause and effect *phrases*, and not just single words or entities. This is an important contribution of the present work, which is illustrated through the following example. For the sentence "The AIDS pandemic is caused by the spread of HIV infection", while most of the earlier models reported in literature finds "pandemic" as the cause and "infection" as effect, the proposed model can correctly identify "AIDS pandemic" as the cause and "HIV infection" as effect, which are obviously more precise. The third contribution of the paper lies in experimenting with cross-domain learning capability of the model. We show that by training the model over a mixed corpus, the model learns the essence of causality in a domain-independent way.

The joint model for causality detection and causal component identification is designed as a sequence-labeling architecture cascaded with fine-tuned Bidirectional Encoder Representations from Transformers (BERT) language model [9]. While a sentence classifier is trained to identify a causal sentence, the sequence labeling layer assigns a label cause (C), effect (E), causal connector (CC) or none (N) to each word. The labeling of connectives is a unique proposition of the work, which along with its companion cause and effect pair, helps in detection of causal relations from complex sentences more effectively. Most of the earlier work only identify causes and effects. As we will discuss later, the causal connectives play an important role in designing downstream applications with the extracted relations. The proposed model is also capable of extracting multiple causal relations from a single sentence in a more robust fashion by identifying all causal relations that bind cause-effect pairs through the causal connectives. The BERT-base model is fine-tuned with sentences from a mixed corpus, and further trained for learning both the above objectives. The fine-tuned model learns the nuances of scientific and/or business language, the typical events, entities and their states. This helps the subsequent layers learn the boundaries of causal phrases more effectively. The proposed model has been evaluated with multiple state-of-the-art baseline neural network architectures. Results show that it outperforms all the baseline models in most of the tasks.

The rest of the paper is organized as follows. Section 2 presents related work in this area. Section 3 presents the proposed joint model for causal sentence and cause-effect relation extraction. Section 4 provides details about datasets. Section 5 presents details of experiments and evaluations. Section 6 presents a short glimpse of how causal insights can be curated for insight generation. Finally section 7 concludes the paper.

2. Related Works

Early references to causality detection from text can be traced back to [10,11,12,13], who championed syntactic rule-based methods for detecting cause - effect pairs. ROTEUS [14] and COATIS [15] were two such systems designed using non-statistical techniques. The diversity of the causal expressions presented earlier clearly show that a syntactic rule based approach cannot detected all kinds of causal relations. Neural representations that can effectively learn both the semantic and syntactic characteristics of causality are expected to do a better job.

An early machine-learning based approach was proposed in [16], which defined the task as one of sequence labeling. The intent was to assign cause or effect labels to words in a sentence, depending on their roles. Khoo et al. in a series of works [17,10,18] reported extraction of explicit causal relations containing known causal connectives like "if-then" constructs, causative adverbs and adjectives etc. The method yielded very low precision of 19% on a test set of Wall Street Journal articles.

Increased focus on domain-independence, scalability and automation made the task of cause-effect identification a prime candidate for various machine learning approaches. In [19] authors proposed a semi-supervised method to automatically identify linguistic patterns that indicate causal relations in text. This work advocated the use of WordNet hierarchical classes like human action, phenomenon, state, psychological feature and event, as distinguishing features. The authors focused on using explicit patterns of the form ⟨*NounPhrase1 - CausativeVerb - NounPhrase2* ⟩. On the other hand, authors of [7] and [5] suggested the use of causatives only. They used a hierarchical organization of several generic semantic templates. Bui et al. presented a novel method exploiting rules to extract and combine relationships between HIV drugs and mutations in viral genomes from articles in [16]. Girju et al.[20] addressed the problem as one of automatic recognition of relations between pairs of nominals in a sentence. Bui et al. [16] employed logistic regression to extract drugs (cause) and virus mutation (effect) occurrences from medical literature. Sorgente et al. [1] combined rule based and machine learning methods to take advantage of both. They used logical rules based on the dependency between words to extract possible cause-effect pairs, after which they applied Bayesian inference to reduce the number of pairs produced by ambiguous patterns. The relatively untouched task of extracting implicit cause-effect from sentences was tackled by Ittoo et al. [21]. Radinsky et al. used statistical inference mechanisms combined with hierarchical clustering to predict future events from news [3].

In SemEval-2007, a relation extraction task was proposed, that included 7 different kinds of relations, of which Cause-Effect was one type [22]. In 2008 Beamer et al.[23] formulated the 2007 SemEval task4 as the task of automatic classification of semantic relations between nouns. They proposed a WordNet-based learning model which relies on the semantic information of the constituent nouns. In 2009 also a similar task was proposed [24], but it was extended to classify causal relation between a pair of phrases in a sentence. One of the most used annotated datasets available for causal relation extraction comes from SemEval-2010 Task 8. However, other than a few exceptions, most of annotations here are over single-word (noun) cause and effect components.

Use of deep neural architectures to detect causal relations started thereafter. Most of the papers report their results for the SEMEVAL-2010 dataset, along with additional datasets created by them to increase the volume of training and test data. Xu et al. employed a combination of shortest dependency paths (SDP) and LSTMs to solve the relation classification task [25]. The shortest dependency path between two entities was identified and then classified using a neural architecture. Along with SDP, words and their parts-of-speech(POS) tags, grammatical relations and WordNet hypernyms were also used. In [8], Zhao et al. worked on predicting future events based on causal relations expressed in text. This work proposed using a new Restricted Hidden Naive Bayes model to extract causality from texts, using word-baed features, contextual features, syntactic features, position features and also causal connectives. In [26], Dasgupta et al. proposed a linguistically informed recursive neural network architecture for automatic extraction of cause-effect relations from text. Beside using content embedding, the BiLSTM based model also exploited other linguistic features.

In 2019, Yu et al. explored the use of causal language to report scientific findings. In [27] they proposed a BERT-based prediction model to classify sentences into four categories - "no relationship", "correlational", "conditional causal", and "direct causal". They reported achieving an accuracy of 0.90 and a macro-F1 of 0.88. Their results were obtained on a corpus of 3,000 PubMed research conclusion sentences, developed by them. Li et al. [28] proposed the SCITE architecture, which uses Self-attentive BiLSTM-CRF wIth Transferred Embeddings to extract cause and effect sequences directly without extracting candidate causal pairs and identifying their relations separately. The task was interpreted as a sequence tagging task where the text sequence is given as input and the model predicts which word in the output sequence is beginning or end of cause and effect phrases. Their proposed architecture also reports F-measure of 0.89 and 0.90 for cause and effect sequences on an extension of the SEMEVAL 2010 dataset. In a recently published paper, Huminski et al. have employed a rule-based method for automatic extraction of causal chains from text [29]. Extensive survey on extraction of causal relations from natural language text can be found in [6], and in the recently published work by Yang et al. in [30].

The following works have looked at different applications of causality detection and its applications. Egami et al. introduced a conceptual framework for making causal inferences with discovered measures as a treatment or outcome [31]. In their position paper [32], Blomqvist et al. highlight the utility of causal relation detection from biomedical text to distinguish causation from correlation. They propose the use of BERT [9], a transformer based language model, to extract causal relations from text, and store them in in the form of a Knowledge Graphs (KG), after being refereed by experts. Guo et al. have also used an unsupervised learning model to extract causal relations between pressure injury and risk factors [33], to construct a causal graph. In [34], Veitch et al. explored the possibility of using causality from text to understand what affects a scientific paper's acceptance. They presented methods to estimate causal effects from observational text data, adjusting for confounding features of the text such as the subject or writing quality. Keith et al. and Weld et al. have explored the possibility of using text data as a source of information to deal with potential confounders while doing causal reasoning in [35] and [36].

To summarize, it can be seen that most of the research work have worked with the assumption that causal sentences are given and the task is to isolate the cause and effect components. Others have used pattern based detection of causal sentences and thereafter isolated the cause-effect components. However, in reality, for any application, it cannot be expected that causal sentences will be detected separately and fed to a model for cause-effect identification. Our intent is to address this issue with joint modeling of the two tasks.

3. Proposed Architecture for Joint Modeling for Causality Detection and Cause-effect Extraction

In this section we present the details of the proposed joint model for causal sentence classification and causal relation extraction based on an enhanced architecture that is built on top of BERT-based language model, presented by Devlin et al. in [9]. The BERT model generates contextual embedding of the input text, which is thereafter fed to a CNNBiLSTM layer followed by a fully connected layer that jointly perform the sentence classification and sequence labeling tasks. Figure 1 presents the proposed architecture.

Causal sentence detection is modeled as a binary classification problem. The predicted label $y^1 \in \{0, 1\}$, where 0 stands for a non-causal sentence and 1 indicates that the sentence contains causal relations. The cause-effect relation extraction is modeled as a sequence labeling task that tags the input word sequence $x = (x_1, x_2, ..., x_T)$ with the label sequence $y^s = (y_1^s, y_2^s, ..., y_T^s)$ where the label $y_i^s \in$ *cause(C), effect(E), causal connective(CC)* and *None(N)*. For example, the labeled output of the sentence *The minister stated that gasoline is up because of refinery issues in Texas* will be *The/N minister/N stated/N that/N Gasoline/E is/E up/E because/CC of/CC refinery/C issues/C in/C Texas/C*. Our intent is to generate correct labels for an entire sequence of words that comprise cause, effect or causal connectives in a sentence. The sequence label prediction of a single word is dependent on predictions for surrounding words. It has been shown that structured prediction models such as cascaded CNN and BiLSTM models can significantly improve the sequence labeling performance. In this work, we have exploited the efficacy of a CNNBiLSTM layer by adding it on top of the BERT model. While the transformer model of BERT creates contextual representation of each word as well as the whole sentence, the spatial collocation properties commonly observed among a set of words bound by a specific relation, are captured by the CNNBiLSTM layer. While analyzing the results we observe that the joint model performs better than single task models as it learns the intricacies of causal dependencies among words and clauses and thereby improves the performance of both the tasks effectively. While more detailed results on standard datasets are presented later, here we present a few unique examples to highlight how the proposed model handles some complex situations correctly :

(1) - *The tornado destruction is followed by widespread disease.* - the model correctly identifies this as a causal sentence, where a causal relation is indicated by the words *is followed by*.

(2) *The leader was followed by his supporters in the march.* - the model correctly identifies that this is not a causal sentence despite the presence of the word *followed by*.

(3) *Climate change due to trapping of Green house gases, threatens people with food and water scarcity, increased flooding, extreme heat, more disease, and economic loss.* - Given this complex sentence without any known causal connectives, the model can not only detect it as causal but also identifies *climate change* as cause, and *threatens people with food and water scarcity, increased flooding, extreme heat, more disease, and economic loss* as effect.

(4) *Human migration and conflict can be a result* - this sentence is identified correctly by the model as non-causal, yet it could identify *conflict* as one of the effects.

Since we use BERT for language modeling, the proposed model is not restricted to work with sentences. It can work on collection of sentences as well. Due to this the model is capable of detecting implicit causalities between sentences also. In [37], Chen et al. had shown that joint modeling was found to outperform other models for the task of intent classification and slot-filling with NERs. Our work also reaffirms this.

3.1. Learning the Joint Model for Sentence Classification and Sequence Labeling Tasks

To solve the causality classification and causal relation extraction tasks together, we have trained the *CNNBiLSTM* layers using a loss functions with two separate components. The cross-entropy loss function is used for the purpose. Given a set of training

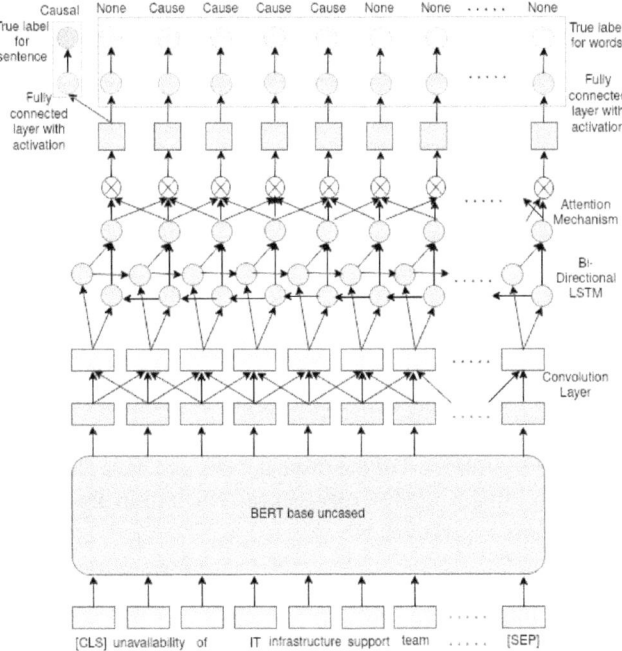

Figure 1. Overview of the neural network architecture for cause-effect relation extraction.

data x_t, w_t^i, $\bar{y}_t$ and $\bar{q}_t^i$, where x_t is the t-th word sequence to be predicted as *causal or not-a causal text*, w_t^i is the i-th word within the sentence to be predicted as *Cause (C), effect (E), causal connective (CN), and None(N)*, $\bar{y}_t$ and $\bar{q}_t^i$ are the one-hot representation of the ground-truth class labels for x_t and w_t^i respectively and y^i and y_n^s are the respective model predictions for both x_t and w_t^i. Thus, the causality classification is predicted as: $y^i = softmax(W_i * h_1 + b_i)$ On the other hand, for the sequence labeling task, we feed the final hidden states of the BERT-CNNBiLSTM network of the other tokens, $h_2, ..., h_T$, into a softmax layer to classify over the sequence labels. To make this procedure compatible with the Word-Piece tokenization, we feed each tokenized input word into a Word-Piece tokenizer and use the hidden state corresponding to the first sub-token as input to the CNNBiLSTM network and finally to a softmax classifier. The output of the model is represented as: $y_n^s = softmax(W^s * h_n + b_s), n \in (1...N)$ where h_n is the hidden state corresponding to the first sub-token of word x_n. Thus, the loss functions for the text classification (L_1) and causal relation extraction task (L_2) are separately defined as: $L_1(\theta) = -\sum_{k=1}^{K} \bar{y}_t^k log(y_t)$ $L_2(\theta) = -\sum_{t=1}^{N} \sum_{j=1}^{J} \bar{q}_t^{i,j} log(q_t^i)$ Where y_t is the vector representation of the predicted output of the model for the input sentence x_t. Similarly, q_t is the vector representation of the predicted output of the model for the input word w_t^i. K and J are the number of class labels for each task. N is the number of words of a given sentence for which the sequence labeling task is performed. The model is fine-tuned end-to-end via minimizing the cross-entropy loss.

We now define the joint loss function using a linear combination of the loss functions of the two tasks as:

$$L_{joint}(\theta) = \lambda * L_1(\theta) + (1 - \lambda) * I_{[y_{sentence}==1]} * L_2(\theta) \tag{1}$$

Where, λ controls the contribution of losses of the individual tasks in the overall joint loss. $I_{[y_{sentence}==1]}$ is an indicator function which activates the causal relation labeling loss only when the corresponding sentence classification label is 1, since we do not want to back-propagate relation labeling loss when the corresponding sentence classification label is 0.

4. Data Description

Though causal relation extraction is acknowledged as an important NLP task, there is not much data available for training or evaluating models. Along with the other datasets mentioned in section 3, a new comprehensive dataset was released for a challenge called Cause-Effect Relation EXtraction (CEREX) during FIRE 2020 [2]. The CEREX-2020 dataset includes the causal dataset from SemEval-2010 task8 and extends it with more causal data from multiple sources. For the present work, we have also added 3000 causal sentences curated from Project Analyst reports available within the organization. Details about the CEREX dataset is given below:

1. **BBC News Article dataset** - this was created by the Trinity College Computer Science Department, from 140 News articles in five topical areas : business, sports, tech, entertainment and politics from 2004-2005 [38]. Out of the 1950 sentences in this collection, around 500 sentences were found to contain causation.

2. **SemEval-2010*:** This is a modified annotation of the original SemEval 2010 Task 8 data, released at CEREX-2020. The SemEval 2010 Task 8 data set proposes a entity based relation extraction task. Altogether there were 4300 sentences out of which only 1331 sentences were found to be having causal relations. While originally, only the entities were annotated as cause or effect, CEREX-2020 provided enhanced annotations for entire clauses. For example, in the sentence *The addition of water to the tank caused a runaway chemical reaction*, the SemEval 2010 annotated cause was "water" while the effect was "chemical reaction". In CEREX-2020, the cause annotation was extended to the complete phrase "The addition of water to the tank" and the effect annotation is "runway chemical reaction".

3. **The adverse drug effect (ADE) dataset** - This was released by [39]. It consists of information about consumption of different drugs and their associated side effects.

4. **Vehicle Recall News** - contains a collection of 1050 sentences collected from News articles that reported recall of different vehicles all over the world, along with the reasons for recall.

It is to be noted that all the above datasets contained only causal sentences, wherein each sentence contained at least one cause or an effect. Additionally, we also collected 10,000 more sentences collectively from the above domains, selecting them carefully so that they do not have any causal information. Table 1 presents brief statistics about the entire dataset used for the task.

---

[2]https://sites.google.com/view/cerex-fire2020/home

No.	Source	Sentence count	Part of CEREX-2020
1.	Project Analyst Report (AR)	3000	No
2.	BBC News(BBC)	503	Yes
3.	SEMEVAL* (SEM)	1331	Yes
4.	Adverse Drug Effect (ADE)	3821	Yes
5.	Recall News (VR)	1126	Yes
6.	Non-causal Sentences	10,000	Yes

Table 1. Data Statistics

5. Experiment and Results

We have designed two different experiments with the datasets described above. The experiments are distinguished from each other by the way, data from different sets are used for training, development and testing purposes.

Experiment-I (Training and Testing on Individual Dataset):, Each of the five data sets are used separately for evaluating the model's performance. Each dataset is randomly divided into 80%, 10% and 10% for training, testing and development respectively. The results are evaluated using five-fold cross-validation. Since, the 10% testing data in fold-1 is different from the 10% testing data in fold-2 or fold-3, we have reported the average performance. While working with the ADE dataset only, we used Bio-BERT, which is another base model, specifically trained on Bio-medical literature, instead of BERT-base.

Experiment-II (Training and Testing on Mixed Datasets): Data from the five sets are combined together and divided into training, development and test sets in the ratio of 80%, 10% and 10% respectively.

The pre-trained BERT-base model, presented in [40], uses 12 layers of transformer blocks, 768 hidden units, and 12 self-attention heads to provide a powerful context-dependent sentence representation. Most of the time, the same is used to fine-tune for the target causality detection tasks. For all the tasks, we have used Xavier initialization [41] for faster convergence. Further, we set the early stopping of fine-tuning to 800 steps in order to prevent over-fitting. We use a batch size 32, a maximum sequence length of 128, and a learning rate of $2 * 10^5$ for fine-tuning this model.

5.1. Baselines

The performance of the proposed joint model was compared with the following baseline models using the aforementioned datasets.

- The causal sentence classification and cause effect relation extraction model that was proposed in [42] had adopted a neural machine translation (**CEREX_NMT**) based architecture and reported results for CEREX dataset.
- A linguistic feature based transfer learning (**CEREX_FTL**) framework for Cause-Effect Relation Extraction was proposed in [43].
- A linguistically informed BiLSTM (**Li-BiLSTM**) model was proposed in [26], which uses word embeddings along with linguistic features.
- Self-attentive BiLSTM-CRF (**SCITE**) model, proposed in [28], employ different deep learning modelsto extract cause and effect components. This paper reported results for the SemEval-2010 Task 8 dataset. We took the openly available model, further trained it over the CEREX dataset and have presented the test data results in table 3. Since, this model does not implement detection of causal sentences, so it is considered only for Task 2.

Most of the models discussed above uses standard pre-trained word embeddings like, Glove, Word2Vec and Flair. Moreover, most of these models are trained to either classify sentences as causal/non-causal or to extract the respective cause-effect relations, but not perform both simultaneously.

In addition to the LSTM-based models, we also used a number of BERT based language models as our baseline, to evaluate the effect of the joint cost function, as well as contribution of the added CNNBiLSTM layers on top of BERT.

- **Single Task** $BERT_{base}$: This is the vanilla BERT model that has been specifically fine-tuned for two independent tasks to be conducted one after another. The first task is to perform causal sentence classification and then further trained to perform the sequence labeling task for causal relation extraction. This doesn't use CNN or BiLSTMs.
- **Single task BERT-CNNBiLSTM**: Here, in addition to the above vanilla BERT models, we have added a layer of CNN and an attention based BiLSTM units to both the units.
- **Joint** $BERT_{base}$: This is similar to the proposed joint model for sentence classification and sequence labeling tasks, however, without the top CNNBiLSTM layer.

We have performed a number of experiments to evaluate and compare the performance of our proposed system with the models presented above.

5.2. Results

Table 2 presents the results for task 1, i.e. causal sentence detection for Experiment-I. It is clear that the Joint BERT-CNN-BiLSTM model performs best as compared to the BiLSTM based neural networks as well as BERT based single task architectures. The joint model shows an average improvement of around 0.08 for F-score, as compared to the baseline single task BERT-CNN-BiLSTM model. Further, it is seen that the proposed model achieves high individual F-scores for all the datasets. For the SEMEVAL dataset, the joint BERT-Base classifier performs best with F1 score 0.95. Overall, it is obvious that joint task modeling definitely helps.

Table 3 presents the results for Experiment-1 of task 2 i.e. cause-effect relation extraction. Once again, the proposed joint BERT-CNN-BiLSTM model achieves the best F-measures of 0.82, 0.84, 0.94, and 0.88 for project analyst reports, BBC News, SEMEVAL and Recall news respectively. For SEMEVAL dataset, the earlier highest F1 measures reported for cause and effect was 0.89 and 0.90 by [27]. Having achieved F1 measure of 0.94 for causes, the proposed model clearly outperforms them in finding cause sequences, while remaining comparable in detecting effects. It was observed that the proposed joint BERT-CNNBiLSTM model significantly reduces the false negative scores and achieves a high true positive score, thereby achieving a higher F-measure as compared to the baseline single task models.

Table 4 presents the results for Experiment II, in which 80% of the entire combined dataset was used for training and the remaining 20% for testing. The aim was to see whether using a large dataset helps. Since joint BERT-CNNBiLSTM performed best so we report the results for only this model here. The first row shows the overall performance of the model, while the subsequent rows show break-up of the results for both the tasks. Though we see a general dip in the performance, F1 score for classification of

Models	Dataset	Precision	Recall	F1-Score
CEREX_NMT [42]	Analyst Reports(AR)	-	-	-
	BBC News (BBC)	0.31± 0.04	0.42± 0.03	0.35± 0.08
	SEMEVAL*(SEM)	0.39± 0.11	0.47± 0.14	0.41± 0.01
	Adverse Drug(ADE)	0.23± 0.07	0.36± 0.03	0.25± 0.06
	Recall News (VR)	0.37± 0.02	0.43± 0.14	0.40± 0.10
CEREX_FTL [43]	Analyst Reports(AR)	-	-	-
	BBC News (BBC)	0.61± 0.14	0.72± 0.03	0.65± 0.08
	SEMEVAL*(SEM)	0.69± 0.11	0.77± 0.14	0.71± 0.01
	Adverse Drug(ADE)	0.63± 0.07	0.76± 0.03	0.65± 0.06
	Recall News (VR)	0.77± 0.02	0.83± 0.14	0.80± 0.10
Li-BiLSTM [26]	Analyst Reports(AR)	0.71 ± 0.11	0.87± 0.09	0.78 ± 0.11
	BBC News (BBC)	0.71± 0.14	0.82± 0.03	0.75± 0.08
	SEMEVAL*(SEM)	0.79± 0.11	0.87± 0.14	0.81± 0.01
	Adverse Drug(ADE)	0.73± 0.07	0.86± 0.03	0.75± 0.06
	Recall News (VR)	0.87± 0.02	0.93± 0.14	0.87± 0.10
Single Task BERT-CNNBiLSTM	Analyst Reports(AR)	0.84± 0.11	0.87± 0.04	0.82± 0.03
	BBC News (BBC)	0.81± 0.01	0.82± 0.03	0.79± 0.04
	SEMEVAL*(SEM)	0.89± 0.03	0.87± 0.01	0.86± 0.05
	Adverse Drug(ADE)	0.83± 0.07	0.96± 0.02	0.90± 0.05
	Recall News (VR)	0.87± 0.08	0.93± 0.05	0.89± 0.06
Joint Task J-BERT	Analyst Report	0.87± 0.14	0.92± 0.09	0.85± 0.07
	BBC News (BBC)	0.81± 0.01	0.92± 0.05	0.84± 0.06
	SEMEVAL*(SEM)	0.81± 0.05	0.97± 0.03	0.89± 0.02
	Adverse Drug(ADE)	0.91± 0.03	0.96± 0.06	0.93± 0.05
	Recall News (VR)	0.87± 0.04	0.93± 0.05	0.90± 0.07
Joint Task J-BERT+CNNBiLSTM	Analyst Report	0.91± 0.05	0.97± 0.07	**0.90± 0.02**
	BBC News (BBC)	0.94± 0.13	0.97± 0.16	**0.94± 0.09**
	SEMEVAL*(SEM)	0.91± 0.15	0.97± 0.07	**0.94± 0.05**
	Adverse Drug (ADE)	0.89± 0.05	0.97± 0.01	**0.97± 0.05**
	Recall News (VR)	0.89± 0.02	0.95± 0.01	**0.92± 0.02**

Table 2. Reported results for Task-1: Causal sentence classification. Results are depicted for experiment-I, reported in terms of Precision, Recall and F1-Scores (along with the standard deviations). *Note that the baseline SCITE [28] model does not perform causal relation classification task, hence is not considered for the Task-1 evaluation. Further, the CEREX_NMT and CEREX_FTL models predate the *analyst report* dataset, and the models are not available, so results for this dataset could not be provided.

causal connectives have gone up significantly for most of the sets, other than for ADE. This can be explained as follows. The larger dataset exposed the model to a large variety of causal connectives, mostly coming from sentences which were a part of NEWS articles, and contributed to the overall gain. The ADE dataset uses terms specific to bio-medical domain to indicate causality, hence showed no improvement. The cause and effect parts for each domain mostly contain domain-specific nouns and entities - hence these fields also did not show any gains. Causal sentence classification shows significant improvement for the Analyst project reports, while for others it remains same. This gain can possibly be attributed to the improved knowledge about causal connectors from the larger dataset. The only domain which loses is ADE. Given that it had attained a high F1 score of 0.97 for causal sentence classification, with BioBERT as the language modeler, our overall conclusion is that augmenting the language model with domain nuances is important for specialized domains.

Deeper dive into the results reveal that in around 12% cases the proposed model incorrectly predicted a cause or an effect event, whereas in only 5% of the sentences, the model incorrectly identified as "not a cause/effect" despite being marked as "cause/effect" by the experts. Sentences in the second category were found to contain ambiguous causal connectives such as: *from, by, based on the fact that* etc. The model can be further trained to recognize implicit causalities in phrases like *share-price manipulation scandal*, which contains a cause *manipulation of share price* and an effect *scandal*, without any causal connector between them.

Models	Dataset	Cause (C)	Effect (E)	Connectives (CC)
CEREX_NMT [42]	AR	-	-	-
	BBC	0.25± 0.10	0.28± 0.04	0.27± 0.02
	SEM*	0.31± 0.02	0.33± 0.07	0.35± 0.12
	ADE	0.29± 0.22	0.33± 0.01	0.31± 0.06
	VR	0.36± 0.03	0.42± 0.12	0.40± 0.02
CEREX_FTL	AR	-	-	-
	BBC	0.29± 0.11	0.36± 0.15	0.31± 0.12
	SEM*	0.33± 0.16	0.35± 0.31	0.33± 0.22
	ADE	0.39± 0.14	0.46± 0.22	0.41± 0.27
	VR	0.41± 0.07	0.43± 0.08	0.41± 0.02
Li-BiLSTM [26]	AR	0.73± 0.02	0.72± 0.02	0.61± 0.02
	BBC	0.68± 0.02	0.69± 0.02	0.74± 0.02
	SEM*	0.87± 0.02	0.83± 0.02	0.77± 0.02
	ADE	0.69± 0.02	0.74± 0.02	0.77± 0.02
	VR	0.80± 0.02	0.80± 0.02	0.76± 0.02
SCITE [28]	AR	0.75 ± 0.02	0.79± 0.14	0.77 ± 0.09
	BBC	0.71 ±0.07	0.76± 0.34	0.71 ± 0.21
	SEM*	0.78 ±0.10	0.79 ±0.20	0.80 ± 0.18
	ADE	0.81 ± 0.18	0.88 ±0.10	0.81 ± 0.05
	VR	0.86 ± 0.16	0.87 ±0.16	0.86 ± 0.07
Single Task BERT-CNNBiLSTM	AR	0.78 ±0.02	0.80± 0.15	0.78 ± 0.20
	BBC	0.78 ±0.12	0.77± 0.03	0.74 ± 0.19
	SEM*	0.81 ±0.23	0.86 ±0.06	0.83 ± 0.12
	ADE	0.89 ± 0.50	0.90 ± 0.01	0.82 ± 0.13
	VR	0.84 ± 0.13	0.88 ±0.03	0.90 ± 0.08
Joint Task BERT	AR	0.79 ±0.10	0.85± 0.13	0.79 ± 0.10
	BBC	0.80 ±0.18	0.78± 0.91	0.72 ± 0.02
	SEM*	0.91 ±0.02	0.88 ±0.05	0.84 ± 0.07
	ADE	0.94 ±0.80	0.93 ±0.16	0.86 ± 0.02
	VR	0.85 ± 0.08	0.88 ±0.16	0.92± 0.01
Joint Task J-BERT+CNNBiLSTM	AR	**0.87 ± 0.09**	**0.88 ± 0.10**	**0.89 ± 0.10**
	BBC	**0.84 ± 0.13**	**0.89± 0.19**	**0.79 ± 0.22**
	SEM*	**0.94 ± 0.22**	**0.88 ± 0.16**	**0.85 ± 0.09**
	ADE	**0.97 ± 0.13**	**0.97 ± 0.05**	**0.89 ± 0.01**
	VR	**0.88 ± 0.91**	**0.89 ± 0.16**	**0.94± 0.03**

Table 3. Reported results for Task-II: Comparing F-scores of the Cause (C), Effect(E) and Connective (CC) extraction by the proposed Joint model with the baseline systems. The results are for Experiment-I.

Dataset	Task-1 Causal Sentence Classification	Task-2 Cause	Effect	Connective
Overall	**0.88**	**0.79**	**0.82**	**0.86**
AR	0.91	0.80	0.82	0.91
BBC	0.90	0.79	0.83	0.89
SEM*	0.92	0.81	0.86	0.87
ADE	0.80	0.75	0.76	0.72
VR	0.90	0.81	0.85	0.92

Table 4. Reported F1 scores for Experiment-II for the proposed Joint BERT-CNNBiLSTM for causal sentence classification (Task-1) and cause-effect extraction task (Task-2).

5.3. Extracting causal relations from a new unmarked text repository

We applied the joint BERT-CNNBiLSTM, with BioBERT as the language model, over a repository of 5000 article abstracts, taken from the Cord19 corpus released by a coalition of leading research groups and The White House to help in treatment of COVID 19 pandemic. Table 5 shows a few causal sentences along with the extracted components, each encapsulated within square brackets with the respective subscripts cause or effect. It can be seen that long clauses are correctly identified, irrespective of their positions, as shown in sentence 4. Additionally, the bio-medical entities drug(D), chemical(C), disease(I) and symptom(S), which were identified by the bio-medical Named Entity Recognizer (NER) called SciSpacy[44] are also marked in Table 5. Figure 2 shows a sample causal graph that is built from this output, where a causal relation is added between a drug or chemical and a disease or symptom, if the entities were part of a cause-effect pair in any sentence. Such causal graphs can be useful for drawing inference from large collections of text. This is still work in progress. We share the results to show that the model works well on

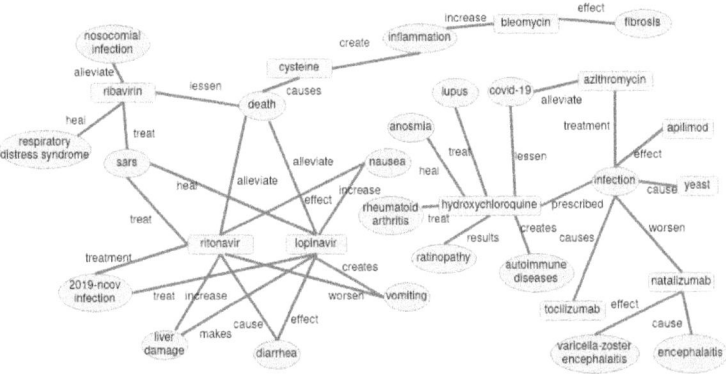

Figure 2. A partial network of a few representative clusters from the COVID-19 bio-medical journal dataset.

Sentences
1). We found that both [prophylactic and therapeutic $(Remdesivir)_{drug}$ had protective effects against Mers-cov replication and associated pathology]$_{cause}$, generally [resulting in]$_{connective}$ [less $(lung\ damage)_{symptom}$ and better $(pulmonary\ function)_{symptom}$]$_{effect}$ compared to controls.
2). The resulting [perturbation of the $(calcium)_{chemical}$ metabolism]$_{cause}$ can [cause]$_{connective}$ [various complications ranging from $(weakness)_{symptom}$ to $(osteoporosis)_{disease}$]$_{effect}$.
3). In addition , since they [received $(Lopinavir)_{drug}$/ $(Ritonavir)_{drug}$]$_{cause}$ which can also [cause]$_{connective}$ [$(diarrhea)_{disease}$]$_{effect}$, how much of gastrointestinal tract symptom was in fact related to Sars-Cov-2 or drug side effect?
4). [Severity of disease, viral replication, and $(lung\ damage)_{disease}$]$_{effect}$ were [reduced]$_{connective}$ when the [drug was administered either before or after infection with Mers-cov]$_{cause}$.
5). The [$(leukocytosis)_{disease}$ was unlikely to]$_{effect}$ be [caused by]$_{connective}$ [$(bacterial\ infection)_{disease}$]$_{effect}$ because [we excluded common bacteria or viruses associated with community acquired $(pneumonia)_{disease}$ and procalcitonin level of all patients in our study was no greater than 0.5 ng/ml.]$_{cause}$
6). [Combined usage with $(Ribavirin)_{drug}$]$_{cause}$ was also [associated with]$_{connective}$ [lower incidence of $(acute\ respiratory\ distress\ syndrome)_{disease}$, $(nosocomial\ infection)_{disease}$ and $(death)_{disease}$, amongst other favorable outcomes.]$_{effect}$
7). [$(Tocilizumab)_{drug}$ are not ideal]$_{cause}$ either as it can suppress the immune system and [lead to]$_{connective}$ [an increased risk of $(infection)_{disease}$]$_{effect}$.
8). [$(Remdesivir)_{drug}$ is a novel $(nucleotide)_{chemical}$ analog prodrug]$_{cause}$ that was intended to be used [for]$_{connective}$ the [treatment of $(ebola\ virus\ disease)_{disease}$]$_{effect}$.
9). [$(Diarrhea)_{drug}$, $(nausea)_{disease}$, $(vomiting)_{disease}$, $(liver\ damage)_{disease}$, and other adverse reactions]$_{effect}$ can occur following [combined therapy with $(Lopinavir/Ritonavir)_{drug}$]$_{cause}$.
10). Technically , we have little knowledge on the pathogen and pathogenesis , [without specific effectively drugs or vaccine against the $(virus\ infection)_{disease}$]$_{cause}$, which [cause]$_{connective}$ [difficulties in rescuing the severe cases]$_{effect}$ which [account for]$_{connective}$ [about 20 % of the $(infections)_{disease}$ ·]$_{effect}$

Table 5. Sample causes and effects mined from CORD19 corpus with Drugs, Chemicals, Diseases and Symptoms identified using SciSpacy

highly complex sentences from a completely unknown repository. The results are highly promising, though further improvements can be effected with more training.

6. Conclusion

In this paper, we present a multi-task learning architecture based on BERT enhanced with CNNBiLSTM layers to solve the dual problem of causal sentence classification and sequence labeling for cause, effect and connectives. The proposed model exploits the dependencies between the two tasks and improves the performance over baselines models. The performance of the joint model improves the state of the art results heretofore reported for SEMEVAL 2010 dataset. This work is now being extended to detect causal chains and implicit causalities. Chains need a different type of labeling scheme since a single clause may be an effect and a cause simultaneously. Current annotated datasets mostly contain simple sentences, with not too many implicit causalities. We are also extending this work to detect causal relations spread over multiple sentences. Annotation for the above tasks is under way. The other area we are working on is towards building causal knowledge graphs to be used for further reasoning, with humans in the loop. The first step however will be to build an indexed causal knowledge repository, which can be used for querying.

References

[1]   Sorgente A, Vettigli G, Mele F. Automatic Extraction of Cause-Effect Relations in Natural Language Text. DART@ AI* IA. 2013;2013:37-48.
[2]   Blanco E, Castell N, Moldovan D. Causal Relation Extraction. In: Lrec; 2008. .
[3]   Radinsky K, Davidovich S, Markovitch S. Learning to predict from textual data. Journal of Artificial Intelligence Research. 2012;45:641-84.
[4]   Girju R, Moldovan D. Mining answers for causation questions. In: AAAI symposium on mining answers from texts and knowledge bases; 2002. .
[5]   Chan K, Low BT, Lam W, Lam KP. Extracting causation knowledge from natural language texts. In: Pacific-Asia Conference on Knowledge Discovery and Data Mining. Springer; 2002. p. 555-60.
[6]   Asghar N. Automatic Extraction of Causal Relations from Natural Language Texts: A Comprehensive Survey. arXiv preprint arXiv:160507895. 2016.
[7]   Low BT, Chan K, Choi LL, Chin MY, Lay SL. Semantic expectation-based causation knowledge extraction: A study on Hong Kong stock movement analysis. In: PAKDD; 2001. p. 114-23.
[8]   Zhao S, Liu T, Zhao S, Chen Y, Nie JY. Event causality extraction based on connectives analysis. Neurocomputing. 2016;173:1943-50.
[9]   Devlin J, Chang MW, Lee K, Toutanova K. Bert: Pre-training of deep bidirectional transformers for language understanding. arXiv preprint arXiv:181004805. 2018.
[10] Khoo CS, Kornfilt J, Oddy RN, Myaeng SH. Automatic extraction of cause-effect information from newspaper text without knowledge-based inferencing. Literary and Linguistic Computing. 1998;13(4):177-86.
[11] Do QX, Chan YS, Roth D. Minimally supervised event causality identification. In: Proceedings of the Conference on Empirical Methods in Natural Language Processing. Association for Computational Linguistics; 2011. p. 294-303.
[12] Girju R. Automatic detection of causal relations for question answering. In: Proceedings of the ACL 2003 workshop on Multilingual summarization and question answering-Volume 12. Association for Computational Linguistics; 2003. .
[13] Hobbs JR. Toward a useful concept of causality for lexical semantics. Journal of Semantics. 2005;22(2):181-209.
[14] Grishman R. Domain modeling for language analysis. DTIC Document; 1988.
[15] Garcia D. COATIS, an NLP system to locate expressions of actions connected by causality links. Knowledge acquisition, modeling and management. 1997.
[16] Bui QC, Nualláin BÓ, Boucher CA, Sloot PM. Extracting causal relations on HIV drug resistance from literature. BMC bioinformatics. 2010;11(1).
[17] Khoo CS. Automatic identification of causal relations in text and their use for improving precision in information retrieval; 1995.
[18] Khoo CS, Myaeng SH, Oddy RN. Using cause-effect relations in text to improve information retrieval precision. Information processing & management. 2001;37(1):119-45.
[19] Girju R, Moldovan DI, et al. Text mining for causal relations. In: FLAIRS Conference; 2002. p. 360-4.

[20] Girju R, Nakov P, Nastase V, Szpakowicz S, Turney P, Yuret D. Classification of semantic relations between nominals. Language Resources and Evaluation. 2009;43(2):105-21.

[21] Ittoo A, Bouma G. Extracting explicit and implicit causal relations from sparse, domain-specific texts. In: International Conference on Application of Natural Language to Information Systems. Springer; 2011. p. 52-63.

[22] Girju R, Nakov P, Nastase V, Szpakowicz S, Turney P, Yuret D. Semeval-2007 task 04: Classification of semantic relations between nominals. In: Proceedings of the 4th International Workshop on Semantic Evaluations. Association for Computational Linguistics; 2007. p. 13-8.

[23] Beamer B, Rozovskaya A, Girju R. Automatic Semantic Relation Extraction with Multiple Boundary Generation. In: AAAI; 2008. p. 824-9.

[24] Hendrickx I, Kim SN, Kozareva Z, Nakov P, Ó Séaghdha D, Padó S, et al. Semeval-2010 task 8: Multi-way classification of semantic relations between pairs of nominals. In: Workshop on Semantic Evaluations: Recent Achievements and Future Directions. ACL; 2009. p. 94-9.

[25] Xu Y, Mou L, Li G, Chen Y, Peng H, Jin Z. Classifying relations via long short term memory networks along shortest dependency paths. In: Proceedings of the 2015 conference on empirical methods in natural language processing; 2015. p. 1785-94.

[26] Dasgupta T, Saha R, Dey L, Naskar A. Automatic Extraction of Causal Relations from Text using Linguistically Informed Deep Neural Networks. In: Proceedings of the 19th Annual SIGdial Meeting on Discourse and Dialogue; 2018. p. 306-16.

[27] Yu B, Li Y, Wang J. Detecting Causal Language Use in Science Findings. In: 2019 Conference on Empirical Methods in Natural Language Processing (EMNLP-IJCNLP). Hong Kong, China; 2019. p. 4664-74.

[28] Li Z, Li Q, Zou X, Ren J. Causality extraction based on self-attentive BiLSTM-CRF with transferred embeddings. Neurocomputing. 2021;423:207-19.

[29] Huminski A, Bin NY. Automatic Extraction of Causal Chains from Text. LIBRES: Library & Information Science Research Electronic Journal. 2020;29(2).

[30] Yang J, Han SC, Poon J. A survey on extraction of causal relations from natural language text. arXiv preprint arXiv:210106426. 2021.

[31] Egami N, Fong CJ, Grimmer J, Roberts ME, Stewart BM. How to make causal inferences using texts. arXiv preprint arXiv:180202163. 2018.

[32] Blomqvist E, Alirezaie M, Santini M. Towards Causal Knowledge Graphs-Position Paper. In: Proceedings of Workshop on The Knowledge Discovery in Healthcare Data (KDH)@ ECAI; 2020. .

[33] Guo S, Jin L, Yang J, Jiang M, Han L, An N. Causal Extraction from the Literature of Pressure Injury and Risk Factors. In: International Conference on Knowledge Graph (ICKG). IEEE; 2020. p. 581-5.

[34] Veitch V, Sridhar D, Blei DM. Using text embeddings for causal inference. arXiv preprint arXiv:190512741. 2019.

[35] Keith KA, Jensen D, O'Connor B. Text and Causal Inference: A Review of Using Text to Remove Confounding from Causal Estimates. arXiv preprint arXiv:200500649. 2020.

[36] Weld G, West P, Glenski M, Arbour D, Rossi R, Althoff T. Adjusting for Confounders with Text: Challenges and an Empirical Evaluation Framework for Causal Inference. arXiv preprint arXiv:200909961. 2020.

[37] Chen Q, Zhuo Z, Wang W. Bert for joint intent classification and slot filling. arXiv preprint arXiv:190210909. 2019.

[38] Greene D, Cunningham P. Practical solutions to the problem of diagonal dominance in kernel document clustering. In: ICML. ACM; 2006. p. 377-84.

[39] Gurulingappa H, Rajput AM, Roberts A, Fluck J, Hofmann-Apitius M, Toldo L. Development of a benchmark corpus to support the automatic extraction of drug-related adverse effects from medical case reports. Journal of biomedical informatics. 2012;45(5):885-92.

[40] Vaswani A, Shazeer N, Parmar N, Uszkoreit J, Jones L, Gomez AN, et al. Attention is all you need. In: Advances in Neural Information Processing Systems; 2017. p. 5998-6008.

[41] Jones A. An Explanation of Xavier Initialization. Retrieved from Andy's blog. 2015.

[42] Thenmozhi D, Arunima S, Amlan Sengupta AB. ssn_nlp@ FIRE2020: Automatic extraction of causal relations using deep learning and machine translation approaches. 2020.

[43] Aziz A, Sultana A, Hossain MA, Ayman N, Chy AN. Feature Fusion with Hand-crafted and Transfer Learning Embeddings for Cause-Effect Relation Extraction. In: FIRE (Working Notes); 2020. p. 756-64.

[44] Neumann M, King D, Beltagy I, Ammar W. ScispaCy: fast and robust models for biomedical natural language processing. arXiv preprint arXiv:190207669. 2019.

Towards a Knowledge-Aware AI
A. Dimou et al. (Eds.)
© *2022 The Authors.*
This article is published online with Open Access by IOS Press and distributed under the terms
of the Creative Commons Attribution License 4.0 (CC BY 4.0).
doi:10.3233/SSW220022

Distinguishing the Types of Coordinated Verbs with a Shared Argument by Means of New ZeugBERT Language Model and ZeugmaDataset

Helena MEDKOVÁ [a,1] and Aleš HORÁK [b]

[a] *Masaryk University, Faculty of Arts, Brno, Czech Republic*
[b] *Masaryk University, Faculty of Informatics, Brno, Czech Republic*

Abstract. Sentences where two verbs share a single argument represent a complex and highly ambiguous syntactic phenomenon. The argument sharing relations must be considered during the detection process from both a syntactic and semantic perspective. Such expressions can represent ungrammatical constructions, denoted as zeugma, or idiomatic elliptical phrase combinations. Rule-based classification methods prove ineffective because of the necessity to reflect meaning relations of the analyzed sentence constituents.

This paper presents the development and evaluation of ZeugBERT, a language model tuned for the sentence classification task using a pre-trained Czech transformer model for language representation. The model was trained with a newly prepared dataset, which is also published with this paper, of 7,849 Czech sentences to classify Czech syntactic structures containing coordinated verbs that share a valency argument (or an optional adjunct) in the context of coordination. ZeugBERT here reaches 88 % of test set accuracy. The text describes the process of the new dataset creation and annotation, and it offers a detailed error analysis of the developed classification model.

Keywords. natural language understanding, coordinated verbs with shared argument, zeugma, BERT language model, dataset

1. Introduction

Coordinated structures are a widely occurring phenomenon in the language, yet they pose problems to syntactic parsers [22,13] to correctly analyze the dependents for all conjuncts because of high ambiguity, and even to their exact realisations in grammar formalisms [25,3] and treebank annotation [5]. One such problematic structure is called zeugma, usually regarded as a figure of speech. Zeugma refers to a coordination of two expressions joined together by a single ambiguous expression where each conjunct is simultaneously related to a different meaning of the joining word. An example of such intended use of zeugma is depicted by the sentence

---

[1] Corresponding Author: Helena Medková, Masaryk University, Faculty of Arts, Brno, Czech Republic;
E-mail: gerzova@phil.muni.cz.

(1)   She drew a gun and a picture of a gun.

Here, the verb "drew" bears two different senses: a) "to pull out a weapon," and b) "to paint a picture." The whole sentence is thus an ambiguous expression yoking together two expressions with different meanings. The resulting construction appears strange from the semantic point of view [24] and, as such, it attracts attention. Besides neglecting the collocability of expressions, zeugma may also indicate an erroneous violation of syntactic rules leading to ungrammatical sentences. Our motivation is to detect such structures comprehensively, which can be valuable for refining syntactic parsers or improving grammar checking proofreader modules.

This paper presents a new linguistic model, ZeugBERT, developed specifically for the sentence analysis of coordinated verbal phrases with a (possible) shared argument. Previous approaches solved this task by rule-based techniques [17,1]. ZeugBERT is designed to solve the classification task of distinguishing sentences with coordinated verbal phrases into three classes: 1) coordination of verbal phrases that do not share a constituent (*coordSent*), 2) coordination of verbal phrases with a shared argument (*coordComArg*), and 3) coordination of verbal phrases with a shared argument that crosses the argument structure for both verbs, the rhetorical concept called zeugma (*coordZeug* class).

For the purpose of ZeugBERT development, we have created a manually tagged dataset of Czech sentences, denoted as ZeugmaDataset, used for training and testing the model. The dataset is publicly available at the website[2] of Natural Language Processing Centre, Masaryk University.

2. Coordinated structures

Coordination is a syntactic relation between two or more conjuncts that have equal syntactic status, primarily in terms of functional likeness [8]. With the ZeugBERT model, we concentrate on three kinds of verb coordinations with a possible shared argument. The specification of these types is explicated in the following subsections.

2.1. Coordination of verbs with the shared argument

The observed structure within this phenomenon is a shared noun phrase (NP) or prepositional phrase (PP) in the right (or left) periphery of coordination of the two verbs conjoined by *and, or* conjunctions as in the typical example (2) [7]:

(2)   Vosy **vykusují a vysávají** přezrálé **ovoce**. (Wasps bite and suck out overripe fruit.)

The Czech dependency grammar theory considers such structures as the result of unifying transformation (fusion), which can be viewed as elliptical structures [11,10]. It means that the argument, that would be repeated in the sentence is elided from the surface structure of the first (or second conjunct) to avoid redundancy. From the generative grammar perspective, the pattern of the sentence (2) represents the Right node raising (RNR), where the object of the first conjunct is moved to the end of the coordination [8]. Such structure is a typical representative of the studied phenomenon and also the most

---

[2]https://nlp.fi.muni.cz/projects/zeugma

frequent configuration in the dataset. Two coordinated verbs *vykusují a vysávají* (bite and suck out) share a single noun phrase *overripe fruit* as their dependent. According to Gerdes and Kahane [6], a shared dependent is governed by both heads of verbal phrases, nevertheless it creates a prosodic unit with the nearest conjunct. The relation here is defined as a pure dependency, while the relation between the other conjunct and the shared dependent as an inherited dependency.

2.2. Zeugma

The second examined structure is the coordination of verbs that share a complement, however, their argument structure does not correspond to each other as can be seen in Example (3). The Czech verb *zmírňovat* (to relieve) binds with an obligatory accusative object, unlike the verb *předcházet* (to prevent) which binds a dative object. This phenomenon is denoted as zeugma [19] and it is usually considered as an ill-formed structure. The ungrammaticality typically rises on the side of the coordination where the dependency between a conjunct and a shared dependent is inherited, i.e. where the conjunct and the dependent do not create one syntactic (prosodic) unit [6]. According to Karlík [10], the dependent element adopts the form required by the adjacent expression.

(3)   ****Zmírňují a předchází bolestem** šíje. (*They relieve and prevent neck pain)[3]

(4)   *Cestující **nastupovali a vystupovali z vlaku**. (*Passengers were getting on and exiting the train.)

The shared dependent can be (besides a complement as presented in Example (3)) also an adjunct, but the dependency strength between the verbs and the adjunct is much weaker than in the case of verbs and complements [7]. It is also the source of frequent issues when deciding whether or not is the dependent shared or not. Sentence (4) is an example of a zeugma, where the shared dependent is the adjunct in form of the prepositional phrase [PP *z vlaku*] (from the train).

2.3. Coordination of verbs without the shared dependent

The last case is represented by coordinated verbal phrases without a shared dependent (i.e. not just the coordination of the heads) [9]. In the ZeugmaDataset, such sentences contain a coordination of two main clauses where the conjuncts are usually two clauses with verbs on their boundaries. The case, where the verbs stand on the borders of the clauses is represented by Example (5).

(5)   **Ptáci** kolem **umlkli** a **zvedl se** lehký **vánek**. (The birds around became silent and a light breeze arose.)

(6)   **Pánové doktoři** ze sálu **vtipkovali** a **ujistili mě o své šílenosti**. (The doctors in the room joked and assured me of their insanity.)

Another option for coordinated verbs is a compound sentence, where the verbs share the left side of their valence structure, i.e. the subject part of their dependency structure

---

[3]The * (star) here explicitly marks a sentence which is considered ill-formed.

Table 1. Statistics of the training, testing and validation subsets (numbers of sentences)

	train_set	test_set	valid_set	whole dataset
coordSent	3,062	875	437	4,374
coordComArg	1,744	499	248	2,491
coordZeug	689	197	98	984
all classes	5,495	1,571	783	7,849

(as can be seen in Example (6). In the generative grammar, this type of clause-level coordination is known as a Forward Conjunction Reduction (FCR), where the right-hand conjunct [VP *ujistili...*] (they assured) inherits the subject [NP *Pánové doktoři...*] (the doctors) [12].

3. ZeugmaDataset – manually annotated dataset of coordinated structures

In this section, we want to introduce the ZeugmaDataset that was specially created with the aim to distinguish the three sentence classes: *coordSent, coordComArg*, and *co-ordZeug*. ZeugmaDataset consists of corpus-based samples of Czech coordinated structures with two coordinated verbs from the largest Czech web corpus csTenTen17 [21], which was crawled in 2017, therefore it reflects the language reality until that year.

A direct search using the Corpus Query Language (CQL) for two verbs connected with the conjunction *and* or *or*[4] revealed 15,703,841 verb coordinations in the corpus. In the successive step, all passive constructions were removed with a negative filter leading to 15,206,270 sentences out of which 7,849 were randomly selected for further processing. The resulting dataset was then manually annotated by a single annotator with the three class labels.

The preceding version of the dataset was prepared as a benchmark dataset for the rule-based detection of zeugma [15]. The dataset contained 2,762 sentences of which 1,081 were positive cases of zeugma and 1,681 sentences covered non-zeugmatic coordinations of verbs. In the current ZeugmaDataset, the class of non-zeugmatic coordinations was split into two other classes (verbs with a shared argument, coordComArg, and compound sentences, coordSent). The whole dataset was extended, cleaned and refined with the methods that are described in [16]. The UDPipe2 web service [20] was used for tokenization, lemmatization, and morphological and syntactic analysis. The dataset for download thus follows the UDPipe2 CoNLL-U format[5] with the sentence class annotations marked as specific dependency relation of the verb in the DEPREL field.

3.1. The statistics of the dataset

The whole ZeugmaDataset is divided into three balanced subsets for training, testing and validation in a ratio of 70:20:10, see Table 1. The split data were selected manually, especially for the *coordZeug* class it was important to choose the sentences uniformly, to avoid an occurrence of the same coordinated verbs in the subset instead of variability.

---

[4]The exact query was [tag="k5.*"] [word="a|nebo"] [tag="k5.*"], i.e. a *verb*$_1$ *a|nebo verb*$_2$, where "*a*" and "*nebo*" stand for "and" and "or".

[5]https://universaldependencies.org/format.html

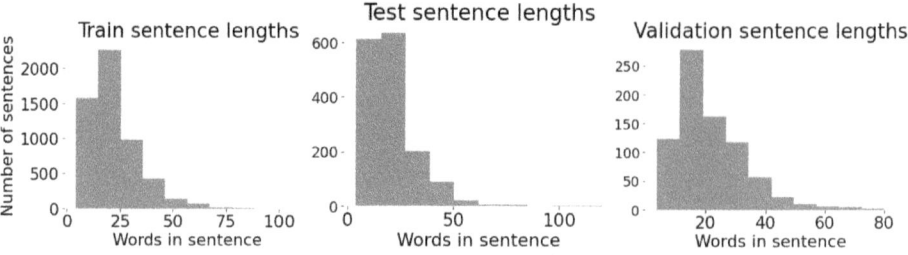

Figure 1. Sentences lengths of the training, testing and validation subsets

Table 2. The count of unseen verb lemmata versus the count of unique coordinated verb lemmata in the train, test, and valid subsets.

Class	Test dataset		Valid dataset	
	unseen in train	total	unseen in train	total
coordSent	836	865	412	433
coordComArg	406	469	212	241
coordZeug	90	138	35	81

Since various details may impact the whole learning process, we made a quantitative comparison of the most frequent sentence lengths of the language data to see if any subsets contained disproportionately short or long sentences. As shown in Figure 1, sentences with lengths of 20–30 words are the most frequent in all subsets. The average length of simple sentences in Czech fiction is 5–8 words [23] so for the presented data, the character of the training sentences should be taken into account, and the fact that they are uncorrected compound sentences from the web corpus.

The dataset split was also driven by the requirement of introducing unknown verb lemmata [6] in the validation and testing subsets to avoid possible lexical bias in training. The learning task was particularly difficult for the zeugma class since this phenomenon appears more frequently in the corpus with some specific verb coordinations. Therefore, we ensured that the coordinations of verbs in the test and validation sets were as unique as possible (see Table 2 for detailed statistics).

3.2. Rules for the annotation of the shared argument

Since a high degree of ambiguity is a characteristic feature of coordinated structures, distinguishing between the classes can be challenging. Therefore, in this section, we outline the procedures we followed to annotate the dataset.

An essential guideline in this matter is using the *Vallex 3.0* valency dictionary [14], according to which we check the types of arguments for specific verbs. We identify a coordination with shared argument when there is a semantically compatible verb complement (required by the verb's argument structure), a typical adjunct (often occurring in combination with the verb), or another optional element of the verbal structure according to the valency dictionary in the left-hand (or right-hand) context of the coordination.

The least problematic are verb complements with an obligatory argument on the right-hand side of the coordination, as illustrated in the sentence (7a). We also observe

---

[6]The dictionary verb form in the infinitive.

the co-occurrence of coordinate verbs on the left side of the coordination, see sentence (7b), although they are less frequent in the dataset.

(7a)   [. . .] umožňují zlepšovat ~~kvalitu pitné vody~~ a měnit kvalitu pitné vody. ([...] they allow to improve ~~drinking water quality~~ and change drinking water quality.)

(7b)   [. . .] **kvalitu pitné vody** umožňují **zlepšovat a měnit** ~~kvalitu pitné vody~~. ([...] the quality of drinking water they allow to improve [the quality of drinking water] and change ~~the quality of drinking water~~.)

(8)   [. . .] jeho vlákna **izolují a regulují teplotu**. ([...] its fibers isolate and regulate temperature.)

In some cases, the common accusative argument identification is a matter of sentence interpretation. We have decided to classify verb coordinations in the way which avoids creating figurative senses.

A borderline example is illustrated by the sentence (8), where both verbs, *to isolate* and *to regulate*, have obligatory complements but are not fully collocable from a semantic point of view. According to corpus evidence, a typical strong collocation in accusative to the verb *isolate* is *"teplo"* (heat) (with the logDice score [18] of 7.7), and not *"teplota"* (temperature). However, it is questionable to what extent the conjunction is semantically incompatible since the expected complement for the verb *isolate* is semantically concrete and *temperature* is an abstract concept. The shared argument in this sentence is thus not a nonsense but rather a conceptual confusion. *To regulate temperature* here forms a syntagm, the subject of the verb *isolate* is considered to be implicit in this case.

(9)   *Cestující nastupovali a vystupovali [PP z vlaku]. (*The passengers were entering and exiting [PP from the train]).

(10)   Ugrofinské jazyky se také mohly vyvinout a rozšířit až [PP po skončení doby ledové]. (Ugrofin languages might also develop and spread [PP after the end of the Ice Age].)

Expressions may bind to verbs as complements in their syntactic structure, see corpus sentence (7a), or adjoin the verbs (9).

In Example (9), we can observe a direction crossover (from where, to where) between verbs. According to *Vallex 3.0*, the prepositional phrase is obligatory; therefore, we consider the adjunct as shared.

In some cases, however, it is not clear whether the prepositional phrase is a shared adjunct or whether it only adjoins the conjunct on the left or right side of the coordination, see Example (10). In such cases, it depends primarily on the interpretation of the sentence, so we consider adjuncts to be shared adjuncts even potentially.

Since the strength of the adjunction in these additions tends to be more a matter of scale [7], it is not always easy to label an adjunct as shared or unshared. In these cases, therefore, the intuition of the annotator plays a significant role.

Table 3. Comparison of the previous rule-based technique and the current ZeugBert model to zeugma detection

	precision	recall	F1-score	support
Rule-based zeugma detection with preceding dataset	0.98	0.38	0.55	1013
Rule-based zeugma detection with current test subset	1.00	0.30	0.46	197
ZeugBert with current test subset	0.82	0.83	0.83	197

Table 4. The results of the ZeugBERT model with the test set data

	precision	recall	F1-score	support
coordSent	0.92	0.92	0.92	875
coordComArg	0.85	0.85	0.85	499
coordZeug	0.82	0.83	0.83	197
accuracy			**0.88**	1,571
macro avg	0.86	0.87	0.86	1,571
weighted avg	0.88	0.88	**0.88**	1,571

4. The ZeugBERT language model

The main goal was to design a tool that recognizes ill-formed structures among coordinated verb phrases. We initially developed a rule-based method with 83 manually created rules for the zeugma detection task. The disadvantage of this approach was the specificity to particular verbs, a low recall, complicated and time-consuming extensibility of the rules, and zero reflection of the semantics. Another problematic aspect was the strong prerequisite of building the rules on top of the (correct) output of a morphological analyzer [15].

The evaluation of the rule-based approach with the preceding version of the dataset (see Section 3) revealed an F1-score of 0.55 with high precision of 0.98 but at the cost of a significantly low recall of 0.38. To offer a fair comparison, we have now reevaluated the rule-based approach with the current ZeugBert test subset, and it reached almost the same results: F1-score of 0.46, i.e. precision of 1.00 and recall of 0.30 (see Table 3).

To achieve satisfactory results, we have employed machine learning methods currently widely prefered in NLP tasks solutions. In the development of the ZeugBERT model, we have adopted the concept of the Bidirectional Encoder Representations Transformers (BERT) language model [4], specifically the SlavicBERT pre-trained model[7] [2] for Czech (and other Slavic languages). The ZeugBERT mode has been fine-tuned to the sentence classification task with the ZeugmaDataset described above and the *huggingface transformers* library [26].

The input to the training process was formed by the word sequences of the sentences without any special preprocessing. The model was trained for 3 epochs. the batch-size 16, 500 warm-up steps and the weight decay of 0.01.

Compared to the rule-based approach, the ZeugBERT method proved to be very efficient in distinguishing between zeugma and other types of coordinated verbs. Table 4 summarizes the ZeugBERT performance with the testing set where it achieved an overall accuracy of 88 %.

---

[7]https://huggingface.co/DeepPavlov/bert-base-bg-cs-pl-ru-cased

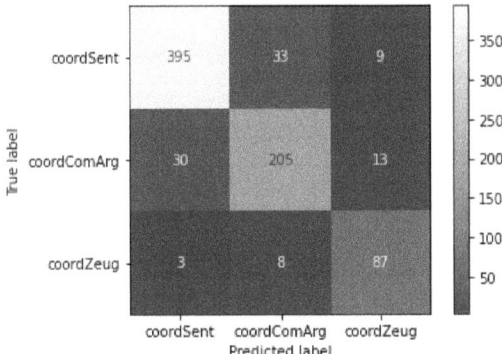

Figure 2. Confusion matrix of ZeugBERT results with the validation subset (numbers of classified sentences)

The model detects zeugma with 83 % accuracy, and we noticed a significant improvement in the recall of detected cases, which also reaches 83 % with the test set data. Based on these results, the ZeugBERT method proved to be an effective solution to the problems of low recall and difficult extensibility of the previous rule-based approach to zeugma detection. Since the rule-based method distinguished just zeugma vs nonzeugma classes, we cannot compare its results for the full three class setup of the ZeugmaDataset and compute a comparable overall accuracy, macro average and weighted average measures. The ZeugBERT model detects the *coordSent* class (the most frequented class in the dataset) with the highest f-score of 92 %. For the *coordComArg* class, the model reaches comparable recognition results as with zeugma.

5. Error analysis

We have examined in detail the cases where the model made a misclassification with the validation set sentences, see Figure 2 for the confusion matrix. An exhaustive error analysis outlining the possible causes of the errors made by the model is presented and discussed in the following subsections, with summary lists in Tables 5–7.

By observation of misclassified sentences, we have identified several regular structure configurations where the model made a mistake, even though in some cases the reasons for the misclassification could not be reliably recognized. Such sentences are labelled as *Uncertain causation* in the tables.

5.1. The compound sentences, coordSent

The model made one of the major traceable errors in distinguishing between structures where sentences potentially share (or do not share) an adjunct (19 %). A typical example of such sentence is presented in (11). "*Long-term diarrhoea*" could cause mortality in wildlife, but it is not necessarily the (only) cause of weight loss. Therefore, errors of this nature are not entirely misclassifications because sentences of this type are semantically ambiguous, and we could potentially consider the adjunct as shared.

(11)   Postižená zvěř **hubne a hyne v důsledku** vyčerpávajících dlouhodobých **průjmů**. (Affected animals lose weight and die as a result of exhausting long-term diarrhoea.) [coordComArg → coordSent][8]

Table 5. Error analysis of *coordSent*

	Reason for model confusion	Count	%
1	Coordination of verbs with a potentially shared adjunct	8	19.0
2	Coordination of verbs with an accusative argument that is semantically incompatible	7	16.7
3	The first verb in coordination without obligatory right-hand argument	8	19.0
4	The potentiality of a zeugma	5	11.9
5	Coordination of verbs with an elided shared argument in surface structure	1	2.4
7	Confusion of the adjunct with an ungrammatically conjoined expression (typically a prepositional phrase)	3	7.1
8	Questionable collocability of potentially shared argument	1	2.4
9	Uncertain causation	9	21.4

(12)   Ráda ve volném čase **maluji a čtu knihy**. (I like to paint and read books in my spare time.) [coordComArg → coordSent]

Sentence (12) illustrates the coordination of two verbs with an accusative complement in their argument structure that is not semantically compatible. The model tags this coordination as *coordComArg*. However, the words *paint books* are not semantically compatible. The model could be confused by considering the prepositional phrase *ve volném čase* (*in the spare time*) as a shared adjunct. Therefore, we tested the sentence without the prepositional phrase, but the model still labels it as *coordComArg*.

(13)   A Egon Bondy **běhal a kopal do vzduchu** a držel se za koleno: Dostal jsem z toho do lejtka křeč, ale proč do nosu ? (And Egon Bondy was running and kicking in the air and holding his knee: I got a cramp in my calf, but why in my nose?) [coordComArg → coordSent]

(14)   [...] za současné situace si asi většina lidí **připlatí a koupí K750i**. ([...] in the current situation, most people will probably pay extra and buy a K750i) [coordZeug → coordSent]

(15)   Před každým použitím **protřepejte a nanášejte na pokrmy** ze vzdálenosti 20–25 cm, nestříkejte do otevřeného ohně nebo na žhavé předměty. (Before each use, shake and apply to food from a distance of 20–25 cm, do not spray on open flames or hot objects.) [coordComArg → coordSent]

(16)   [...] až děti **vyrostou a odejdou z domova**. (When children grow up and leave home) [coordZeug → coordSent].

In some cases, the model marked the verb coordination as *coordComArg* in which the first verb is without an obligatory right-hand complement (or adjunct), as illustrated by sentence (13). These cases may also include verbs with a null object.

In some cases, again, there can be an issue with the ambiguity of sentence interpretation (14). The model has identified the structure as a zeugma which potentially could be correct. However, since the first verb can optionally omit the argument from its surface structure, such a structure is not classified as a zeugma in the dataset.

In sentence (15), we exemplify the case where the model has identified the sentence as a verb with a shared argument. Verbs can potentially refer to the same elided object.

---

[8]Here by [*class_predicted → class_ground_truth*], we indicate the misclassification case where the correct *class_ground_truth* was predicted as *class_predicted* by the ZeugBERT model.

Table 6. Error analysis of *coordComArg*

	Reason for model confusion	Count	%
1	Valency argument on the left-hand side of the coordination	11	25.6
2	Unrecognized argument on the right-hand side	9	20.9
3	Zeugma confusion with coordination of verbs with prepositional phrases on the right side of the coordination	9	20.9
4	Interpretation issue of the common adjunct	6	14.0
5	Zeugma misclassification based on formal similarity	4	9.3
6	Uncertain causation	4	9.3

However, since the accusative has a complement omitted from the surface structure, the correct classification of such cases is *coordSent*.

Example (16) illustrates the case where the model incorrectly identified a zeugma, typically involving a structure with a prepositional phrase adjacent to the second verb in coordination. Similar to the sentence (8), the model here has identified a common argument for the coordinating verbs, but the collocability of the first verb with the argument is semantically questionable, as we have explained above.

5.2. Verb with a shared argument, coordComArg

In the classification of the *coordComArg* class, the model struggled most with coordinations where the complement of both verbs took place in the left-hand context, in 25.6% of cases, see Example (17). The misclassification here is probably caused by low frequency of such configurations in the dataset.

(17) [. . .] **příběh dopíši a vydám** na Vánoce, stejně jako minule. (I will finish the story and publish it on Christmas, just like last time) [coordSent → coordComArg]

In contrast, the model did not recognize the accusative argument at the right periphery of the coordination in 20.9 %, see Example (18), even though this is the most frequently represented example of a shared argument in the dataset.

Since many sentences in the dataset are very long, we tried to test only coordination with arguments without further context, and the model then determined the class correctly. Thus, we assume that in these cases, the broad context of the coordination is the cause of the misclassification.

(18) [. . .], **sdílet a vyměňovat** si **informace** a **nápady**, [. . .] (to share and exchange information and ideas) [coordSent → coordComArg]

With the same frequency, the model misclassified coordinated verbs that share a prepositional valency complement on the right-hand side of the coordination as zeugma (19). The causation may be traceable to the ellipsis of the first obligatory accusative complement of the verbs *to request* and *beg*, or the similarity of the syntactic configuration to ungrammatical structures.

(19) "**Žádám a prosím o respekt** soukromí všech, koho se to týká," vzkázala Moore. ("I request and beg for respect of the privacy of all the concerned," Moore said) [coordZeug → coordComArg]

As with the *coordSent* class, we encounter the problem of recognizing and interpreting the common adjunct. In case of Example (20), the prepositional phrase [until lunch] is labelled as a common adjunct. The Czech verbs *přemýšlet* (to think) and *diskutovat* (to

Table 7. Error analysis of *coordZeug*

	Reason for model confusion	Count	%
1	Unrecognized syntactically or semantically incompatible argument	6	54.5
2	Coordination of a verb with an elided argument of the first verb	2	18.2
3	Binding crossover at the first argument of a ditransitive verb	1	9.1
4	Uncertain causation	2	18.2

discuss) have an elided shared argument *o něčem* (about something). We assume that both these actions in relation to the elided object of discussion finish in the time that the adjunct expresses. However, this is again a subjective interpretation of the sentence.

(20)   Proto Patricij s Bbloudem **přemýšleli a diskutovali až do oběda**. (Therefore, Patricius and Bbloud were thinking and discussing until lunchtime.) [coordSent → coordComArg]

5.3. Zeugma constructions, coordZeug

A considerably large group of misclassified ill-formed zeugma structures is formed by verb coordinations which allow for interpreting the sentence in the way where the first verb of the coordination has its valency complement omitted from the surface. An example can be seen in the sentence (21) in which the verb *porozumět* (to understand) forms a syntagm with the expression *problém* (problem) (i.e. *to understand the problem*), but at the same time, it could bind the complement *vám* (*you*) that elided from the surface as expressed in Example (21). Similar cases form 55 % of all errors in this class.

(21a)   Abych lépe **porozuměl a prošetřil problém**. (To better understand and investigate the problem.) [coordSent → coordZeug]

(21b)   Abych ~~vám~~ lépe **porozuměl a prošetřil problém**. (To better understand ~~you~~ and investigate the problem.)

A less frequent error group consists in a zeugma which the model recognized as a common argument, probably due to the lack of this kind of syntactic configuration in the training data, see Example (22).

(22)   "Za toto je odpovědný policejní prezident, proto **žádáme a trváme na** jeho **odchodu**," zdůraznil John. ("The police president is responsible for this, so we demand and insist on his leave," John emphasized.) [coordComArg → coordZeug]

We have also identified a case in which the model classified the coordination as *coordComArg* where the coordinated verbs had a shared grammatically correct second argument in their structure. Nevertheless, the first argument diverged, causing cross-linkage. An example is in sentence (23), where the argument structure of the verb *doporučit* (to recommend) follows an obligatory frame *něco někomu* (something to someone), but the verb *chtít* (to ask) expects the valency of *něco po někom* (something <u>from</u> someone).

(23) Proto vláda přijala usnesení, kde **doporučila a chtěla po Ministerstvu obrany** garanci [. . .] (Therefore, the government passed a resolution recommending and asking the Ministry of Defence to guarantee [...]) [coordComArg → coordZeug]

6. Conclusions

In the presented paper, we have investigated the possibilities of machine learning methods for the task to distinguish grammatical and ungrammatical coordinated structures. A significant contribution is the creation of a benchmark ZeugmaDataset for fine-tuning and evaluating new language models and the new ZeugBERT language model based on it. We have proved that solving this task by deep learning techniques achieves remarkable improvements that ultimately outperform all approaches applied so far on zeugma detection reaching the accuracy of 88 % with the testing set. Additionally, we provide detailed error analysis where we discuss the patterns where the model made an error which will contribute to further improvements of the model's performance.

The examined phenomena occur across many languages. Even though we focus mainly on detecting non-grammatical structures in Czech, we assume comparable results for the equivalent structures in other languages because of the universality of the classification method. In general, zeugma detection may also be beneficial, for example, for the machine translation output checking.

In the future, we will focus on extending the current dataset to involve the coordination of other phrasal forms than just verb phrases. Since the deep learning method has proven effective for detecting ungrammatical structures, we will continue to develop foundational datasets for detecting other non-grammatical structures such as attraction or verb binding errors.

Acknowledgements

This work was partly supported by the Ministry of Education of CR within the LINDAT-CLARIAH-CZ project LM2018101 and by Masaryk University in the project of specific research *Využití strojového učení při detekci společného argumentu v koordinovaných strukturách* (The application of machine learning methods to shared argument detection in verbal coordination structures, project no. MUNI/A/1184/2020).

References

[1] A. Abeillé. In defense of lexical coordination. *Empirical issues in syntax and semantics*, 6:7–36, 2006.

[2] M. Arkhipov, M. Trofimova, Y. Kuratov, and A. Sorokin. Tuning multilingual transformers for language-specific named entity recognition. In *Proceedings of the 7th Workshop on Balto-Slavic Natural Language Processing*, pages 89–93, Florence, Italy, Aug. 2019. Association for Computational Linguistics.

[3] B. Crysmann. An asymmetric theory of peripheral sharing in HPSG: Conjunction reduction and coordination of unlikes. In *Proceedings of fgvienna: The 8th conference on formal grammar*, pages 45–64. CSLI Publications Stanford, California, 2003.

[4] J. Devlin, M.-W. Chang, K. Lee, and K. Toutanova. BERT: Pre-training of deep bidirectional transformers for language understanding. In *Proceedings of the 2019 Conference of the North American Chapter of the Association for Computational Linguistics: Human Language Technologies, Volume 1 (Long and Short Papers)*, pages 4171–4186, Minneapolis, Minnesota, June 2019. Association for Computational Linguistics.

[5]   J. Ficler and Y. Goldberg. Coordination Annotation Extension in the Penn Tree Bank. *arXiv preprint arXiv:1606.02529*, 2016.

[6]   K. Gerdes and S. Kahane. Non-constituent coordination and other coordinative constructions as Dependency Graphs. In *Depling 2015*, Proceedings of Depling 2015, Uppsala, Sweden, 2015.

[7]   J. Hrbáček. K otázce několikanásobného přísudku (On the topic of multiple prepositions). *Naše řeč*, 32(43):4–18, 1960.

[8]   R. Huddleston and G. K. Pullum. *Coordination and Subordination*, chapter 9, pages 198–219. John Wiley & Sons, Ltd, 2006.

[9]   R. Kaplan and J. Maxwell. Constituent coordination in lexical-functional grammar. 1, 01 2003.

[10] P. Karlík. *Nový encyklopedický slovník češtiny (New Encyclopaedic Dictionary of Czech)*, chapter Zeugma. 2017.

[11] P. Karlík and H. Gruet Škrabalová. *Nový encyklopedický slovník češtiny (New Encyclopaedic Dictionary of Czech)*, chapter Koordinace. Praha, 2017.

[12] G. Kempen. Conjunction reduction and gapping in clause-level coordination: an inheritance-based approach. *Computational Intelligence*, 7(4):357–360, 1991.

[13] S. Kübler, E. Hinrichs, W. Maier, and E. Klett. Parsing coordinations. In *Proceedings of the 12th Conference of the European Chapter of the ACL (EACL 2009)*, pages 406–414, 2009.

[14] M. Lopatková, V. Kettnerová, E. Bejček, A. Vernerová, and Z. Žabokrtský. *Valenční slovník českých sloves VALLEX (Valency dictionary of Czech verbs VALLEX)*. Karolinum, Praha, 2016.

[15] H. Medková. Automatic detection of zeugma. In A. Horák, P. Rychlý, and A. Rambousek, editors, *Proceedings of the Fourteenth Workshop on Recent Advances in Slavonic Natural Languages Processing, RASLAN 2020*, pages 79–86, Brno, 2020. Tribun EU.

[16] H. Medková. Building a dataset for detection of verb coordinations with a shared argument. In A. Horák, P. Rychlý, and A. Rambousek, editors, *Recent Advances in Slavonic Natural Language Processing (RASLAN 2021)*, pages 125–133, Brno, 2021. Tribun EU.

[17] F. Mouret. A phrase structure approach to argument cluster coordination. In *The Proceedings of the 13th International Conference on Head-Driven Phrase Structure Grammar*, pages 247–267. Citeseer, 2006.

[18] P. Rychlý. A lexicographer-friendly association score. In *RASLAN 2008*, pages 6–9, Brno, 2008. Masarykova Univerzita.

[19] Y. Shen. Zeugma: Prototypes, categories, and metaphors. *Metaphor and symbol*, 13(1):31–47, 1998.

[20] M. Straka. UDPipe 2.0 prototype at CoNLL 2018 UD shared task. In *Proceedings of the CoNLL 2018 Shared Task: Multilingual Parsing from Raw Text to Universal Dependencies*, pages 197–207, 2018.

[21] V. Suchomel. csTenTen17, a Recent Czech Web Corpus. In P. R. Aleš Horák and A. Rambousek, editors, *Proceedings of the Twelfth Workshop on Recent Advances in Slavonic Natural Languages Processing, RASLAN 2018*, pages 111–123, Brno, 2018. Tribun EU.

[22] H. Teranishi, H. Shindo, and Y. Matsumoto. Decomposed local models for coordinate structure parsing. In *Proceedings of the 2019 Conference of the North American Chapter of the Association for Computational Linguistics: Human Language Technologies, Volume 1 (Long and Short Papers)*, pages 3394–3403, 2019.

[23] L. Uhlířová. O délce věty (About the length of a sentence). *Slovo a slovesnost*, 32(3):232–240, 1971.

[24] E. Viebahn. Ambiguity and zeugma. *Pacific Philosophical Quarterly*, 99(4):749–762, 2018.

[25] M. White. Efficient realization of coordinate structures in Combinatory Categorial Grammar. *Research on Language and Computation*, 4(1):39–75, 2006.

[26] T. Wolf, L. Debut, V. Sanh, J. Chaumond, C. Delangue, A. Moi, P. Cistac, T. Rault, R. Louf, M. Funtowicz, et al. Transformers: State-of-the-art natural language processing. In *Proceedings of the 2020 conference on empirical methods in natural language processing: system demonstrations*, pages 38–45, 2020.

Towards a Knowledge-Aware AI
A. Dimou et al. (Eds.)
© *2022 The Authors.*
This article is published online with Open Access by IOS Press and distributed under the terms
of the Creative Commons Attribution License 4.0 (CC BY 4.0).

Subject Index

© 2022 The Authors.
This article is published online with Open Access by IOS Press and distributed under the terms
of the Creative Commons Attribution License 4.0 (CC BY 4.0).

Author Index

www.ingramcontent.com/pod-product-compliance
Ingram Content Group UK Ltd.
Pitfield, Milton Keynes, MK11 3LW, UK
UKHW050045180526
471099UK00006B/219